McDougal Littell

WORLD HISTORY

PATTERNS OF INTERACTION

Reading Study Guide

McDougal Littell
A DIVISION OF HOUGHTON MIFFLIN COMPANY

ISBN-13: 978-0-618-40933-4   ISBN-10: 0-618-40933-5

Printed in the United States of America

9 10 – VEI – 10 09 08 07

Contents

UNIT 6 Industrialism and the Race for Empire, 1700–1914

UNIT 7 The World at War, 1900–1945

UNIT 8 Perspectives on the Present, 1945–Present

Chapter 35 Struggles for Democracy, 1945–Present

Chapter 36 Global Interdependence, 1960–Present

Being a Strategic Reader
Strategies for Reading Your History Book

Understanding the Big Picture

History is filled with people, events, facts, and details. Sometimes you can get lost in all the details. This is why the most important Strategy to remember as you read a history textbook is to form the "big picture" of history. As you read, keep asking yourself, "What is the main idea?" When you do this, the details will make more sense.

Use the strategies shown here to help you read *World History: Patterns of Interaction.*.

Strategy: Look for key terms and names, which are in dark type in the section. The text gives clues to the important terms and names in the section.
Try This: Read the terms. Then look at pages 542 and 543. Which of the terms appears on these pages? How did you recognize it?

Strategy: Read "Main Idea" and "Why It Matters Now" to begin forming the "big picture" of the section.
Try This: What do you think will be the subject of this section?

Strategy: Look at the heads and subheads in each section to get a general understanding of the subject..
Try This: Preview the head and subheads on pages 542 and 543. What do you expect to learn in this section?

Strategy: Look closely at the graphic organizers, art, and other illustrations in the text. Be sure to read the captions.
Try This: Look at the chart under "Taking Notes." What will you compare in the chart?

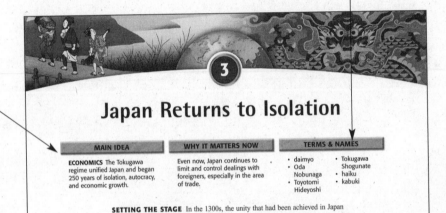

Japan Returns to Isolation

MAIN IDEA	WHY IT MATTERS NOW	TERMS & NAMES
ECONOMICS The Tokugawa regime unified Japan and began 250 years of isolation, autocracy, and economic growth.	Even now, Japan continues to limit and control dealings with foreigners, especially in the area of trade.	• daimyo • Tokugawa Shogunate • Oda Nobunaga • haiku • Toyotomi Hideyoshi • kabuki

SETTING THE STAGE In the 1300s, the unity that had been achieved in Japan in the previous century broke down. Shoguns, or military leaders, in the north and south fiercely fought one another for power. Although these two rival courts later came back together at the end of the century, a series of politically weak shoguns let control of the country slip from their grasp. The whole land was torn by factional strife and economic unrest. It would be centuries before Japan would again be unified.

TAKING NOTES

Comparing Use a chart to compare the achievements of the daimyos who unified Japan.

Daimyo	Achievements

A New Feudalism Under Strong Leaders

In 1467, civil war shattered Japan's old feudal system. The country collapsed into chaos. Centralized rule ended. Power drained away from the shogun to territorial lords in hundreds of separate domains.

Local Lords Rule A violent era of disorder followed. This time in Japanese history, which lasted from 1467 to 1568, is known as the Sengoku, or "Warring States," period. Powerful samurai seized control of old feudal estates. They offered peasants and others protection in return for their loyalty. These warrior-chieftains, called **daimyo** (DYE•mee•oh), became lords in a new kind of Japanese feudalism. Daimyo meant "great name." Under this system, security came from this group of powerful warlords. The emperor at Kyoto became a figurehead, having a leadership title but no actual power.

The new Japanese feudalism resembled European feudalism in many ways. The daimyo built fortified castles and created small armies of samurai on horses. Later they added foot soldiers with muskets (guns) to their ranks. Rival daimyo often fought each other for territory. This led to disorder throughout the land.

New Leaders Restore Order A number of ambitious daimyo hoped to gather enough power to take control of the entire country. One, the brutal and ambitious **Oda Nobunaga** (oh•dah noh•boo•nah•gah) defeated his rivals and seized the imperial capital Kyoto in 1568.

Following his own motto "Rule the empire by force," Nobunaga sought to eliminate his remaining enemies. These included rival daimyo as well as wealthy Buddhist monasteries aligned with them. In 1575, Nobunaga's 3,000 soldiers armed with muskets crushed an enemy force of samurai cavalry. This was the first time firearms had been used effectively in battle in Japan. However,

A samurai warrior ▼

542 Chapter 19

Japan in the
17th Century

Land controlled by Tokugawa or related households
— Five highways
Daimyo boundary

Hokkaido

*Sea of
Japan*

KOREA

Honshu

Edo (Tokyo)

Kyoto

Osaka

Kyushu

Shikoku

*PACIFIC
OCEAN*

Nagasaki

N

200 Miles

400 Kilometers

Strategy: Preview the maps in each section. Think about how geography affected historical events.
Try This: Look closely at the map. What does the map show?

▲ Himeji Castle, completed in the 17th century, is near Kyoto.

GEOGRAPHY SKILLBUILDER: Interpreting Maps
1. **Place** *Why might Edo have been a better site for a capital in the 17th century than Kyoto?*
2. **Region** *About what percentage of Japan was controlled by Tokugawa or related households when Tokugawa Ieyasu took power in the early 1600s?*

Nobunaga was not able to unify Japan. He committed *seppuku,* the ritual suicide of a samurai, in 1582, when one of his own generals turned on him.

Nobunaga's best general, **Toyotomi Hideyoshi** (toh•you•toh•mee hee•deh•yoh•shee), continued his fallen leader's mission. Hideyoshi set out to destroy the daimyo that remained hostile. By 1590, by combining brute force with shrewd political alliances, he controlled most of the country. Hideyoshi did not stop with Japan. With the idea of eventually conquering China, he invaded Korea in 1592 and began a long campaign against the Koreans and their Ming Chinese allies. When Hideyoshi died in 1598, his troops withdrew from Korea.

Tokugawa Shogunate Unites Japan One of Hideyoshi's strongest daimyo allies, Tokugawa Ieyasu (toh•koo•gah•wah ee•yeh•yah•soo), completed the unification of Japan. In 1600, Ieyasu defeated his rivals at the Battle of Sekigahara. His victory earned him the loyalty of daimyo throughout Japan. Three years later, Ieyasu became the sole ruler, or shogun. He then moved Japan's capital to his power base at Edo, a small fishing village that would later become the city of Tokyo.

MAIN IDEA
Drawing Conclusions
Ⓐ How would the "alternate attendance policy" restrict the daimyo?

Japan was unified, but the daimyo still governed at the local level. To keep them from rebelling, Ieyasu required that they spend every other year in the capital. Even when they returned to their lands, they had to leave their families behind as hostages in Edo. Through this "alternate attendance policy" and other restrictions, Ieyasu tamed the daimyo. This was a major step toward restoring centralized government to Japan. As a result, the rule of law overcame the rule of the sword. Ⓐ

An Age of Explorations and Isolation **543**

Strategy: Look at charts and graphs that present ideas in visual ways.
Try This: Study the chart below. What does the chart show?

Strategy: Use the Main Idea questions to check your understanding as you read.
Try This: Read Question A. How would the details in the text help you answer the question?

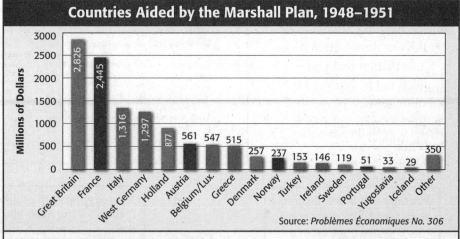

Countries Aided by the Marshall Plan, 1948–1951

Millions of Dollars

Country	Amount
Great Britain	2,826
France	2,445
Italy	1,316
West Germany	1,297
Holland	877
Austria	561
Belgium/Lux.	547
Greece	515
Denmark	257
Norway	237
Turkey	153
Ireland	146
Sweden	119
Portugal	51
Yugoslavia	33
Iceland	29
Other	350

Source: *Problèmes Économiques No. 306*

SKILLBUILDER: Interpreting Charts
1. **Drawing Conclusions** *Which country received the most aid from the United States?*
2. **Making Inferences** *Why do you think Great Britain and France received so much aid?*

How to Use This *Reading Study Guide*

The purpose of this *Reading Study Guide* is to help you read and understand your history textbook, *World History: Patterns of Interaction*. You can use this *Reading Study Guide* in two ways.

1. Use the *Reading Study Guide* side-by-side with your history book
- Turn to the section that you are going to read in the textbook. Then, next to the book, put the pages from the *Reading Study Guide* that accompany that section. All of the heads in the *Reading Study Guide* match the heads in the textbook.
- Use the *Reading Study Guide* to help you read and organize the information in the textbook.

2. Use the *Reading Study Guide* to study for tests on the textbook.
- Reread the summary of every chapter.
- Review the definitions of the Terms and Names in the *Reading Study Guide*.
- Review the diagram of information that you filled out as you read the summaries.
- Review your answers to questions.

Strategy: Read the Terms and Names and the definition of each. The Terms and Names are in dark type in the section.
Try This: What are the definitions of "indulgence" and "annul"?

Name _____ Date _____

CHAPTER 17 Section 3 (pages 488–494)

Luther Starts the Reformation

BEFORE YOU READ

In the last section, you saw how the Renaissance spread to Northern Europe.

In this section, you will see how Renaissance ideas helped bring about the Reformation.

AS YOU READ

Use the chart below to take notes on the responses to Luther's challenge.

TERMS AND NAMES

indulgence Release from punishments due for a sin

Reformation 16th-century movement for religious reform, leading to the founding of new Christian churches

Lutheran Member of a Protestant church founded on the teachings of Martin Luther

Protestant Member of a Christian church founded on the principles of the Reformation

Peace of Augsburg Agreement in 1555 declaring that the religion of each German state would be decided by its ruler

annul Cancel or put an end to

Anglican Relating to the Church of England

BATTLE/ POLITICAL ISSUE	EFFECT
Responses to Luther's Challenge	The Pope threatens Luther with excommunication.

Causes of the Reformation
(pages 488–489)

Why was the Church criticized?

By 1500, the influence of the Church on the lives of people had weakened. Some people resented paying taxes to support the Church in Rome. Others sharply criticized the Church for some of its practices. Popes seemed more concerned with luxury and political power than with spiritual matters. The lower *clergy* had faults too. Many local priests lacked education and were not able to teach people. Some lived immoral lives.

Reformers urged the Church to change its ways to become more spiritual and humble. Christian humanists such as Erasmus and Thomas More added their voices to calls for change. In the early 1500s, the calls grew louder.

1. What kinds of changes did Church critics want to make?

_____

_____

_____

CHAPTER 17 EUROPEAN RENAISSANCE AND REFORMATION **161**

Strategy: Fill in the diagram as you read. The diagram will help you organize information in the section.
Try This: What is the purpose of this diagram?

Strategy: Read the summary. It contains the main ideas and the key information under the head.
Try This: What do you think this section will be about?

Luther Challenges the Church
(page 489)

How did the Reformation begin?

In 1517, a German monk named Martin Luther protested the actions of a Church official. That person was selling **indulgences**. An indulgence was a kind of forgiveness. By paying money to the Church, people thought they could win *salvation*.

Luther challenged this practice and others. He posted a written protest on the door of a castle church. His words were printed and spread throughout Germany. This was the beginning of the **Reformation**, a movement for reform that led to the founding of new Christian churches.

2. What role did Martin Luther play in the Reformation?

_____

_____

The Response to Luther (pages 490–492)

What effects did Luther's protest have?

Pope Leo X punished Luther for his views, but he refused to change them. Holy Roman Emperor Charles V, a strong Catholic, called Luther an outlaw. Luther's books were burned. But it was too late. Many of his ideas were already being practiced. The **Lutheran** Church started around 1522. In 1524, *peasants* in Germany hoped to use Luther's ideas about Christian freedom to change society. They demanded an end to serfdom—a condition like slavery. When it was not granted, they revolted. Luther disagreed with this *revolt*. German princes killed thousands in putting the revolt down.

Some *nobles* supported Luther's ideas. They saw a chance to weaken the emperor's power over them. Other German princes joined forces against Luther's supporters. They signed an agreement to remain loyal to the pope and the emperor. Supporters of Luther's ideas *protested* this agreement. They were called the Protestants. Eventually, the term **Protestant** meant Christians who belonged to non-Catholic churches.

War broke out between Catholic and Protestant forces in Germany. It finally ended in 1555 with the **Peace of Augsburg**. This treaty granted each prince the right to decide whether his subjects would be Catholic or Protestant.

3. Why did Luther's ideas lead to war?

_____

_____

England Becomes Protestant
(pages 51–52)

How did England become Protestant?

The Catholic Church faced another challenge to its power in England. Henry VIII, the king, was married to a Spanish princess. She gave birth to a daughter. England had never had a female ruler. Henry feared a civil war would start if he had no son. He believed his wife was too old to have another child. He tried to get the pope to **annul**, or put an end to the marriage, so he could remarry. The pope refused.

To remarry, Henry had to get out of the Catholic church. In 1534, Henry had *Parliament* pass laws that created the Church of England. These laws made the king or queen, not the pope, head of the Church of England. Henry no longer had to obey the pope. Henry remarried five times. His only son was from his third wife.

One of Henry's daughters, Elizabeth, became queen in 1558. She finished creating a separate English church. The new church was called **Anglican**. It had some practices that would appeal to both Protestants and Catholics. In this way, Elizabeth hoped to end religious conflict.

4. What role did Henry VIII play in creating the Church of England?

_____

_____

Strategy: When you see a word in italic type, read the definition in the Glossary at the the end of the chapter.
Try This: What does *Parliament* mean? Look at the Glossary on the next page to find the definition.

Strategy: Answer the question at the end of each part.
Try This: Write an answer to Question 4.

Strategy: Underline main ideas and key information as you read.
Try This: Read the summary under the head "The Response to Luther." Underline information that you think is important. One important idea is already underlined.

Being a Strategic Reader

How to Use This Reading Study Guide

At the end of every chapter in the Reading Study Guide, you will find a Glossary and a section called After You Read. The Glossary gives definitions of all the words in italic type in the chapter summaries.

After You Read is a two-page chapter review. Use After You Read to identify those parts of the chapter that you need to study more for the test on the chapter.

Strategy: Review all of the Terms and Names before completing Parts A and B of After You Read.
Try This: Use the Reading Study Guide for Chapter 17 to answer Questions A 1–5.

Strategy: Review the chapter summaries before completing the Main Ideas questions. Write a complete sentence for every answer.
Try This: In your own words, what is Question 1 asking for?

Strategy: Write one or two paragraphs for every Thinking Critically question.
Try This: In your own words, what is Question 1 asking for?

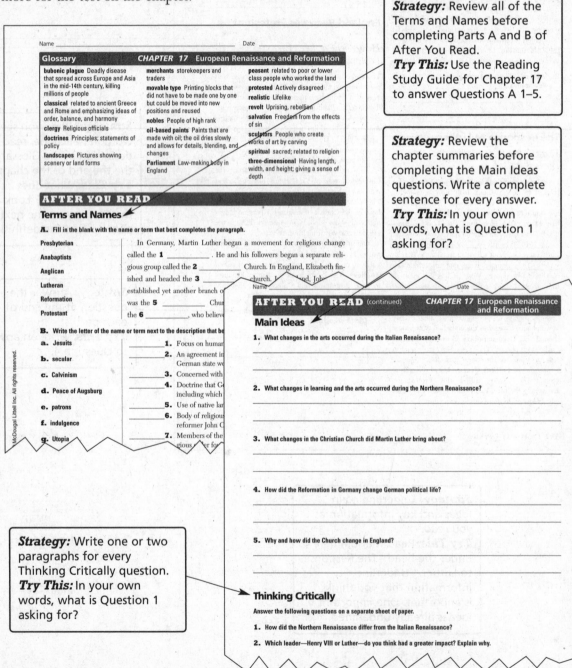

Name _____ Date _____

Glossary   **CHAPTER 17** European Renaissance and Reformation

bubonic plague Deadly disease that spread across Europe and Asia in the mid-14th century, killing millions of people

classical related to ancient Greece and Rome and emphasizing ideas of order, balance, and harmony

clergy Religious officials

doctrines Principles; statements of policy

landscapes Pictures showing scenery or land forms

merchants storekeepers and traders

movable type Printing blocks that did not have to be made one by one but could be moved into new positions and reused

nobles People of high rank

oil-based paints Paints that are made with oil; the oil dries slowly and allows for details, blending, and changes

Parliament Law-making body in England

peasant related to poor or lower class people who worked the land

protested Actively disagreed

realistic Lifelike

revolt Uprising, rebellion

salvation Freedom from the effects of sin

sculptors People who create works of art by carving

spiritual sacred; related to religion

three-dimensional Having length, width, and height; giving a sense of depth

AFTER YOU READ

Terms and Names

A. Fill in the blank with the name or term that best completes the paragraph.

Presbyterian
Anabaptists
Anglican
Lutheran
Reformation
Protestant

In Germany, Martin Luther began a movement for religious change called the **1** _____ . He and his followers began a separate religious group called the **2** _____ Church. In England, Elizabeth finished and headed the **3** _____ church. ... and, Joh... established yet another branch of ... was the **5** _____ Chur... the **6** _____ , who believ...

B. Write the letter of the name or term next to the description that be...

a. Jesuits
b. secular
c. Calvinism
d. Peace of Augsburg
e. patrons
f. indulgence
g. Utopia

___ **1.** Focus on human...
___ **2.** An agreement in ... German state w...
___ **3.** Concerned with ...
___ **4.** Doctrine that G... including which ...
___ **5.** Use of native lar...
___ **6.** Body of religious ... reformer John C...
___ **7.** Members of the ... gious ...er fo...

Name _____ Date _____

AFTER YOU READ (continued)   **CHAPTER 17** European Renaissance and Reformation

Main Ideas

1. What changes in the arts occurred during the Italian Renaissance?

2. What changes in learning and the arts occurred during the Northern Renaissance?

3. What changes in the Christian Church did Martin Luther bring about?

4. How did the Reformation in Germany change German political life?

5. Why and how did the Church change in England?

Thinking Critically

Answer the following questions on a separate sheet of paper.

1. How did the Northern Renaissance differ from the Italian Renaissance?

2. Which leader—Henry VIII or Luther—do you think had a greater impact? Explain why.

CHAPTER 1   Section 1 (pages 5–13)

Human Origins in Africa

BEFORE YOU READ

In this section, you will read about the earliest humans.

AS YOU READ

Use the time line below to take notes on the earliest humans.

TERMS AND NAMES

artifact Remains, such as tools, jewelry, and other human-made objects

culture People's way of life

hominid Human or other creature that walks upright

Paleolithic Age Old Stone Age

Neolithic Age New Stone Age

technology Ways of applying knowledge, tools, and inventions to meet needs

Homo sapiens Species name for modern humans

3.5 million years ago	16 million years ago
Hominids live in East Africa	

25 million years ago	40,000 years ago

Scientists Search for Human Origins (pages 5–7)

How do scientists learn about early humans?

People can learn about the past by using written records. But these records cover only the last 5,000 years or so of human life. To learn about the time before written records, scientists called *archaeologists* use special skills and tools.

Archaeologists work at places called *digs*. They uncover **artifacts:** tools, jewelry, or other things made by people. Archaeologists also dig up bones—the bones of ancient humans and of the animals that lived with them. Some of these bones have become *fossils*, meaning they have survived over time because they were preserved in stone. By studying bones and artifacts, scientists learn about the **culture,** or way of life, of early humans.

In the early 1970s, archaeologists in East Africa found the footprints of humanlike beings, called *australopithencines*. Humans and other creatures that walk upright, such as australopithecines, are called **hominids.** These footprints were made about 3.5 million years ago.

Because these early beings walked upright, they could travel long distances more easily than four-footed ones. They could also use their free arms to carry food, tools, and children. They also had an *opposable thumb* that could move across the palms of their hands and touch their other fingers. The opposable thumb allowed them to pick up and hold objects.

Analyzing Key Concepts: Culture
Culture is the way of life of a group of people.

---

1. **What were the first humanlike beings, and where were they found?**

_____

The Old Stone Age Begins (pages 7–8)

What advances did hominids make during the Stone Age?

Humans made important advances during a period called the Stone Age, when people used tools made of stone. At this time, they also began to use fire and learned to speak.

Scientists divide the Stone Age into two parts. The **Paleolithic Age,** or Old Stone Age, began about 2.5 million years ago and lasted until about 8000 B.C. The **Neolithic Age,** or New Stone Age, went from about 8000 B.C. to around 3000 B.C.

Much of the Old Stone Age overlapped the Ice Age, when the earth was colder than it is now. Huge sheets of ice—*glaciers*—covered much of the land. About 10,000 years ago, the earth's temperature increased. The ice sheets grew smaller. People began to roam wider stretches of land.

In East Africa, archaeologists found a hominid fossil they named *Homo habilis.* It means "man of skill." The fossil was given this name because the site also held tools made of lava rock. *Homo habilis* lived about 2.5 million years ago.

About 1.6 million years ago, another kind of hominid lived. This one was *Homo erectus. Homo erectus* began to use tools for special purposes. That is when **technology** began. *Homo erectus* dug for food in the ground, cut meat from animal bones, and scraped animal skins. *Homo erectus* also used fire and may have had spoken language.

2. Who were *Homo habilis* and *Homo erectus?*

_____

_____

_____

_____

The Dawn of Modern Humans; New Findings Add to Knowledge (pages 8–13)

Who were the Neanderthals and Cro-Magnons?

Many scientists believe that *Homo erectus* eventually developed into humans, or **Homo sapiens.**

Scientists once thought that Neanderthals were ancestors of modern humans but no longer do. These hominids appeared 200,000 years ago. They lived in caves or built shelters of wood or animal skins. At one time, they were thought to be rough and wild people. Now scientists think that they may have held religious beliefs. These people found ways to survive the freezing cold of the Ice Age. About 30,000 years ago, though, the Neanderthals strangely disappeared.

About 10,000 years before these people vanished, the *Cro-Magnons* appeared. Their bodies were just like those of modern people. Scientists think that these people worked with one another in planning large-scale hunts of animals. They may have also had more skill at speaking than did the Neanderthals. Because they had these skills, the Cro-Magnons were better at finding food. That may explain why Cro-Magnons survived and Neanderthals did not.

Scientists are continuing to work on many sites in Africa. New discoveries continually add to what we know about human origins.

3. How is the species *Homo sapiens* different from earlier hominids?

_____

_____

_____

_____

_____

Humans Try to Control Nature

BEFORE YOU READ

In the last section, you read about the earliest humans.

In this section, you will read about the development of agriculture and a settled way of life.

AS YOU READ

Use the web below to take notes on changes in human culture.

TERMS AND NAMES

nomad Person who wanders from place to place

hunter-gatherer Person whose food supply depends on hunting animals and collecting plant foods

Neolithic Revolution Agricultural revolution that occurred during the Neolithic period

slash-and-burn farming Early farming method that some groups used to clear fields

domestication Taming of animals

Early Advances in Technology and Art (pages 14–15)

What advances occurred in technology and art?

The first humans had faced a struggle for survival. For thousands and thousands of years, they had two concerns: finding food and protecting themselves. They used fire, built shelters, made clothes, and developed spoken language. These areas of life are all part of culture. Human culture changed over time as new tools replaced old and people tested new ideas. Later some modern humans increased the pace of change.

The people who had lived in the early part of the Old Stone Age were **nomads.** They moved from place to place. They were **hunter-gatherers.**

They found food by hunting and gathering nuts, berries, and roots. The Cro-Magnon people, who came later, made tools to help them in their search.

These early modern humans used many tools—more than 100 different ones. They used stone, bone, and wood. They made knives, hooks, and bone needles.

Cro-Magnon people also created works of art, including paintings. Thousands of years ago, Stone Age artists mixed charcoal, mud, and animal blood to make paint. They used this paint to draw pictures of animals on cave walls and rocks.

1. In what ways did Cro-Magnon people change human culture?

_____

_____

_____

The Beginnings of Agriculture

(pages 15–16)

What was the Neolithic Revolution?

For centuries, humans lived by hunting and gathering. Humans lived in small groups of 25 to 70 people. They often returned to a certain area in the same season each year because they knew it would be rich in food at that time.

Over the years, some humans realized that they could leave plant seeds in an area one year and find plants growing there the next year. This was the beginning of a new part of human life: farming.

Scientists think that the climate became warmer all around the world at about the same time. Humans' new knowledge about planting seeds combined with this warmer climate to create the **Neolithic Revolution**—the agricultural revolution that occurred during the Neolithic period.

Instead of relying on gathering food, people began to produce food. One early farming method was **slash-and-burn farming.** That meant cutting trees and burning them to clear a field. The ashes were used to fertilize the soil.

Along with growing food, they also began to raise animals. They tamed horses, dogs, goats, and pigs. **Domestication** is the taming of animals.

Archaeologists have studied a site in the northeastern part of modern Iraq. It is called Jarmo. The people who lived in this region began farming and raising animals about 9,000 years ago.

2. How did life change during the Neolithic Revolution?

_____

_____

Villages Grow and Prosper

(pages 16–18)

How did the growth of farming villages change life?

People began to farm in many spots all over the world. The study of one village in modern-day Turkey shows what early farming communities were like.

The village called Catal Huyuk grew on the good land near a river. Some workers grew wheat, barley, and peas. Others raised sheep and cattle. Because these workers produced enough food for all the people, others could begin developing other kinds of skills. Some made pots out of clay that they baked. Others worked as weavers. Some artists decorated the village. Archaeologists have found wall paintings that show animals and hunting scenes. They have found evidence that the people had a religion, too.

Early farming villagers had problems, too. If the farm crop failed or the lack of rain caused a drought, people starved. Floods and fires caused damage and death. With more people living near each other than before, diseases spread easily. Still, some of these early villages grew into great cities.

3. What problems did early farming villages face?

_____

_____

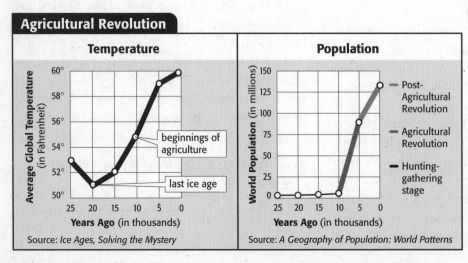

Agricultural Revolution

Temperature

Average Global Temperature (in Fahrenheit)

60° 58° 56° 54° 52° 50°

beginnings of agriculture

last ice age

25 20 15 10 5 0
Years Ago (in thousands)

Source: *Ice Ages, Solving the Mystery*

Population

World Population (in millions)

150 125 100 75 50 25 0

○ = Post-Agricultural Revolution
○ = Agricultural Revolution
○ = Hunting-gathering stage

25 20 15 10 5 0
Years Ago (in thousands)

Source: *A Geography of Population: World Patterns*

Skillbuilder

1. When did the Agricultural Revolution begin?

_____

2. When was population growth the greatest?

_____

CHAPTER 1 Section 3 (pages 19–23)

Civilization Case Study: Ur in Sumer

BEFORE YOU READ

In the last section, you read about the development of agriculture and a settled way of life.

In this section, you will read about factors leading to the rise of civilizations.

AS YOU READ

Use the chart below to take notes on how civilizations develop.

TERMS AND NAMES

civilization Culture with advanced cities, specialized workers, complex institutions, record keeping, and improved technology

specialization Development of skills in a specific kind of work

artisan Skilled worker that makes goods by hand

institution Long-lasting pattern of organization in a community

scribe Professional record keeper

cuneiform Wedge-shaped writing developed in Sumer

Bronze Age Time when people began using bronze

barter Trading goods and services without money

ziggurat Pyramid-shaped monument; part of a temple in Sumer

FEATURES OF CIVILIZATION	EXAMPLES FROM UR
1. Advanced Cities	
2.	
3.	
4.	
5.	

Villages Grow into Cities (pages 19–20)

What changed as villages grew into cities?

Over time, farmers developed new tools—hoes, sickles, and plow sticks. These helped them grow even more food. They decided to plant larger areas of land. The people in some villages began to irri-gate the land, bringing water to new areas. People invented the wheel for carts and the sail for boats. These new inventions made it easier to travel between distant villages and to trade.

Life became more complex as the villages began to grow. People were divided into social classes. Some people had more wealth and power than others. People began to worship gods and goddesses that they felt would protect their crops and make their harvests large.

1. How did life become more complex?

_____

_____

_____

_____

How Civilization Develops (pages 20–21)

What makes a civilization?

One of the first civilizations arose in Sumer. It was in Mesopotamia, between the Tigris and Euphrates rivers of modern Iraq. A **civilization** has five features.

First, a civilization has advanced cities that contain many people and serve as centers for trade.

Second, civilizations have specialized workers. **Specialization** is the development of skills needed for one specific kind of work. Skilled workers who make goods by hand are called **artisans.**

Third, civilizations have complex institutions. Government, organized religion, and an economy are examples of complex **institutions.**

A fourth feature of civilizations is record keeping, which is needed to keep track of laws, debts, and payments. It also creates the need for writing. **Scribes** were people who used writing to keep records. **Cuneiform,** which means "wedge shaped," was a form of writing invented in Sumer.

Fifth, civilizations have improved technology that can provide new tools and methods to solve problems.

Sumer had all the features of a civilization. One of the new technologies in Sumer was making a metal called bronze. The term **Bronze Age** refers to the time when people began using bronze to make tools and weapons.

Analyzing Key Concepts: Civilization
Civilization is defined as a complex culture with five characteristics—advanced cities, specialized workers, complex institutions, record keeping, and improved technology.

---

2. Name the five features of a civilization.

_____

_____

_____

_____

Civilization Emerges in Ur
(pages 22–23)

What was civilization like in Ur?

One of the early cities of Sumer was named Ur. The city was surrounded by walls built of mud dried into bricks. Ur held about 30,000 people. Social classes included rulers and priests, traders, craft workers, and artists.

Farmers outside the city walls raised the food for them all. Some workers dug ditches to carry water to the fields. Officials of the city government planned all this activity.

Inside the city, metalworkers made bronze points for spears. Potters made clay pots. Traders met people from other areas. They traded the spear points and pots for goods that Ur could not produce. This way of trading goods and services without money is called **barter.** Sometimes their deals were written down by scribes.

Ur's most important building was the temple. Part of the temple was a **ziggurat,** a pyramid-shaped structure. Priests there led the city's religious life.

3. What social classes existed in Ur?

_____

_____

_____

_____

_____

_____

Glossary   **CHAPTER 1** The Peopling of the World

archaeologists Scientists who learn about past human life and activities

australopithecines A type of prehistoric hominid

Cro-Magnons Early humans who walked erect and appeared about 40,000 years ago

digs Explorations usually done by digging dirt or sand in search of evidence from the past

fossils Remains of life preserved in stone

glaciers Huge sheets of ice

Homo erectus Early human who used tools for special purposes

Homo habilis Hominid called "man of skill"

Jarmo Site in Iraq where people were farming and raising animals by 7000 B.C.

Neanderthals Early humans who walked erect and vanished mysteriously

opposable thumb Physical feature that sets humans apart from animals by enabling them to pick up and hold objects

pottery Pots and other objects made from baked clay

AFTER YOU READ

Terms and Names

A. Write the name or term in each blank that best completes the meaning of the paragraph.

Neolithic Age

Paleolithic Age

hominids

technology

Homo sapiens

Homo habilis, Homo erectus, Neanderthals, and Cro-Magnons are all examples of **1**_____. Evidence of these early humans was discovered by archaeologists. This evidence dates back to both the **2**_____, which lasted until about 8000 B.C. and the later **3**_____. One important change between *Homo habilis* and *Homo erectus* was probably in developing **4**_____. *Homo erectus* is believed to have used intelligence to create tools. After *Homo habilis* and *Homo erectus*, **5**_____ appeared.

B. Write the letter of the name or term next to the description that explains it best.

a. institution

b. domestication

c. ziggurat

d. specialization

e. cuneiform

_____ **1.** Development of skills for a specific type of work

_____ **2.** Pyramid-shaped structure that was part of a Sumerian temple

_____ **3.** Taming of animals

_____ **4.** Wedge-shaped writing developed in Sumer

_____ **5.** Long-lasting pattern of organization in a community

Main Ideas

1. How and where do scientists find evidence of early human life?

_____

_____

_____

2. What hominids developed during the Old Stone Age?

_____

_____

_____

_____

3. How were the Neanderthals and the Cro-Magnons alike and different?

_____

_____

_____

_____

4. People who lived in the early part of the Old Stone Age were nomads. What was their life like?

_____

_____

_____

_____

5. Name five features of Ur that show it was a civilization.

_____

_____

_____

Thinking Critically

Answer the following questions on a separate sheet of paper.

1. How did the Cro-Magnons differ from early hunter-gatherers?

2. Why was the development of farming so important?

City-States in Mesopotamia

BEFORE YOU READ

In the last chapter, you read about the earliest humans and the first civilization.

In this section, you will learn more about early civilization in a part of Mesopotamia called Sumer.

AS YOU READ

Use the chart below to take notes on Sumer.

SUMER	NOTES
Geography	• part of Fertile Crescent • rich soil from flooding of rivers • problems: needed irrigate, defend, find materials they did not have

Geography of the Fertile Crescent (pages 29–30)

What problems did the Sumerians face?

There is an *arc* of rich land in Southwest Asia that is called the **Fertile Crescent.** Two of its rivers, the Tigris and the Euphrates, flood in the spring. This flooding leaves rich mud, called *silt*, in the plain between the rivers. Because of this, many thousands of years ago humans began to settle in

that plain, known as **Mesopotamia.** They grew wheat and barley. It was here that the first civilization began.

About 3300 B.C., the Sumerians moved into this region and settled. They faced three problems. First, the floods were not regular, and once they passed, the hot sun quickly baked the land into clay. Second, the small farming villages had no protection against enemies. Third, the area lacked stone, wood, and metal to use for tools.

The Sumerians solved these problems. They dug irrigation ditches from the river to their fields so they could bring water to their crops. They built walls of baked mud around their villages for *defense*. Because they could grow more food than they needed, they traded the extra for stone, wood, and metal from other lands.

1. How did the Sumerians solve the problems they faced?

_____

_____

Sumerians Create City-States

(page 30)

How did the Sumerians govern?

Several large city-states were at the center of the Sumerian world. These **city-states** had control over a surrounding area. They could act independently, much like a country does today. Slowly, some people rose to power in a number of the city-states. They became rulers, as did their children after them. Rule of an area by the same family is called a **dynasty.**

As population and trade grew, Sumerians came into contact with other peoples. Their own ideas affected others. The Sumerians also got ideas from other cultures. This process of spreading ideas or products is called **cultural diffusion.**

2. Who governed the city-states?

_____

_____

Sumerian Culture (pages 31–32)

What did the Sumerians believe and accomplish?

The Sumerians believed in **polytheism,** or many gods. Each god had power over different forces of nature or parts of their lives. Sumerians believed that people were just the servants of the gods. Souls of the dead went to a joyless place under the earth's crust. These views spread to other areas and shaped the ideas of other peoples.

Society was divided into social classes. At the top were the priests and kings, after whom came wealthy merchants. Next were workers in fields and workshops. Slaves made up the lowest level. Women could enter most careers and could own property. But there were some limits on them.

The people of Sumer invented the sail, the wheel, and the plow. They were the first to use bronze. They also developed the first writing system—on clay tablets. They invented arithmetic and geometry, which they used to help build large structures.

3. How was Sumerian society organized?

_____

_____

The First Empire Builders (pages 32–34)

Who built the world's first empire?

Centuries of fighting between the city-states made the Sumerians weak. In 2350 B.C., the conqueror Sargon defeated Sumer and captured other cities to the north. He built the world's first **empire.** An empire brings together several peoples, nations, or previously independent states. It puts them under the control of one ruler.

A few hundred years later, a different group of people conquered the Sumerians. These people built a capital at Babylon, establishing the Babylonian Empire. They were led by a king named **Hammurabi.** He is famous for his code of laws. It was a harsh code that punished people for wrongdoing. However, it also made it clear that the government had some responsibility for taking care of its people.

4. Why was Hammurabi's Code important?

_____

_____

CHAPTER 2 Section 2 (pages 35–41)

Pyramids on the Nile

BEFORE YOU READ

In the last section, you read about the city-states that arose in Mesopotamia.

In this section, you will learn about early civilization along the Nile.

AS YOU READ

Use the web below to show how Egypt was unified, what its culture was like, and how it fell.

TERMS AND NAMES

delta Marshy area at the mouth of a river

Narmer King of Upper Egypt who united Upper and Lower Egypt

pharaoh Egyptian ruler thought of as a god

theocracy Government in which the ruler is considered to be a divine figure

pyramid Resting place for Egyptian kings after death

mummification Process by which a body is preserved after death

hieroglyphics Egyptian writing system

papyrus Plant used to make a paper-like material

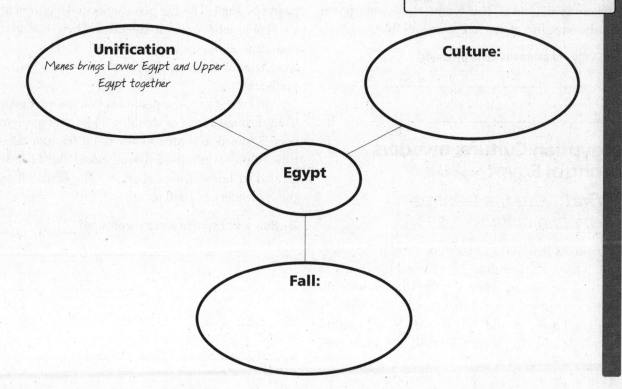

Unification
Menes brings Lower Egypt and Upper Egypt together

Culture:

Egypt

Fall:

The Geography of Egypt (pages 35–37)

What was the key feature of early Egypt's geography?

Another civilization arose along the banks of the Nile River of East Africa. The Nile flows to the North, toward the Mediterranean Sea. It, too, floods each year. The waters leave rich soil on the river banks. There the people of ancient Egypt grew food and began to build their own culture. They worshiped the Nile as a life-giving god.

For many centuries, the people of Egypt lived in two kingdoms, Upper Egypt and Lower Egypt. Upper Egypt extended north from the Nile's first area of rapids, or cataracts, to the Nile **delta.** The delta is a broad, marshy, triangular area of rich land. Lower Egypt began here and continued north to the Mediterranean, just 100 miles away.

1. How did the Nile create boundaries?

_____

_____

Egypt Unites into a Kingdom
(pages 37–38)

Who ruled the kingdom?

About 3000 B.C., the king of Upper Egypt, **Narmer,** united the two kingdoms. In the years between 2660 and 2180 B.C., the basic marks of the culture of Egypt arose. Ruling over the land was the **pharaoh.** He was not only a king but was also seen as a god. A government in which a ruler is seen as a divine figure is a **theocracy.**

Pharaohs believed they would rule the land after their death. So these kings built themselves magnificent tombs. The tombs were huge **pyramids** made out of _massive_ limestone blocks.

2. Why did pharaohs build pyramids?

_____

_____

Egyptian Culture; Invaders Control Egypt (pages 38–41)

What were the features of Egyptian culture?

Egyptians believed in many gods and in an afterlife. One god, they thought, weighed the hearts of each dead person. Hearts judged heavy with sin were eaten by a beast. Good people, with _featherweight_ hearts, would live forever in a beautiful Other World. To prepare for this, Egyptians preserved a dead person's body by **mummification.** This kept the body from decaying.

The pharaoh and his family were at the top of Egyptian society. Below them were people of wealth who owned large amounts of land, the priests, and members of the government and army. Then came the middle class—_merchants_ and people who worked in crafts. At the bottom were the peasants. In later times, the Egyptians had slaves. People could move from one rank of society to another. Those who could read and write held important positions.

The Egyptians, like the Sumerians, developed a way of writing. In their writing system, **hieroglyphics,** pictures stood for sounds or ideas. The pictures could be put together to make words and sentences. At first they wrote on stone. Later they began to make a kind of paper from the **papyrus** plant. The Egyptians invented a system of written numbers and a calendar. Their calendar had 12 months, each of which had 30 days. They were famous in the ancient world for their ideas in medicine.

After 2180 B.C., the pharaohs lost power. Egypt went through a time of troubles. Then strong rulers once again took control. They ruled for four centuries until a group of Asians called the Hyksos arrived in horse-drawn chariots. The land fell to these invaders in 1640 B.C.

3. How was Egyptian society organized?

_____

_____

_____

_____

Planned Cities on the Indus

TERMS AND NAMES
subcontinent Land mass that is a distinct part of a continent
monsoon Seasonal wind
Harappan civilization Ancient settlements in the Indus River Valley

BEFORE YOU READ

In the last section, you read about the development of culture along the Nile.

In this section, you will learn about the first civilization in India.

AS YOU READ

Use the chart below to take notes on the civilization of the Indus.

INDUS CIVILIZATION	NOTES
geography	• subcontinent separate from other areas • rich soil from flooding of rivers • problems: unpredictable river, winds

The Geography of the Indian Subcontinent (pages 44–45)

What is a subcontinent?

South Asia—modern India, Pakistan, and Bangladesh—is a **subcontinent.** It is separated from the rest of Asia by tall mountains. Just below the mountains are two large plains that hold the Ganges and Indus rivers. The high mountains gave the people safety from invaders. Because they lived close to the sea, the people could travel over the water to trade with other peoples.

The people along the Indus River faced many of the same challenges that the people in Mesopotamia did. Their river flooded each year and left soil good for farming. But the floods did not occur at the same time each year. Also, the river sometimes changed course. The region's weather caused problems, too. Each winter, strong winds blew dry air across the area. Each spring, the winds brought heavy rains. These seasonal winds are called **monsoons.**

1. What challenges did the people along the Indus River face?

_____

_____

Civilization Emerges on the Indus; Harappan Culture (pages 46–48)

What *were cities like on the Indus?*

Historians cannot understand the writings of the people who settled in the Indus Valley. So, they have not learned much about these people. They do know that they were farming along the river by about 3200 B.C. The culture is called **Harappan civilization** because many discoveries were made near the city of Harappa. They also know that the culture of these people covered an area larger than either Mesopotamia or Egypt.

About 2500 B.C., these people began building their first cities. In Mesopotamia, cities were a jumble of winding streets. In the Indus Valley, however, the builders carefully planned their cities. They made a *grid* of streets. They built an area called a *citadel* that was easy to defend. All the important buildings were here. They also had systems for carrying water and sewage.

Because the houses were mostly alike, scholars think that the Indus culture did not have big differences between social classes.

These early people left an important mark on the region. Some religious objects include symbols that became part of later Indian culture. Historians also think that the people of the area had extensive trade with people in the region and with the people of Mesopotamia.

2. Name two conclusions that have been drawn about Harappan civilization.

_____

_____

Mysterious End to Indus Valley Culture (page 49)

How *did Indus Valley culture end?*

Around 1750 B.C., the cities began to show signs of decline. The Indus Valley civilization collapsed around 1500 B.C. Satellite images suggest a shift in the earth's crust that caused earthquakes. Because of the quakes the Indus River may have changed its course. This would stop the good effects of the yearly floods. The people may have overworked the land. This would have left the soil too poor to produce crops.

3. Name two reasons why Indus Valley civilization may have ended.

_____

_____

In their private baths, people took showers by pouring pitchers of water over their head.

Wastes drained through clay pipes into brick sewers running below the streets.

Skillbuilder

Use the illustration to answer the questions.

1. Drawing Conclusions What advance in technology is shown in this illustration?

_____

_____

2. Clarifying What happened to the wastewater?

_____

_____

River Dynasties in China

TERMS AND NAMES

loess Fertile soil

oracle bone Animal bone used by ancient Chinese priests to communicate with the gods

Mandate of Heaven Divine approval of the ruler

dynastic cycle Pattern of rise, fall, and replacement of dynasties

feudalism Political system in which nobles or lords are granted the use of lands that belong to the king

BEFORE YOU READ

In the last section, you read about Indus Valley culture.

In this section, you will learn about the earliest cultures in China.

AS YOU READ

Use the chart below to take notes on how geography and early cultures influenced the development of Chinese culture.

```
┌─────────────────┐   ┌─────────────────┐   ┌─────────────────┐
│   Geography     │   │  Shang Culture  │   │   Zhou Culture  │
│ Developed apart │   │                 │   │                 │
│  from other     │   │                 │   │                 │
│    cultures     │   │                 │   │                 │
└─────────────────┘   └─────────────────┘   └─────────────────┘
          \                   │                    /
                   ┌───────────────────┐
                   │  Chinese Culture  │
                   └───────────────────┘
```

The Geography of China (pages 50–51)

How did geography affect China's past?

The last of the great early civilizations arose in China and continues to this day. China's geography caused it to develop apart from other cultures.

A great ocean, huge deserts, and high mountains isolate China from other areas. The mountains did not protect China totally, however. People living to the north and west invaded the land many times during Chinese history.

There are two rich rivers within China—the Huang He and the Yangtze. Almost all the good farmland in China lies between these rivers. The Huang He deposited huge amounts of *silt* when it

overflowed. This silt is fertile soil called **loess.** The Chinese people also made use of the flood waters of these rivers.

1. Why did China develop apart from other cultures?

_____

_____

Civilization Emerges in Shang Times (pages 51–52)

What was the Shang Dynasty?

A few thousand years ago, some people began to farm along China's rivers. About 2000 B.C., the first dynasty of rulers brought government to China.

Around 1500 B.C., a new dynasty, the Shang, began to rule. This dynasty left the first written records in China. Objects found in their palaces and tombs also tell us much about their society. Chinese people built their buildings of wood, not mud-dried brick as the other early cultures did. Huge walls made of earth surrounded these buildings to protect them. The walls were needed because it was a time of constant war.

The king and the *nobles* who helped him fight these wars were at the top of Shang society. At the bottom was the mass of peasants who lived in simple huts outside the city walls. They worked hard on the farms, using wooden tools because the Shang believed that bronze was too good to be used for farming.

2. What were three features of Shang culture?

_____

_____

_____

The Development of Chinese Culture (pages 52–54)

What beliefs shaped Shang society?

Shang society was held together by a strong belief in the importance of the group—all the people—and not any single person. The most important part of society was the family. Children grew up learning to respect their parents.

The family played a central role in Chinese religion, too. The Chinese thought that family members who had died could still influence the lives of family members who were alive. They gave respect to dead members of the family, hoping to keep them happy. Through the spirits of their *ancestors*, the Shang also asked for advice from the gods. They used **oracle bones** to do this. These were animal bones and shells. Priests wrote questions on them. Then they touched them with something hot. The priest interpreted the cracks that resulted to find their answers.

The Chinese system of writing differed from those of other groups. Symbols stood for ideas, not sounds. This allowed the many different groups in China to understand the same writing even though each had a special spoken language. The written language had thousands of symbols, however. This made it very hard to learn. Only specially trained people learned to read and write.

3. Name three important values of Shang culture.

_____

_____

_____

Zhou and the Dynastic Cycle

(pages 54–55)

What is the Mandate of Heaven?

About 1027 B.C., a new group, the Zhou, took control of China. They adopted Shang culture. They also started an idea of royalty that was new to China. Good rulers, they said, got authority to rule from heaven. This was known as the **Mandate of Heaven.** They claimed the Shang rulers were not just and had lost the favor of the gods. That is why they had to be replaced. From then on, the Chinese believed in *divine* rule. However, it also meant that disasters such as floods or war pointed to a ruler that had lost the support of the gods and needed to be replaced. Until the early 1900s, the Chinese had one dynasty after another. This pattern of rise, fall, and replacement of dynasties is known as the **dynastic cycle.**

The Zhou gave members of the royal family and other nobles the rights to large areas of land. They established **feudalism.** Feudalism is a political system in which the nobles owe loyalty to the king. The nobles promise to fight for the rulers and to protect the peasants who live on the land.

Eventually the Zhou rulers lost all power. The nobles fought each other for control of China in a period called the *"time of the warring states."* It lasted many hundred years. The Chinese people suffered during this time.

4. Name two important changes brought about by the Zhou.

_____

_____

_____

Glossary		**CHAPTER 2** Early River Valley Civilizations
ancestors Long-ago relatives **arc** Curved shape **citadel** Fort or other stronghold **defense** Protection against enemies **divine** Godlike **featherweight** Extremely light; as light as a feather	**grid** Large square or rectangle evenly divided into squares or rectangles **massive** Huge **merchants** People who sell goods; shopkeepers **nobles** People just below rulers or kings in wealth and power	**silt** thick bed of rich mud deposited on the plain as a result of a river's flooding **_"time of the warring states"_** Time after the Zhou lost power when nobles fought each other for control of China

AFTER YOU READ

TERMS AND NAMES

A. Write the name or term in each blank that best completes the meaning of the paragraph.

mummification

theocracy

pharaoh

Narmer

pyramids

A king named **1**_____brought together Upper Egypt and Lower Egypt to create one kingdom. The ruler of the kingdom was the **2**_____. This ruler was seen as a divine figure. This meant the government was a **3**_____. It also helps explain why the rulers built **4**_____for themselves. They were preparing for rule after their death. To preserve their bodies for this future life, a process called **5**_____ was used.

B. Write the letter of the term next to the description that explains it best.

a. monsoon

b. loess

c. irrigation

d. dynasty

e. empire

_____ **1.** Several peoples or nations brought together under one rule

_____ **2.** System of bringing water to fields

_____ **3.** Fertile soil deposited by flooding

_____ **4.** Seasonal wind

_____ **5.** Series of rulers from a single family

Main Ideas

1. In Sumer, what was a city-state?

_____

_____

_____

2. What did Sargon and Hammurabi have in common?

_____

_____

_____

3. Name three effects of the Nile on the life and culture of ancient Egypt.

_____

_____

_____

4. How were Indus Valley cities constructed?

_____

_____

_____

5. What is a dynastic cycle, and where did it occur?

_____

_____

_____

Thinking Critically

Answer the following questions on a separate sheet of paper.

1. Describe the impact of the environment on river valley civilizations.

2. Explain the importance of family in early Chinese culture.

The Indo-Europeans

BEFORE YOU READ

In the last chapter, you read about peoples who built civilizations in the great river valleys.

In this section, you will learn about the movements of two groups of people who lived on the grasslands of Asia.

AS YOU READ

Use the chart below to take notes on where each group migrated and on the features of its culture.

TERMS AND NAMES

Indo-Europeans Group of Asian peoples who migrated to many different places

steppes Dry grasslands

migration Movement of people from one place to another

Hittites Group of Indo-European peoples who occupied Anatolia

Anatolia Large peninsula in modern-day Turkey

Aryans Group of Indo-Europeans

Vedas Sacred literature of the Aryans

Brahmin Priest

caste Class

Mahabharata Poem that tells the story of a great war

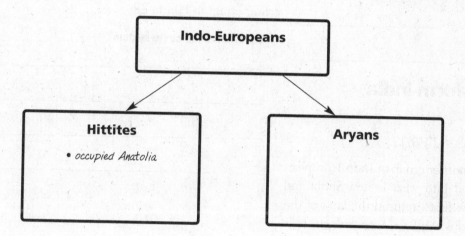

Indo-Europeans → Hittites (• occupied Anatolia), Aryans

Indo-Europeans Migrate (pages 61–62)

Who were the Indo-Europeans?

The Indo-Europeans were a group of peoples who came from the **steppes**—the dry grasslands of western Asia. The Indo-Europeans rode horses and tended cattle, sheep, and goats. They spoke many different languages, but all of them came from the same original language.

For some reason, starting about 1700 B.C., the Indo-Europeans began to leave their homeland. They moved into some of the settled areas and began to conquer them. These **migrations,** move-

ments of people from one region to another, took place over a long period of time.

1. What happened to the Indo-Europeans?

_____

_____

The Hittite Empire (pages 62–63)

Who were the Hittites?

The **Hittites** were one of these Indo-European peoples. They rode two-wheeled chariots and used iron weapons to conquer **Anatolia.** Anatolia is also called Asia Minor. It is a huge *peninsula* in modern-day Turkey. The Hittites moved farther and took the ancient lands of Mesopotamia. When they moved to the south, they ran into the Egyptians. Neither side was able to defeat the other. So, they decided to make peace.

The Hittites adopted many features of the culture that had grown in Mesopotamia before they arrived. They changed others to suit their own ideas. Their laws, for instance, were less harsh than the code of Hammurabi. The Hittites ruled their Southwest Asian empire from about 2000 to 1190 B.C. Then they fell to a new wave of invaders.

2. How did the Hittites react to the culture they found in Mesopotamia?

_____

_____

_____

_____

Aryans Transform India

(pages 63–65)

Who were the Aryans?

The **Aryans** were another group of Indo-European people. They moved into what is now India and *transformed* it. They first captured the land of the people of the Indus Valley. *Archaeology* tells almost nothing about the Aryans. But their sacred literature, the **Vedas,** tells a lot about them.

The Aryans were divided into three classes of people. There were priests (**Brahmins**), warriors, and peasants or traders. They viewed the non-Aryans living in the area as a fourth class. Over time, they made many rules for how people in these classes, or **castes,** could interact with one another. People were born into their caste for life. Some "impure" people lived in a group outside this class system. They were butchers, grave diggers, and trash collectors. Because they did work that was thought unclean, they were called *"untouchables."*

Over many centuries, the Aryans took more and more of what is now India. Eventually many powerful people tried to create their own kingdoms. They fought each other until one kingdom, Magadha, won control over almost all of India. Around this time, an *epic* poem, the **Mahabharata,** was written. It tells of the blending of cultures at the time. It also sets down ideals that were to become important in Hindu life.

3. What is the caste system?

_____

_____

_____

_____

Hinduism and Buddhism Develop

BEFORE YOU READ

In the last section, you read about the Hittites and the Aryans.

In this section, you will learn about the roots of Hinduism and Buddhism.

AS YOU READ

Use the chart below to show features of Hinduism, Buddhism, and also Jainism.

```
              ┌─────────────────────┐
              │   World Religions    │
              └─────────────────────┘
            ↙            ↓            ↘
  ┌──────────────┐ ┌──────────────┐ ┌──────────────┐
  │   Hinduism   │ │   Buddhism   │ │   Jainism    │
  │ collection of│ │              │ │              │
  │   beliefs    │ │              │ │              │
  └──────────────┘ └──────────────┘ └──────────────┘
```

Hinduism Evolves Over Centuries (pages 66–68)

What is Hinduism?

Hinduism is a collection of religious beliefs that forms no one system. Unlike many religions, it was not founded by only one person. It is a religion that allows great variety for its followers. Certain ideas became common to the beliefs of all Hindus.

Hindus believe that each person has a soul. However, there is also a larger soul, called *Brahman*, that brings together all the individual souls. A person's goal is to become free of desire and not bothered by suffering. When that takes place, the person's soul wins escape from life on Earth. Hindus believe in **reincarnation.** They believe the soul is born again into another body after death. In the next life, the soul has another chance to learn its lessons. According to Hindus, how a person behaves in one life has an effect on the person's next life. This is the soul's **karma**— good or bad deeds.

Another religion that arose in India was **Jainism**. It was started by Mahavira, a man who lived from about 599 to 527 B.C. He believed that every creature in the world—even an animal—has a soul. Because of that, people must be sure not to harm any creature. Today, Jains take jobs that are certain not to hurt living things.

1. Name three Hindu beliefs.

_____

_____

_____

The Buddha Seeks Enlightenment (pages 68–71)

What is Buddhism?

Another new religion, Buddhism, arose about the same time as Hinduism and Jainism. Buddhism has millions of followers all around the world. It was started around 528 B.C. by **Siddhartha Gautama.**

Siddhartha searched for a way that would allow him to escape the suffering of human life. He spent many years searching for this answer. He was looking for **enlightenment,** or wisdom. Finally, he sat down and *meditated* under a tree. After 49 days, he had his answer. He was now called the Buddha, which means the "enlightened one."

The Buddha began to teach others how to attain enlightenment. They were to follow a plan of behavior called the Eightfold Path—right views, right resolve, right speech, right conduct, right livelihood, right effort, right mindfulness, and right

concentration. This would lead to **nirvana,** or a release from selfishness and pain.

As with Hinduism, the Buddha taught that the soul would be reborn into a new life. This chain of new lives would continue until the soul, like Buddha, reached understanding.

These ideas attracted many followers. Many people who lived in the lower classes of Indian society saw these ideas as a chance to escape from the limits placed on them. This teaching also spread in southern India. There the Aryans did not have much influence. Some followers took the ideas to other lands.

In the centuries after Buddha's death in 483 B.C., Buddhism appeared in Southeast Asia. Later it was carried to China and then to Korea and Japan. Merchants and traders played an important role in spreading the religion. Strangely, in India where Buddhism was founded, the religion faded. Many places that are important to Buddhism remain in India, however. Buddhists from around the world come there to visit locations connected to the life of Buddha.

2. Name four basic beliefs of Buddhism.

_____

_____

_____

_____

Four Noble Truths of Buddhism	
First Noble Truth	Life is filled with suffering and sorrow.
Second Noble Truth	The cause of all suffering is people's selfish desire for the temporary pleasures of this world.
Third Noble Truth	The way to end all suffering is to end all desires.
Fourth Noble Truth	The way to overcome such desires and attain enlightenment is to follow the Eightfold Path, which is called the Middle Way between desires and self-denial.

Skillbuilder

Use the chart to answer the questions,

1. What is the subject of the first three noble truths?

_____

_____

2. What is the Eightfold Path?

_____

_____

CHAPTER 3 Section 3 (pages 72–76)

Seafaring Traders

BEFORE YOU READ

In the last section, you read about major religions that developed in India.

In this section, you will learn about traders whose influence spread throughout the Mediterranean.

AS YOU READ

Use the web below to take notes on how trade spread both products and culture.

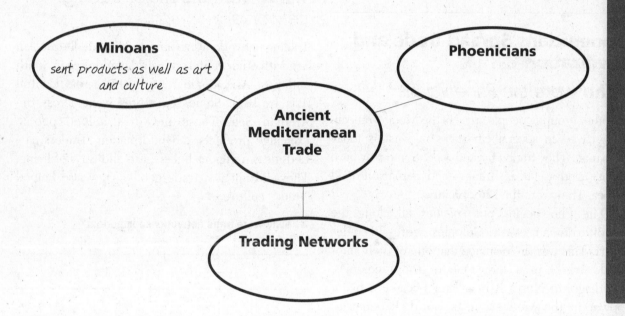

Minoans — *sent products as well as art and culture*

Phoenicians

Ancient Mediterranean Trade

Trading Networks

Minoans Trade in the Mediterranean (pages 72–73)

Who were the Minoans?

In the Mediterranean area, a new culture arose on the island of Crete. The **Minoans** were peaceful people who lived in rich cities that were safe from invaders. They controlled trade in their area, Crete. Crete is a large island on the southern edge of the **Aegean Sea.** The Minoans sent their fine pottery, swords, and metal drinking cups to other lands. They also sent other countries their style of art and architecture. This style later had influence on the art of Greece.

Archaeologists have explored the ruins of **Knossos,** the capital city of the Minoans. It was the archaeologists that first called the culture Minoan, after its famous ruler, **King Minos.** They found beautiful wall paintings that offer views of Minoan culture. One interesting feature of Minoan life was the high position that women appear to have held. An earth goddess seems to have headed all the gods of Crete, and women ruled over some important religious places. Women did not play such important roles among other peoples who lived nearby.

Minoan cities were damaged in 1470 B.C. by a series of disasters. First, a number of earthquakes rocked the island, destroying buildings. Then a volcano exploded on a nearby island. That was followed by huge waves and clouds of white ash from the volcano's fire. These shocks seem to have been too much for the Minoans. The Minoan civilization ended about 1200 B.C.

1. What were three important features of Minoan culture?

_____

_____

_____

_____

Phoenicians Spread Trade and Civilization (pages 73–76)

Who were the Phoenicians?

Another group of people arose in the Mediterranean. They lived in several city-states in what is today Lebanon. They traded far and wide. Some may have even sailed as far as Britain—and perhaps around Africa. They were the **Phoenicians.**

The Phoenicians put *colonies* all along the Mediterranean coast. Colonies were 30 miles apart. This was the distance that one of their ships could travel in a day. One of those colonies, Carthage, in North Africa, later became a major power in the Mediterranean world. Phoenicians traded such goods as wine, weapons, metals, ivory, slaves, and objects made of wood and glass. They also made a purple dye that was highly valued.

The important achievement of the Phoenicians was their alphabet. They used symbols to stand for the sounds of consonants. They brought their system of writing to other lands such as Greece, where Greeks changed the form of some letters. The alphabet that we use today, however, had its beginnings in Phoenician writing.

2. How did the Phoenicians spread their culture?

_____

_____

_____

_____

Ancient Trade Routes (page 76)

What were the major trading networks?

Trading networks also connected the Mediterranean Sea with other centers of world commerce in South and East Asia. Some routes went across Central Asia by land. Some sea routes went across the Arabian Sea. These networks helped people exchange products and information. Traders carried ideas, religious beliefs, art, and ways of living. They did not just trade goods. They also helped "trade" culture.

3. Why were trade networks so important?

_____

_____

_____

_____

The Origins of Judaism

BEFORE YOU READ

In the last section, you read about the spread of culture through trade.

In this section, you will learn about the *origins* of Judaism.

AS YOU READ

Uses the chart below to take notes on the beginnings of Judaism.

TERMS AND NAMES

Palestine Region on the eastern end of the Mediterranean Sea

Canaan Ancient home of the Hebrews

Torah First five books of the Hebrew Bible

Abraham "Father" or the first of the Hebrew people

monotheism Belief in a single god

covenant Mutual promise between god and the Hebrews

Moses According to the Torah, the man that led the Jews out of slavery

Israel Region on the eastern end of the Mediterranean Sea

Judah Hebrew kingdom in Palestine

tribute Payment made by a weaker power to a stronger power

Promised Land	Kingdom of Israel	Babylonian Captivity
• Canaan in Palestine		

The Search for a Promised Land

(pages 77–78)

Where did the Hebrews claim land?

The Hebrews made a claim to an important piece of land, the area now called **Palestine.** They believed the land had been promised to them by God. Their ancient home was the area of Palestine called **Canaan.** This region sat on the eastern edge of the Mediterranean Sea and on the Red Sea, which led to the Indian Ocean. It opened to the trade of many lands. Most of what we know about the early history of the Hebrews comes from the **Torah,** the sacred book of the Hebrews.

The story of the Hebrews began in Mesopotamia. There, according to the Torah, God chose a man named **Abraham** to be the "father," or the first of the Hebrews. God told Abraham to move his family to Palestine. Abraham promised that he and his people would always obey God. (The Hebrews were among the world's earliest peoples to believe in one god, or **monotheism.**) God, in turn, promised to always protect them from their enemies. This was the first of many **covenants**—promises between God and the Hebrews.

1. What role did Abraham play in early Hebrew history?

_____

_____

Moses and the Exodus (pages 78–80)

Who was Moses?

When their crops failed, the Hebrews moved to Egypt around 1650 B.C. Over time, they were forced to become slaves. After many years, they fled. The Hebrews called this mass departure *"the Exodus."*

According to the Torah, a man named Moses led them out of Egypt between 1300 and 1200 B.C. They wandered 40 years in a wilderness. During that time, the Torah says, God gave **Moses** the Ten Commandments. These were the laws that the Hebrews were to follow. For the second time, God promised to protect them in return for their obedience to his laws.

After Moses died, the Hebrews finally reached Palestine and settled. There they began to adopt new ways of life. They often fought with other peoples living in the area, as each group tried to control the best land and other resources.

The Hebrews were organized into twelve groups, called *tribes*. Each tribe was separate from the others. But in times of danger they would unite under leaders called *judges*. One of those judges was a woman named Deborah. It was unusual for women in Hebrew society to hold such a position. Women usually were expected to stay home and raise children.

The Hebrews had other leaders called *prophets*. They said that they were messengers sent by God to tell the people how he wanted them to act. These prophets told the people that they had two duties: to worship God and to deal in just and fair ways with one another. With this message, religion was changing. Instead of being a part of life run by priests, it was now a matter of each person living a *moral* life.

2. What were the Ten Commandments?

_____

_____

_____

_____

_____

The Kingdom of Israel (pages 81–82)

How was Israel formed?

After the exile, the only large tribe left was the tribe of Judah. As a result, the Hebrews came to be known as the Jews. Their religion was called Judaism.

From about 1020 to 922 B.C., the Jews were united into one kingdom, **Israel.** Three kings helped unite them. The first, Saul, drove off their enemies. The second, David, made Jerusalem the capital. The third, Solomon, built a magnificent temple to be used to worship God.

After Solomon's death, though, the kingdom split into two parts. Israel was in the north, and **Judah** was in the south. For the next two centuries, each of the kingdoms had times of prosperity, followed by low periods.

3. How was Israel split?

_____

_____

_____

The Babylonian Captivity (page 82)

Who conquered Israel and Judah?

Disaster came when both kingdoms lost their independence. Israel and Judah began to pay tribute to Assyria. **Tribute** is money paid by a weaker power to a stronger power to make sure it does not attack.

Eventually, the northern kingdom fell to the Assyrians. Later, the southern kingdom fell to the Babylonians. Many Jews were forced into exile in Babylon. They lived there for many years during what was known as the Babylonian *Captivity*. Then the Babylonians themselves were conquered by the Persian king Cyrus the Great. The new ruler let 40,000 Jews return home.

4. What was the Babylonian Captivity?

_____

_____

Glossary   CHAPTER 3   People and Ideas on the Move

archaeology Study of past human life and activities

Brahman Larger soul that brings together individual souls, in Hinduism.

captivity State of being kept against one's will

colonies Lands under the control of another power

epic Long poem that tells a story; long story written in poetry

Exodus Mass departure of Jews from Egypt

judge Leader of a Hebrew tribe

meditated Cleared the mind of everyday thought

moral Based on principles of right and wrong

origins Beginnings

peninsula Body of land surrounded on three sides by water

prophet Leader whom the Hebrews believed to be a messenger of god

transform Change

tribe One of twelve original groups of Hebrews

untouchables People thought of as unclean and therefore outside the caste system

AFTER YOU READ

Terms and Names

A. Write the name or term in each blank that best completes the meaning of the paragraph.

Anatolia

Aryans

Indo-Europeans

steppes

migrations

Thousands of years ago, there were peoples in Asia called **1**_____. They herded animals on dry grasslands known as **2**_____. Over several centuries, a number of **3**_____ of these peoples took place. They settled in many different areas. One group occupied Asia Minor, or **4**_____. They were the Hittites. Another group settled in the Indus River Valley of what is now India. They were the **5**_____.

B. Write the letter of the name or term next to the description that explains it best.

a. monotheism

b. reincarnation

c. karma

d. nirvana

e. covenant

_____ **1.** Release from selfishness and pain

_____ **2.** Agreement between God and the Hebrew people

_____ **3.** Good or bad deeds

_____ **4.** Belief that an individual soul is reborn again and again

_____ **5.** Belief in one god

AFTER YOU READ (cont.) **CHAPTER 3** People and Ideas on the Move

Main Ideas

1. How did Aryan invaders change India?

_____

_____

_____

2. What makes Hinduism different from other religions?

_____

_____

_____

3. What was Siddhartha Gautama looking for, and how did he find it?

_____

_____

_____

4. What may have caused the end of Minoan civilization?

_____

_____

_____

5. What role did Moses play in early Jewish history?

_____

_____

_____

Thinking Critically

Answer the following questions on a separate sheet of paper.

1. What effect did the Minoans and Phoenicians have on neighboring cultures?

2. What was unique about the religious beliefs of the Hebrews?

Name _____   Date _____

The Egyptian and Nubian Empires

BEFORE YOU READ

In the last section, you read about the religion of the ancient Hebrews.

In this section, you will read about the interaction of Egypt and Nubia.

AS YOU READ

Use the time line below to take notes on changes in Egypt and Nubia.

> ### TERMS AND NAMES
>
> **Hyksos** Invaders that ruled Egypt from 1640 to 1570 B.C.
>
> **New Kingdom** Period after the Hyksos rulers
>
> **Hatshepsut** New Kingdom ruler who encouraged trade
>
> **Thutmose III** Warlike ruler; stepson of Hatshepsut
>
> **Nubia** Region of Africa bordering Egypt
>
> **Ramses II** Pharaoh and great builder of Egypt
>
> **Kush** Nubian kingdom
>
> **Piankhi** Kushite king who forced the Libyans out of Egypt
>
> **Meroë** Home and trading center of the Kush kingdom

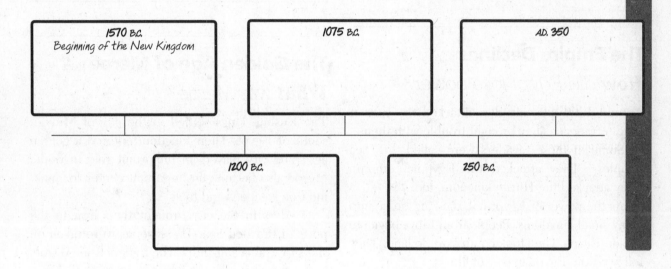

| 1570 B.C. Beginning of the New Kingdom | 1075 B.C. | AD. 350 |

| 1200 B.C. | 250 B.C. |

Nomadic Invaders Rule Egypt

(page 89)

Who were the Hyksos?

At the end of its second period of glory, power struggles weakened Egypt. New invaders, the **Hyksos,** arrived. They had the chariot. Egyptians had never seen this war machine before. The Hyksos ruled Egypt for many years. Some historians believe that the Hyksos encouraged the Hebrews to settle there.

Around 1600 B.C., a series of warlike rulers began to restore Egypt's power. Eventually, the Hyksos were driven completely out of Egypt. The pharaohs began some *conquests* of their own.

1. How did Egypt fall to the Hyksos?

_____

_____

The New Kingdom of Egypt

(pages 90–91)

The time from 1570 to 1075 B.C. is called the **New Kingdom.** In this third period, Egypt was richer and more powerful than ever.

Hatshepsut was one of the rulers of the New Kingdom. She encouraged trade. Her stepson, **Thutmose III,** was a much more warlike ruler. He and other pharaohs of this New Kingdom brought

Egyptian rule to Syria and Palestine in the east. They also moved south into **Nubia.** This was a part of Africa near where the Nile began. Egypt had traded with Nubia and influenced the region since the time of the Middle Kingdom.

The pharaohs of the New Kingdom did not build pyramids, like those who had come before. Instead, they built great tombs in a secret place called the *Valley of the Kings.* Some pharaohs also built huge palaces for themselves or temples to the Egyptian gods.

Ramses II stood out among the great builders of the New Kingdom. He reigned from about 1290 to 1244 B.C.

2. What was the relationship between Nubia and Egypt during the New Kingdom?

_____

_____

_____

The Empire Declines (pages 91–92)

How did Egypt lose power?

Around 1200 B.C., invaders attacked the eastern Mediterranean. They brought trouble with them.

Some of these invaders were called the "Sea Peoples." They attacked the Egyptian empire. They attacked the Hittite kingdom, too.

As the power of Egypt fell, the land broke into many small kingdoms. People from Libya began to invade Egypt. They took control of the land. They followed the Egyptian way of life.

3. Who invaded Egypt?

_____

_____

The Kushites Conquer the Nile Region (pages 92–93)

How did the Kushites rule?

As Egypt grew weaker, the Nubian kingdom of **Kush** became more powerful. Under Egyptian rule, the people of Kush accepted many Egyptian traditions and customs. They felt that they had to protect Egyptian values.

A Kushite king named **Piankhi** moved into Egypt to force out the Libyans. He united the Nile Valley. He wanted to bring back Egypt's glory. The Kushites ruled Egypt for a few decades. Then the Assyrians invaded. They forced the Kushites back to their home.

4. How did the Kushites view Egyptian culture?

_____

_____

_____

The Golden Age of Meroë (page 94)

What was Meroë?

The Kushite kings settled in the city of **Meroë,** south of Egypt. Their kingdom entered a golden age. The city played an important role in trade. Meroë also became an important center for making iron weapons and tools.

Traders in the city brought their iron to the ports of the Red Sea. These goods were taken on ships to Arabia and India. The traders from Meroë, in the meantime, brought back jewelry, cloth, silver lamps, and glass bottles. The city thrived from about 250 B.C. to about A.D. 150. By A.D. 350 Meroë had fallen to rival Aksum, a seaport farther south.

5. Why was Meroë important?

_____

_____

_____

The Assyrian Empire

BEFORE YOU READ

In the last section, you read about Egypt and Nubia,

In this section, you will read about the Assyrians, the people who took over Egypt.

AS YOU READ

Use the chart below to take notes on Assyria.

TERMS AND NAMES

Assyria Powerful empire in northern Mesopotamia

Sennacherib Assyrian king and empire builder

Nineveh Assyria's capital on the Tigris River

Ashurbanipal Assyrian king who gathered writing tablets from many lands

Medes People who helped to destroy the Assyrian empire

Chaldeans People who helped to destroy the Assyrian empire

Nebuchadnezzar Chaldean king who rebuilt Babylon

ASSYRIA	
Military might	defended themselves first; then conquered others

A Mighty Military Machine

(pages 95–96)

Who were the Assyrians?

For a time, **Assyria** was the greatest power in Southwest Asia. The Assyrians began as a farming people in the northern part of Mesopotamia. Because their homes were open to attack, they formed a strong fighting force. Soon they turned to conquest. Assyrian kings, including the fierce **Sennacherib,** built an empire that stretched from east and north of the Tigris River all the way to central Egypt.

The Assyrians used many different methods to win their battles. Their soldiers carried strong iron-tipped spears and iron swords. They used large numbers of men with bows. They dug tunnels under city walls to weaken them. They used heavy battering rams to knock down the wooden gates of the city.

The Assyrians conquered almost everything in their path. They usually killed or enslaved those they defeated. Some Assyrian kings bragged about their cruelty toward people they captured.

Sometimes conquered peoples would revolt. Assyrians wanted to stop these rebellions and *dominate* the peoples. They forced groups of captives to leave their homelands. Then the captives were too far away to cause trouble.

1. **What made the Assyrians such a strong fighting force?**

_____

_____

The Empire Expands (page 96)

Whom did the Assyrians conquer?

Between 850 and 650 B.C., the Assyrians conquered all of Mesopotamia along with Syria and Palestine. Then they took modern Turkey and Egypt. They ruled by putting in power kings who would support them. They also collected taxes and tribute—yearly payments from peoples who were weaker. If a city did not pay, the Assyrian army moved in and destroyed it.

The Assyrian kings were builders, too. One built the city of **Nineveh** on the north branch of the Tigris River. It was the largest city of its day. The city was surrounded with walls.

Another king, **Ashurbanipal,** gathered thousands of writing tablets from the lands that had been taken. Some of these tablets were dictionaries. The collection provided historians with much information about the earliest civilizations in Southwest Asia. The library was also the first to have many of the features of a modern library, including a cataloging system.

2. **Besides conquering other people, what did the Assyrians accomplish?**

_____

_____

_____

_____

The Empire Crumbles (pages 97–98)

Why did the Assyrians fall?

The Assyrians had also made many enemies over the years. After a while, those enemies banded together. An army made up of **Medes, Chaldeans,** and others struck back. In 612 B.C., they destroyed the city of Nineveh. Many people in the area were glad that the city was in ruins.

The Chaldeans, who had ruled the area earlier, took control of Mesopotamia again. A Chaldean king named **Nebuchadnezzar** rebuilt the city of Babylon. Once more it was one of the greatest cities of the world. The city included famous hanging gardens with many different plants from the cool mountain regions, Slaves watered the plants with hidden pumps.

Babylon also featured a *ziggurat*. This stepshaped pyramid soared 300 feet into the air. It was the tallest building in Babylon. At night, priests would study the stars and the planets. They recorded what they saw. This was the beginning of the science of *astronomy*.

3. **Who were the Chaldeans?**

_____

_____

_____

_____

The Persian Empire

BEFORE YOU READ

In the last section, you read about the military might of the Assyrians.

In this section, you will read about the wise rule of the Persians.

AS YOU READ

Use the chart below to take notes on key people in the rise of Persia, its rule, and its religion.

Cyrus	*general and king who conquered a huge empire*
Cambyses	
Darius	
Zoroaster	

TERMS AND NAMES

Cyrus Persian king who created a huge empire

Cambyses Cyrus's son

Darius Persian king who put satraps in place and built the Royal Road

satrap Governor who ruled locally

Royal Road Road that helped unify the Persian Empire

Zoroaster Persian prophet and religious reformer

The Rise of Persia (pages 99–100)

How did Persia come to power?

Persia, a new power, arose east of Mesopotamia, in modern Iran. The area had good farmland. It was also rich in minerals. There were mines of copper, lead, gold, and silver.

The Persians joined with other forces to help defeat the Assyrians. About 550 B.C., the Persians began their own conquests.

Their king was **Cyrus,** an excellent general.

Cyrus led his army to conquer a huge empire. It stretched from the Indus River in India all the way to Anatolia. The empire covered about 2,000 miles. Cyrus took all this land in just over 10 years.

Cyrus won this vast land in part because of the wise way he treated the people there. Cyrus did not follow the examples of the Assyrians. They destroyed towns and cities. Cyrus, however, made sure that his army did not harm the people he conquered. He allowed the people to practice their old religions, too. Cyrus let the Hebrews return to

Jerusalem and rebuild their temple there. Cyrus was also a great warrior. He was killed in battle.

1. What made Cyrus a great leader?

_____

_____

_____

Persian Rule (pages 100–101)

Who was Darius?

Cyrus died in 530 B.C. The kings who followed him had to decide how to run the vast new empire. His son, **Cambyses,** conquered Egypt. Cambyses was not like his father. He was not wise or understanding. He did not respect the Egyptians and their way of life.

The next king, **Darius,** proved as able as Cyrus. Darius put down several revolts. He won more land for the empire and created a government for the empire. Only Greece escaped Persian control.

Darius divided the land into 20 *provinces,* each holding a certain group of people. He allowed each group to practice its own religion, speak its own language, and obey many of its own laws. He also put royal governors—**satraps**—in place to make sure that the people obeyed his laws.

Darius built the **Royal Road** to unite his large empire. This excellent road system ran 1,677 miles. Royal messengers on horses could travel this distance in about seven days. The Royal Road made communication better within the empire. Transportation became easier too.

Darius also had metal coins made that could be used for business anywhere in the empire. The coins had a standard value. This money system, along with the Royal Road, helped increase trade.

2. How did Darius change Persia?

_____

_____

_____

The Persian Legacy (page 103)

What is the legacy of the Persian Empire?

During the Persian Empire, a new religion arose in Southwest Asia. A prophet named **Zoroaster** said there were two powerful spirits. One stood for truth and light. The other represented evil and darkness. The two spirits were in a constant struggle. People needed to take part in the struggle. They would be judged on how well they fought. These ideas influenced later religions.

The Persians left their mark in history. They were fair and understanding. The Persians showed respect for other cultures. Their government brought order to Southwest Asia.

3. What mark did the Persians leave on history?

_____

_____

_____

The Unification of China

BEFORE YOU READ

In the last section, you read about the Persian empire.

In this section, you will learn how China was restored to order.

AS YOU READ

Use a chart like the one below to take notes on new ideas and changes in China that restored order.

TERMS AND NAMES

Confucius China's most influential scholar

filial piety Children's respect for their parents and elders

bureaucracy Organization of government into agencies and departments

Daoism Philosophy of Laozi that puts people in touch with the forces of nature

Legalism Chinese idea that a highly efficient and powerful government is the key to social order

I Ching Chinese book that gave advice on practical and everyday problems

yin and yang Powers that govern the natural rhythms of life and must be balanced

Qin dynasty Dynasty that unified China

Shi Huangdi First emperor of China; leader of the Qin Dynasty

autocracy Government in which the ruler has unlimited power

Ideas about social order	Ideas about government	Ideas about nature	New political rule
Confucius stresses five basic relationships			

Order in China

Confucius and the Social Order

(pages 104–105)

How did Confucius try to restore order in China?

After the fall of the Zhou dynasty, China became a land of troubles. Ancient Chinese values were forgotten. Civilization seemed doomed. Yet some thinkers tried to find ways to restore these values.

One of the most important thinkers was **Confucius.** He was born in 551 B.C. Confucius believed that order could return. But first, the peo-

ple would have to work at five basic relationships. These were ruler and subject, father and son, husband and wife, older and younger brothers, and friend and friend. The family relationships, he thought, were the most important. Confucius stressed that children should practice **filial piety.** This is respect for parents and elders.

Confucius also tried to make government better. He helped create the basis of a **bureaucracy.** This is a system of departments and agencies for running the government. Education was important for the people who held jobs in this kind of government.

Over time, the ideas of Confucius spread to other countries of East Asia.

1. How did Confucius try to restore ancient Chinese values?

_____

_____

_____

Other Ethical Systems (pages 105–107)

What other ethical systems developed?

Another thinker of this period was Laozi. He said nature follows a universal force called the Dao, or "the Way." His beliefs are called **Daoism.**

Other thinkers formed a set of beliefs called **Legalism.** They said the government should use the law to restore order in China.

Some Chinese people looked for practical advice in solving problems. They might refer to a book called *I Ching.* Other people turned to the idea of **yin and yang.** These two powers represented the harmony between opposite forces in the universe.

2. What was the basic purpose of all these ethical systems?

_____

_____

_____

The Qin Dynasty Unifies China

(pages 107–109)

What happened during the Qin Dynasty?

A 13-year-old ruler became ruler of the **Qin Dynasty.** He ended the troubles of the warring states. This young ruler used the ideas of Legalism to unite China. After ruling for 20 years, he took a new name—**Shi Huangdi.** This means "First Emperor."

Shi Huangdi doubled the size of China. He established an **autocracy.** In this kind of government, a ruler has unlimited power. Shi Huangdi forced wealthy *nobles* to give up their land in the country and move to his capital city. He destroyed his enemies. The emperor wanted to control ideas, too. He ordered his government to burn books.

Shi Huangdi also had peasants build a network of roads that linked one corner of the empire to another. He set standards for writing, law, money, and weights and measures to be followed throughout the empire.

In the past, some Chinese rulers had built sections of wall to try to block attacks from northern nomads. Shi Huangdi had hundreds of thousands of poor people connect these sections of wall and make a huge barrier. When finished, the Great Wall of China stretched for thousands of miles.

These steps won the emperor little support. When he died, his son took the throne. Just three years into his *reign,* peasants revolted and managed to overthrow the emperor. By 202 B.C., the Qin dynasty had given way to the Han dynasty.

3. Name two changes that Shi Huangdi made.

_____

_____

_____

Daoism	Legalism
• The natural order is more important than the social order	• A highly efficient and powerful government is the key to social order.
• A universal force guides all things.	• Punishments are useful to maintain social order.
• Human beings should live simply and in harmony with nature.	• Thinkers and their ideas should be strictly controlled by the government.

Skillbuilder

Use the chart to answer the questions.

1. Which set of ideas places more importance on social order?

_____

2. In what ways are these ideas opposite?

_____

Glossary

astronomy Study of heavenly bodies

conquests Acts of conquering or taking over

dominate Has control over

nobles Wealthy landowners just below the level of emperor or king

province Outside territory controlled or ruled by another area or country

reign Rule by a king or other power

unifies Brings together as one

Valley of the Kings Place where New Kingdom pharaohs built tombs

ziggurat Step-shaped pyramid

AFTER YOU READ

Names and Terms

A. Write the name or term in each blank that best completes the meaning of the paragraph.

bureaucracy

Legalism

autocracy

Confucius

Shi Huangdi

After the warring states period in China, new ideas were formed. Many of these came from an important thinker named **1**_____. He wanted to organize society around five basic relationships. He also favored creating a **2**_____ in the government. More ideas about changing government came from **3**_____. This way of thinking urged rich rewards for those who carried out their duties and strong punishments for those who did not. The leader of the Qin Dynasty and the new emperor of China, **4**_____, also had strong ideas about government. He established an **5**_____, a government in which the ruler has unlimited power.

B. Write the letter of the name next to the description that explains it best.

a. Cyrus

b. Sennacherib

c. Nineveh

d. Darius

e. Nebuchadnezzar

_____ **1.** Persian ruler and builder of the Royal Road

_____ **2.** Founder of the Persian empire

_____ **3.** Capital of Assyria

_____ **4.** Chaldean king who restored Babylon

_____ **5.** Assyrian king and warrior

Main Ideas

1. What was Meroë?

_____

_____

_____

2. What did Nebuchadnezzar accomplish?

_____

_____

3. Name three things for which Cyrus might be remembered.

_____

_____

_____

4. Explain the ideas of Zoroaster.

_____

_____

_____

5. Name the five relationships that Confucius said people should work at.

_____

_____

_____

Thinking Critically

Answer the following questions on a separate sheet of paper.

1. Explain the relationship of Kush to Egypt.

2. How did Shi Huangdi unite his empire?

Cultures of the Mountains and the Sea

BEFORE YOU READ

In the last section, you read about belief systems in ancient China and the Qin dynasty.

In this section, you will read about the development of culture in ancient Greece.

AS YOU READ

Use the chart below to take notes on ancient Greek life.

GEOGRAPHY	MYCENAEANS	DORIANS
mountains and valleys separated areas		

Geography Shapes Greek Life

(pages 123–124)

How did geography influence the Greeks?

The lives of the ancient Greeks were shaped by the geography of their land. Greece is a rocky land with high mountains and deep valleys. These landforms were like barriers. Moving over the land was difficult. For these reasons, Greeks living in different areas could not be easily *united*.

Good farmland covered only about one-fourth of Greece and could not support many people. The need for more living space and the lack of good farmland may have influenced the Greeks to find new colonies.

The Greeks had easy access to the sea, however. They became excellent sailors. Trade became important because Greece had few natural resources.

The climate is mild. As a result, Greek people spent much time outdoors. They attended public events and even *conducted* government outside.

1. Why was sea trade important for the Greeks?

_____

_____

_____

_____

Mycenaean Civilization Develops (pages 124–125)

Who were the Mycenaeans?

A large wave of people moved from Europe, India, and Southwest Asia. Some of these people settled on the Greek mainland around 2000 B.C. They were later called **Mycenaeans.** They were ruled by powerful warrior-kings.

The Mycenaeans developed a strong culture. They borrowed from the Minoan culture of Crete. They adapted the Minoan form of writing and artistic design. The Mycenaeans also became interested in trade.

According to legend, Mycenaeans fought a long war with the people of Troy, a city in Turkey. This conflict was called the **Trojan War.**

The war was said to have started because a Trojan youth kidnapped a Greek woman. Her name was Helen. She was the beautiful wife of a Greek king. The Greek army later destroyed Troy.

2. How were the Mycenaeans influenced by the Minoans?

_____

_____

_____

_____

Greek Culture Declines Under the Dorians (pages 125–126)

What was Greece like under the Dorians?

The culture of the Mycenaeans fell about 1200 B.C. Sea raiders destroyed their palaces. A less advanced people called the **Dorians** occupied the land. For the next 400 years, Greece went into decline. No written records exist from this period. Little is known about this era.

The spoken word lived on, however. A great storyteller named **Homer** made up **epics,** long poems, based on tales he heard. Epics are about heroes and their deeds. One of Homer's great epics was the _Iliad._ It centers on the heroes of the Trojan War. The heroes of the _Iliad_ are warriors. Homer tells about their courage and noble actions in battle.

The Greeks also created a rich set of **myths.** These stories explain the actions of gods and events in nature. In Greek myths, gods often act like humans. For example, they show feelings, such as love, hate, and jealousy. Unlike humans, though, the Greek gods lived forever.

3. How did Homer keep Greek culture alive under the Dorians?

_____

_____

_____

_____

Name ______________________ Date ____________

CHAPTER 5 Section 2 (pages 127–133)

Warring City-States

TERMS AND NAMES

polis City-state of ancient Greece

acropolis Fortified hilltop in an ancient Greek city

monarchy Government ruled by a king or queen

aristocracy Government ruled by a small group of noble families

oligarchy Government ruled by a few powerful people

tyrant Powerful ruler who gained control of a city-state's government by asking the common people for support

democracy Rule by the people

helot Peasant forced to stay on the land

phalanx Side-by-side fighting formation of Greek foot soldiers

Persian Wars Wars between Greece and the Persian Empire

BEFORE YOU READ

In the last section, you read about the rise of early cultures in Greece.

In this section, you will read about city-states and their governments.

AS YOU READ

Use the chart below to take notes on the city-states,

GOVERNMENT	*city-state—main political unit* *ways to rule city-states—monarchy, aristocracy, oligarchy, democracy*
SPARTA	
ATHENS	
PERSIAN WAR	

Rule and Order in Greek City-States (page 127)

How were city-states governed?

The center of Greek life was the **polis,** or city-state. A polis was made up of a city and the countryside villages surrounding it. Men would gather in the marketplace or on a fortified hilltop in the polis, called an **acropolis,** to conduct business.

The city-states had different kinds of government. Some had a **monarchy,** a government ruled by a king or queen. Some had an **aristocracy,** a government ruled by a small group of *noble* families. Later, some merchants and craft workers formed an **oligarchy,** a government ruled by a few powerful people.

Sometimes, the common people clashed with the rulers of the city-states. Powerful individuals called **tyrants** sometimes appealed to the common people for support. Tyrants would then rule the city-state. Unlike today, tyrants generally were not considered harsh or cruel. Rather, they were looked upon as leaders who did things for the ordinary people.

1. What types of government existed in the city-states?

_____

_____

_____

Athens Builds a Limited Democracy (pages 128–129)

How was Athens governed?

In some city-states, most notably Athens, the idea of representative government took hold. In Athens, as in other city-states, wealthy nobles and poor people *clashed*. The people of Athens avoided major political problems, however, by making reforms. Reformers in Athens tried to build a **democracy,** or government by the people.

In 594 B.C., a trusted statesman named Solon came to power. He introduced far-reaching changes to the government of Athens. He gave citizens a greater voice. He made it possible for any citizen of Athens to join discussions in the assembly, which approved laws. About 90 years later a leader named Cleisthenes took power and introduced further democratic reforms.

Athenian citizens, then, were able to participate in a limited democracy. Not everyone was involved in making political decisions, though. Only free adult men were citizens. Women and slaves had few rights. They played little or no role in political life.

2. Why was Athens not a full democracy?

_____

_____

_____

Sparta Builds a Military State

(pages 129, 131)

How was Sparta governed?

Sparta was a very strong city-state in the south of Greece. It conquered its neighbor Messenia. The people of Messenia became **helots.** They were peasants forced to stay on the land they worked. They had to give the Spartans half their crops.

An *assembly*, the Council of Elders, and elected officials governed Sparta. Two kings ruled over Sparta's military. Sparta prized military skills. Boys joined the army at the age of seven and went through a long period of training as soldiers. Spartan women ran the family estates, freeing their husbands to serve in the army.

3. What was Sparta's focus as a city-state?

_____

_____

_____

The Persian Wars (pages 131–133)

Who fought the Persian Wars?

Over the years, the Greeks developed the ability to make iron weapons. Because these cost less than weapons made of bronze, more people could afford them. Soon each city-state had its own army. In this army, soldiers stood side by side. They had a spear in one hand and a shield in the other. Together they formed a **phalanx.**

The Persian Wars were fought between Greece and the Persian Empire. In 490 B.C., Persian ships landed 25,000 soldiers on the coast of Greece. At the Battle of Marathon, the Greeks won a tremendous victory that saved Athens.

Ten years later, the Persians returned. The Greeks lost a battle on land, despite the heroic efforts of a small band of Spartans. The Persians also burned Athens. However, the ships of Athens won a great sea battle. The Greeks followed it with another victory on land. The threat from Persia was over.

4. What was the outcome of the Persian Wars?

_____

_____

_____

CHAPTER 5   Section 3 (pages 134–139)

Democracy and Greece's Golden Age

BEFORE YOU READ

In the last section, you read about the government of the city-states.

In this section, you will read about democracy and the Golden Age of Greece.

AS YOU READ

Use the web below to show characteristics and events of Greece's Golden Age.

TERMS AND NAMES

direct democracy Form of government in which citizens rule directly

classical art Art in which harmony, order, and balance were emphasized

tragedy Serious drama dealing with such themes as love, hate, war, or betrayal

comedy Light and amusing play that may poke fun at serious subjects

Peloponnesian War War in which Athens and its allies were defeated by Sparta and its allies

philosopher Thinker who uses logic and reason to explore life's important questions

Socrates Greek thinker who explored truth and justice and developed a method of questioning and answering

Plato Socrates's student who wrote *The Republic,* a view of the ideal society

Aristotle Plato's student who developed a method for testing and organizing ideas.

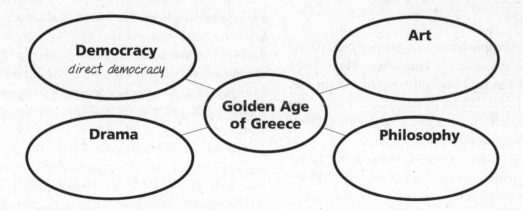

Democracy
direct democracy

Drama

Golden Age of Greece

Art

Philosophy

Pericles' Plan for Athens (pages 134–135)

How did Pericles change Athens?

Pericles led Athens during its golden age. He served in this role from 461 to 429 B.C. Greek culture reached new heights under his leadership. Pericles had a great influence over Athens. Pericles took many steps to make Athens better.

He set three goals. One goal was to make Athens much more democratic. More people served in the government. Pericles helped bring about **direct democracy.** This meant that citizens ruled directly and not through representatives. An assembly of male citizens had a voice in making laws for Athens.

Another goal was to make Athens stronger. Pericles tried to increase its wealth and power. He helped build up Athens's navy. It became the strongest in the Mediterranean.

Another goal was to make Athens beautiful. Pericles used money from the empire to buy gold, ivory, and marble. He helped fund great works of art.

1. What were Pericles' three main goals for Athens?

_____

_____

_____

Glorious Art and Architecture

(pages 135–136)

How was Greek art unique?

One of the glories of Athens was the *Parthenon*. This temple was built to honor the goddess Athena. It is a masterpiece of art. Like other buildings and sculptures in Greece, it is an example of **classical art.** It reflects order, balance, and *proportion*.

2. Why was the Parthenon built?

_____

_____

_____

Drama and History (page 136)

What kinds of drama did Greeks produce?

Athens also became home to a group of very skilled playwrights. Some wrote **tragedies.** These plays were about the pain and suffering of human life. Love, hate, and war were common themes. The main characters were called tragic heroes. They had flaws that caused their downfall.

Other playwrights wrote **comedies.** These plays made audiences laugh about important ideas. Some plays were critical of customs, politics, and people. Such performances showed that Athens was a free and open society.

Also, such writers as Herodotus and Thucydides pioneered the accurate reporting of events. Their works led to the development of the subject of history.

3. What was the purpose of Greek comedies?

_____

_____

_____

Athenians and Spartans Go to War (pages 137–138)

What was the Peloponnesian War?

After being *rivals* for many years, Sparta and Athens finally went to war. The **Peloponnesian War** began in 431 B.C. The conflict ended badly for Athens. In 430 B.C. a horrible *plague* killed a great many people in Athens. After several battles, the two sides signed a truce. However, they were soon back at war. Finally, Athens gave up in 404 B.C. Athens had lost its empire.

4. What was the result of the Peloponnesian War?

_____

_____

_____

Philosophers Search for Truth

(pages 138–139)

What did philosophers contribute to Greek culture?

After Athens's defeat, this city-state became home to several **philosophers.** They were thinkers who tried to understand human life. One of these great thinkers was **Socrates.** He believed deeply in truth and justice. Yet many people did not trust him. They thought his teachings were a danger to young people. Socrates was brought to trial and condemned to death.

His pupil, **Plato,** recorded many of Socrates's ideas. Plato became an important thinker in his own right. Plato's student, **Aristotle,** wrote books that summarized the knowledge of the Greeks. He also developed a way of reasoning. His system of logic became the foundation of scientific thought used today.

5. Who were three important Greek philosophers?

_____

_____

_____

Alexander's Empire

TERMS AND NAMES

Philip II King of Macedonia who conquered Greece

Macedonia Kingdom located just north of Greece

Alexander the Great Philip II's son who established a huge empire

Darius III Persian king

BEFORE YOU READ

In the last section, you read about the Golden Age of Greece and the fall of Athens.

In this section, you will learn about Alexander the Great and his empire.

AS YOU READ

Use the diagram below to take notes on Alexander's Invasions.

Persia	Egypt	India
in 334 B.C. soldiers invade Anatolia		

Alexander's Invasions

Philip Builds Macedonian Power

(pages 142–143)

Who were the Macedonians?

In 359 B.C., **Philip II** became king of **Macedonia,** a kingdom located just to the north of Greece. He was a strong leader and trained his troops to be tough fighters. Philip prepared his army to invade Greece.

The Athenian *orator* Demosthenes tried to warn the Greeks. He told them about Philip's plans. But they united too late to save themselves. The Macedonians won. Greek independence was now over.

Philip planned to invade Persia next. He never got the chance. He was killed. His son Alexander became king at age 20. He became known as **Alexander the Great.**

1. How did Greek independence end?

_____

_____

Alexander Defeats Persia (pages 143–144)

How did Alexander defeat Persia?

Alexander was a brilliant general, just like his father. He was prepared to carry out his father's dream of world *conquest*. In 334 B.C., Alexander invaded Persia. After Alexander's first victory, the king of Persia, **Darius III,** raised a huge army to face him. Alexander then used a surprise attack. Darius III had to retreat.

Alexander then moved south to enter Egypt. He was crowned pharaoh and founded a city that he named for himself—Alexandria. He then turned back to Persia and won another great battle. It ended all Persian resistance. The empire was his.

2. **What two kingdoms did Alexander defeat?**

_____

_____

Alexander's Other Conquests

(pages 144–145)

How far east did Alexander push?

Alexander pushed east, taking his army as far as India. He moved deep into that country. After many years of marching and fighting, however, his soldiers wanted to return home. Alexander agreed and turned back. On the way home, he began to make plans for how to govern his new empire. Then he suddenly fell ill and died. He was not yet 33 years old.

Three of Alexander's generals divided his empire. One ruled Macedonia and Greece. Another took control of Egypt. The third became ruler of the lands that used to be in the Persian Empire. Alexander's empire was not long lasting. Yet it had important effects. After Alexander, the people of Greece and Persia and all the lands between mixed together and shared ideas and culture.

3. **How did Alexander's power come to an end?**

_____

_____

CHAPTER 5 Section 5 (pages 146–149)

The Spread of Hellenistic Culture

TERMS AND NAMES

Hellenistic Relating to the culture that blended Greek with Egyptian, Persian, and Indian influences

Alexandria Egyptian city that was the center of Hellenistic culture

Euclid Greek mathematician and pioneer in geometry

Archimedes Greek scientist, inventor, and mathematician

Colossus of Rhodes Huge bronze statue created on the island of Rhodes

BEFORE YOU READ

In the last section, you read about the military conquests of Alexander the Great.

In this section, you will learn about the spread of Hellenistic culture.

AS YOU READ

Use the web below to take notes on developments in Hellenistic culture.

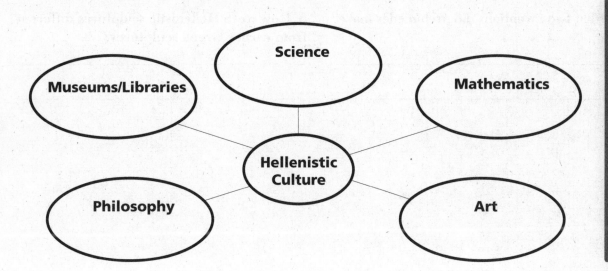

Hellenistic Culture in Alexandria

(pages 146–147)

What was Hellenistic culture?

A new culture arose—the **Hellenistic** culture. It blended Greek with Egyptian, Persian, and Indian influences. The center of this culture was **Alexandria,** Egypt. This city was located near the mouth of the Nile River on the Mediterranean Sea. Alexandria had a ship harbor. Trade was lively. Alexandria had a large population. These people were from many different countries.

Alexandria was also a beautiful city. Its huge lighthouse towered over the harbor. Its famous museum had works of art, a zoo, and a garden. Alexandria had the first true research library. It held half-million papyrus scrolls. These contained everything known in the Hellenistic world.

1. Give two reasons why Alexandria became a center of Hellenistic culture.

_____

_____

Science and Technology

(pages 147–148)

What new ideas arose in science, technology, and mathematics?

While scholars kept what was known about science alive, others learned new ideas. Some used an *observatory* to look at the stars and planets. One of these *astronomers* developed the idea that the sun was actually larger than Earth. No one had believed this before.

The thinkers in Alexandria also made advances in mathematics. **Euclid** wrote a book with the basic ideas of geometry. His approach is still used today. **Archimedes** invented many clever machines. One was the pulley. Another is called Archimedes screw. Its purpose was to bring water from a lower level to a higher one.

2. What two inventions did Archimedes make?

_____

_____

Philosophy and Art (pages 148–149)

What new developments occurred in philosophy and the arts?

Two new schools of philosophy arose in these times. The *Stoics* argued that people should live a good life to keep themselves in harmony with natural laws. Desire, power, and wealth led people down the wrong path. The *Epicureans* said that people could rely only on what they learned from their five senses. They urged everyone to live moral lives.

The arts were also important in Hellenistic times. Great achievements occurred in sculpture. Sculpture in the earlier Greek style aimed at showing perfect forms. In the Hellenistic age, sculpted figures were more realistic and emotional. The largest known Hellenistic statue is the **Colossus of Rhodes.** It stood over 100 feet high.

3. How were Hellenistic sculptures different from earlier Greek sculptures?

_____

_____

Name _____ Date _____

assembly Law-making body in ancient Greece

astronomers Scientists who study the stars and planets

clashed Disagreed strongly

conducted Did the work of

conquest Act of conquering or taking over

Epicureans Philosophers who said people could rely only on what they learned through their five senses

noble Of very high rank

observatory Place for observing the movement of heavenly bodies

orator Public speaker; speech maker

Parthenon Temple in ancient Greece that is a masterpiece of classical art

plague Deadly disease that spreads quickly killing many

proportion A pleasing arrangement

rivals Competitors; people or groups determined to outdo each other

Stoics Philosophers who said people should live a moral life to keep them in harmony with natural laws

united Brought together as one

AFTER YOU READ

Names and Terms

A. Write the name or term in each blank that best completes the meaning of the paragraph.

Aristotle

classical art

Socrates

direct democracy

Plato

Three of the greatest gifts to western culture from ancient Greece were developments in democracy, philosophy, and art. The Athenians had a form of democracy in which all citizens, and not just their representatives, participated. This was **1** _____. In art, the Greeks valued balance, order, and proportion. The gave the world **2** _____. In philosophy, three Greek thinkers have influenced Western thought. The philosopher **3** _____ encouraged his thinkers to examine their beliefs and developed a method of questioning and answering still used today. His student, **4** _____, was also an important thinker. The philosopher **5** _____ invented a way of thinking logically.

B. Write the letter of the name next to the description that describes it best.

a. Archimedes

b. Philip II

c. Darius III

d. Euclid

e. Homer

_____ **1.** Leader of Macedonia who conquered Greece

_____ **2.** Persian king who fought Alexander the Great

_____ **3.** Greek poet

_____ **4.** Inventor of the pulley

_____ **5.** Mathematician who wrote the book *Elements*

AFTER YOU READ (cont.)   *CHAPTER 5* Classical Greece

Main Ideas

1. Give three examples of how the geography of Greece affected its civilization.

_____

_____

_____

2. What war did Athens and Sparta fight, and how did it end?

_____

_____

_____

_____

3. How was Athens governed under Pericles?

_____

_____

_____

4. Where did Alexander the Great turn back and why?

_____

_____

_____

_____

5. Name an advance made in science, technology, and mathematics during Hellenistic times.

_____

_____

_____

Thinking Critically

Answer the following questions on a separate sheet of paper.

1. Compare and contrast Athens and Sparta.

2. Discuss the features of Alexandria that show it was a center of Hellenistic culture.

Name ______________________ Date ____________

CHAPTER 6 Section 1 (pages 155–159)

The Roman Republic

TERMS AND NAMES

republic Government in which citizens have the right to select their own leader

patrician Aristocratic landowner

plebeian Farmer, artisan, or merchant; commoner

tribune Official who helped the plebeians protect their rights

consul Official who was like a king

senate Aristocratic branch of Rome's government

dictator Roman leader who had absolute power to make laws and command the army for a brief period

legion Military unit of the ancient Roman army

Punic Wars Series of wars between Rome and Carthage

Hannibal Carthaginian general who invaded northern Italy

BEFORE YOU READ

In the last section, you read about Hellenistic culture. In this section, you will read about the Roman republic.

AS YOU READ

Use the chart below to take notes on early Rome.

EARLY ROME	
Geography	On river Midpoint of the Mediterranean
Government	
Growth	

The Origins of Rome (pages 155–156)

Where was Rome founded?

The city of Rome was founded by the Latin people on a river in the center of Italy. It was a good location, which gave them a chance to control all of Italy. It put them near to the midpoint of the Mediterranean Sea. Two other groups lived in what is now Italy: the Greeks in the south, and the *Etruscans* in the north. The Romans borrowed some ideas from both peoples.

1. What were the advantages of Rome's location?

____

____

The Early Republic (pages 156–157)

How was Rome governed?

In 509 B.C., Romans overthrew the Etruscan king who had ruled over his people and over Rome. The Romans said Rome was now a **republic.** The people had the power to vote and choose leaders.

Two groups struggled for power in the new republic. One was the **patricians.** They were the *aristocratic* landowners who held most of the power. The other group was the **plebeians.** They were the common farmers, *artisans,* and merchants who made up most of the population. At first, the patricians had the most power. Over time, the plebeians got the right to form their own *assembly*. They could elect representatives called **tribunes.**

The basis for Roman law was the *Twelve Tables*. This set of rules said that all free citizens were protected by law.

The government had three parts, Two **consuls,** or officials, were elected each year. They led the government and the army.

The second part of the government was the **senate.** It usually had 300 members chosen from the upper classes, The senate passed laws.

The third, and most democratic, part of government was the assemblies. The assemblies included members from different parts of society, such as citizen-soldiers or plebeians. The assemblies could also make laws.

If there were a crisis, the republic could appoint a **dictator.** This was a leader with absolute power. The dictator made laws and commanded the army. But his power lasted for only six months.

Any citizen who owned property had to serve in the army. Roman soldiers were organized into military units called legions. The Roman **legion** was made up of some 5,000 heavily armed foot soldiers.

2. **What were the three main parts of Roman government?**

_____

_____

_____

_____

Rome Spreads Its Power (pages 158–159)

How did Rome spread its power?

In the fourth century B.C., Rome began to get larger. Within 150 years, it had captured almost all of Italy. Rome allowed some of the conquered peoples to enjoy the benefits of citizenship. With its good location, Rome saw a growth in trade. This brought it into conflict with Carthage, a trading city in North Africa.

From 264 to 146 B.C., Rome and Carthage fought three bitter wars called the **Punic Wars.** In the first, Rome won control of the island of Sicily, In the second, **Hannibal,** a brilliant Carthaginian general invaded northern Italy. He and his soldiers did much damage. But he was unable to take Rome. It took an equally brilliant Roman general, Scipio, to defeat him. By the time of the third war, Carthage was no longer a threat to Rome. Even so, Rome destroyed the city and made its people slaves. Carthage became a new Roman province.

3. **What happened as a result of the wars with Carthage?**

_____

_____

_____

_____

_____

CHAPTER 6 Section 2 (pages 160–165)

The Roman Empire

TERMS AND NAMES

civil war Conflict between two groups in the same country

Julius Caesar Ambitious leader who brought order to Rome

triumvirate Group of three rulers

Augustus First ruler of imperial Rome

Pax Romana Period of Roman peace and prosperity

BEFORE YOU READ

In the last section, you read about the creation of the Roman republic.

In this section, you will read about the transformation of Rome from a republic to an empire.

AS YOU READ

Use the chart below to take notes on the end of the Roman republic and the emergence of the Roman Empire.

Collapse of the Republic	*conflict between rich and poor*
A Powerful Empire	*power struggles*
Life in Imperial Rome	*civil wars*

The Republic Collapses (pages 160–162)

What conflicts existed in Rome?

Rome's victory in Carthage brought conflict between the rich and poor in Rome. **Civil war,** or fighting between groups in the same country, broke out. Leading generals fought for power.

Julius Caesar tried to take control. First he joined with two others—Crassus, a wealthy man, and Pompey, a successful general. They formed a **triumvirate,** a group of three leaders. For the next ten years, the triumvirate ruled Rome.

Caesar gained fame with several victories in battle. Pompey feared Caesar as a result. The two fought another civil war that lasted several years.

Caesar won the civil war and then governed as an absolute ruler, or a leader who holds all power.

Caesar made some reforms that increased his popularity. But some members of the senate mistrusted him. They killed him because they feared he wanted to become king.

Once again, Rome suffered civil war. Caesar's nephew was the winner. He took the title **Augustus,** meaning *"exalted* one." The Roman Empire was now ruled by one man.

1. How did Caesar's rule lead to the end of the republic?

_____

_____

A Vast and Powerful Empire

(pages 162–163)

What was the Pax Romana?

For about 200 years, the Roman empire was a great power. Its population of between 60 and 80 million enjoyed peace and prosperity. This period is known as the **Pax Romana**—Roman peace.

The empire stretched around the Mediterranean, from modern Syria and Turkey west and north to England and Germany. It relied on farming, which employed 90 percent of all workers.

Trade was also important. Traders used common coins to buy and sell goods. Coins made trading easier.

Rome had a vast trading network. Goods traveled throughout the empire by ship and along the Roman roads. The Roman navy protected trading ships.

The army defended all the people and Roman territories from attack. Many of the army's troops came from the conquered peoples. Once they finished their time in the army, they became Roman citizens.

Augustus was Rome's ablest emperor. He brought peace to the frontier, built many public buildings, and created a lasting government. He also set up a civil service. That is, he paid workers to manage the affairs of government.

Between A.D. 96 and A.D. 180, the Five Good Emperors ruled Rome. The death of Marcus Aurelius in A.D. 180 marked the beginning of the decline of the Roman Empire and the end of *Pax Romana.*

2   How were the people of the empire employed?

_____

_____

_____

_____

The Roman World (pages 163–165)

How did the quality of Roman life vary?

Throughout its history, Romans valued discipline, strength, and loyalty, The family was the center of Roman society. The oldest man in the family had complete authority in the household. He controlled all the property, too.

The Romans made more use of slaves than any civilization before. About one third of the people were slaves. Most slaves came from conquered lands. Slaves worked in the city and on farms. Some slaves were forced to become gladiators. Gladiators were professional fighters who fought to the death in public contests, Slaves did revolt from time to time. None of these revolts succeeded.

Quality of life in *imperial* Rome depended on social position. The wealthy ate well and enjoyed luxuries. The poor—including many people in Rome itself—had no jobs and received food from the government. Housing was poor. People lived in constant danger of fire. To distract people from their problems, the government gave many celebrations and *spectacles*.

3. Who were the slaves, and what work did they do?

_____

_____

_____

_____

_____

Name _____ Date _____

CHAPTER 6 Section 3 (pages 168–172)

The Rise of Christianity

BEFORE YOU READ

In the last section, you read about the *Pax Romana*. In this section, you will read about the development of Christianity.

AS YOU READ

Use the chart below to take notes on the beginnings and the spread of Christianity.

| TERMS AND NAMES |

TERMS AND NAMES

Jesus Leader who came to be known as Christ and was believed to be a savior

apostle Close follower of Jesus

Peter First apostle who helped spread Christianity through Syria and Palestine

Paul Apostle who played a key role in the spread of Christianity throughout the Roman Empire

Diaspora Moving away of the Jews from their homeland in Palestine

bishop Head of all churches in one area

pope Head of the Christian Church

Constantine Roman emperor who ended persecution of Christians

LEADER	RELIGIOUS INFLUENCE
Jesus	spread message of love believed by some to be Messiah
Peter	
Paul	
Constantine	

The Life and Teachings of Jesus

(pages 168–169)

Why did people believe Jesus was the savior?

One group of people that lost its land to the Romans was the Jews. Many Jews wanted the Romans to leave their land.

Others hoped for the coming of the *Messiah*— the savior. According to Jewish tradition. God promised that the Messiah would restore the kingdom of the Jews.

Jesus was born in Judea. At about age 30, Jesus began to preach. His message included many ideas from Jewish traditions, such as the principles of the Ten Commandments and the belief in one God. According to close followers, who were later called **apostles,** Jesus performed many miracles, His fame grew. Some believed him to be the long-awaited Messiah.

Jewish leaders did not believe that his teachings were those of God. Roman leaders feared he would *incite* the people. The Romans arrested Jesus and put him to death.

© McDougal Littell Inc. All rights reserved.

CHAPTER 6 ANCIENT ROME AND EARLY CHRISTIANITY 59

After his death, Jesus's followers said that he appeared to them again and then went to heaven. They said this proved he was the Messiah. They called him Christ. This is the Greek word for savior. His followers came to be called Christians. Led by **Peter,** the first apostle, they spread his teachings throughout Palestine and Syria.

1. Why was Jesus put to death?

_____

_____

_____

_____

Christianity Spreads Through the Empire (pages 169–170)

How did Christianity spread through the empire?

At first Jesus's followers were all Jewish. Later, under one apostle, **Paul,** Christians began to look to all people, even non-Jews, to join the church. The leaders of the early church traveled throughout the empire spreading the teachings of Jesus.

During this time, Jews made attempts to break free of the Romans. These movements did not succeed. Most Jews were driven from their homeland into *exile.* This scattering of the Jews is called the **Diaspora.**

At the same time, Roman leaders tried to punish the Christians. Some were put to death or killed by wild animals in the arena. But Christianity continued to spread. After almost 200 years, millions of people across the empire became Christians.

2. What did the Romans do to the Jews?

_____

_____

_____

_____

_____

A World Religion (pages 170–172)

Why did Christianity spread?

Christianity spread for several reasons. First, it accepted all believers: rich or poor, male or female. Second, it gave hope to the powerless. Third, it appealed to those who were bothered by the lack of *morality* in Rome. Fourth, it offered a personal relationship with god. Fifth, it offered the promise of life after death.

As the church grew, it became more organized. Priests were in charge of small churches. **Bishops** were in charge of all the churches in one area. The **pope** was in charge of all, The pope was the head of the Christian Church.

In A.D. 313, Christianity entered a new era. The Roman emperor **Constantine** said that Christians would no longer be *persecuted.* He gave his official approval to Christianity. A few decades later, Christianity became the empire's official religion.

While Christianity grew in power, it went through changes. Church leaders sometimes disagreed over basic beliefs and argued about them. Church leaders called any belief that appeared to contradict the basic teachings a heresy. From time to time, councils met to end disagreements and define beliefs.

3. How was the church organized?

_____

_____

_____

_____

_____

_____

Name _____ Date _____

The Fall of the Roman Empire

BEFORE YOU READ

In the last section, you read about the spread of Christianity.

In this section, you will learn how the Roman Empire collapsed.

AS YOU READ

Use the time line below to take notes on the fall of the empire.

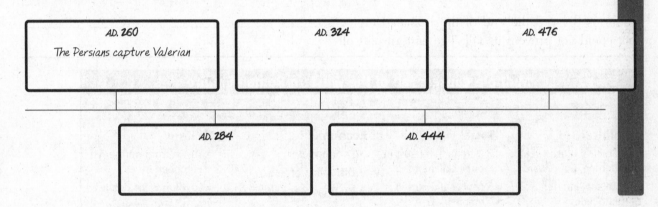

AD. 260 — The Persians capture Valerian

AD. 324

AD. 476

AD. 284

AD. 444

A Century of Crisis (page173)

What problems did Rome face?

Rome entered a period of decline after the reign of Marcus Aurelius ended in 180 A.D. Rome suffered economic problems. Trade slowed as raiders threatened ships and *caravans* on sea and land. The economy suffered from **inflation,** a drastic drop in the value of money and a rise in prices. Food supplies also dropped as tired soil, warfare, and high taxes cut the amount of grain and other foods produced on farms.

The empire also had military problems. German tribes caused trouble on the frontiers. Persians defeated the Romans in A.D. 260 and captured the emperor. Roman soldiers could no longer be counted on. Instead, **mercenaries**—soldiers who

fight for money—had to be hired. At the same time, Roman generals fought one another for control of the empire.

1. What economic problems did Rome face?

_____

_____

Emperors Attempt Reform
(pages 174–175)

What changes did the emperors make?

Diocletian took the throne as emperor in 284. He passed many new laws to try to fix the economy. He tried to restore the status of the emperor by naming himself a son of the chief Roman god. He even divided the empire into eastern and western halves to make it easier to govern.

Constantine continued many of these changes. He became emperor of both halves of the empire in 324. A few years later, Constantine moved the capital of the empire to a new city in northwestern Turkey where Europe and Asia meet. The city was *Byzantium.* It was given a new name— **Constantinople,** the city of Constantine.

2. Who was Constantine?

_____

_____

The Western Empire Crumbles

(pages 175–176)

Who overran Rome?

Reforms delayed the end of the Roman Empire but could not prevent its fall. The eastern part of the empire remained strong and unified. But troubles continued in the west. Germanic tribes moved into the empire. They were trying to escape from the *Huns,* fierce nomadic people from central Asia, who were moving into their land.

The Roman armies in the west collapsed. German armies twice entered Rome itself. In 408 Visigoths led by their king, Alaric, put the city under siege. In 444, the Huns united under a powerful chieftain named **Attila.** Attila and his armies terrorized both halves of the empire.

The invasions continued after Attila's death. The Germans had arrived for good. By 476 German peoples controlled many areas of Europe. That year a German general removed the last western Roman emperor from the throne.

3. What role did Attila play in the collapse of Rome?

_____

_____

Multiple Causes: Fall of the Western Roman Empire			
Contributing Factors			
Political	**Social**	**Economic**	**Military**
• Political office seen as burden, not reward	• Decline in interest in public affairs	• Poor harvests	• Threat from northern European tribes
• Military interference in politics	• Low confidence in empire	• Disruption of trade	• Low funds for defense
• Civil war and unrest	• Disloyalty, lack of patriotism, corruption	• No more war plunder	• Problems recruiting Roman citizens; recruiting of non-Romans
• Division of empire	• Contrast between rich and poor	• Gold and silver drain	• Decline of patriotism and loyalty among soldiers
• Moving of capital to Byzantium	• Decline in population due to disease and food shortage	• Inflation	
		• Crushing tax burden	
		• Widening gap between rich and poor and increasingly impoverished Western Empire	

Immediate Cause

Invasion by Germanic tribes and by Huns

FALL OF ROMAN EMPIRE

Skillbuilder

1. What was the immediate cause of the fall of the Roman Empire?

_____

2. Which of the social factors do you think was most important? Why?

_____

Rome and the Roots of Western Civilization

TERMS AND NAMES

Greco-Roman culture Culture developed from the blending of Greek, Hellenistic, and Roman cultures

Pompeii Roman town covered by the eruption of Mount Vesuvius

Virgil Roman poet who wrote the Aeneid

Tacitus Roman historian who recorded the good and bad of imperial Rome

aqueduct Pipeline or channel built to carry water

BEFORE YOU READ

In the last section, you read about the fall of Rome. In this section, you will learn about the contributions of Rome to Western civilization.

AS YOU READ

Use the web below to take notes on Rome's influence on the western world.

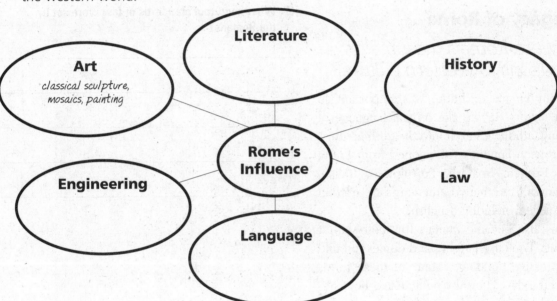

The Legacy of Greco-Roman Civilization (pages 178–181)

What is Greco-Roman culture?

Rome took aspects of Greek and Hellenistic culture and added ideas of its own. The mixing of Greek, Hellenistic, and Roman culture produced a new culture called **Greco-Roman culture.** This is also often called classical civilization.

Roman artists, philosophers, and writers did not just copy Greek works. They created a style of their own for their own purposes. Much of Roman art had practical purposes. It was aimed at educating the public.

One example of the mixing of cultures occurred in sculpture. Romans borrowed Greek ideas but made their sculptures more realistic. The Romans also developed a kind of sculpture in which images stood out from a flat background.

Romans were skilled at creating pictures made from tiny tiles, a process called *mosaic*. But Romans were perhaps most skilled at painting. The best examples of Roman painting are found in the Roman town of **Pompeii.** Pompeii was covered with ash after a volcanic eruption. The ash preserved many works of art and culture.

In both literature and philosophy, Romans were inspired by the Greeks. The poet **Virgil** wrote the most famous work of Latin literature, the *Aeneid*. It was modeled on the Greek epics of Homer.

The Romans also produced some important histories. **Tacitus** is an important Roman historian. Among ancient historians, he is known for presenting accurate facts. He described the good and bad parts of imperial Rome in his *Annals* and *Histories*.

1. Name three Roman cultural achievements.

_____

_____

_____

_____

The Legacy of Rome (pages 181–183)

What were Rome's most major contributions to Western culture?

The Roman language, Latin, was important in European history. It was the official language of the Roman Catholic Church into the 20th century. Many European languages developed from Latin, including French, Spanish, Portuguese, Italian, and Romanian. And many Latin words are used in other languages, including English.

Romans also became famous for their skill at engineering. They used arches and domes to build large, impressive buildings. Many of these forms are still used today. They also built an excellent system of roads and several **aqueducts.** Aqueducts carried water from distant lakes or rivers to large cities.

But Rome's most lasting influence was in the field of law. The Roman government set standards of law that still influence people today. Some of the most important principles of Roman law were:

- All persons had the right to equal treatment under the law.
- A person was considered innocent until proven guilty.
- The burden of proof rested with the accuser rather than the accused.
- A person should be punished only for actions, not for thoughts.
- Any law that seemed unreasonable or unfair could be set aside.

2. What important standards of law were set by the Romans?

_____

_____

_____

_____

Name _____ Date _____

Glossary

aristocratic Belonging to the highest class

artisans Skilled workers

assembly Gathering; group of people organized to make laws for a community

Byzantium City in northwestern Turkey that was renamed Constantinople after Constantine made it the capital of the Roman empire

caravans Traders traveling together

Etruscans People who lived in the north of what is now Italy before the Romans

exalted Honored, praised, glorified

exile State of being sent away from or removed from one's own country

imperial Related to an empire

incite To provoke or urge on

Messiah Savior; name given by some to Jesus

morality Code of right and wrong, good and evil

mosaic Type of art in which designs are made using tiny tiles

persecuted Oppressed or harassed unfairly, especially for beliefs or heritage

spectacle Something to be seen or viewed

testify Make a statement in court

Twelve Tables Set of rules protecting all Roman citizens

AFTER YOU READ

Terms and Names

A. Write the name or term in each blank that best completes the meaning of the paragraph.

triumvirate

Augustus

Hannibal

civil war

Julius Caesar

After years of fighting, Rome defeated Carthage and its brilliant military leader **1**_____. Soon after the victory, **2**_____ broke out in Rome. When it ended, **3**_____ tried to take control. First, he joined with two others to form a **4**_____. When this government collapsed, he became an absolute ruler. Because he then had so much power, some feared he wanted to be king and killed him. Eventually, his rule was followed by that of **5**_____, the new emperor.

B. Write the letter of the term next to the description that explains it best.

a. patricians

b. plebeians

c. apostles

d. mercenaries

e. aqueduct

_____ **1.** Pipeline or channel built to carry water

_____ **2.** Aristocratic landowners in ancient Rome

_____ **3.** Foreign soldiers who fought for money

_____ **4.** First close followers of Jesus

_____ **5.** Common artisans, farmers, and merchants in ancient Rome

AFTER YOU READ (cont.)   *CHAPTER 6* Ancient Rome and Early Christianity

Main Ideas

1. What was the Roman legion, and who served in it?

_____

_____

_____

2. What was the *Pax Romana?*

_____

_____

_____

3. Name three reactions to the teachings of Jesus.

_____

_____

_____

4. What changes did Diocletian make?

_____

_____

_____

5. Explain what is meant by the term Greco-Roman culture.

_____

_____

_____

Thinking Critically

Answer the following questions on a separate sheet of paper.

1. Why was Paul so important in the history of Christianity?

2. Explain this statement: Rome's most lasting influence was in the field of law.

India's First Empires

BEFORE YOU READ

In the last section, you read about the influence of ancient Rome.

In this section, you will read about the Mauryan and Gupta Empires in India.

AS YOU READ

Use the time line below to take notes on the first empires of India.

TERMS AND NAMES

Mauryan Empire First empire in India, founded by Chandragupta Maurya

Asoka Grandson of Chandragupta; leader who brought the Mauryan Empire to its greatest height

religious toleration Acceptance of the right of people to have differing religious beliefs

Tamil Language of southern India; also the people who speak that language

Gupta Empire Second empire in India, founded by Chandra Gupta

patriarchal Relating to a social system in which the father is the head of the family

matriarchal Relating to a social system in which the mother is the head of the family

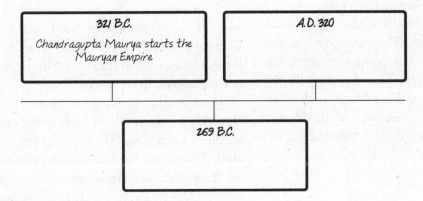

321 B.C.	A.D. 320
Chandragupta Maurya starts the Mauryan Empire	

269 B.C.

The Mauryan Empire Is Established (pages 189–192)

How did the Mauryan Empire begin?

In 321 B.C., Chandragupta Maurya used his army to defeat a powerful king in eastern India. He became king, and this started the **Mauryan Empire.**

Chandragupta then moved northwest. In 305 B.C., he began to challenge Seleucus, one of Alexander the Great's generals. The two armies fought for several years. Eventually Chandragupta won. For the first time, northeastern and northwestern India were joined under the rule of one person.

Chandragupta was a harsh ruler. He charged a heavy tax on farmers—one-half of the crop they grew each year. He used this wealth to build a huge army. He controlled his government by carefully choosing officials and watching them closely. He split his empire into four *provinces*, each ruled by a prince. These areas, in turn, were divided into smaller pieces that were run by members of the government. Life in Chandragupta's court was rich. The palace and capital city were beautiful.

Chandragupta's grandson, **Asoka,** took the throne in 269 B.C. He brought the Mauryan Empire to its greatest height. At first he was a warlike king and fought many fierce battles with an enemy to the south. Then he decided to accept the teachings of the Buddha.

Asoka promised to rule in a fair and just way. He issued laws that urged his subjects to avoid violence. He urged **religious toleration.** This is acceptance of people's rights to differing religious beliefs. He made great roads so that people could travel easily. Soon after Asoka died, however, his empire collapsed.

1. What changes did Asoka make in the Mauryan Empire?

_____

_____

_____

A Period of Turmoil (page 191)

What troubles did India face?

For 500 years after Asoka, India was a land of troubles. In the center of India, a new dynasty—the Andhra Dynasty—*dominated* the region. In the northwest, many Greeks, Persians, and Central Asians entered the land. They were fleeing the invasions of others. These peoples added new ideas and languages to India's rich mix of culture. In the south, three different kingdoms fought each other off and on. The people who lived in this region spoke the **Tamil** language. They are called the Tamil people.

2. Who are the Tamils?

_____

_____

_____

The Gupta Empire is Established

(pages 191–192)

What was life like in the Gupta Empire?

Around A.D. 320, Chandra Gupta I came to power in the north. He was not related to the first emperor. He took the title of king and began to conquer other areas.

His son, Samudra Gupta, followed the same policy. For 40 years, he fought to win new lands for the **Gupta Empire.** Samudra's son, Chandra Gupta II, brought the empire to its largest size. He added parts of western India, including some important ports on the Indian Ocean, to his empire. With these, the Guptas were able to take part in the rich trade that connected India, Southwest Asia, and the world of the Mediterranean Sea. The Gupta empire stretched all across northern India.

Most Indians lived in villages and were farmers. Part of each crop that they grew had to be paid to the king each year. Farmers also had to set aside part of each month to work on community resources, such as wells or dams. Craft workers and those who worked in trade lived in special sections of each village, town, or city.

Most families in northern India were **patriarchal.** They were headed by the oldest male. But in southern India, some Tamil families were **matriarchal.** This meant the mother was head of the family. Property, and sometimes the throne, were passed through the female side of the family.

The Gupta kings were *patrons* of the arts. Artists *flourished* during the Gupta rule. However, after the death of Chandra Gupta II, another wave of invaders moved into India. Over the next hundred years, the great Gupta Empire broke up into several smaller kingdoms. The empire ended about 535.

3. How did the Gupta Empire end?

_____

_____

_____

CHAPTER 7 Section 2 (pages 193–199)

Trade Spreads Indian Religions and Culture

BEFORE YOU READ

In the last section, you read about the Mauryan and Gupta Empires of India.

In this section, you will learn how trade caused changes in Indian religion and culture.

AS YOU READ

Use the chart below to show changes in India.

TERMS AND NAMES

Mahayana Sect of Buddhism that offers salvation to all and allows popular worship

Theravada Sect of Buddhism focusing on strict spiritual discipline

Brahma Creator of the world, in Hinduism

Vishnu Preserver of the world, in Hinduism

Shiva Destroyer of the world, in Hinduism

Kalidasa One of India's greatest poets and playwrights

Silk Roads Caravan routes that crisscrossed central Asia

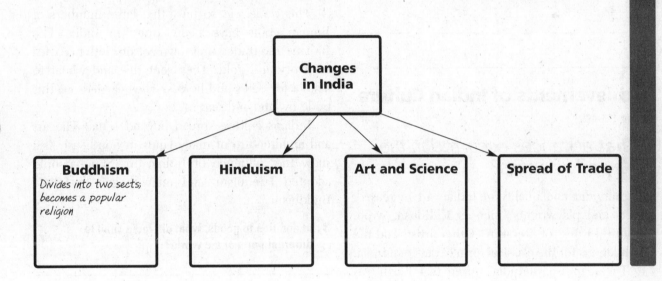

Changes in India

Buddhism	Hinduism	Art and Science	Spread of Trade
Divides into two sects; becomes a popular religion			

Buddhism and Hinduism Change (pages 193–194)

What were the changes in religious thought?

Over time, the religions of Hinduism and Buddhism became more and more distant from the common people. Priests dominated Hinduism. Followers of the Buddha found it difficult to find the promised goal of release from this world. As new peoples moved into India, they brought new ideas. These ideas had an impact on these religions.

The Buddha had taught that a tough spiritual life was the way to escape from the suffering of the world. But *self-denial* was difficult for most people. Many people came to worship the Buddha himself as a god, even though he had forbidden it. Some came to believe that other people could become Buddhas themselves. They could do this through good works and sacrifice.

These ideas created a new kind of Buddhism, the **Mahayana** *sect*. Those who held on to the stricter beliefs belonged to the **Theravada** sect. The new Mahayana approach helped Buddhism become a popular religion. All believers had the chance to be saved. This change caused an increase in art. Buddhists with money built temples and shrines and then paid artists to decorate them with sculptures and paintings.

Hinduism changed, too. By the time of the Mauryan empire, only priests were involved in many rituals of the faith. For centuries, Hinduism had been a religion of many gods. Now other religions based on only one god were becoming more important. Many Hindus began to emphasize three gods in particular. One was **Brahma,** creator of the world. Another was **Vishnu,** preserver of the world. The third was **Shiva,** destroyer of the world. By devoting themselves to these gods, people began to feel the religion more directly in their lives.

1. What changes did the split in Buddhism bring?

_____

_____

_____

Achievements of Indian Culture

(pages 194–195)

What advances occurred in the arts and sciences?

The amount and quality of Indian art increased. Poets and playwrights, such as **Kalidasa,** wrote beautiful works of literature. Other artists laid the foundations for the classical form of dance in India.

The scientists of India proved that Earth was indeed round 1,000 years before Columbus. They made great advances in mathematics, too. They invented the idea of zero and of decimal numbers. The doctors of India became highly skilled. They knew more than 1,000 diseases and used hundreds of medicines from plants to help their patients.

2. What advances did scientists and mathematicians make?

_____

_____

_____

The Spread of Indian Trade

(pages 195–197)

How did India's trade increase?

Soon Indians learned about the **Silk Roads.** These were *caravan* routes that crisscrossed central Asia. Indian traders joined in the trade along these routes. Indians traded cotton cloth and animals to China for silk. Traders brought spices from Southeast Asia to India and then sold them to Rome and other western peoples.

This trade was so busy that large numbers of Roman coins have been found in India. The Indians also traded their own cotton cloth in Africa for ivory and gold. They sent rice and wheat to Arabia for dates and horses. They carried out this trade by land and sea.

Indians culture spread beyond India. The art and architecture of many lands in Southeast Asia show the influence of Indian art. Some people adopted Hinduism, and many began to follow Buddhism.

3. In addition to goods, what did India send to different parts of the world?

_____

_____

_____

Han Emperors in China

TERMS AND NAMES

Han Dynasty Chinese dynasty that ruled for most of the period from 202 B.C. to A.D. 220

centralized government Government that concentrates power in a central authority

civil service Administrative departments of a government; also, word describing government jobs and employees

monopoly One group's complete control over the production and distribution of certain goods

assimilation Policy of encouraging conquered peoples to adopt the institutions and customs of the conquering nation

BEFORE YOU READ

In the last section, you read about the spread of Indian religions and culture.

In this section, you will read about the Han Dynasty in China.

AS YOU READ

Use the web below to take notes on the Han Dynasty.

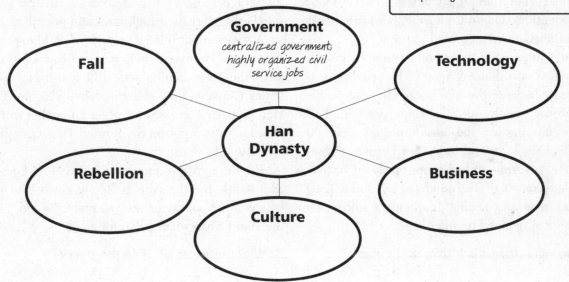

Government
centralized government; highly organized civil service jobs

Fall

Technology

Han Dynasty

Rebellion

Business

Culture

The Han Restore Unity to China

(pages 200–202)

What changes did Han leaders make?

A strong empire also arose in China. The Chinese had been united briefly under the Qin empire. But it fell apart in a period of civil war. In 202 B.C., Liu Bang named himself the first emperor of the **Han Dynasty.** The Han would rule parts of China for the next 400 years. They set many patterns for Chinese culture for centuries to come,

Liu Bang created a **centralized government,** Local officials reported to the emperor. The rule of the previous emperor had been very harsh. Liu Bang took a different approach. He lowered taxes. He gave lighter penalties for crimes. Life became easier for the Chinese people.

From 141 to 87 B.C., the emperor Wudi ruled Han China. He made his empire almost the size of modern China. He defeated nomads in the north. He moved troops and settlers to the west. He sent soldiers to the north into modern Korea and to the south to modern Vietnam.

1. What changes did Liu Bang make?

_____

_____

A Highly Structured Society; Han Technology, Commerce, and Culture (pages 202–205)

What advances took place?

Chinese society under the Han dynasty was very structured. The emperor was at the top. He had a large number of officials, who reached down to the smallest village. They filled **civil service** jobs. Those who wanted these jobs had to pass an exam. The exam tested them on their knowledge of the writings of the Chinese philosopher Confucius.

To support a large government, the emperor collected taxes. Farmers paid part of the crops they gathered. Merchants paid taxes on the goods they traded. Peasants also had to work one month a year on government projects, such as dams and roads.

Under Han rule, the Chinese created many new inventions. One was paper. Paper made books more available and increased learning.

The Chinese also improved farming by inventing a new two-bladed plow. This change was important because the number of Chinese people had grown greatly. As Han emperors told their people, farming was the most important work. At the same time, several industries became important. The government had a **monopoly** on, or took complete control of, the mining of salt and making of iron, coins, and alcohol. It also made silk, which was in great demand in other lands.

2. Why were changes in farming so important?

_____

_____

_____

The Han Unifies Chinese Culture; The Fall of The Han and Their Return (pages 205–207)

Why did problems develop?

China now included many different peoples. The Han rulers encouraged **assimilation**—making sure that these people learned Chinese ways. They urged the Chinese to marry them.

One group that did not do well in Han China was women. According to Confucius, women were limited to meeting the needs of their husband and children. Some upper-class women, however, were able to become involved in other areas of life.

The Han empire began to have problems. Rich people got richer, while the poor were forced to pay heavy taxes. Members of the court were caught up in plots to gain power. Eventually, the peasants rebelled against their high taxes and poor lives.

A government official named Wang Mang took the throne. He tried to help the poor by taking land from the large landholders. But a terrible flood struck China and the peasants rebelled again. The Han Dynasty was *restored* when a member of the Han family was put on the throne. This was called the Later Han Dynasty.

For the next few decades, China enjoyed peace and wealth. But the same problems arose. The gap between rich and poor was too great. By A.D. 220, the Han Dynasty had fallen for good.

3. What caused the fall of the Han Dynasty?

_____

_____

_____

Two Great Empires: Han China and Rome	
Han Dynasty—202 B.C. to A.D. 220	**Roman Empire—27 B.C. to A.D. 476**
• Empire replaced rival kingdoms	• Empire replaced republic
• Centralized, bureaucratic government	• Centralized, bureaucratic government
• Built roads and defensive walls	• Built roads and defensive walls
• Conquered many diverse peoples in regions bordering China	• Conquered many diverse peoples in regions of three continents
• At its height—area of 1,500,000 square miles and 60,000,000 people	• At its height—area of 3,400,000 square miles and 55,000,000 people
• Chinese became common written language throughout empire	• Latin did not replace other written languages in empire
• Ongoing conflict with nomads	• Ongoing conflict with nomads

Skillbuilder

1. Which empire at its height covered more land?

_____

_____

2. What did the two empires have in common?

_____

_____

Name _____ Date _____

caravan Word describing a route on which many traders traveled in groups

commerce Business

dominated Controlled

flourished Did extremely well

patrons Financial supporters

provinces Political divisions like states

restored Brought back

sect Branch that breaks off from a larger group, usually due to disagreements

self-denial Not taking part in life's pleasures

AFTER YOU READ

Terms and Names

A. Write the name or term in each blank that best completes the meaning of the paragraph.

Vishnu

Theravada

Mahayana

Brahma

Shiva

Both Hinduism and Buddhism underwent changes. Because the Buddha's teachings were so difficult to follow in real life, a new sect, **1** _____ Buddhism, arose. It offered salvation to more people. Those who held on to the stricter teachings of the Buddha belonged to the **2** _____ sect. Changes also occurred in Hinduism. Gradually, Hindus shifted from the worship of hundreds of gods to concentration on three main gods. These were **3** _____, creator of the world; **4** _____, preserver of the world; and **5** _____ destroyer of the world.

B. Write the letter of the name or term next to the description that explains it best.

a. monopoly

b. assimilation

c. patriarchal

d. matriarchal

e. civil service

_____ **1.** Administrative parts of a government; also describes government jobs and employees

_____ **2.** Relating to a social system in which the father is the head of the family

_____ **3.** Relating to a social system in which the mother is the head of the family

_____ **4.** One group's complete control over the making and selling of a certain good

_____ **5.** Policy to get conquered peoples to adopt the culture of the conquering nation

AFTER YOU READ (cont.)   *CHAPTER 7* India and China Establish Empires

Main Ideas

1. Describe the rule of Chandragupta Maurya.

_____

_____

_____

2. What happened in the 500 years between the Mauryan and Gupta Empires?

_____

_____

_____

3. Explain the role of the Silk Roads in changing and spreading Indian culture.

_____

_____

_____

4. Explain how Wudi changed his empire.

_____

_____

_____

5. What were two cultural facts of life in Han China?

_____

_____

_____

Thinking Critically

Answer the following questions on a separate sheet of paper.

1. Compare and contrast the rule of Chandragupta Maurya and Asoka.

2. What basic problem was there in Han China that led to its fall?

Diverse Societies in Africa

BEFORE YOU READ

In the last section, you read about empires in China.

In this section, you will learn how African people developed diverse societies.

AS YOU READ

Use the web below to show some of the features of Africa's geography.

TERMS AND NAMES

Sahara Large desert in Africa

savanna Grassy plain

Sahel Land at the southern edge of the Sahara

animism Religion in which spirits play a role in daily life

griot West African storyteller

Nok African people who lived in what is now Nigeria from 500 B.C. to a.d. 200

Djenné-Djeno Oldest known city in Africa south of the Sahara

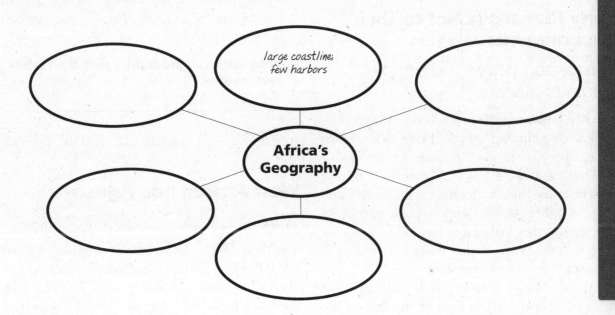

large coastline; few harbors

Africa's Geography

A Land of Geographic Contrasts

(pages 213–215)

What are some of the geographic contrasts in Africa?

Africa is the second largest continent in the world. It stretches 4,600 miles from east to west and 5,000 miles from north to south. It has about one-fifth of the earth's land. Much of the land is a high plateau, with lower land near the coasts. The rivers that flow along this high land often form waterfalls or rapids. As a result, boats cannot use these rivers to travel either to or from the coast. Also, the coast has few harbors for so large a landmass.

Africa has many different environments. There are hot, dry deserts; steamy, wet rain forests; and high, cool mountains.

About a third of Africa's land is desert. Few people live there. Deserts form a barrier to people who want to move from one area to another. The **Sahara** Desert in the north of Africa is about one-third the size of the United States. Dense rain forests cover much of the central part of Africa.

The northern and southern regions of Africa have large numbers of people. Most Africans live on the **savannas,** grasslands that cover almost half of the continent. They grow grains, including rice and wheat, and tend cattle.

The land at the southern edge of the Sahara Desert is the **Sahel.** Each year, the Sahara Desert takes over a little more of this Sahel.

1. Name three contrasting features of African geography.

_____

_____

Early Humans Adapt to Their Environments (pages 215–216)

When and where did people begin to farm?

The first humans in Africa got food by hunting animals and gathering plants. Even today, some African peoples still use this method to get food.

Over time, these people learned to tame animals and raise them for food. Like the hunters and gatherers, these herders were *nomadic* people. As they moved, they looked for grass and for water for their animals. When food or water was used up in one area, they moved to another.

About 10,000 B.C., some people in Africa began to farm. People used to farm in the area of the Sahara before it became a desert. They also farmed in the Nile Valley and West Africa or on the grasslands. Some moved to the rain forest.

2. Where did African people settle and begin farming?

_____

_____

Early Societies in West Africa

(pages 216–217)

How did early societies live?

The *diverse* environments of Africa created much variety in the way different African peoples lived. The people who lived south of the Sahara, though, had these features in common:

- The family was the most important unit of society. The family was an extended family that included grandparents, aunts, uncles, and cousins. In some groups, family included all the people who came from common *ancestors*. This is called a *clan*.
- They believed that one god created the world. Their beliefs included **animism.** They felt that plants, animals, and other natural forces all have spirits that play an important role in life.
- They relied on oral storytelling, rather than writing, to pass on the traditions of their people. In West Africa, for example, storytellers, or **griots,** kept history alive.

3. What features did people living south of the Sahara have in common?

_____

_____

West African Iron Age (pages 217–219)

Who were the Iron Age societies?

The West African **Nok** culture existed from about 500 B.C. to a.d. 200. The Nok people made pottery figures and were the first people in Africa who knew how to make iron. Some styles of Nok pottery are still found in Africa today.

Djenné-Djeno is the oldest known African city south of the Sahara. It was located on the banks of the Niger River. It dates from about 250 B.C. About 50,000 people lived there at its height. At first, they lived in round huts made of *reeds* and covered with mud. Later they lived in houses of mud bricks. They grew rice, raised cattle, and made iron. They traded these goods for gold and copper.

4. What is Djenné-Djeno?

_____

_____

Migration

Case Study: Bantu-Speaking Peoples

BEFORE YOU READ

In the last section, you read about African societies populating the continent. In this section, you will read about the causes and effects of migration in Africa among Bantu-speaking peoples.

AS YOU READ

Use the chart below to record reasons for the movement of Bantu-speaking peoples.

TERMS AND NAMES

migration A permanent move from one area to another

push-pull factors Reasons attracting or driving people to move

Bantu-speaking peoples People who speak one of a group of languages related to Bantu

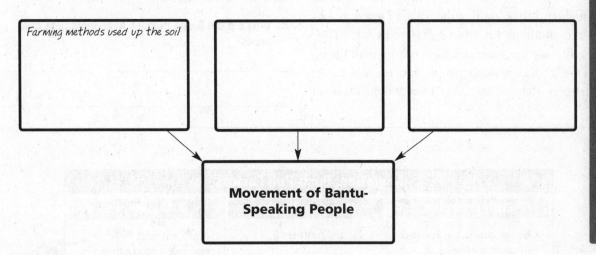

Farming methods used up the soil

Movement of Bantu-Speaking People

People on the Move (pages 220–221)

What are the main reasons for migrations?

Throughout human history, many peoples have felt the urge to move from their homes to a new land. This movement is called **migration.** There are many reasons that people make such a move. But they can be grouped into three main causes. They are environmental change, economic pressure, political and religious *persecution*.

Reasons people move into or out of an area are called **push-pull factors.** People may be attracted or pulled into an area because they see economic advantages. Or they may move because they want freedom. Sometimes people are pushed out of an

area because the environment changes and it is impossible to live there. Other times people may leave to find security or peace that can not be found in their area. These are examples of push factors.

In studying times before written history, researchers look for clues to migrations. One clue they use is language. People take their language with them when they move to a new place. When historians find two languages from two distant areas that have words that are somewhat similar, they can conclude that those two languages may have both come from the same language. However, some time later the original speakers of the language moved apart. Then the two languages changed independently. This kind of clue has given historians a way of understanding the early history of Africa.

1. Name three key reasons for migration.

_____

_____

_____

Massive Migrations (pages 220–224)

Who were the Bantu-speaking peoples?

Many languages spoken in Africa today developed from the same parent language called *Proto-Bantu.* The speakers of all these different languages are called the **Bantu-speaking peoples.** The people who spoke Bantu first lived in a part of modern Nigeria. In the first few centuries a.d., they began to move south and east. Over time, they spread throughout Africa south of the Sahara Desert, reaching the southern tip around 500 years ago. They brought their language and their culture with them.

One of the reasons people moved had to do with their style of farming. They would clear an area and use it until the soil no longer could produce good crops. The people then needed to move to a new area to clear new ground.

Another reason they moved was that their farming was so successful. Farming helped them produce more food than they could by hunting and gathering. With more to eat, groups became larger and the land more crowded. They could not move north, where the Sahara Desert made a barrier. So they had to move farther and farther south.

As they reached new areas, the Bantu peoples met other peoples. Sometimes these meetings were violent. The Bantus, who knew how to make iron, had better weapons than those they met, who only had stone tools. Some of the peoples that they met are still found in Africa. But they live in small areas with very harsh environments. The Bantus took the better land.

2. Why did the Bantu peoples keep moving to new areas?

_____

_____

_____

Migration: Push-Pull Factors

Push Examples	Migration Factors	Pull Examples
Climate changes, exhausted resources, earthquakes, volcanoes, drought/famine	Environmental	Abundant land, new resources, good climate
Unemployment, slavery	Economic	Employment opportunities
Religious, ethnic, or political persecution, war	Political	Political and/or religious freedom

PUSH

PULL

Skillbuilder

1. Categorizing   Which pull example is associated with economic factors?

_____

2. Drawing Conclusions   Why would climate changes be considered a push factor?

_____

CHAPTER 8 Section 3 (pages 225–229)

The Kingdom of Aksum

BEFORE YOU READ

In the last section, you read about the migration of Bantu-speakers across parts of southern Africa. In this section, you will learn about the kingdom of Aksum and its role in trade.

AS YOU READ

Use the time line below to show the rise and fall of Aksum.

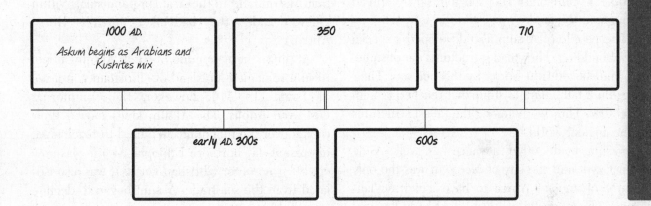

1000 A.D.	350	710
Askum begins as Arabians and Kushites mix		

early A.D. 300s	600s

The Rise of the Kingdom of Aksum (pages 225–226)

How did Aksum arise?

The peoples in East Africa had a great deal of contact with people from other areas. The Kushite kingdom of Nubia had close relations with Egypt. Its kings even ruled Egypt for a while. That kingdom continued for many centuries as a trading power. It was then replaced by the kingdom of **Aksum** in what is now modern Ethiopia. The dynasty that ruled Aksum and later Ethiopia included the 20th-century ruler Haile Selassie.

Aksum may have begun as early as 1000 B.C. when Arabian traders mixed with the people of Kush. It became an important part of world trade.

Salt, emeralds, brass, copper, gold, cloth, olive oil, and wine all moved through Aksum. Its trade routes helped link Rome to India. Traders crowded into its chief seaport, **Adulis.**

In the early A.D. 300s, Aksum had a strong new king named **Ezana.** He brought the kingdom to its height during his rule. Ezana captured more land on the Arabian peninsula, and then conquered Kush in 350.

1. Why was Aksum an important trading center?

_____

_____

_____

_____

An International Culture Develops (pages 227–228)

What was unique about Aksum's culture?

Aksum was an international trading center. It was home to peoples from many different cultures. There were people from Aksum's widespread trading partners, including Egypt, Arabia, Greece, Rome, Persia, India, and even Byzantium. At the time of King Ezana, these different peoples all spoke to one another in Greek.

The Aksumites, like other ancient Africans, traditionally believed in one god. They also worshiped the spirits of nature and honored their dead ancestors. During his rule, King Ezana decided to become a Christian. The religion slowly spread throughout the land.

The people of Aksum also developed a special way of building. They made structures out of stone, not mud baked into bricks by the hot sun. Their kings built tall *pillars* of stone that reached as high as 60 feet. They were among the tallest structures in the ancient world.

Aksum made other advances as well. Aside from Egypt and the city of *Meroë*, it was the only culture of ancient Africa to have a written language. The language of Aksum had been brought to the land by Arab traders many hundreds of years before. Aksum was also the first state south of the Sahara to *mint* its own coins.

The people of Aksum also developed a new way of farming. They cut **terraces,** steplike ridges, into the steep mountainsides in their country. The terraces helped the land hold water instead of letting it run down the mountain in a heavy rain. This was called terrace farming. The people of Aksum also used dams and stone tanks to store water and used ditches to channel it to their fields.

2. What achievements and advances were made in Aksum?

_____

_____

_____

_____

The Fall of Aksum (page 229)

Why did Aksum fall?

Aksum remained an important power in East Africa for 800 years. It was first challenged in the 600s, after the new religion of Islam came to Arabia. The followers of Islam captured the lands that Aksum held in the Arabian peninsula. Within a few decades, they had taken much of North Africa.

At first, these conquerors left Aksum alone. Aksum remained an island of Christianity in a sea of Islam. In 710, however, the conquerors destroyed Adulis. The Aksum kings moved their capital over the mountains to a hard-to-reach area, in present-day northern Ethiopia. Aksum was now cut off from other Christian lands. It was also isolated from the sea trade. Aksum began to decline as a world power.

3. Why did the rulers of Aksum move their capital?

_____

_____

_____

_____

_____

Glossary

ancestors Relatives who came before or long ago

clan Group that shares common ancestors

decline Weaken, lose power

diverse Varied; different

Meroë City on the Nile River in ancient Africa

mint Produce money by stamping metal

nomadic Wandering

pillars Thin columns

Proto-Bantu Parent language from which the Bantu languages came

reeds Plants with long, hollow stems

AFTER YOU READ

Terms and Names

A. Write the name or term in each blank that best completes the meaning of the paragraph.

Nok

animism

savanna

griot

Djenné-Djeno

Early dwellers in Africa spread across the continent. They settled in grassland areas called **1** _____. Societies that developed south of the Sahara shared certain characteristics. One characteristics was the belief in one creator and shared beliefs in **2** _____, a religion in which spirits played an important role in daily life. Early cultures kept their traditions alive by having a storyteller called a **3** _____ . Early cultures have been found south of the Sahara in West Africa. These include the city of **4** _____ on the Niger River. Scientists have also unearthed remains of Africa's earliest known culture, the **5** _____ culture.

B. Write the letter of the name or term next to the description that explains it best.

a. migration

b. push-pull factors

c. Adulis

d. Sahel

e. Ezana

_____ 1. reasons for migration

_____ 2. Land at the southern edge of the Sahara

_____ 3. permanent move to another area

_____ 4. King of Aksum who conquered Kush

_____ 5. Chief seaport of Aksum

AFTER YOU READ (cont.)　　　　　*CHAPTER 8* African Civilizations

Main Ideas

1. Where do large numbers of Africans live?

_____

_____

_____

2. What was the Nok culture?

_____

_____

_____

3. Who was Ezana, and what did he accomplish?

_____

_____

_____

4. Name three features of the culture that developed in Aksum.

_____

_____

_____

5. What are some examples of push-pull factors of migration?

_____

_____

_____

Thinking Critically

Answer the following questions on a separate sheet of paper.

1. What impact did geography have on the way human societies developed in Africa?

2. Why was Aksum important?

The Earliest Americans

TERMS AND NAMES

Beringia Land bridge between Asia and the Americas

Ice Age Time when sheets of ice covered large portions of North America

maize Corn; the most important crop of the Americas

BEFORE YOU READ

In the last chapter, you read about African civilizations. In this section, you will read about the Americas' first inhabitants.

AS YOU READ

Use the chart below to take notes on changes related to or brought about by the end of the Ice Age.

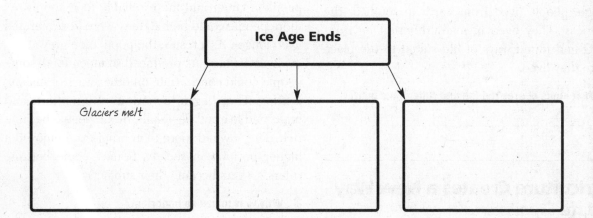

Ice Age Ends

Glaciers melt

A Land Bridge (pages 235–236)

How did the earliest people come to the Americas?

North and South America form a single stretch of land. It stretches from the Arctic Circle in the north to the waters around Antarctica in the south. The Atlantic and Pacific Oceans separate the Americas from Africa, Asia, and Europe.

But that was not always the case. From around 1.6 million years ago until about 10,000 years ago, the earth went through an **Ice Age.** During this time, huge sheets of ice called *glaciers* spread south from the Arctic Circle. The level of the world's oceans went down. The lowered oceans *exposed* land that is today again covered by water.

One strip of land, called **Beringia,** connected Asia and North America. Wild animals crossed this

rocky *land bridge* and entered North America for the first time. Some of the Asian people who hunted these animals followed them. The people became the first Americans.

No one knows for sure when these first people arrived. Some scholars say the people came to the Americas as long ago as 40,000 B.C. Others say as late as 12,000 B.C. A discovery in Chile suggests that people were well-settled in that part of the Americas by 10,500 B.C. Since Chile lies far south of the land bridge, some experts say that people needed many thousands of years to travel that far. For this reason, they think that the first people must have crossed the land bridge in about 20,000 B.C.

1. Where did the first Americans come from?

_____

_____

Hunters and Gatherers (page 236)

How did early Americans live?

These first Americans lived as hunters. One of their favorite hunting targets was the huge mammoth. Over time, all the mammoths died. People were forced to look for other food. They began to hunt smaller animals and to fish. They also began to gather plants and fruits to eat. They no longer had to roam over large areas to search for the mammoth, so they settled for part of the year in one spot.

Between 12,000 and 10,000 B.C., the climate changed. The Ice Age ended, and the world warmed up again. The huge sheets of ice melted, and the oceans rose again to cover the land bridge that connected Asia to the Americas. By this time, though, people lived from north to south in the Americas. They lived in many different environments and found ways of life suited to the place where they lived.

2. **What kinds of prey did the first Americans hunt?**

_____

_____

Agriculture Creates a New Way of Life (pages 238–239)

How did agriculture change ways of life?

About 7000 B.C., the people living in central Mexico started a quiet revolution—farming. It was the same kind of *radical* change that had happened in several spots in Asia and Africa. By 3400 B.C., they had several foods that they grew, including squashes, beans, chilies, and the most important one—**maize,** or corn. Corn grew so well that a family of three could, in four months, grow enough corn to feed it for two years.

Over many centuries, farming spread throughout the Americas. In what is now the eastern United States and in the region of the Andes, people may have discovered the idea of farming on their own. In central Mexico, farmers became so skilled at growing corn that they could enjoy three harvests each year.

Farming had the same results in the Americas that it did in Asia and Africa. Growing food gave people a larger and more reliable food supply. As more people could be fed, they were healthier and lived longer. As a result, the population grew.

Because farmers produced so much food, some people could concentrate on other ways of making a living. They began to work in different arts and crafts and learned new skills. Some people became rich. They owned more than others and enjoyed a higher position in society. Some people became rulers. Others became their subjects.

3. **Why was maize so important?**

_____

_____

The Effects of Agriculture	
Before Agriculture	**After Agriculture**
• People hunted or gathered what they ate. • Families continually moved in search of big game. • Groups remained small due to the scarcity of reliable sources of food. • Humans devoted much of their time to obtaining food.	• People enjoyed a more reliable and steady source of food. • Families settled down and formed larger communities. • Humans concentrated on new skills: arts and crafts, architecture, social organization. • Complex societies eventually arose.

Skillbuilder

1. **How did the development of agriculture lead to population growth?**

_____

2. **How did the development of agriculture change daily life?**

_____

Early Mesoamerican Civilizations

TERMS AND NAMES

Mesoamerica Area that stretches south from central Mexico to the northern part of modern-day Honduras

Olmec People who flourished along the Mesoamerican coast of the Gulf of Mexico from 1200 B.C. to 400 B.C.

Zapotec Early Mesoamerican civilization that was centered in the Oaxaca Valley of what is now Mexico

Monte Alban First urban center in the Americas, built by the Zapotec

BEFORE YOU READ

In the last section, you read about the first inhabitants of the Americas.

In this section, you will read about the first civilizations in America.

AS YOU READ

Use the time line below to take notes on the rise and fall of early Mesoamerican civilizations.

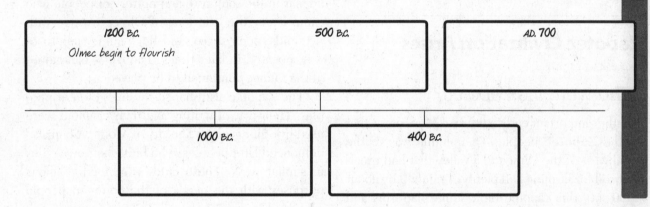

1200 B.C.
Olmec begin to flourish

500 B.C.

A.D. 700

1000 B.C.

400 B.C.

The Olmec (pages 240–241)

Who were the Olmec?

The story of American civilizations begins in Mesoamerica. This area stretches south from central Mexico to the northern part of present-day Honduras.

The earliest known American civilizations arose in southern Mexico, an area of hot rain forests. The people are called the Olmec. They *flourished* from about 1200 to 400 B.C. Their culture had a great influence on their neighbors and on peoples who lived long after them.

The Olmec lived along the coast of the Gulf of Mexico in a land of *dense* forests and heavy rains.

The land gave them many benefits. It had good clay that could be used for pottery. Wood and rubber could be taken from the forest. The mountains to the north had stone for building. The rivers could be used to move people and goods. The soil was excellent for growing food.

Archaeologists have found earthen *mounds*, courtyards, and pyramids built of stones. On top of the mounds were many monuments made of stone. Some of these stone structures are very large. They weigh as much as 44 tons.

Researchers are not sure whether the Olmec sites were monuments to rulers or areas important for religious reasons. They do think that the Olmec had many gods who stood for important forces of nature. The most important god, it seems, was the jaguar spirit. Many stone monuments show figures that are half-human and half-jaguar.

The Olmec traded with other people in the region. In return for the products they made, they received iron ore and different kinds of stone. Along with their trade goods, they spread their culture to other people. For some reason, the Olmec disappeared around 400 B.C. Historians still do not understand why. But their influence lived on.

1. **What evidence of Olmec civilization has been found?**

_____

_____

_____

_____

Zapotec Civilization Arises

(pages 242–243)

Who were the Zapotec?

Another important early culture of Mexico was that of the **Zapotec** people. Their home was to the southwest of the Olmec in a valley that had excellent soil for farming and plenty of rainfall. By about 1000 B.C. the Zapotec built stone platforms and temples. A few hundred years later, they developed a kind of writing and a calendar.

Around 500 B.C., the Zapotec built the first city in the Americas. The city was called **Monte Alban.** As many as 25,000 people lived there. The city lasted as late as A.D. 700. Monte Alban had tall pyramids, temples, and palaces made out of stone. It had an *observatory* that could be used to look at the stars. But the Zapotec culture collapsed. As with the Olmec, historians do not know why.

2. **What evidence of Zapotec civilization has been found?**

_____

_____

_____

_____

The Early Mesoamericans' Legacy (page 243)

How did the early Mesoamericans influence later peoples?

Both of these cultures left their mark on later cultures. The jaguar figure of the Olmec continued to appear in the sculpture and pottery of people who came later. Also, the look of Olmec towns—with pyramids, open space, and huge stone sculptures was repeated in later times. The *ritual* ball games of the Olmec continued to be played.

The Zapotec also shaped the lives of later peoples. Their way of writing and their calendar were used by other groups. The city of Monte Alban also influenced later peoples, who built their own cities in similar ways. These cities combined religious purposes with the needs of the common people who lived in them.

3. **How did the Zapotec influence later peoples?**

_____

_____

_____

_____

CHAPTER 9 Section 3 (pages 246–249)

Early Civilizations of the Andes

TERMS AND NAMES

Chavín First influential culture in South America, which flourished from around 900 B.C. to 200 B.C.

Nazca Culture that flourished along the southern coast of Peru from around 200 B.C. to A.D. 600

Moche Culture that flourished along the northern coast of Peru from around A.D. 100 to A.D. 700

BEFORE YOU READ

In the last section, you read about the first Mesoamerican civilizations.

In this section, you will read about the civilizations of the Andes.

AS YOU READ

Use the time line below to take notes on the early civilizations of the Andes.

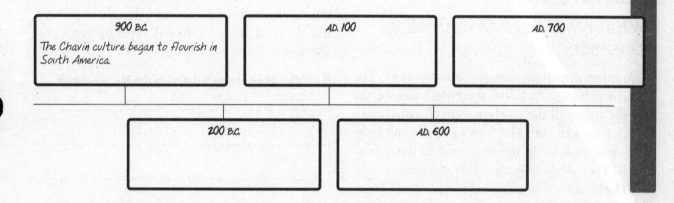

900 B.C.
The Chavin culture began to flourish in South America.

AD. 100

AD. 700

200 B.C.

AD. 600

Societies Arise in the Andes

(pages 246–249)

What geographic factors made it unlikely for a civilization to arise?

Other interesting civilizations arose in the Americas far to the south of the Olmec and Zapotec peoples. These civilizations grew in a very harsh environment—the *Andes* in South America. This mountain range has many peaks that are more than 20,000 feet high.

Toward the northern part of South America, along these mountains, lies the modern country of Peru. In this area, the mountains are steep and very rocky. Ice and snow cover the tops of the mountains during the entire year. Travel is hard.

The climate changes quickly from being hot during the day to bitter cold at night. The soil is poor.

It was in the mountains of this difficult land that a new civilization arose. That culture is called Chavín. It takes its name from a major ruin, Chavín de Hwintar, in the Andes. At this site, researchers have found pyramids, open spaces, and large mounds made of earth. The Chavín culture was at its height from 900 B.C. to 200 B.C. It is considered the first influential civilization in South America.

Scientists have found objects that suggest that the Chavín culture helped shape other cultures to the north and south of this site. At these other sites are the art styles and symbols of religion found at Chavín. Scientists think that the main site was not the center of a political empire but was the chief site of a spiritual or religious movement. People from other areas may have made trips to the main site to pay their respects. The Chavín culture, like the Olmec in Mexico, may have been a "mother culture," one that gave the first form to the ideas and styles of the area.

1. **What theories do scientists have about the Chavín culture?**

_____

_____

_____

_____

_____

Other Andean Civilizations Flourish (pages 24_ _9)

What other *A*ndean civilizations developed*

Two other important cultures arose in Peru. The **Nazca** culture developed along the coast of the Pacific Ocean in the south of Peru. It lasted from 200 B. to A.D. 600. The Nazca people built large and complex systems to bring water to their farm-land. They made beautiful cloth and pottery.

The Nazca are most famous for the *Nazca Lines.* They are huge pictures scraped on the surface of a rocky plain. The drawings include a monkey, a spider, some birds, and other creatures. The pictures are so large that they can be seen and appreciated only from high in the air. Some experts think that the Nazca drew these pictures for their gods to see.

The other culture of early Peru arose along the Pacific Coast but far to the north. This was the **Moche** culture. It lasted from A.D. 100 to A.D. 700. The Moche tapped into rivers that flowed down from the mountains. They built ditches to bring water to their fields. They raised corn, beans, pota-toes, squash, and peanuts. They also fished, caught wild ducks and pigs, and hunted deer.

Archaeologists have found some tombs of the Moche people. They show that the culture had great wealth. They have found objects made of gold, silver, and jewels. The Moche people made beautiful pottery that showed scenes of everyday life. So, even though they never had a written lan-guage, it is possible to learn much about how they lived.

Eventually, the Moche culture also fell. As with the other peoples of the Americas, the reason for this fall is not known. For the next hundred years, other cultures would rise and fall in the Americas. But most of them remained separate from one another.

2. **Name three characteristics of the Moche people.**

_____

_____

_____

_____

_____

Glossary — CHAPTER 9 The Americas: A Separate World

Andes Mountain range in South America

archaeologists Scientists who learn about past human life and activities

dense Thick

exposed Uncovered

flourished Did well

glaciers Huge sheets of ice

land bridge Strip of land linking two larger land masses

mammoth Large prehistoric animal like an elephant

mounds Raised masses of earth created by humans for burial, ceremonial, or other purposes

Nazca Lines Huge drawings made by the Nazca people by scraping the surface of a rocky plain and which can only be properly observed from the air

observatory Place to observe heavenly bodies

radical Extreme

ritual An event or ceremony with order, form, and significance

AFTER YOU READ

Terms and Names

A. Write the name or term in each blank that best completes the meaning of the paragraph.

Zapotec

Nazca

Olmec

Chavín

Moche

Early civilizations in the Americas developed in the Andes of South America as well as in Mesoamerica. In the Andes, the **1**_____ culture was the first to develop. This culture was followed by two other significant Andean civilizations. Both the **2**_____ and the **3**_____ developed in what is now Peru. In Mesoamerica, the **4**_____ culture, which has come to regarded as a "mother culture," developed a little ahead of the **5**_____ culture.

B. Write the letter of the name or term next to the description that explains it best.

a. Monte Alban

b. Mesoamerica

c. maize

d. Ice Age

e. Beringia

____**1.** Corn

____**2.** Area stretching from present-day central Mexico to northern Honduras

____**3.** Land bridge between Asia and the Americas

____**4.** Period when sheets of ice covered large portions of North America

____**5.** First urban center in the Americas

AFTER YOU READ (cont.)   *CHAPTER 9*   The Americas: A Separate World

Main Ideas

1. Explain how scholars know when the first people arrived in the Americas.

_____

_____

_____

2. What changes did the rise of farming cause in the Americas?

_____

_____

_____

3. What geographic advantages did the Olmec enjoy?

_____

_____

_____

4. What is the significance of Monte Albán?

_____

_____

_____

5. What made the Andes an unlikely place for civilizations to arise?

_____

_____

_____

Thinking Critically

Answer the following questions on a separate sheet of paper.

1. What did the first Americans hunt, and what happened when that supply of food disappeared?

2. What do the Olmec and Chavín cultures have in common?

CHAPTER 10 Section 1 (pages 263–268)

The Rise of Islam

BEFORE YOU READ

In the last section, you read about early civilizations in South America.

In this section, you will read about the rise of Islam.

AS YOU READ

Use the chart below to take notes on the rise of Islam.

TERMS AND NAMES
Allah One god of Islam
Muhammad Arab prophet who founded Islam
Islam Religion based on the belief in Allah
Muslim Follower of the religion Islam
Hijrah Muhammad's move from Mecca to Yathrib (Medina) in 622
mosque Islamic house of worship
hajj Pilgrimage to Mecca
Qur'an Holy book of Islam
Sunna Islamic model for living based on the life and teachings of Muhammad
shari'a Body of Islamic law

BATTLE / POLITICAL ISSUE	EFFECT
geography of the Arabian peninsula	desert nomadic way of life near trade routes
Muhammad	
Islamic beliefs	

Deserts, Towns, and Trade Routes (pages 263–264)

How did the desert help shape Arab life?

The harsh environment of the Arabian Peninsula left its mark on the Arab peoples. The land is almost completely covered by desert. The desert people were nomads. They herded animals, leading them from one *fertile* spot, or *oasis*, to another. Over time, many of these people, called *Bedouins*, began to live in towns and cities. They also began to trade goods.

By the early 600s, trade became an important activity in the Arabian Peninsula. Merchants from the north brought goods to Arabia. They traded for spices and other goods. They also brought new ideas.

At this time, some Arabs believed in one God, called Allah in Arabic. Others believed in many gods. Religious pilgrims came to Mecca to worship at an ancient shrine called the *Ka'aba*.

1. When and how did trade become important?

_____

_____

The Prophet Muhammad

(pages 264–265)

Who was Muhammad?

Around the year 570, **Muhammad** was born into this Arab society. At around age 40, he took religion as his life's mission and became a *prophet*. According to Muslim belief, the angel Gabriel visited Muhammad and told him to speak the word of God to his people.

Muhammad began to teach that **Allah** was the one and only God. The religion based on his teachings is called **Islam**. Its followers are called **Muslims.**

At first many people in Mecca opposed Muhammad's views. They feared Meccans would neglect traditional Arab gods. Muhammad and his followers were forced to leave Mecca for Yathrib (later called Medina) in 622. This became known as the **Hijrah.** The Hijrah was a turning point for Muhammad.

Gradually Muhammad and his followers gained power. Finally, in 630, Muhammad went to the Ka'aba in Mecca and destroyed the *idols*. Many of the people of Mecca adopted Islam. They began to worship Allah as the only God. Muhammad died soon after, in 632. Much of the Arabian Peninsula was already united under Islam.

2. What was the Hijrah?

_____

_____

_____

_____

Beliefs and Practices of Islam

(pages 267–268)

What do Muslims believe and practice?

Muslims have five duties to perform. These duties include faith, prayer, *alms, fasting,* and pilgrimage to Mecca. The duties show a person's acceptance of the will of Allah:

- A Muslim must state the belief that, "There is no God but Allah, and Muhammad is the Messenger of Allah."
- A Muslim must pray to Allah, facing Mecca, five times every day. This may be done at a **mosque,** an Islamic house of worship.
- A Muslim must give alms, or money for the poor, through a tax.
- A Muslim must fast during the holy month of Ramadan. Muslims eat only one meal a day, after sunset, every day during this month.
- A Muslim should perform the **hajj**—a trip to the holy city of Mecca—at least once in his or her life.

The central ideas of Islam are found in the **Qur'an.** Muslims believe this book states the will of Allah as revealed to Muhammad. Muslims are also guided by the example of Muhammad's life, called the **Sunna,** and by a set of laws and rules, the **shari'a.**

Muslims believe that Allah is the same God that Jews and Christians worship. To Muslims, the Qur'an perfects the earlier teachings of God found in the Jewish Torah and the Christian Bible. Because their holy books were related to the Qur'an, Jews and Christians enjoyed special status in Muslim societies.

3. What are the five duties of Muslims?

_____

_____

_____

_____

_____

CHAPTER 10 Section 2 (pages 269–272)

Islam Expands

BEFORE YOU READ

In the last section, you read about the rise of Islam, In this section, you will read about the spread of Islam.

AS YOU READ

Use the chart below to take notes on how Islam spread.

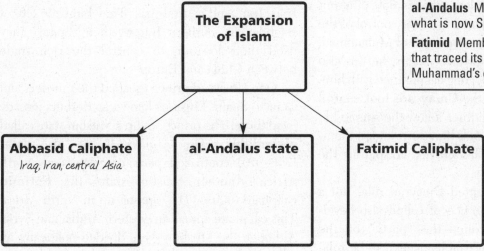

The Expansion of Islam

Abbasid Caliphate
Iraq, Iran, central Asia

al-Andalus state

Fatimid Caliphate

TERMS AND NAMES

caliph Highest political and religious leader in a Muslim government

Umayyads Dynasty that ruled the Muslim Empire from A.D. 661 to 750

Shi'a Branch of Islam whose members believe the first four caliphs are the rightful successors of Muhammad

Sunni Branch of Islam whose members believe Ali and his descendants are the rightful successors of Muhammad

Sufi Muslim who tries to achieve direct contact with God

Abbasids Dynasty that ruled much of the Muslim Empire from A.D. 750 to 1258

al-Andalus Muslim-ruled area in what is now Spain

Fatimid Member of a Muslim dynasty that traced its ancestry to Muhammad's daughter Fatima

Muhammad's Successors Spread Islam (pages 269–270)

How did other leaders spread Islam?

When Muhammad died, his followers elected a new leader, Abu-Bakr. He had been loyal to Muhammad. He was given the title **caliph.** This means *"successor"* or *"deputy."* A successor is a person who comes after and takes the place of someone else. A deputy is an assistant who acts on behalf of a leader who is absent.

Abu-Bakr reacted quickly when a group of Arabs abandoned Islam. He defeated them in battle over a two-year period. Abu-Bakr died soon after. But his army began to conquer new lands. By 750, the Muslim Empire stretched from the Indus River in India west to the Atlantic Ocean.

Many of the people conquered by the Muslims accepted Islam. Some found the message of Islam appealing. Others liked the fact that by becoming Muslims they avoided paying a tax put only on non-Muslims. But the Qur'an prevented Muslims from forcing others to accept the religion. Muslim rulers allowed people to follow whatever beliefs they chose.

1. How did Abu-Bakr spread Islam?

_____

_____

_____

_____

Internal Conflict Creates a Crisis

(pages 270–271)

What disagreements arose?

After the murder of a ruling caliph in 656, different Muslim groups began to struggle for control of the empire. Ali, a cousin and son-in-law of Muhammad, was chosen caliph. After a few years, he was also killed. The system of electing caliphs died with him.

A family known as the **Umayyads** took control of the empire. They did not follow the simple life of earlier caliphs. Instead, they surrounded themselves with wealth. This created a split in the Muslim community.

Most Muslims accepted Umayyad rule. But a different view of the office of caliph also developed. The **Shi'a** group—the "party" of the deceased Ali—felt that caliphs needed to be relatives of Muhammad. Those who did not openly resist Umayyad rule became known as the **Sunni.** Among them were many Muslims who felt that the Umayyads had lost touch with their religion. Another group, the **Sufi,** reacted to the Umayyads' life of luxury. The Sufis emphasized a more spiritual way of life.

2. How did the Shi'a and Sunni groups arise?

_____

_____

_____

_____

Control Extends Over Three Continents (pages 271–272)

What Muslim states arose?

After 750, there were Muslim caliphates on three continents. The **Abbasids** (750–1258) took power and murdered members of the Umayyad family.

The Abassids controlled the lands of modern Iraq, Iran, and central Asia. They built the city of Baghdad in southern Iraq as their capital. They used their location to control the rich trade between China and Europe.

One Umayyad prince escaped the murders and went to Spain. Muslims known as Berbers already lived there. The prince set up a Muslim state called **al-Andalus.** The Umayyads of al-Andalus (756–976) controlled parts of Spain and North Africa. Another Muslim state—the **Fatimid** caliphate (909–1171)—sprang up in North Africa, This caliphate spread to western Arabia and Syria. Although the Muslims were divided politically, all of the different communities were linked by religion, language, culture, and trade.

3. Who were the Abbasids?

_____

_____

_____

_____

CHAPTER 10 Section 3 (pages 273–279)

TERMS AND NAMES
House of Wisdom Center of learning established in Baghdad in the 800s
calligraphy Art of beautiful handwriting

Muslim Culture

BEFORE YOU READ

In the last section, you read about the expansion of Islam.

In this section, you will read about the cultural achievements of Muslim society.

AS YOU READ

Use the web below to take notes on the cultural achievements and advances made by Muslims.

```
                    Scholarship
              Collected, translated, and
                 saved ancient works

   Art                                      Science

                     Muslim
                     Culture

   Literature                               Math
```

Muslim Society (pages 273–274)

Where and how did Muslims live?

The Muslim Empire included people of many different lands and cultures. Major cities arose in the Muslim world. They included Córdoba and Cairo, centers of Muslim rule in Spain and North Africa, and Baghdad, the Abbasid capital.

Muslim society was divided into four groups, At the top were people who were Muslims from birth. Next came those who converted to Islam. The third group included Jews, Christians, and Zoroastrians—protected because Muslims shared some of their beliefs. The fourth group was slaves, none of whom were Muslims.

According to Muslim law, women should obey men. But Muslim women still enjoyed more rights than did those living in European society at the time. The Qur'an gave Muslim women some economic and property rights. In early Muslim society, women could also have an education and take part in public life. Later they lost those rights.

1. Name the four groups of Muslim society.

_____

_____

Muslim Scholarship Extends Knowledge (pages 274–276)

How did Muslim scholars keep learning alive?

Muslims placed a high value on learning and *scholarship*. Muslim scholars added much to human knowledge. Europe was in chaos and much of the knowledge of Europeans was in danger of being lost. During this time, Muslim scholars collected ancient Greek, Indian, and Persian works of science and philosophy. The scholars translated these works into Arabic. One center of this study was the **House of Wisdom** in Baghdad. Later, this ancient learning returned to Europe when the works of Muslim scholars were translated,

2. Explain how Muslim scholars helped save the learning of the West.

_____

_____

Arts and Sciences Flourish

(pages 276–278)

What were some achievements of Muslim society?

Literature was a strong tradition before Islam. Later, the Qur'an became the standard for all Arabic literature and poetry. The collection *The Thousand and One Nights* included many entertaining stories, fairy tales, and legends.

Muslims had their own special practices in art. For instance, artists could not draw pictures of people. Only Allah, the religion said, could create life. Unable to draw these images, Muslims developed a new art form. They practiced **calligraphy,** or the art of beautiful handwriting.

Muslim scholars made great advances in medicine and mathematics, The physician al-Razi wrote an encyclopedia that collected all that was known about medicine from Greece to India. In science, Muslims studied the work of ancient Greek scientists but used logic rather than experiments to reach conclusions. One Muslim scientist made new discoveries about how people see. His findings helped lead to the invention of the telescope and microscope. A mathematician named al-Khwarizmi wrote a textbook that developed algebra.

3. Name four achievements of Muslim scientists and mathematicians.

_____

_____

Philosophy and Religion Blend Views (pages 278–279)

How did philosophy blend with Islam?

Philosophers at the House of Wisdom also translated works of the ancient Greek philosophers. Muslim philosopher Ibn Rushd was criticized for trying to join their ideas with Muslim ideas. But he argued that Greek philosophy and Islam both searched for the truth. The Jewish philosopher Maimonides, who lived in the Muslim Empire, was also criticized for his ideas. He wrote a book that blended philosophy, religion, and science. Philosophers reflected the different people who lived in the Muslim Empire. Muslims came to recognize the value of their differences.

4. Why was Ibn Rushd criticized?

_____

_____

Glossary

alms Money for the poor

Bedouins Nomadic people of Arabia, North Africa, or Syria

deputy An assistant or representative who can take over when the leader is absent

fasting Restricting what one eats

fertile Word that describes soil that is good for growing crops

flourish Do well

idols Images or objects that people worship

Ka'aba Muslim shrine

oasis Place in a desert with end_ water to support plant life

prophet Person said to speak t_ word of God

scholarship Learning

successor Person who comes __er and takes the place of someor __se

AFTER YOU READ

Terms and Names

A. Write the name or term in each blank that best completes the meaning of the pa__raph.

shari'a

Islam

hajj

Allah

Muslim

Muhammad is the prophet of the religion __ed **1** _____. The word that names a follower of this religion is _____. One of the central beliefs of this religion is that t__e is only __e god, **3** _____. Among the required practices __follower__ s the giving of alms, or aid, for the poor. Followers __t al__ make a **4** _____, or pilgrimage, to Mecca at least c__e __ a lifetime. Believers also follow a body of law known as **5** _____. It gives guidance on practical matters of daily life.

B. Write the letter of the name or term next to the description that explains it best.

a. Umayyad

b. Fatimid

c. Abbasid

d. Hijrah

e. Sufi

_____ **1.** Muhammad's move from Mecca to Yathrib (Med__ _)

_____ **2.** Member of a Muslim caliphate that traced __s ances__ to Muhammad's daughter

_____ **3.** Caliphate that ruled much of the Muslim Emp__ _ from A.D. 7__ to 1258

_____ **4.** Caliphate that ruled the Muslim Empire from A.D. 661 to 750

_____ **5.** Muslim who pursues a life of poverty and spirituality.

AFTER YOU READ (cont.)   *CHAPTER 10* The Muslim World

Main Ideas

1. Who was Muhammad, and what did he teach?

_____

_____

_____

2. Explain the importance of the Qur'an and Sunna in Muslim life.

_____

_____

_____

_____

3. Why did many conquered peoples accept Islam? What happened to those who did not?

_____

_____

_____

_____

4. What factors linked the three separate caliphates—the Abbasids, the Umayyads of al-Andalus, and the Fatimids?

_____

_____

_____

_____

5. What rights did women have in early Muslim society?

_____

_____

_____

_____

Thinking Critically

Answer the following questions on a separate sheet of paper.

1. Explain the importance of Mecca and Yathrib (Medina) in the life of Muhammad.

2. Explain the relationship between these terms: Umayyads, caliph, Sunni, and Shi'a.

The Byzantine Empire

BEFORE YOU READ

In the last chapter, you read about the Muslim world.
In this section, you will learn about the Byzantine Empire.

AS YOU READ

Use the chart below to take notes on people, places, and developments in the Byzantine Empire.

TERMS AND NAMES

Justinian powerful ruler of Byzantine empire

Justinian Code Body of Roman law collected and organized by Justinian around A.D.534

Hagia Sophia Church destroyed by mobs of rioters in 532 and rebuilt by Justinian

patriarch Leader of the Eastern church

icon Religious image used in practices by eastern Christians

excommunication Formal declaration that someone is no longer a member of the Church

Cyrillic alphabet Alphabet invented by Saints Cyril and Methodius, in which most Slavic languages, including Russian, are written

---

THE BYZANTINE EMPIRE	
Action	**Result**
Justinian moves the capital	
Justinian creates the law	
The empire is weakened	
The church divides	

A New Rome in a New Setting

(page 301)

How did the Roman Empire change?

In the A.D. 300s, the emperor Constantine moved the capital of the Roman Empire to the east. He was worried about the growing power of German tribes. He thought that he could better meet that threat in the east. He built a great new capital city, Constantinople. It was on the site of the old port city of Byzantium. Constantinople became the center of the empire. Power moved eastward.

The Roman Empire was officially divided in 395. The western area was overrun by German tribes. It did not exist after 476. However, the Byzantine, or eastern, part remained strong. It lasted for hundreds of years.

In 527, **Justinian** became the Byzantine emperor. He sent an army to try to regain control of Italy. He hoped to restore the Roman Empire once again. By about 550, Justinian ruled over almost all of the territory of the old Roman Empire.

1. Who was Justinian?

_____

_____

Life in the New Rome
(pages 302–303)

What changes did Justinian bring?

Justinian directed legal experts to create a complete code of laws based on the laws of ancient Rome. This body of civil law—**the Justinian Code**—served the empire for 900 years.

Justinian also worked at making Constantinople a strong but also a beautiful capital. He built high, sturdy walls to protect the city from attack. He constructed a huge palace, public baths, courts, schools, hospitals, and many churches. The main street of the city was lined with shops and open-air markets. People bought and sold goods from Asia, Africa, and Europe there.

In 532, riots broke out against the emperor. Justinian's troops maintained control of the city, killing thousands of rioters. A church called **Hagia Sophia** ("Holy Wisdom," in Greek) had been destroyed by the mobs. Justinian rebuilt it to become the most beautiful church in the Christian world.

2. How did Justinian make Constantinople a strong and beautiful capital?

_____

_____

The Empire Falls (page 304)

What weakened the empire?

The Byzantine Empire faced many dangers. A terrible disease broke out in 542. It was probably caused by rats. The illness killed thousands of people and returned every 8 to 12 years until about 700. This weakened the empire.

Also, the empire was forced to *confront* many enemies over the centuries. German tribes, the Sassanid Persians, and Muslim armies all tried to gain control of Byzantine land. Constantinople remained safe during this time despite many attacks. Eventually, though, the empire shrank. By

1350, the empire included only the capital city and lands in the *Balkans*—part of southeastern Europe.

3. What were the two biggest problems the empire faced?

_____

_____

The Church Divides (pages 304–306)

Why did the church divide?

Although it was based on the Roman Empire, the Byzantine Empire had developed a culture of its own. People in the Byzantine Empire spoke Greek, not Latin. They belonged to the Eastern Orthodox Church, not the Catholic Church. The Eastern Church was led by the **patriarch,** the leading bishop. However, even the patriarch had to obey the emperor.

The feeling of separateness from Rome grew worse when one emperor *banned* the use of **icons.** Icons are religious images used by eastern Christians to aid their *devotions*. The emperor thought this was like *idol* worship. Iconoclasts, or "icon breakers" went into churches destroying images. This caused the people to riot and the *clergy* to rebel. The pope became involved. He supported the use of icons. One pope even ordered the **excommunication** of a Byzantine emperor. That means that the pope said the emperor could no longer be a member of the Church.

Slowly the Eastern and Roman churches grew further apart. In 1054, the schism, or split, became permanent.

Some *missionaries* traveled from the Byzantine Empire to the north. Two missionaries, Saint Methodius and Saint Cyril, met the Slavic peoples who lived in Russia. They developed an alphabet for the Slavic languages. Many Slavic languages, including Russian, are now written in what is called the **Cyrillic alphabet.**

4. What are two differences between the Eastern and Roman churches?

_____

_____

The Russian Empire

BEFORE YOU READ

In the last section, you read about the establishment and decline of the Byzantine Empire.

In this section, you will learn about the emergence of Russia.

AS YOU READ

Use the time line below to show key events in the early development of Russia.

TERMS AND NAMES

Slavs People from the forests north of the Black Sea

Vladimir Grandson of Olga who ordered all his subjects to adopt Christianity

Yaroslav the Wise Russian ruler who helped Kiev gain power and wealth

Alexander Nevsky Russian noble who gained power in Moscow

Ivan III Moscow prince who led rebellion against Mongol rule

czar Russian emperor

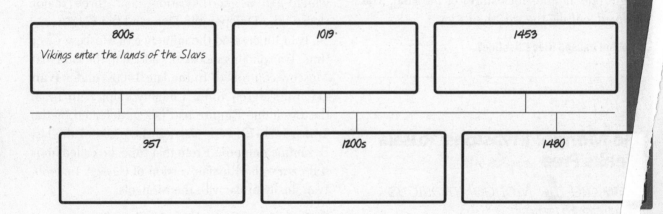

800s	1019	1453
Vikings enter the lands of the Slavs		

957	1200s	1480

Russia's Birth (pages 307–308)

Who were the Slavs?

The **Slavs** lived in what is today eastern Russia. The area was bounded by the Ural Mountains and the Black Sea on the south and the Baltic Sea on the north.

The Slavs lived in the forest areas. They worked as farmers and traders. In the 800s, some Vikings called the Rus came from the north. They built forts along the rivers and blended with the *Slavic* people. They founded the cities of Novgorod and Kiev and became the rulers of the land. They began to trade in Constantinople. With them, they brought furs, timber, and the Slavs who were their

subjects. They sold these people as slaves. In fact, the word slave comes from Slav.

Over time, the Vikings adopted the culture of the Slavs. Divisions between Vikings and Slavs disappeared. In 957 Princess Olga of Kiev *converted* to Christianity. Her grandson, **Vladimir,** also converted to Byzantine Christianity. He was the ruler of Russia. He ordered all of his subjects to adopt this religion. Now more than trade linked Russia to the Byzantine Empire.

Russia also looked to Constantinople for religious leadership. Teachers from the empire gave the Russian people instructions in the new religion. The king liked the idea that the ruler of the empire was also the head of the church.

1. How did Olga and Vladimir influence the Slavic people?

_____

_____

Kiev's Power and Decline (pages 308–309)

What caused Kiev's rise?

Under the influence of Byzantine culture, Kiev grew to be a large, wealthy, and cultured city. It continued to grow as Vladimir took land to the west and to the north. His son, **Yaroslav the Wise,** came to power in 1019. He proved to be an able ruler as well. Under him, Kiev grew even more wealthy through trade and *alliances* made with western nations.

Then the state centered in Kiev began to have problems. After Yaroslav's death in 1054, his sons fought one another for control of the land. Trade *declined,* cutting the wealth of Kiev.

2. What caused Kiev's decline?

_____

_____

The Mongol Invasions; Russia Breaks Free (pages 309–311)

How did the Mongol invasions change Russia?

In the middle 1200s, the *Mongols* reached Kiev. They quickly overran the Russian state, killing many people. The Mongols held control of the area for more than 200 years.

The Mongols had been fierce conquerors, but they were not harsh rulers. As long as the Russian people did not rebel, the Mongols let them keep their customs, including their Eastern Christian religion.

The Mongols made the Russians pay tribute, a sum of money that was owed every year. They used Russian nobles to collect the *tribute*. One of those nobles, **Alexander Nevsky,** gained power. His *heirs* became princes of Moscow. They later used this city as their base of power.

Control by the Mongols had important effects on Russia. It isolated the Russians from western Europe. Russian society developed in its own way. Rule by the Mongols united many different areas of Russia under one central authority. Before then, what is now Russia had been ruled by a number of princes. Mongol rule also led to the rise of Moscow, which had a good location near three major rivers—the Dnieper, the Don, and the Volga.

Ivan I increased the influence of Moscow. Over time, Ivan and his successors added to the land that Moscow controlled. In the late 1400s, under **Ivan III,** Russia grew to be a mighty empire. In 1453, the Byzantine Empire had fallen, defeated by the Turks. In 1472, Ivan married the niece of the last Byzantine emperor. From that time, he called himself **czar**—the Russian version of *Caesar*. In 1480, Ivan finally broke with the Mongols.

3. Name three effects of Mongol rule on Russia.

_____

_____

Skillbuilder

Use the illustration to answer these questions.

1. What kinds of items are the Vikings carrying in their boat?

_____

2. What conclusions can you draw about the Vikings from this woodcut?

_____

CHAPTER 11 Section 3 (pages 314–317)

Turkish Empires Rise in Anatolia

TERMS AND NAMES

Seljuks Turkish group that migrated into the Abbasid Empire in the 10th century and later established their own empire

vizier Prime minister in a Muslim kingdom or empire

Malik Shah Famous Seljuk sultan

BEFORE YOU READ

In the last section, you read about the growth of Russia.

In this section, you will learn about the Turks in Anatolia.

AS YOU READ

Use the time line below to record important events in the rise and fall of the Seljuk Turks.

945		1095
Persians take control of the Abbasid Empire		

	1055		1258

The Rise of the Turks (pages 314–315)

Who were the Seljuk Turks?

The Turks were nomads from central Asia. They lived by herding sheep and goats. They traded with the settled peoples of the Abbasid Empire.

Beginning in the 900s, they moved into the lands of that empire and began converting to Islam.

The Turks were fierce and highly skilled fighters. The rulers of the empire began to buy them as children to train them for their armies. These Turkish military slaves were known as mamelukes. The Turks became an important political factor in the empire. Turkish soldiers many times removed caliphs from the throne in Baghdad and put new rulers in their place.

While the Turkish influence was growing, the empire itself was shrinking. Local leaders in several areas split off to establish their own states. In 945, a Persian army seized control of the empire. Members of the Abbasid family continued to hold the position of caliph and act as religious leaders. The new rulers of the government were from outside the dynasty. They were called *sultans*.

Large numbers of Turks settled in the empire as these changes took place. They were called **Seljuks** after the name of the family that led them. In 1055, the Seljuks captured Baghdad and took control of the government. In the next few decades, the Seljuks used their force to take land from another empire—the Byzantine Empire. They won almost all of Anatolia. Anatolia was the name for the peninsula where modern Turkey is located. In this position, the Seljuks stood almost at the gates of Constantinople.

The Seljuks relied on the government experience of Persians in ruling their empire. They chose the Persian city of Isfahan as the capital of their kingdom. They gave Persians important positions in the government. For example, Nizam al-Mulk was a Persian who served as **vizier,** or prime minister. In return, Persians became loyal supporters of Turkish rule.

The Turks also adopted Persian culture. The nomadic Seljuk Turks had arrived in Southwest Asia as basically *illiterate*. They were not familiar with the traditions of Islam, which they had just adopted. They looked to Persian scholars to teach them the proper way to follow Islam. They began to use the Persian language for art and education. Turkish rulers even took the Persian word for "king"—*shah*—as their title.

One of the greatest Seljuk rulers, **Malik Shah,** became a *patron* of the arts. He made the capital city more beautiful by building many mosques, or Muslim houses of worship. Persian became so important that Arabic—the language of the Qur'an—almost died out in Seljuk lands.

1. **What influence did Persians and Persian culture have on the Seljuks?**

_____

_____

_____

_____

Seljuks Confront Crusaders and Mongols (pages 316–317)

Why did the Seljuk Empire collapse?

After Malik Shah died unexpectedly in 1092, the Seljuk Empire collapsed quickly. Weak rulers could not maintain it. Collapse was also due to the *Crusades*. Rulers in western Europe sent armies to capture the lands of ancient Palestine. These were places sacred to Christians.

The First Crusade began in 1095, and the Christian armies captured Jerusalem. They established a Latin Kingdom that lasted about a century. Eventually, the Turks gathered enough strength to fight back. They retook the city in 1187.

Just when the Crusades became less of a threat to the Muslim world, the Mongols moved in from the east. They were led by a brutal leader, Genghis Khan. They killed tens of thousands of people and overran huge stretches of territory. Baghdad was captured in 1258. The Mongols killed the last caliph and took control of the government from the Seljuk Turks.

2. **What brought the Seljuk Empire to an end?**

_____

_____

_____

Name _____ Date _____

alliances Agreements, usually for the sake of trade or protection

Balkans Region of southeastern Europe now occupied by Greece, Bulgaria, Albania, Romania, the European part of Turkey, and the former republics of Yugoslavia

banned Forbade completely; outlawed the use or practice of

civil law Law dealing with the rights of private citizens

clergy Officials of the church

confronts Faces; meets

converted Officially changed from one religion to another

Crusades Series of attempts made by Western rulers to capture the Holy Land

decline Weakening; lessening power

devotions Prayers and other acts of worship

heirs People, usually relatives, who inherit the power or holdings of those who died before them

idol Image or object used in worship

illiterate Unable to read or write

missionaries People who bring Christianity to others

patron Supporter

shah Persian word for "king;" title of some Persian and Turkish rulers

Slavic Relating to the Slavs

sultans Rulers of a Moslem country, especially what is now Turkey

tribute Payment made by a conquered people to its rulers

AFTER YOU READ

Terms and Names

A. Write the name or term in each blank that best completes the meaning of the paragraph.

patriarch

excommunication

Cyrillic alphabet

icons

There were many reasons for the split that occurred between the Eastern Orthodox Church and the Roman Catholic Church. One reason was the leader of the Eastern Church, the **1** _____ had to be subject to the emperor. The authority of the emperor was tested when one emperor banned the use of **2** _____. These were important in the religious practices of eastern Christians. Worshipers were outraged when iconoclasts went into churches breaking these images. Another outrage occurred when a Roman pope ordered the **3** _____ of a Byzantine emperor. As the two churches grew apart, missionaries for the Orthodox Church traveled to the land of the Slavs. There, they created the **4** _____, which helped give the Slavs a written language.

B. Write the letter of the name next to the description that explains it best.

a. Hagia Sophia

b. Alexander Nevsky

c. Malik Shah

d. Vladimir

e. Yaroslav the Wise

_____ **1.** Seljuk sultan

_____ **2.** Grandson of Olga who ordered all his subjects to adopt Christianity

_____ **3.** Church rebuilt by Justinian

_____ **4.** Russian ruler who helped Kiev gain power

_____ **5.** Russian noble who gained power in Moscow

AFTER YOU READ (cont.)   *CHAPTER 11* Byzantines, Russians, and Turks Interact

Main Ideas

1. What was the importance of Constantinople?

_____

_____

_____

2. Describe the accomplishments of the emperor Justinian.

_____

_____

_____

_____

3. What relationship did the Slavs have to the Vikings?

_____

_____

_____

4. Explain the changes that occurred in Russia during the rules of Ivan I and Ivan III.

_____

_____

_____

5. Explain the role the mamelukes played in the Abbasid Empire.

_____

_____

_____

Thinking Critically

Answer the following questions on a separate sheet of paper.

1. What influences combined to produce Russian culture?

2. Explain how the Turks eventually displaced both the Abbasids and the Byzantine Empire.

CHAPTER 12 Section 1 (pages 323–329)

Tang and Song China

TERMS AND NAMES

Tang Taizong Great emperor of the Tang Dynasty

Wu Zhao Tang ruler and only woman in China ever to assume the title of emperor

movable type Wood or metal blocks, each with a single character, that can be arranged to make up a page for printing

gentry Powerful upper class

BEFORE YOU READ

In the last section, you read about the Turkish empires. In this section, you will read about changes in China during the Tang and Song dynasties.

AS YOU READ

Use the web below to show developments during the Song Dynasty.

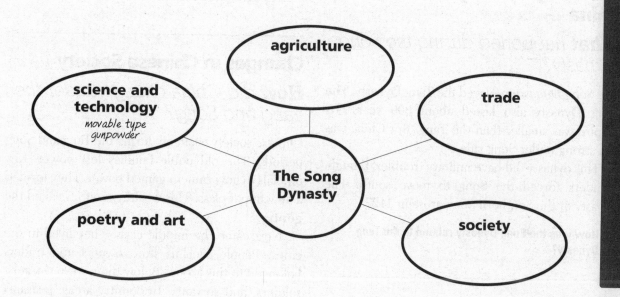

agriculture

science and technology
movable type
gunpowder

trade

The Song Dynasty

poetry and art

society

The Tang Dynasty Expands China (pages 323–324)

What changes occurred during the Tang Dynasty?

Starting in A.D. 220, China went through a long period of troubles. There were no strong rulers. China was not united. Then in 589, Wendi brought order. He united the northern and southern regions. He also named himself the first emperor of the *Sui Dynasty.*

This dynasty lasted only about 30 years. Just two rulers reigned. Both were important. They built the *Grand Canal.* This waterway connected China's two major rivers. The canal was a trade route between northern and southern China. Cities were in the north. Areas that grew rice were in the south.

The *Tang Dynasty* followed. It lasted for 300 years. **Tang Taizong** was a mighty emperor. He and other Tang rulers made the empire larger. They gained back lands lost since the fall of the Han Dynasty. **Wu Zhao** was another great Tang leader. She was the only woman ever to rule China as emperor. During her reign, parts of Korea were added to the dynasty.

Early Tang rulers made the government stronger. They extended the network of roads and canals, helping to tie the empire together.

Schools were set up to train people for political jobs. They had to pass tough tests. Only then could people work for the government.

By the mid-700s, the Tang Dynasty had begun to weaken. Rulers charged heavy taxes. The Chinese people faced more hardship. Invaders attacked the empire's lands. Chinese rebels became violent. In 907, they killed the last Tang ruler.

1. How did Tang rulers change China?

_____

_____

The Song Dynasty Restores China (pages 324–325)

What happened during the Song Dynasty?

The *Song Dynasty* replaced the Tang Dynasty. The Song Dynasty also lasted about 300 years. Its empire was smaller than the Tang. But China was still strong under Song rule.

This dynasty did have military troubles, though. Invaders forced the Song to move south. The dynasty of the Southern Song arose in 1127.

2. How was the Song Dynasty related to the Tang Dynasty?

_____

_____

An Era of Prosperity and Innovation (pages 325–326)

What advances occurred during the Tang and Song periods?

During the Tang and Song rule, the Chinese made many advances. They invented useful things. **Movable type** made printing faster. Gunpowder was another important invention. It led to the design of exploding weapons. The Chinese made progress in farming, too. They improved ways of growing rice.

Trade increased under the Tang and Song emperors. Goods were carried over land routes. Later, ocean trade became important. Ideas were also exchanged. Buddhism spread. This religion traveled from China to Japan, Korea, and Vietnam.

The Tang and Song dynasties were creative periods. Great poets wrote about life. Artists made beautiful paintings.

3. Name three advances in technology.

_____

_____

_____

Changes in Chinese Society (page 327)

How did China change under the Tang and Song?

Chinese society changed during the Tang and Song periods. The old noble families lost power. Key officials in government gained power. They formed a new upper class. This wealthy group is called the **gentry.**

Next came the middle class. They lived in the cities. People such as store owners and traders belonged to this group. Below them were workers, soldiers, and servants. In country areas, peasants made up the largest class. The position of women became worse.

4. What social changes occurred in China during the Tang and Song periods?

_____

_____

_____

CHAPTER 12 Section 2 (pages 330–334)

The Mongol Conquests

BEFORE YOU READ

In the last section, you read about the Tang and Song dynasties.

In this section, you will read about the rise and conquests of the Mongols.

AS YOU READ

Use the chart below to record facts about the Mongols and their empire.

TERMS AND NAMES

pastoralist Person who herds tamed animals

clan Large group of people related to a common ancestor

Genghis Khan Leader who brought together the Mongol clans

Pax Mongolica "Mongol Peace," a period from mid-1200s to mid-1300s when Mongols imposed order across much of Eurasia

Life as Nomads	Herded animals Lived on dry grassland
The Rise of the Mongols	
The Mongol Empire	

Nomads of the Asian Steppe

(pages 330–331)

How did the nomads of the Asian steppe live?

Much of Central Asia is covered by dry grassland. Such a region is called the *steppe*. Very little rain falls on the steppe. Only short hardy grasses grow in this dry region. It gets very cold in winter and very hot in the summer.

Herders lived in this area. They were **pastoralists.** They herded *domesticated* animals. The herders were *nomads*. They moved from place to place. They searched for grass to feed the sheep and goats.

Herders often rode on horseback. They traveled together in large groups. These groups formed

clans. The clans were made up of people related to a common ancestor.

The nomads often rode out from the steppes and made contact with the settled people who lived in towns and villages. Often they traded peacefully with one another. But sometimes the nomads attacked the villages and took what they wanted by force. A nomadic group, called the Mongols, became very powerful.

1. Name three characteristics of the nomads of the steppes.

_____

_____

_____

The Rise of the Mongols

(pages 331–332)

Who united the Mongols?

Around 1200, a leader tried to bring the Mongol clans together. His name was Temujin. In 1206, he took the title **Genghis Khan.** This means "universal ruler." Over the next 21 years, he ruled the Mongols. They conquered much of Central Asia, including parts of China.

Genghis Khan enjoyed military success for several reasons. First, he organized his soldiers well. He followed the Chinese model of creating armies of 10,000 men. The armies were broken into brigades of 1,000 men, companies of 100 men, and platoons of 10 men.

Second, Genghis Khan was able to trick his enemies. He set traps for his opponents. He sometimes had his cavalry retreat. Then, when the enemy gave chase, the rest of the Mongol army would appear and charge the enemy.

Third, he used cruelty. His terror made many of his enemies surrender.

2. Name three reasons for the success of the Mongols as conquerors.

_____

_____

_____

The Mongol Empire (pages 332–334)

How did the Mongol Empire spread and divide?

Genghis Khan died in 1227. In less than 50 years, his successors conquered territory from China to Poland. In doing so, they created the largest unified land empire in history.

By 1260, the Mongol Empire was divided into four areas. These were called *khanates*. Each was ruled by a descendant of Genghis Khan.

The Mongols destroyed many things in their invasions. Some towns were completely wiped out. They destroyed irrigation systems in the Tigris and Euphrates valleys. People could no longer live in some of those areas.

Over time, Mongol rulers borrowed from the cultures in the areas they ruled. Rulers in the west became Muslims. Those in China used Chinese inventions. Differences in culture split up the Empire.

The Mongols were able rulers. They brought about a long period of peace, called the **Pax Mongolica,** in Central Asia. Trade thrived. The exchange of ideas between Asia and Europe increased. However, the Mongols may have also brought the *bubonic plague* to Europe. In the 1300s, this deadly disease killed many people in Europe.

3. What were two effects of the Mongol empire on Central Asia?

_____

_____

_____

Name _____ Date _____

The Mongol Empire

TERMS AND NAMES
Kublai Khan Mongol leader and Chinese emperor
Marco Polo Traveler from Venice who served Kublai Khan for 17 years

BEFORE YOU READ

In the last section, you read about the rise of the Mongols and their conquests.

In this section, you will read about the Mongol leader who became emperor of China.

AS YOU READ

Use this diagram to show the effects of Kublai Khan's rise to power and rule.

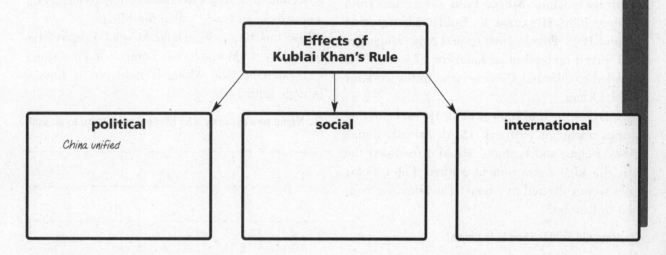

Effects of Kublai Khan's Rule

political — *China unified*

social

international

Kublai Khan Becomes Emperor

(pages 299–300)

How did Kublai Khan rule China?

Genghis Khan began the conquest of China in 1215. His grandson, **Kublai Khan,** conquered all of China in 1279. He was the first foreigner to rule the whole country.

Kublai Khan became China's new emperor. He began the *Yuan Dynasty.* It ruled China for less than 100 years. This era was important. Kublai Khan united China for the first time in 300 years. He opened China to more foreign trade. The Mongols did not *disrupt* Chinese government or culture. Kublai Khan built a new capital. It was

located in the modern city of Beijing.

The Mongols tried to conquer other lands. Kublai Khan attacked Japan in 1274 and 1281. The Mongols forced the Koreans to build and supply ships for the planned invasions. It was very expensive and almost ruined Korea. Both attacks failed. The second failed because a typhoon destroyed the Mongol fleet.

1. Why was the Yuan Dynasty important in Chinese history?

_____

_____

_____

Mongol Rule in China (pages 336–337)

What changes occurred under Mongol rule?

Mongol rulers were very different from the Chinese. The Mongols kept the top government jobs for themselves. They also hired many people from other lands for these posts. Mongol rulers did not trust the Chinese.

Kublai Khan was a great leader. He restored the Great Canal. He helped foreign trade increase. Chinese goods such as silk and porcelain were in demand. Western Asia and Europe wanted Chinese inventions. These included gunpowder and paper money.

Kublai Khan welcomed merchants from other countries to China. **Marco Polo** was a trader from Venice, Italy. He came to Kublai Khan's court around 1275. Polo learned several Asian languages and served under Kublai Kahn for 17 years. Polo traveled to different Chinese cities in his work for Kublai Khan.

Polo returned to Italy in 1292. He told amazing stories about his journeys. He described China's cities, riches, and customs. He also recorded the way the Khan's government worked. Later, Polo's tales were collected in a book. The book was popular in Europe.

2. How did Kublai Khan help China?

_____

_____

_____

_____

The End of Mongol Rule (pages 337–338)

How did Mongol rule end?

In the last years of his rule, Kublai Khan ran into trouble. Attacks on Southeast Asia failed. Many lives and much equipment were lost.

To pay for these wars, as well as public works and the luxuries enjoyed by the Yuan court, the Khan raised taxes. The Chinese resented the heavy burden these taxes placed on them.

Kublai Khan died in 1294. Afterward, Mongol leaders struggled for power. They fought over control of the empire. These fights weakened Mongol rule.

Rebellions broke out in many parts of China in the 1300s. In 1368, Chinese rebels took over the government. Mongol rule ended. The rebels set up a new dynasty. It was called the Ming.

By this time, the whole Mongol Empire was falling apart. Mongols lost control of Persia and Central Asia. The Mongols held on to Russia, though, until 1480.

3. Name two reasons why Mongol rule came to an end.

_____

_____

_____

_____

_____

CHAPTER 12 Section 4 (pages 339–343)

Feudal Powers in Japan

TERMS AND NAMES

Shinto Japan's earliest religion, based on respect for nature and worship of ancestors

samurai Japanese warrior who served a lord

Bushido Code that samurai lived by—"the way of the warrior"

shogun Highest military commander in feudal Japan, ruling in the name of the emperor

BEFORE YOU READ

In the last section, you read about Mongol rule in China. In this section, you will learn about the early Japanese and their system of government.

AS YOU READ

Use the chart below to take notes on the development of Japan.

Geography	Made up of islands
Early Religion	
Early Emperors	
Feudalism	

The Growth of Japanese Civilization (pages 339–340)

How did geography help shape Japan?

Japan benefited from its location. It was near China. Thus Chinese culture influenced Japan. However, there was enough distance between these two countries to make Chinese attacks difficult.

Japan is made up of about 4,000 islands. They vary in size. Most people live on the four largest islands. The country has many mountains. There is not much good farmland. The islands have few natural resources, such as coal and oil.

Early Japan was broken up into many small areas. Each was controlled by a clan. These clans believed in their own gods. Later, all these beliefs became combined. They formed Japan's earliest religion, called **Shinto.** The main ideas of Shinto are respect for nature and the worship of ancestors.

In the 400s, the *Yamato clan* became the most powerful clan. The Yamato claimed that they were related to a sun goddess. By the 600s, Yamato leaders began to call themselves emperors. The emperor remained an important figure in Japan.

1. Who were the Yamato?

_____

_____

Japanese Culture; Life in the Heian Period (pages 340–341)

How did Chinese culture influence Japanese culture?

By the 400s, contact between China and Japan grew. Japan became more aware of Chinese ways. Buddhism from China reached Japan. It became an important religion in Japan.

Japan's emperor sent people to China. They learned about the culture. The Japanese adopted the Chinese system of writing. Japanese artists imitated Chinese paintings. For a while, Japan even used China's government as a model. Yet Japan still held on to its own traditions.

The years from 794 to 1185 are called the *Heian Period*. Heian was the new capital of the royal court. Japanese culture thrived there.

The gentleman and ladies of the court lived in splendor. Art and good manners formed the center of their lives. The best accounts of Heian society come from the writings of women of the court.

2. Name two parts of Chinese culture that Japan adopted.

_____

_____

Feudalism Erodes Imperial Authority (pages 341–343)

How did feudalism arise in Japan?

Over time, the power of Japan's central government decreased. Wealthy landowners lived away from the capital. They set up their own armies. These soldiers began to *terrorize* farmers.

In exchange for protection, farmers gave up some of their land to the lords. This is how the feudal system began in Japan. It was similar to the feudal system in Europe during the Middle Ages.

Each lord used a group of trained soldiers. They were called **samurai.** They protected their lord from attacks by other lords. Samurai followed a strict code of behavior. It was called **Bushido.** This word means "way of the warrior."

After a period of war, one of these lords arose as the most powerful. The emperor named him the **shogun.** This means "supreme general of the emperor's army." The emperor remained in power in name. But the new shogun ran the country. This pattern continued in Japan from 1192 to 1868.

3. Who were the samurai?

_____

_____

Kingdoms of Southeast Asia and Korea

TERMS AND NAMES
Khmer Empire Empire that ruled what is now Cambodia
Angkor Wat Temple complex of the Khmer Empire
Koryu Dynasty Dynasty that ruled Korea from 935 to 1392

BEFORE YOU READ

In the last section, you read about early Japan and the rise of feudalism.

In this section, you will learn about smaller kingdoms in East and Southeast Asia.

AS YOU READ

Make a web like the one below. Use it to take notes on Southeast Asia and Korea.

Srivijaya Empire

Khmer Empire
Main power on mainland Southeast Asia (800 to 1200)

Dai Viet

Southeast Asian Kingdoms

Korea under the Han

Koryu Dynasty

Kingdoms of Southeast Asia

(pages 344–347)

What was the Khmer Empire?

The region of Southeast Asia lies to the south of China. It includes mainland areas and many islands.

The region has never been united culturally or politically. Rivers and valleys cut through the mainland from north to south. Between the valleys are hills and mountains that make travel difficult in the region.

Political power in the area has often come from control of trade routes. This is because Southeast Asia lies on the most direct sea route between the Indian Ocean and the South China Sea.

India had a great influence on Southeast Asia. Hindu and Buddhist missionaries spread their faiths. Kingdoms in the area followed these religions as well as Indian political ideas. This early Indian influence on Southeast Asia is seen today in the region's religions, languages, and art forms.

Chinese ideas spread to the area through trade and migration. Sometimes the Chinese exerted political influence over the region.

From about 800 to 1200, the **Khmer Empire** was the main power. It was located on the mainland of Southeast Asia in what is now Cambodia. Growing rice was its chief source of wealth. The Khmer used large irrigation works to bring water to their fields. Rulers built huge temples and palaces. One of these is called **Angkor Wat.** It is among the world's greatest achievements in architecture.

At the same time, a dynasty called *Srivijaya* arose on Java. Java is an island. This dynasty reached its height from the 600s to the 1200s. Nearby islands fell under its rule. The capital, Palembang, was located on Sumatra. Palembang was a center for the study of Buddhism.

Vietnam fell under the influence of China. China controlled the area from about 100 B.C. to A.D. 900. Vietnam became an independent kingdom, known as Dai Viet, in 939.

The Vietnamese borrowed from Chinese culture. For example, Buddhism became important. The Vietnamese, though, kept their own culture. Women in Vietnam, for instance, had more rights than women in China.

1. What kingdoms arose in Southeast Asia?

_____

_____

_____

_____

Korean Dynasties (pages 346–347)

How did China influence Korea?

Korea, like Japan and Vietnam, was influenced by China. Korea also preserved its own traditions. In 108 B.C., the Han Dynasty of China conquered Korea. Leaders set up a military government. From China, the Koreans learned about two religions—Buddhism and Confucianism. Koreans also learned about China's central government and system of writing.

Korean tribes began to gather into groups. One group, the Silla, chased out the Chinese in the 600s and took control of the Korean peninsula.

By the 900s, Silla rule had weakened. A rebel leader named Wang Kon took power and set up the **Koryu Dynasty.** It ruled Korea from 935 to 1392. It had a government similar to China's. Korea used examinations to fill government jobs. But this did not keep wealthy landowners from controlling society. The dynasty, though, produced great works of art—including celadon pottery, fine poetry, and wood blocks to print the entire Buddhist canon.

Korea fell to the Mongols. They were under the Mongols until the 1350s. The Mongols demanded heavy taxes. The Koreans rebelled. The Mongols lost power. Then a new dynasty, the Choson, took over Korea. It ruled for 518 years.

2. What was the Koryu Dynasty?

_____

_____

_____

_____

Glossary

bubonic plague Deadly disease that struck Europe in the 1300s

disrupt Break up

domesticated Tamed for human use

Grand Canal Long waterway connecting China's major rivers and linking the north and south

Heian Period Time in Japanese history of great cultural achievement from 794 to 1195

khanates Four areas into which the Mongol Empire was divided

nomads Groups who move from place to place

Song Dynasty Important and long-lasting Chinese dynasty that followed the Tang

Srivijaya Powerful island dynasty in Southeast Asia

steppe Large, dry area of grassland

Sui Dynasty Short-lived Chinese dynasty that gave way to the Tang Dynasty

Tang Dynasty Important Chinese dynasty that followed the Sui Dynasty

terrorize Use of force or threats to frighten people

Yamato clan Powerful early Japanese clan

Yuan Dynasty Chinese dynasty founded by Kublai Khan

AFTER YOU READ

Names and Terms

A. Write the name or term in each blank that best completes the meaning of the paragraph.

Genghis Khan

Kublai Khan

Marco Polo

clans

pastoralists

The Mongol Empire arose on the grasslands of Asia. There, nomads lived as **1** _____. They moved from place to place in large family units called **2** _____. A ruler who adopted the name **3** _____ brought these groups together into one empire. He conquered China and Central Asia. Later, his grandson, **4** _____, ruled China and founded the Yuan Dynasty. One important visitor to China at this time was the European traveler **5** _____.

B. Write the letter of the name or term next to the description that explains it best.

a. Koryu Dynasty

b. Tang Taizong

c. Khmer Empire

d. Bushido

e. Wu Zhao

_____ **1.** Early and brilliant emperor of the Tang Dynasty

_____ **2.** Samurai code of honor

_____ **3.** Korean dynasty

_____ **4.** Tang emperor; only female emperor of China

_____ **5.** Southeast Asian empire that ruled in the area now known as Cambodia.

AFTER YOU READ (cont.)   *CHAPTER 12*   Empires in East Asia

Main Ideas

1. Name three social changes that occurred in China during the Song Dynasty.

_____

_____

_____

2. How did Genghis Khan change the Mongols?

_____

_____

_____

3. Why did the Mongol Empire fall?

_____

_____

_____

4. Explain Shinto and its main ideas.

_____

_____

_____

5. What happened in Korea before the Koryu Dynasty?

_____

_____

_____

Thinking Critically

Answer the following questions on a separate sheet of paper.

1. Compare and contrast the Tang and Song Dynasties.

2. What was the relationship between a Japanese shogun and the emperor?

Charlemagne Unites Germanic Kingdoms

BEFORE YOU READ

In the last section, you read about Southeast Asian kingdoms and Korean dynasties.

In this section, you will read about the rise and fall of Charlemagne's empire.

AS YOU READ

Take notes on the time line below. Fill it in with key events related to the rise of Germanic kingdoms and Charlemagne's empire.

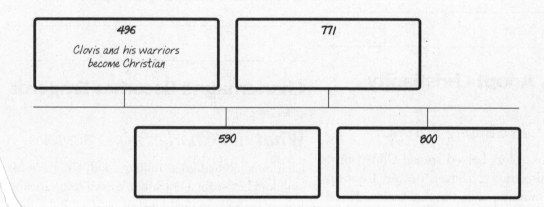

496	771
Clovis and his warriors become Christian	

590	800

<table>
<tr><td colspan="2">TERMS AND NAMES</td></tr>
<tr><td>Middle Ages Period of European history from 500 to 1500</td></tr>
<tr><td>Franks Germanic people who held power in the Roman province called Gaul</td></tr>
<tr><td>monastery Religious community of people devoting their lives to worship and prayer</td></tr>
<tr><td>secular Concerned with worldly things</td></tr>
<tr><td>Carolingian Dynasty Dynasty of Frankish rulers, lasting from 751 to 987</td></tr>
<tr><td>Charlemagne Powerful Frankish ruler who built a huge empire</td></tr>
</table>

Invasions of Western Europe

(page 353)

How did invasions by Germanic groups change Europe?

The slow decline of the Roman Empire marked the beginning of a new era in European history. This period is called the **Middle Ages.** It lasted from around 500 to 1500.

By the end of the fifth century, various Germanic groups invaded the Roman Empire in the west. These invasions led to a series of changes. Trade was halted. Moving goods from place to place became unsafe. Cities were no longer centers of trade and government. Many people then fled to the countryside. They returned to rural ways of life. People also became less educated.

As Germanic groups settled in different areas, they began to blend Latin with phrases of their own language. Many kinds of *dialects* developed. Europe no longer had a single language understood by all.

1. Name three effects of the Germanic invasions.

_____

_____

Germanic Kingdoms Emerge

(page 354)

Who were these Germanic peoples?

As Rome's power faded, a new kind of government appeared. Warring Germanic groups carved out kingdoms. The borders of these kingdoms changed often because of warfare. There was no central rule. Family ties and loyalty to a local leader bound Germanic peoples together. Europe was in *chaos*. The Church provided a sense of order, though.

The **Franks,** a Germanic people, established a large kingdom. It was located in the Roman province of Gaul. In 496, Clovis, the king of the Franks, and his warriors became Christian. From then on, the pope in Rome supported Clovis.

2. What new kind of government arose during Rome's decline?

_____

_____

_____

Germans Adopt Christianity

(pages 354–355)

How did Christianity spread?

Other Frankish rulers helped spread Christianity. The Church also tried to convert people. It set up religious communities called **monasteries.** There Christian men called *monks* devoted their lives to God. *Nuns* were women who led this religious way of life. Monasteries became centers of learning. Their libraries preserved some writings of ancient Rome.

The Church grew in importance when Gregory I became pope in 590. He made the pope the *guardian* of the spiritual lives of all Christians. He also made the pope a worldly, or **secular,** power in governing part of Italy. Gregory used Church wealth to raise armies and fix roads. He took part in making peace treaties with invaders. His influence in politics grew.

3. What role did monasteries play during this period?

_____

_____

An Empire Evolves (pages 355–356)

How did the Carolingian Dynasty arise?

The kingdom of the Franks covered much of modern France. By the 700s, the most powerful official was the mayor of the palace. He made laws and controlled the army.

In 719, Charles Martel became mayor of the palace. He expanded the lands controlled by the Franks. He also won a battle in 732. He defeated a Muslim force moving north from Spain. This victory ended the Muslim threat to Europe and made Charles Martel a Christian hero.

His son, Pepin, was crowned king. Pepin began the reign of the Frankish rulers called the **Carolingian Dynasty.** One of Pepin's sons, **Charlemagne,** became king of the whole Frankish kingdom in 771.

4. Who were Charles Martel and Pepin?

_____

_____

Charlemagne Becomes Emperor

(pages 356–357)

What did Charlemagne achieve?

Charlemagne had great military skill. He made his kingdom larger than any other known since ancient Rome. By 800, he held most of modern Italy, all of modern France, and parts of modern Spain and Germany. Pope Leo III crowned him emperor. This event marked the joining of Germanic power, the Church, and the *heritage* of the Roman Empire.

Charlemagne cut the power of the nobles in his empire and increased his own. He traveled throughout his lands, visiting the people and judging cases. He brought well-read men to his court and *revived* learning. However, Charlemagne's empire fell apart soon after his death.

5. What was important about Charlemagne's being crowned as emperor?

_____

_____

Feudalism in Europe

BEFORE YOU READ

In the last section, you read about Charlemagne and his empire.

In this section, you will read about feudalism.

AS YOU READ

Use the chart below to take notes on feudalism.

BATTLE/POLITICAL ISSUE	EFFECT
Feudal relationships	• Lord promised land and protection to his vassal • Vassal helped his lord in battle
Social classes	
Manor system	

Invaders Attack Western Europe

(pages 358–360)

Who invaded Western Europe?

Between 800 and 1000, new invasions threatened Europe. From the north came the most feared fighters of all. They were the Vikings, or Norsemen.

The Vikings raided villages and monasteries. By around the year 1000, though, the Vikings had settled down in many parts of Europe. They adopted Christianity and stopped raiding to become traders and farmers.

The Magyars were Turkish nomads. They attacked from the east and reached as far as Italy and western France. They sold local people as slaves. The Muslims struck from the south. They attacked areas along the Atlantic and Mediterranean coast.

The attacks by Vikings, Muslims, and Magyars made life in western Europe difficult. People suffered and feared for their futures. With no strong central government, they went to local leaders for protection.

1. Why did the people need to turn to local leaders for help?

_____

A New Social Order: Feudalism

(page 360)

How did feudalism affect society?

Europe's feudal system arose around the ninth and tenth centuries. Feudalism was based on an agreement between a **lord,** or landowner, and a **vassal,** a person who received land from a lord. In exchange for land, or a fief, a vassal promised to help his lord in battle.

Under feudalism, society in western Europe was divided into three groups. Those who fought were the nobles and **knights.** Those who prayed were the officials of the Church. Those who worked were the peasants. Peasants were by far the largest group. Most peasants were **serfs,** who were not free to move about as they wished. They were tied to the land of their lord.

2. What were the three main groups of feudal society?

_____

_____

_____

Manors: The Economic Side of Feudalism (pages 360–363)

What was life like on a manor?

The lord's land was called the **manor.** Manors became the centers of economic life. The lord gave peasants some land, a home, and protection from raiders. The lord controlled much of their lives. The peasants worked the land to grow food, giving part of each year's crop to the lord. They paid taxes on their grain. Peasants also paid a tax, called a **tithe,** to the Church.

Peasants lived in small villages of 15 to 30 families. They produced almost everything they needed. Peasants rarely traveled far from their homes.

Life on the manor was often harsh. Peasants' cottages had just one or two rooms with only straw mats for sleeping. They had poor diets. Peasants *endured* these conditions. They believed that God had set their place in society.

3. What was the job of peasants on the manor?

_____

_____

_____

Skillbuilder

Use the diagram to answer the questions.

1. How are rank and position organized on this pyramid?

_____

_____

2. What members of feudal society are not represented on this chart?

_____

_____

_____

The Age of Chivalry

BEFORE YOU READ

In the last section, you read how feudalism shaped society.

In this section, you will read about the code of chivalry for knights and its influence.

AS YOU READ

Use the web below to take notes on knighthood during the Middle Ages.

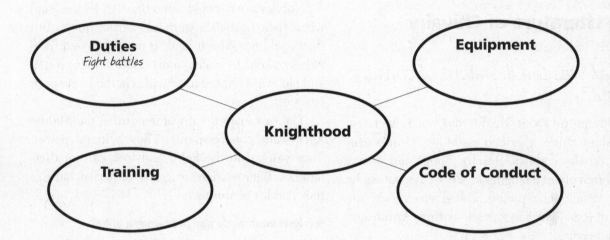

Knights: Warriors on Horseback

(pages 364–365)

What was the role of knights?

Nobles were constantly at war with one another. They raised private armies. The armies included knights, soldiers who fought on horseback. These knights became the most important warriors during the Middle Ages.

By the 11th century, nobles used their armies of *mounted* knights to fight for control of land. When nobles won battles, they gave some of the new land to their knights. The knights could use the wealth from this land to pay for weapons, armor, and horses. Knights devoted much of their time to improving their skill at fighting.

1. What was the main duty of knights?

_____

_____

Knighthood and the Code of Chivalry (pages 365–367)

What was required of a knight?

By the 1100s, a new code of *conduct* for knights arose. This code of **chivalry** required that knights fight bravely for three masters: their lord, God, and their chosen lady. Knights were also required to protect the weak and poor. While the code set high standards, most knights failed to meet all of the standards.

The son of a noble began training to become a knight at an early age. At around age 7, his parents sent him off to the castle of another lord. There he would learn good manners. The boy would also practice fighting skills. At around age 14, he would become the servant of a knight. Then at age 21, he would finally become a knight himself.

Knights gained experience by fighting in staged combats called **tournaments.** These fights were fierce, but real battles, especially those fought at castles, were far more violent. To protect their lands and homes, nobles built stone castles.

2. Give two examples of training for knighthood.

_____

_____

The Literature of Chivalry

(pages 367–368)

What was the literature of chivalry about?

The literature about knights did not reflect real life. Many stories glorified castle life. Others centered on the code of chivalry. Songs and poems were often about a knight's loyalty to the woman he loved. Some long poems, called epics, told the story of legendary kings, such as King Arthur and Charlemagne.

Troubadours were poet-musicians at the castles and courts of Europe. They wrote and sang about the joys and sorrows of romantic love. Many troubadours traveled to the court of Eleanor of Aquitaine. She was the rich, powerful ruler of a land in southern France.

3. Who were the troubadour's songs about?

_____

_____

Women's Role in Feudal Society

(pages 368–369)

What were the roles of women?

Most women in feudal society had little power. The Church taught that they were inferior. But they played important roles in the lives of both noble and peasant families.

Noblewomen could sometimes rule the land when their husbands were away from home. But they could not inherit land. It usually passed from father to son. In reality, most noblewomen, young and old, were limited to activities in the home or in convents.

The vast majority of women during the Middle Ages were poor peasants. They held no power. They worked in the fields and took care of their families. Poor women struggled to survive—just as they had for centuries.

4. How were noble and poor women alike?

_____

_____

The Power of the Church

BEFORE YOU READ

In the last section, you read about knighthood and the literature of chivalry.

In this section, you will learn about power struggles between church leaders and political leaders.

AS YOU READ

Use the chart below to take notes on the authority of the Church.

CHURCH STRUCTURE	CHURCH LAWS
Different ranks of clergy—priest, bishops, pope	

The Far-Reaching Authority of the Church (pages 370–371)

How *did the Church control most aspects of life?*

With the central governments of Europe weak, the Church became the most important force in *unifying* European society. An early pope believed that God had made two areas of influence in the world—religious and political. The pope was in charge of spiritual matters. The emperor and other rulers were in charge of political affairs. Over the years, though, the difference was not so clear. Popes often tried to influence the actions of rulers, who *clashed* with them in struggles for power.

The Church established its own organization. It consisted of different ranks of **clergy,** or church officials. At the bottom were the priests who led services at local churches. Above them were bishops, who oversaw all the priests in a large area. At the top was the pope. He was the head of the Church.

The Middle Ages was an Age of Faith. People were bound together by their belief in God and the teachings of the Church. Though their lives were hard, Christians during this time hoped for *salvation*—eternal life in heaven. One path for achieving this goal was through the **sacraments.** These were important religious ceremonies.

The law of the Church, called **canon law,** was a set of standards that applied to all Christians during the Middle Ages. These standards guided such matters as marriage and religious practices. The Church also set up courts. People who broke canon law were put on trial.

Two punishments were especially harsh. If the Church *excommunicated* a person, he or she was out of the Church forever. The person was denied the chance for eternal life in heaven. Popes often used this power to threaten rulers. The other punishment was interdiction. When a ruler disobeyed the pope, the Church leader could place the land under *interdiction*. That meant that no sacred actions of the Church could officially take place there. The people of the area deeply feared this. They might then be doomed to eternal suffering in hell.

1. What powerful punishments could the Church hand down?

_____

_____

The Church and the Holy Roman Empire; The Emperor Clashes with the Pope (pages 371–372)

How did conflict develop between the pope and the Holy Roman emperor?

Otto I was the strongest ruler of medieval Germany. He set up an alliance with the Church. In 962, the pope crowned him emperor of what became the Holy Roman Empire.

The **Holy Roman Empire** was the strongest kingdom that arose from Charlemagne's fallen empire. It was mainly made up of what is now Germany and Italy. One of Otto's successors was Henry IV. He and Pope Gregory VII became caught in a conflict.

For a long time, rulers had the power to name the bishops who led the Church in their lands. This power was known as **lay investiture.** In 1075, Pope Gregory VII *banned* this practice. Henry IV was angry. He persuaded his bishops to say that this pope had no real authority. Gregory then excommunicated Henry. Henry's nobles supported Gregory. So Henry begged the pope for forgiveness. The pope forgave him.

The larger issue of lay investiture was left open until 1122. Then an agreement stated that only the pope could name bishops. However, the emperor had the right to turn down any appointment he did not like.

2. Why did Henry IV beg Pope Gregory VII for forgiveness?

_____

_____

Disorder in the Empire (page 373)

Who was Frederick I?

In the late 1100s, a strong German king came to power. His name was Frederick I. He repeatedly invaded the cities of Italy but lost an important battle in 1176. He then made peace with the pope.

When Frederick died in 1190, his empire fell apart. It was broken up into feudal states. These German states did not unify during the Middle Ages.

3. What happened to the Holy Roman Empire after Frederick I's death?

_____

_____

Glossary　　　　　　　　　　　　　　CHAPTER 13　European Middle Ages

chaos Complete disorder

conduct Behavior

convert Change to another religion

dialects Varieties of a language

endured Lived through; managed against odds

excommunicated Banished from the Church

guardian One who watches over the welfare of another

heritage Traditions passed down or received from the past

interdiction Church ruling prohibiting sacred actions of the Church from taking place in a certain area

banned Officially forbidden

monks Christian men devoted to a religious life

mounted On horseback

nuns Christian women devoted to a religious life

province Part of a country with its own government

revived Brought back

rural Having to do with the country

salvation Eternal life in heaven after death

unifying Bringing together

AFTER YOU READ

Names and Terms

A. Write the name or term in each blank that best completes the meaning of the paragraph.

vassal

serf

fief

knight

lord

The feudal system was based on an exchange. The **1** _____, or landowner, granted land to a person called a **2** _____. The land granted to him was his **3** _____. In return, that person gave the landowner military protection. This meant he might go into battle, performing the duties of a **4** _____. People who worked the land were mostly peasants. Among the peasants were many people who were not free to leave the land. The term used to describe one of these peasants is **5** _____.

B. Write the letter of the name or term next to the description that explains it best.

a. Franks

b. Holy Roman Empire

c. Carolingian Dynasty

d. Middle Ages

e. Charlemagne

_____ 1. Period of European history from 500 to 1500

_____ 2. A Frankish ruler who built a huge empire and unified Europe for the first time since the Roman Empire

_____ 3. Dynasty of Frankish rulers, lasting from 751 to 987

_____ 4. Germanic people who held power in the Roman province called Gaul

_____ 5. Empire established in the 10th century mainly consisting of what is now Germany and Italy

AFTER YOU READ (continued)   CHAPTER 13 European Middle Ages

Main Ideas

1. Who was Clovis?

_____

_____

_____

2. Give three examples describing how Charlemagne ruled his empire.

_____

_____

_____

_____

3. Why was life on the manor often harsh for peasants?

_____

_____

_____

_____

4. What did the code of chivalry require?

_____

_____

_____

_____

5. How did Pope Gregory show his power in political affairs?

_____

_____

_____

_____

Thinking Critically

Answer the following questions on a separate sheet of paper.

1. How did invasions contribute to the beginning of the feudal system?

2. Why was the Church so important during in the Middle Ages?

CHAPTER 14 Section 1 (pages 379–385)

Church Reform and the Crusades

TERMS AND NAMES

simony Practice of selling positions in the church

Gothic Style of architecture of the cathedrals during the Middle Ages

Urban II Pope who called for the first Crusade

Crusade A holy war

Saladin Famous Muslim leader of the 1100s

Richard the Lion-Hearted English king who fought Saladin in the Third Crusade

Reconquista Effort by Christian leaders to drive the Muslims out of Spain

Inquisition Church court that tried people suspected of having opposing religious beliefs

BEFORE YOU READ

In the last section you read about the authority and role of the Church during the Middle Ages.

In this section you will read about changes in the Church and the launching of the Crusades.

AS YOU READ

Use the diagram below to take notes on impact of the Age of Faith—a new age of religious feeling.

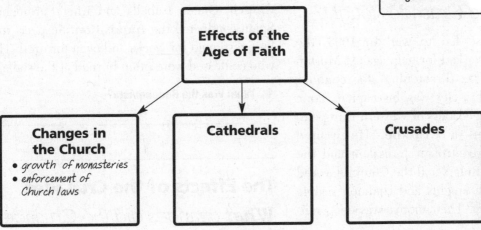

Effects of the Age of Faith

Changes in the Church
- growth of monasteries
- enforcement of Church laws

Cathedrals

Crusades

The Age of Faith (pages 379–380)

What changes did the Church undergo?

Starting in the 1000s, a new age of spiritual feeling arose in Europe. This era was called The Age of Faith. It led to many changes.

Many problems troubled the Church. Popes made reforms. They enforced Church laws. They tried to end certain practices. One was the marriage of priests. Another was **simony,** or the selling of positions in the Church. A third problem was the

appointment of bishops by kings. The Church felt it alone could appoint bishops.

In the early 1200s, a new Church group arose. They were called *friars*. They moved from place to place spreading the ideas of the Church. Friars owned nothing. They begged for food. Women also played a role during the Age of Faith. Many entered convents to devote themselves to God.

1. What three practices showed the Church needed reforming?

_____

_____

Cathedrals—Cities of God

(pages 380–381)

How did the new cathedrals reflect the new Age of Faith?

The Age of Faith was shown in the building of great *cathedrals*. In the early 1100s, these huge churches were built in a new style of architecture. This style was called **Gothic.** The cathedrals were towering. They seemed to reach toward heaven. Light streamed in through colorful stained-glass windows.

2. What was the new style of church architecture?

_____

_____

The Crusades (pages 382–383)

Why were the Crusades fought?

Renewed faith also led to war. In 1093, the Byzantine emperor asked for help against Muslim Turks. They were threatening to conquer Constantinople. This city was his capital. Pope Urban II urged the leaders of Western Europe to begin a holy war—a **Crusade.** He wanted Christians to gain control of Jerusalem and the entire Holy Land. Rulers and the Church favored the Crusades. Both knights and common people joined the Crusades. Their motive was deep religious feeling.

The First Crusade began in 1095. It was badly organized. Yet the Crusaders still captured some of the Holy Land, including Jerusalem. Muslims won back some of this land. Then other Crusades followed. During the Second Crusade, the Muslim leader **Saladin** recaptured Jerusalem.

Three powerful European rulers led the Third Crusade. One was the English king. His name was **Richard the Lion-Hearted.** He fought Saladin. The two reached a *truce.* But the Crusades were not over.

The Fourth Crusade ended in disaster. In 1204, knights *looted* Constantinople. This helped make a lasting split between western and eastern Christian churches.

3. Why did people support the Crusades?

_____

_____

The Crusading Spirit Dwindles

(pages 383–384)

What happened to Muslims and Jews in Spain?

A later Crusade took place in Spain. Christian rulers tried to drive the Muslims out of Spain. This long fight was called the **Reconquista.** It lasted from the 1100s until 1492.

Thousands of Jews lived in Spain. During the late 1400s, many Spanish Jews and Muslims became Christians. Jewish and Muslim converts were suspected of *heresy*. They were believed to hold beliefs that differed from the teachings of the Church. Queen Isabella and King Ferdinand of Spain conducted the **Inquisition.** Suspects might be questioned for weeks and even tortured. Those who confessed were often burned at the stake.

4. What was the Reconquista?

_____

_____

The Effects of the Crusades

What changes did the Crusades bring?

The Crusades had many effects on Europe. At first the Crusades showed the power of the Church in the lives of the believers. The failure of later Crusades cut the pope's power. The deaths of many knights reduced the nobles' power. Contact with the East revived trade. The Christians' harsh treatment of Muslims in the Holy Land led to bitterness that has lasted to the present.

5. What are four effects of the Crusades?

_____

_____

Changes in Medieval Society

BEFORE YOU READ

In the last section, you read about the Crusades.

In this section, you will read about the rise of towns and trade.

AS YOU READ

Use the diagram below to take notes on changes occurring in towns and cities during the Middle Ages.

TERMS AND NAMES

three-field system Farmland divided into three equal-sized fields, in which crops were rotated

guild An organization working to get the best prices or working conditions

Commercial Revolution The expansion of trade and changes in business practices

burgher Merchant class person who lived in a town

vernacular Everyday language

Thomas Aquinas Scholar who argued that the most basic religious truths could be proved by sound reasoning

scholastics Scholars who gathered and taught at universities

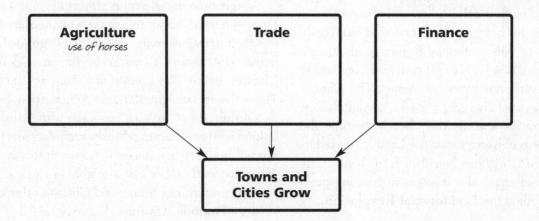

Agriculture
use of horses

Trade

Finance

Towns and Cities Grow

A Growing Food Supply (page 387)

Why did the food supply increase?

The climate in Europe became warmer between the years 800 and 1200. This helped farming. Farmers also developed better ways to produce crops. Horses pulled plows. Horses could do twice the work of oxen. A new harness made the use of horses possible.

Farmers also used a new method of rotating the crops planted in an area. They planted two-thirds of their fields, leaving one-third unplanted. This **three-field system** help farmers grow greater amounts of food.

1. Give three reasons why the food supply increased.

_____

_____

_____

_____

The Guilds (page 388)

What were the guilds?

Changes in the way goods were produced and sold happened in the medieval period. Merchants banded together in an organization called a **guild.** A merchant guild worked to get the best prices for their goods. Later, workers formed craft guilds.

They were made up of groups of workers who did the same job These included bakers, tailors, and glassmakers. Members set standards and prices for their products. They also made rules for young people learning the craft.

2. What were the two kinds of guilds?

_____

_____

_____

The Commercial Revolution

(pages 389–390)

Why did trade and finance increase?

Along with the growth in the food supply, trade and finance increased. Craft workers began to make more goods. These goods were traded all over Europe. Towns held fairs each year. There merchants sold cloth, food, leather, and other wares.

With more trade, merchants needed more cash. They had to borrow money to buy goods to sell. They needed new ways to get cash and loans and to exchange different types of money. The Church had rules against charging a fee for loaning money. Jews, who were outside the Church, became the chief sources of loans. Later, the Church relaxed its rules. Then Christians began to form banks. The expansion of trade and changes in banking practices was called the **Commercial Revolution.**

3. How did ways of doing business change?

_____

_____

_____

Urban Life Flourishes (pages 390–391)

Why did towns grow larger?

In the early 1100s, the population of western Europe grew quickly. Trade was booming. Towns grew larger and more important. Towns were dirty places, with narrow streets. Wooden houses in the towns were fire hazards.

Many peasants fled to the towns. After living there a year and a day, they became free. Other town _dwellers,_ known as **burghers,** organized themselves. The burghers were of the merchant class. Merchants helped change the social order. They demanded more rights for town dwellers.

4. Why did peasants move to the towns?

_____

_____

_____

The Revival of Learning (pages 391–392)

Why did learning spread?

Growing trade and wealth helped lead to a growing interest in education. New centers of learning arose in Europe. They were called universities.

At this time, most writers were still using Latin. However, some began to use the **vernacular.** This was their native, everyday language. Dante Alighieri wrote _The Divine Comedy_ in Italian. Geoffrey Chaucer wrote _The Canterbury Tales_ in English. These writers brought literature to many people.

During the Crusades, contact with Muslims helped increase learning. Muslim scholars had preserved books from ancient Rome and Greece. These works then became available in Europe.

Ancient writings influenced Christian thinkers, such as **Thomas Aquinas.** He reasoned that the most basic religious truths could be proved by logic. Aquinas and his fellow scholars met at the great universities. They were known as schoolmen, or **scholastics.**

5. How did the use of the vernacular help spread learning?

_____

_____

_____

CHAPTER 14 Section 3 (pages 393–397)

England and France Develop

TERMS AND NAMES

William the Conqueror Duke of Normandy who invaded England in 1066 and claimed the English crown

Henry II English king who added French lands to English holdings by marrying Eleanor of Aquitaine

common law A body of rulings by English judges

Magna Carta Great Charter, which guaranteed certain basic political rights

parliament Body of representatives that makes laws for a nation

Hugh Capet Founder of the dynasty that ruled France from 987–1328

Philip II One of the most powerful Capetian kings

Estates General A council of representatives that advise the French king

BEFORE YOU READ

In the last section, you read about the growth of towns and trade.

In this section, you will read about the development of France and England.

AS YOU READ

Use the time line below to take notes on the development of France and England.

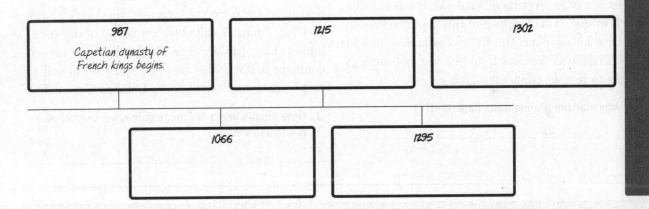

987 — Capetian dynasty of French kings begins.

1215

1302

1066

1295

England Absorbs Waves of Invaders (pages 393–394)

Who invaded England?

England was formed by the blending of cultures. Danish Vikings invaded the island in the 800s. Some Germanic groups arrived there much earlier. Over time, the Vikings and Anglo-Saxons were united under one rule and kingdom.

In 1066, King Edward died. A power struggle followed. This led to one last invasion. The invader was **William the Conqueror.** He was the duke of Normandy, a land in northern France. He won control of England declared it his personal realm.

1. Who invaded England before the William the Conqueror?

_____

_____

England's Evolving Government
(pages 394–395)

What were some of England's earliest steps toward democracy?

Later English kings, *descendants* of William, tried to hold and add to the land they still had in France.

They also wanted to increase their control over the government and the Church in England.

Henry II ruled from 1154 to 1189. He was one of the strongest of William's descendants. He married Eleanor of Aquitaine, who had been married to King Louis VII of France. From this marriage, Henry gained more territory in France. In England, he began the practice of trial by jury. Over the years, the ruling of the English judges formed a body of law called **common law.** These laws form the basis of law in many English-speaking countries.

One of Henry's sons, King John, had serious problems. He was a poor military leader. His harsh rule caused nobles to rebel against him. In 1215, they forced John to sign an important paper called the **Magna Carta.** It put limits on the power of the king. The document protected the power of nobles only. Common people, though, said that parts of the Magna Carta also applied to them.

Another step toward limiting the king came in the 1200s. Edward I needed to raise taxes for a war against the French. He called a meeting of representatives from all parts of England. It was called a **parliament.** The purpose of this meeting was to approve his tax plan. His *Model Parliament* met in 1295. This was the first time bishops, nobles, and common people attended together.

2. Why was the Magna Carta important?

_____

_____

Capetian Dynasty Rules France

(pages 396–397)

What was the Capetian Dynasty?

In France, a new dynasty of kings came to power. They were called the Capetians. They were named for the first of these rulers, **Hugh Capet,** who had been a duke from the middle of France. This dynasty ruled from 987 to 1328.

France was split into 30 separate small territories. Each was ruled by a different lord. The kings held only a small area centered in Paris. They tried to gain control of all the land. Gradually, the growth of royal power would unite France.

One of the most successful kings was **Philip II.** He ruled from 1180 to 1223. He tripled the lands under his control. He also made a stronger central government. This gave the king more control over his lands and the people who lived there.

His grandson, Louis IX, ruled from 1226 to 1270. He carried on Philip's work. Louis set up royal courts. There, people could appeal their lords' decisions. These courts increased the king's power. In 1302, Philip IV called for a meeting of representatives. Like Edward I in England, Philip invited common people. This meeting and the council of representatives was called the **Estates General.**

3. How did the kings of France gain more control over their subjects?

_____

_____

The Development of England and France	
England	**France** 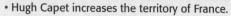
• William the Conqueror invades England in 1066.	• Hugh Capet increases the territory of France.
• Henry II (1154–1189) introduces use of the jury in English courts.	• Philip II (1180–1223) established bailiffs to preside over courts and collect taxes.
• John (1199–1216) agrees to the Magna Carta in 1215.	• Louis IX (1226–1270) creates a French appeals court.
• Edward I (1272–1307) calls the Model Parliament in 1295.	• Philip IV (1285–1314) adds Third Estate to the Estates-General.

Skillbuilder

Use the chart to answer the questions.

1. Determining Main Ideas Which English king signed one of the most important documents in English history?

2. Comparing What is similar about Edward I's and Philip IV's actions?

CHAPTER 14 Section 4 (pages 398–403)

The Hundred Years' War and the Plague

BEFORE YOU READ

In the last section, you read about developments in the governments of France and England.

In this section, you will learn about the plague, religious conflict, and war between England and France.

AS YOU READ

Use the time line to take notes on the events of the 1300s and first half of the 1400s.

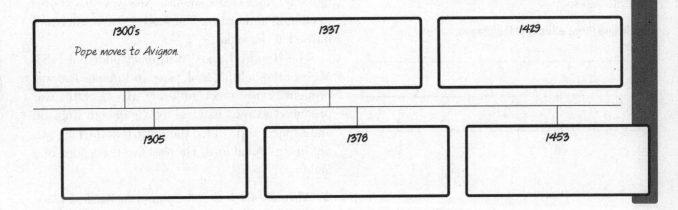

1300's — Pope moves to Avignon.

1337

1429

1305

1378

1453

A Church Divided (pages 398–399)

How was the Church divided?

In 1300, the pope said he had supreme authority over King Philip IV of France. Philip would not obey him. He held the pope prisoner. Philip planned to put him on trial. The pope was rescued but died soon after. The king then forced the election of a French cardinal as pope. In 1305, the new pope moved to **Avignon,** a city in France. There, the new pope was to lead the Church. This action weakened the Church.

In 1378, the French pope at that time died. An Italian was elected the next pope. But the French

elected their own pope. Confusion resulted. Church officials had two popes, one in France and the other in Rome. This situation, called the **Great Schism,** lasted 39 years.

At the same time, the pope's authority was challenged. The English scholar **John Wycliffe** and the Bohemian **John Huss** argued that the Bible, not the pope, was the final authority for Christian teaching.

1. What created the Great Schism?

_____

_____

The Bubonic Plague Strikes

(pages 399–401)

What happened when the plague struck?

People of the late 1300s experienced an even greater shock than the schism in the Church. A deadly disease—the **bubonic plague**—struck. It swept across Europe. The plague started in 1347. It lasted for decades. Millions of people died. The disease wiped out about one-third of Europe's population.

The plague affected Europe's economy. Trade declined, and prices rose. Towns became smaller. Fewer people meant fewer workers. Peasants demanded wages or their freedom. When nobles resisted these demands, peasants often revolted.

The Church lost *prestige* because it could not stop the plague. Jews were persecuted all over Europe. The plague helped bring an end to the Middle Ages.

2. **Name three effects of the plague.**

_____

_____

_____

The Hundred Years' War (pages 401–403)

Why was the Hundred Years' War fought?

A century-long war also helped bring the Middle Ages to an end. The last Capetian king of France died in 1328. He left no *heirs*. Edward III of England claimed the throne. In 1337, he began a war to win control of France. This conflict is known as the **Hundred Years' War.**

English forces won three important battles. At one, their archers used longbows. These weapons launched arrows that killed one-third of the French troops—even armored knights.

By 1429, France was desperate. The French army held the town of Orleans. But England was about to capture it. A teenage peasant girl named **Joan of Arc** arrived on the scene. She led the army of France to victory. Then the French crowned a new king, Charles VII. Later, Joan was captured in battle by *allies* of the English. She was turned over to Church authorities. She was tried as a witch and burned at the stake.

The Hundred Years' War finally ended in 1453. Most of the fighting took place in France. The war brought France much suffering. However, the war produced a strong national feeling in both England and France. It provided the sense that the king was not just a feudal lord. He was also the leader of a nation.

3. **What role did Joan of Arc play in the Hundred Years' War?**

_____

_____

_____

Glossary   CHAPTER 14   The Formation of Western Europe

allies Those who joined in a close relationship, often for national protection

cathedrals Large, towering churches

descendants People who come from a common family

dwellers People who live in a certain place

friars Members of a Church religious order who owned nothing and begged for food

heirs People who inherit the goods or position of another

heresy Beliefs differing from the teachings of the Church

looted Robbed

Model Parliament A meeting of representatives in 1295, called by Edward I of England

prestige High position or status

truce Temporary end of fighting

AFTER YOU READ

Names and Terms

A. Write the name or term in each blank that best completes the meaning of the paragraph.

scholastics

guild

vernacular

Thomas Aquinas

Commercial Revolution

Trade and business began to improve around the middle of the medieval period. One organization that helped this was the **1** _____, which organized either merchants or craftspeople to sell goods or services. The change in the way business and trade was done is called the **2** _____. As towns and trade were reborn, learning was revived. One reason for this revival was that some great authors began to write in their own everyday language instead of in Latin. The use of the **3** _____ enabled more people to read their works. At this time, ancient thinkers influenced Christian thinkers. The scholar **4** _____ developed an argument about the nature of religious truth. He and his fellow thinkers who met at the great universities of the day were known as the **5** _____.

B. Write the letter of the name or term next to the description that explains it best.

a. John Wycliffe

b. William the Conqueror

c. Henry II

d. Saladin

e. Urban II

_____ **1.** Muslim leader who fought in the Crusades

_____ **2.** Pope who called for Europe to begin a holy war

_____ **3.** Duke of Normandy who conquered England in 1066

_____ **4.** Scholar who taught that the Bible was the final authority for Christian life

_____ **5.** English king who married Eleanor of Aquitaine

AFTER YOU READ (cont.)　　CHAPTER 14　The Formation of Western Europe

Main Ideas

1. What started the Crusades?

_____

_____

_____

2. What was the Commercial Revolution?

_____

_____

_____

3. Why was the Model Parliament important ?

_____

_____

_____

4. What were the effects of the bubonic plague on medieval society?

_____

_____

_____

5. Why was the Hundred Years' War fought?

_____

_____

_____

Thinking Critically

Answer the following questions on a separate sheet of paper.

1. Discuss the effects of the Crusades.

2. What do you think was the most serious problem affecting Europe in the 14th century? Explain your answer.

North and Central African Societies

TERMS AND NAMES

lineage Group of people descended from a common ancestor

stateless societies Societies without central governments

patrilineal Tracing ancestry though the father

matrilineal Tracing ancestry though the mother

Maghrib Part of North Africa that is today the Mediterranean coast of Morocco

Almoravids Islamic group that established an empire in North Africa and southern Spain during the 11th century

Almohads Islamic group that overthrew the Almoravids in the 12th century

BEFORE YOU READ

In the last section, you read about disasters in Europe during the 1300s.

In this section, you will read about various societies that arose in North and Central Africa.

AS YOU READ

Use the web below to take notes on the different societies that developed in North and Central Africa.

Hunting-Gathering

Men hunt animals.
Women collect plant foods.

North and Central African Societies

Muslim

Stateless

Hunting-Gathering Societies

(page 409)

What is life like for hunter-gatherers?

People in early African societies depended on hunting and gathering for their food supply. Some societies, such as the Efe, still use these methods today. The Efe live in central Africa. They live in groups of around 50 people. All members of the groups are related to one another. Each family has its own shelter. It is made of grass and brush. The Efe move often in search for food. That is why they keep few belongings.

Women gather plant foods. They look for roots, yams, mushrooms, and wild seeds. These are found in the forest. Men and older boys hunt animals. Sometimes they form groups to hunt. At other times, a hunter goes alone. He uses a poison-tipped arrow as a weapon. The Efe also collect honey.

An older male leads the group. But he does not give orders or act like a chief. Each family makes its own decisions. Families, though, do ask the leader for his advice.

1. How do the Efe get food?

_____

_____

_____

Stateless Societies (page 410)

What are stateless societies?

Family organization is important in African society. In many African societies, families form groups called **lineages.** Members of a lineage believe that they are all descended from a common ancestor. Lineage also includes relatives of the future. These are the children who are not yet born.

Lineage groups sometimes take the place of rulers. They do not have central governments. Such societies are called **stateless societies.** Power in these societies is spread among more than one lineage. This prevents any one family from having too much control and power.

The Igbo people are from southern Nigeria. They first began living in a stateless society in the 800s. Sometimes there were disagreements within an Igbo village. Then the older members from different villages would meet. Together they would solve the problem.

In **patrilineal** societies, lineages are traced through fathers. In **matrilineal** societies, lineages are traced through mothers.

In some societies, children of similar ages belong to groups called age sets. All members of the *age set* take part in ceremonies. These rites mark the movement from one stage of life to the next. Men and women have different life stages.

2. How does lineage help balance the power in some stateless societies?

_____

_____

_____

Muslim States (pages 410–412)

How did Islam spread in north Africa?

Islam was an important influence on African history. Muslims came to northwest Africa in the 600s. By 670, Muslims ruled Egypt. They entered the **Maghrib,** a part of North Africa. This area today is the Mediterranean coast of Libya, Morocco, Tunisia, and Algeria.

In their new states, the Muslims set up *theocracies*. In them, the ruler served as both political and religious leader. The Islamic tradition of obeying the law was important. It helped promote order in the government. The common influence of Islamic law also set up ties between the different North African states.

The *Berbers* were a group of North Africans. They *converted* to Islam. In the 11th century, a group of Berbers devoted themselves to spreading Islam. They were called the **Almoravids.** They had many conquests. They conquered modern Morocco, the empire of Ghana, and parts of Spain.

The **Almohads** were another group of Berbers. They overthrew the Almoravids in the 1100s. The Almohads also captured Morocco and then Spain. Their empire reached east to the cities of Tripoli and Tunis. This empire lasted about 100 years. Then it broke up into smaller states.

3. Who were the Berbers?

_____

_____

_____

CHAPTER 15 Section 2 (pages 413–419)

West African Civilizations

TERMS AND NAMES

Ghana West African empire that grew rich from trade

Mali West African empire that grew rich from trade

Sundiata Founder and first emperor of the kingdom of Mali

Mansa Musa Mali ruler who created a large kingdom and adopted Islam

Ibn Battuta 14th century traveler who visited most of the Islamic world

Songhai West African empire that conquered Mali

Hausa West African people who lived in several city-states of what is now northern Nigeria

Yoruba West African people who formed several kingdoms in what is now Benin

Benin Kingdom that arose near the Niger River delta and became a major West African state

BEFORE YOU READ

In the last section, you read about societies in North and Central Africa.

In this section, you will read about kingdoms in West Africa.

AS YOU READ

Use the chart below to take notes on the kingdoms and states of West Africa.

Ghana	Gained wealth through gold and taxing trade.
Songhai	
Mali	
Benin	
Other States	

Empire of Ghana (pages 413–415)

How did the kingdom of Ghana arise?

Traders crossed the Sahara Desert of North Africa as early as A.D. 200. The desert was harsh. This limited trade. Then the Berbers began using camels. Trade increased.

By the 700s, the rulers of the kingdom of Ghana were growing rich. They taxed the goods that traders carried through their land. The two most important trade goods were gold and salt. Gold was taken from mines and streams in the western and southern parts of West Africa. It was traded for salt from the Sahara region. Arab traders also brought cloth and manufactured goods. These came from cities on the Mediterranean Sea.

The king of Ghana was powerful. Only the king

could own *gold nuggets*. He was the religious, military, and political leader. By the year 800, Ghana had become an empire. It controlled the people of nearby lands.

Over time, Muslim merchants and traders brought their religion to Ghana. By the 1000s, the kings converted to Islam. Many common people in the empire, though, kept their traditional beliefs. Later, Ghana fell to the Almoravids of North Africa. Ghana never regained its former power.

1. What goods were traded in Ghana?

_____

_____

Empire of Mali (pages 415–417)
How did Mali rise to power?

By 1235, a new kingdom began—**Mali.** It arose south of Ghana. Mali's wealth and power were also based on the gold trade. **Sundiata** became Mali's first emperor. He was a great military and political leader.

Later Mali rulers adopted Islam. One of them was **Mansa Musa.** He made Mali twice the size of the old empire of Ghana. To rule this large empire, he named governors to head several *provinces*. Mansa Musa was a devoted Muslim. He built *mosques* in two cities. One was Timbuktu. It became a leading center of Muslim learning.

Ibn Battuta was a later traveler to the area. He described how peaceful Mali was. Mali, though, declined in the 1400s. Mali was replaced by another empire that grew wealthy from gold.

2. What did Mansa Musa achieve?

_____

_____

Empire of Songhai (page 417)
How did Songhai arise?

The next trading empire was **Songhai.** It was farther to the east than Mali. Sonhgai arose in the 1400s. It had two great rulers. One was Sunni Ali. He gained control of new areas. His conquests included the city of Timbuktu.

Songhai's other great ruler was Askia Muhammad. He was a devoted Muslim. He ran the government well.

The Songhai Empire fell, however. Its army lacked modern weapons. In 1591, Moroccan troops used gunpowder and cannons to beat Songhai soldiers. They had only swords and spears. This defeat ended the period when empires ruled West Africa.

3. Why did Songhai fall?

_____

_____

Other Peoples of West Africa
(pages 417–419)

What other states and kingdoms arose?

In other parts of West Africa, city-states developed. The **Hausa** people lived in the region that is now northern Nigeria. Their city-states first arose between the years 1000 and 1200. The Hausa rulers depended on farmers' crops. They also relied on trade goods. These included salt, grain, and cotton cloth.

The **Yoruba** people also first lived in city-states. These were located in what is now Benin and southwestern Nigeria. Over time, some of the small Yoruba communities joined together. Many Yoruba kingdoms were formed. Yoruba people believed their kings were gods.

The kingdom of **Benin** arose in the 1200s. It was located near the delta of the Niger River. In the 1400s, a ruled named Ewuare led Benin. He made the kingdom more powerful. During his reign, Benin became a major West African state. He strengthened Benin City, his capital. High walls surrounded the city. The huge palace contained many works of art.

In the 1480s, trading ships from Portugal came. They sailed into a major port of Benin. Their arrival was historic. It marked the start of a long period of European involvement in Africa.

4. What was important about Benin?

_____

_____

Eastern City-States and Southern Empires

TERMS AND NAMES

Swahili Language that is a blend of Arabic and Bantu

Great Zimbabwe City that grew into an empire built on the gold trade

Mutapa Southern African empire established by the leader Mutota

BEFORE YOU READ

In the last section, you read about West African kingdoms and states.

In this section, you will read about East African city-states and southern African empires.

AS YOU READ

Use the chart below to take notes on East Africa and southern Africa from 1000 to 1500.

East Coast Trade Cities	*Swahili arose.*
Great Zimbabwe	
Mutapa Empire	

East Coast Trade Cities

(pages 422–424)

What cultures blended in East Africa?

The east coast of Africa became a region where cultures blended. Africans speaking Bantu languages moved to this area from central Africa. Muslim Arab and Persian traders settled in port cities along the coast. A new blended language formed. It was called **Swahili**.

Arab traders sold *porcelain* bowls from China. They sold jewels and cotton cloth from India. They bought ivory, gold, and other African goods. The

traders took these goods back to Asia. By 1300, trade was *thriving* in over 35 cities on the coast. Some cities also manufactured products for trade. These goods included woven cloth and iron tools.

Kilwa was one of the richest trading ports. It was located far to the south. Trade goods from southern lands passed through Kilwa.

In 1497, though, the situation changed. Ships arrived on the east coast of Africa from Portugal. Portuguese sailors were looking for a route to India. They wanted to join in the trade for spices and other goods desired in Europe. Soon the Portuguese attacked Kilwa. They also attacked other trading centers along the East African coast.

For the next two centuries, the Portuguese remained a powerful force in the region.

1. Why did Kilwa become an important center of trade?

_____

_____

Islamic Influences (pages 424–425)

How did Muslim traders influence East Africa?

On the east coast of Africa, contact with Muslim traders grew. This resulted in the spread of Islam. A *sultan,* or governor, ruled each city. Most government officials and wealthy merchants were Muslims. As in West Africa, though, most common people kept their traditional beliefs.

Muslim traders also sold slaves from the East African coast. These slaves were brought to markets in areas such as Arabia and Persia. Some slaves did household tasks. Other were sent to India to be soldiers. This slave trade was still small. Only about 1,000 slaves a year were traded. The later European-run slave trade was much larger.

2. Describe the Muslim slave trade.

_____

_____

Southern Africa and Great Zimbabwe (pages 425–426)

What empires arose in Southern Africa?

In southern Africa, a great city-state arose in the 1000s. The Shona people grew crops in their rich land. The also raised cattle. Their city, **Great Zimbabwe,** linked the gold fields inland with the trading cities on the coast. From the 1200s through the 1400s, the city controlled this trade. The city grew wealthy.

Around 1450, though, the people left the city. No one knows why. One explanation is that overuse had destroyed the grasslands, soil, and timber. About 60 acres of ruins remain. The ruins include stone buildings. A high wall carved with figures of birds also still stands.

3. What happened to Great Zimbabwe around 1450?

_____

_____

The Mutapa Empire (page 427)

Who founded the Mutapa empire?

The **Mutapa** Empire followed. It began around 1420. A man named Mutota left the area. He moved farther north looking for salt. Mutota and his successors took control of a large area. It was almost all of the land of the modern Zimbabwe. This empire gained wealth from its gold. The rulers forced the conquered to mine the gold. The southern region of the empire formed its own kingdom.

In the 1500s, the Portuguese moved in. They failed to conquer the empire. Later, through political schemes, they took over the government.

4. How did Mutapa rulers obtain luxury goods from coastal city-states?

_____

_____

TRADE GOODS		
Point of Origin	**Raw Materials**	**Products Made**
• savanna region	• leopard skins	• saddles
• shells of hawksbill sea turtles	• tortoiseshell	• combs
• mines in southern Africa	• gold	• coins, jewelry
• tusks from elephants in savanna region	• ivory	• carved chess pieces and sword hilts

Skillbuilder

Use the chart to answer the questions.

1. Which raw materials came from South African mines?

_____

2. What do most of the raw materials have in common?

_____

Glossary
CHAPTER 15 Societies and Empires of Africa

age sets Groups of similar ages who take part in the same ceremonies

Berbers North African Muslims

converted Officially changed from one religion to another

dominating Taking control

gold nuggets Small lumps of gold

Kilwa Key East African trading port, especially for trade from India

mosques Islamic houses of worship

porcelain Fine pottery

provinces Divisions of a country

successors Leaders who replace others in charge

sultan Muslim ruler

theocracy Government controlled by a religious leader

thriving Busy and growing

AFTER YOU READ

Names and Terms

A. Write the name or term in each blank that best completes the meaning of the paragraph.

Mali

Songhai

Ibn Battuta

Ghana

Sundiata

Three powerful empires arose in West Africa. The first of these was **1** _____. This empire grew rich from taxing the trade goods that went through its territory. Much later, the empire of **2** _____ arose. The powerful leader **3** _____ became its first emperor. **4** _____, an Islamic traveler, described this great kingdom as peaceful. The last of the great empires to arise was **5** _____. It fell to a Moroccan army.

B. Write the letter of the name or term next to the description that explains it best.

a. Almohads

b. Almoravids

c. Mutapa

d. Maghrib

e. Swahili

_____ **1.** Part of North Africa that is today the Mediterranean coast of Morocco, Tunisia, Libya, and Algeria

_____ **2.** Arabic-influenced blended language that is used widely in eastern and central Africa

_____ **3.** Islamic reformers who overthrew the Almoravids to establish an empire in North Africa and southern Spain

_____ **4.** Southern African empire established by Mutota

_____ **5.** Islamic brotherhood that spread Islam in North Africa and southern Spain

Main Ideas

1. What is a stateless society, and how are decisions made in this type of society?

_____

_____

_____

2. What role did the Almoravids and Almohads play in North Africa?

_____

_____

_____

3. Who were the Hausa and Yoruba?

_____

_____

_____

4. Describe the trade that took place in east coast trade cities.

_____

_____

_____

5. What was the Mutapa Empire?

_____

_____

_____

Thinking Critically

Answer the following questions on a separate sheet of paper.

1. What common feature linked the kingdoms and empires of West Africa?

2. How does Swahili reflect the blending of cultures in East Africa?

North American Societies

BEFORE YOU READ

In the last section, you read about diverse societies in Africa.

In this section, you will read about diverse societies in North America.

AS YOU READ

Use the chart below to take notes on Native American societies.

TERMS AND NAMES

potlatch Ceremonial giving practiced by some Native American societies in the Pacific Northwest

Anasazi Early Native American people who lived in the Southwest

pueblos Villages of large apartment-like buildings made of clay and stone by peoples of the American Southwest

Mississippian Related to the Mound Builder culture that flourished in North America between A.D. 800 and 1500

Iroquois Native American peoples from the eastern Great Lakes region of North America who formed an alliance in the late 1500s

totems Animals or other natural objects that serve as symbols of clans or other groups

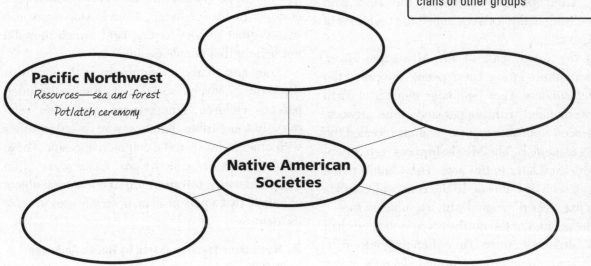

Pacific Northwest
Resources—sea and forest
Potlatch ceremony

Native American Societies

Complex Societies in the West; Mound Builders and Other Woodland Cultures (pages 441–444)

Where did different Native American societies arise?

Between about 40,000 and 12,000 years ago, hunter-gatherers moved from Asia to North America. (At that time the two continents had a land connection.) These were the first Americans. They spread throughout North and South America. They had many different ways of life, each suited to the place where they lived.

The Pacific Northwest stretches from modern Oregon to Alaska. The peoples who lived there used the rich resources of the region. The sea was the most important of these resources. The people there hunted whales. They also gathered food from the forests on the coast. The people of the Pacific Northwest developed societies in which differences in wealth led to the creation of social classes. From time to time, they performed a ceremony called the **potlatch.** In this ceremony, wealthy families could show their rank and prosperity by giving food, drink, and gifts to the community.

The peoples of the Southwest faced a harsh environment. The *Hohokam* people *irrigated,* or watered, their crops. Their use of pottery and baskets showed that they had contact with the Mesoamerican people to the south.

The **Anasazi** lived where the present-day states of Utah, Arizona, Colorado, and New Mexico meet. They built groups of houses in the shallow caves that broke up the rocky walls of deep canyons. By the 900s, the Anasazi were living in **pueblos.** Pueblos were villages with large, apartment-style groupings. They were made of stone and clay baked in the sun. The Anasazi did not have horses, mules, or the wheel. They relied on human power to make their pueblos. They had small windows to keep out the hot sun. One of the largest pueblos had more than 600 rooms and probably housed about 1,000 people.

Many Anasazi pueblos were abandoned around 1200. Later peoples—including the Hopi and Zuni—living in this area continued the traditions of the Anasazi.

In the woods east of the Mississippi River, another culture arose. These people are called the *Mound Builders.* They built large mounds of earth that were filled with copper and stone artwork. When seen from above, some mounds revealed the shapes of animals. The **Mississippians** were a people who lived later in this area. They built thriving villages, such as Cahokia. In the center of Cahokia was a flat-topped pyramid with a temple on top.

The peoples of the northeastern woodlands had many different cultures. They often fought for control of land. Some groups formed *alliances* to put an end to this fighting. The most successful of these alliances was set up in the late 1500s by the **Iroquois** and was called the Iroquois League. The league linked five tribes in upper New York.

1. Explain the cultural differences between the Anasazi and the Mississippians.

_____

_____

_____

Cultural Connections (pages 444–445)

How were Native American groups similar culturally?

These North American groups had some common features. Trade linked people of all regions of North America. Religious ideas were similar across the continent as well. Nearly all native North Americans thought that the world was full of spirits and that people had to follow certain *rituals* and customs to live in peace. Native Americans also shared great respect for the land, which they did not believe that people could own.

They also shared an emphasis on the family as the most important social unit. Family included parents, children, grandparents, and other relatives. In some tribes, families were linked together with others who shared a common ancestor. These larger groups are called *clans*. Clans were often identified with a **totem.** A totem is a natural object or animal that a person, clan, or family uses to show its identity.

2. Name three features shared by Native American groups.

_____

_____

_____

Name _____ Date _____

Maya Kings and Cities

TERMS AND NAMES

Tikal Maya city in present-day Guatemala

glyph Picture symbol used as part of a writing system

codex Book with bark-paper pages; only three of these ancient Maya books have survived

Popul Vuh Book containing a Maya story of creation

BEFORE YOU READ

In the last section, you read about societies in North America.

In this section, you will read about the Maya civilization in Mexico and Central America.

AS YOU READ

Use the chart below to take notes on Maya civilization.

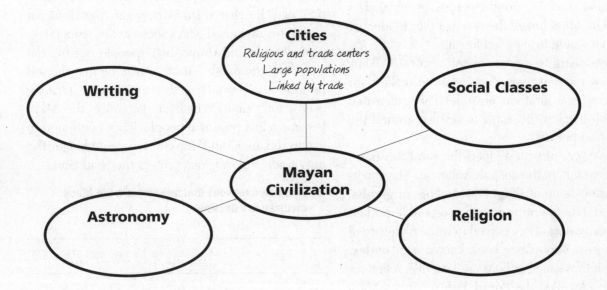

Maya Create City-States (pages 446–447)

Who were the Maya?

A great civilization arose in what is today southern Mexico and northern Central America. This was the Maya civilization. It appeared around A.D. 250. Between then and 900, the Maya built large cities such as **Tikal** and Copán. Each city was independent and ruled by a god-king. Each city was a religious center as well as a trade center for the area around it. These cities were large. Tens of thousands of people lived in these cities. The cities were full of palaces, temples, and pyramids. *Archaeologists* have found at least 50 Maya cities.

Trade linked these cities. Among the trade goods were salt, *flint*, feathers, shells, cotton cloth, and ornaments made of jade. Cacao beans, which are used to make chocolate, were sometimes used as money. Maize, beans, and squash were the main foods.

Maya society was divided into social classes. The best warriors and priests were at the top. The merchants and craft workers were at the next level. Peasant farmers—the majority of the people—were at the bottom.

1. What is known about Maya cities?

_____

_____

Religion Shapes Maya Life

(pages 447–448)

How did religion shape Maya life?

The Maya religion was at the center of their society. There were many gods, including one for each day. The actions of the day's god could be predicted, they thought, by following a calendar. The Maya sometimes cut themselves to offer their blood to the gods in sacrifice. Sometimes they killed enemies and sacrificed them.

The Maya religion led to the development of mathematics, calendars, and astronomy. Maya math included the idea of zero. They had two calendars. One calendar was religious, and it had 13 20-day months. The other calendar was based on the sun. It had 18 months consisting of 20 days each. The Maya linked the two together to identify days that would bring good fortune.

Maya astronomy was very accurate. They observed the sun, moon, and stars to make their calendars as accurate as possible. They calculated the time it takes the earth to revolve around the sun almost perfectly.

The Maya also developed the most advanced writing system in the ancient Americas. Maya writing was made up of about 800 symbols, or **glyphs.** They used their writing system to record important historical events. They carved in stone or recorded events in a bark-paper book known as a **codex.** Three of these ancient books still survive. A famous Maya book called the ***Popul Vuh*** records a Maya story of the creation of the world.

2. How does Maya writing reflect Maya culture?

_____

_____

_____

_____

_____

Mysterious Maya Decline

(page 449)

Why did the civilization decline?

In the late 800s, the Maya civilization began to decline. Historians do not know why. One explanation may be that warfare between the different city-states disrupted Maya society. The wars interrupted trade and drove many people out of the cities into the jungle. Another may be that the soil became less productive due to intensive farming over a long time. Whatever the cause, the Maya became a less powerful people. They continued to live in the area, but their cities were no longer the busy trade and religious centers they had been.

3. Name two reasons that may explain the Maya civilization's decline.

_____

_____

_____

_____

CHAPTER 16 Section 3 (pages 452–458)

The Aztecs Control Central Mexico

TERMS AND NAMES

obsidian Hard, volcanic glass used by early peoples to make sharp weapons

Quetzalcoatl Toltec god.

Triple Alliance Association of city-states that led to the formation of the Aztec Empire

Montezuma II Ruler under whom the Aztec Empire weakened

BEFORE YOU READ

In the last section, you read about Maya civilization. In this section, you will read about societies that arose in central Mexico, including the Aztecs.

AS YOU READ

Use the time line below to take notes on the peoples and empires of Central Mexico.

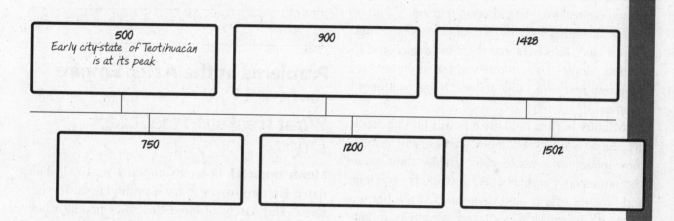

500 Early city-state of Teotihuacán is at its peak	900	1428

750	1200	1502

The Valley of Mexico (pages 452–453)

What civilizations arose in the Valley of Mexico?

The Valley of Mexico is a mountain valley more than a mile above sea level. It is a good place for people to settle because it has lakes and fertile soil. An early city-state called *Teotihuacán* ("City of the Gods") arose in this area in the first century A.D. The city had between 150,000 and 200,000 people at its peak in the sixth century.

The city was the center of a major trade network. The most important trade item was **obsidian.** This green or black volcanic glass was used to make sharp weapons. The huge Pyramid of the Sun, which measured some 200 feet high and 3,000 feet around its base, dominated the city. By 750,

Teotihuacán was abandoned. The reasons why are not clear.

The next people to dominate the area were the *Toltecs.* They rose to power around 900 and ruled over central Mexico for about 300 years. The Toltecs were warlike and based their empire on *conquest.* They worshiped a warlike god.

One Toltec king, *Topiltzin,* tried to replace the warlike god with a peaceful one. The peaceful god was called **Quetzalcoatl,** the Feathered *Serpent.* Followers of the warlike god rebelled and chased Topiltzin away. The Toltecs became warlike again. Over time, Topiltzin and Quetzalcoatl became one in Toltec legends. In these legends, someday Quetzalcoatl would return and bring a new *reign* of peace. This legend lived on in central Mexico for centuries and had important consequences.

1. What was Teotihuacán?

_____

_____

_____

The Aztec Empire; Tenochtitlán: A Planned City (pages 453–455)

How did the Aztecs build an empire?

Around 1200, the Toltecs were losing control of the region. But another people—the Aztecs—began to gain power. The Aztecs founded a city and, in 1428, they joined with two other city-states to form the **Triple Alliance.** The Triple Alliance became the leading power of the Valley of Mexico. It soon gained control over neighboring regions.

By the early 1500s, the Aztecs controlled a large empire that included somewhere between 5 and 15 million people. This empire was based on military conquest and collecting _tribute_ from conquered peoples.

Military leaders held great power in Aztec society. Along with government officials and priests, they made up a noble class. Below them were commoners—merchants, craft workers, soldiers, and farmers who owned their land. At the bottom of society were the slaves taken as captives in battle. At the top was the emperor. He was treated as a god as well as a ruler.

The capital city—Tenochtitlán—was built on an island in a lake. The Aztecs made long _causeways_ to connect the city to the mainland. The city contained between 200,000 and 400,000 people. It was well-planned and had a huge religious complex at its center.

2. How was Aztec society organized?

_____

_____

_____

Religion Rules Aztec Life (page 456)

What was the role of religion in Aztec life?

Religion played a major role in Aztec society. Temples were built in cities for the many different gods. Priests led religious rituals. The most important rituals were for the sun god. Priests made the sacrifice of human blood to make sure that the sun god was happy, and the sun would rise every day. People taken captive in war were sacrificed. The need for a steady supply of victims pushed the Aztecs to fight their neighbors.

3. Why and how did the Aztecs sacrifice to the sun god?

_____

_____

_____

Problems in the Aztec Empire

(pages 456, 458)

What weakened the Aztec Empire?

Montezuma II became emperor in 1502. The Aztec Empire began to have problems during his reign. The Aztecs ordered the other peoples they had conquered to hand over even more people to sacrifice. These other peoples finally rebelled against the Aztecs. In the midst of this conflict, the Spanish arrived and made contact with the Aztecs for the first time. Some saw their arrival as the legendary return of Quetzalcoatl.

4. Why did conquered peoples rebel against the Aztecs?

_____

_____

_____

Name _____ Date _____

The Inca Create a Mountain Empire

BEFORE YOU READ

In the last section, you read about the Aztec Empire.

In this section, you will learn about the empire of the Inca.

AS YOU READ

Use the chart below to show how the Inca created their empire.

> **TERMS AND NAMES**
>
> **Pachacuti** Ruler under whom the Incan Empire grew quickly
>
> **ayllu** Small community or clan whose members worked together for the common good
>
> **mita** Requirement for all Incan subjects to work for the state a certain number of days each year
>
> **quipu** Arrangement of knotted strings on a cord used by the Inca to record numerical information

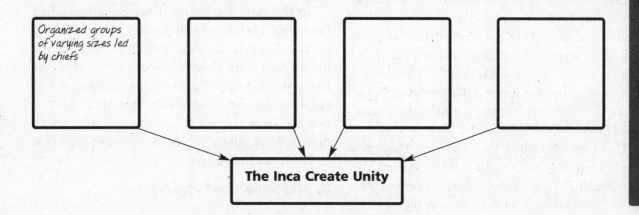

Organized groups of varying sizes led by chiefs

The Inca Create Unity

The Inca Build an Empire (pages 459–460)

Who were the Inca?

The Inca civilization arose in the Andes of South America. It was built on the foundations made by several earlier cultures.

The Inca united much of the Andes under their rule. They first settled in the Valley of Cuzco, in modern Peru. They built a kingdom there by the 1200s. The Inca believed that their ruler was related to the sun god, who would bring wealth and power to them. Only men from one of 11 noble families believed to be descendants of the sun god could serve as king.

In 1438, **Pachacuti** became the ruler of the Inca. He made conquest after conquest. By 1500,

the Inca ruled an empire that stretched along the Andes from modern Ecuador all the way south to Chile and Argentina. It held about 16 million people. The empire did not grow only through military conquest. Often the Inca offered new peoples the chance to join the empire peacefully as long as they swore loyalty to the emperor. Many peoples became part of the empire in this way. Even when force was needed, afterward the Inca tried to win the loyalty of the conquered peoples through friendship rather than fear.

1. What beliefs and practices related to Inca rulers?

_____

_____

Incan Government Creates Unity (pages 460–461)

How did the government unite the empire?

The Inca had a highly organized system to govern their empire. Small groups of people known as **ayllu** worked together for the common good. For example, they built irrigation ditches together. The Inca applied this idea to their empire. Families were placed in groups of 10, 100, 1,000, and so on. A chief led each group.

The Inca usually let local rulers stay in place when they conquered a people—as long as the conquered people met any Incan demands. The most important demand was for all adult workers to spend some days each year working for the state. They might work on state farms or build state roads or buildings. This payment of labor was known as **mita.**

The Inca built a complex network of roads. The roads linked all parts of the empire. The Inca also built all government buildings in the same style. This created a common identity for the government throughout the empire. They made all people speak a common language—the Incan tongue, called *Quechua*.

The Inca controlled the economy. They told people what to grow or make and how it would be distributed. The government also took care of people who needed help, such as the very old or ill.

In spite of all these advances, the Inca never developed a system of writing. All records were kept in peoples' memories. They did have a device for counting. It was a set of knotted strings called a **quipu.** The Inca also had day and night calendars for information about their gods.

2. What was mita, and what forms did it take?

_____

_____

_____

Religion Supports the State; Discord in the Empire (pages 462–463)

How were religion and government connected?

The Incan religion played a central role in Inca life. The Inca believed in fewer gods than the peoples of Mexico. The most important of the Incan gods were the creator god and the sun god. Cuzco, the capital, was the most important religious center. It was decorated with gold and other precious objects.

In the early 1500s, the Incan Empire reached the height of its power under the rule of Huayna Capac. However, he died while traveling through the empire. After Huayna Capac's death, civil war broke out between his two sons, Atahualpa and Huascar. Atahualpa eventually won, but the war tore the empire apart. When the Spanish arrived, they took advantage of Incan weakness to divide and conquer the empire.

3. Why did the Incan Empire fall?

_____

_____

_____

Glossary   *CHAPTER 16* People and Empires in the Americas

alliances Agreements between groups or nations to protect common interests

archaeologists People who study past human societies and cultures

causeways Raised roadways that go across water or swampy land

clans Groups made up of people related to a common ancestor

conquest Act of conquering

flint Hard quartz

Hohokam A group of people from Southwest North America

irrigated Watered

Mound Builders Prehistoric Native American people who built mounds, mainly in the valley of the Mississippi River

Quechua Language of the Inca

reign Rule

rituals Ceremonial acts or traditional ways of doing things

serpent Snake

Teotihuacán Early city-state in the Valley of Mexico that reached its peak around 500

Topiltzin Toltec king

Toltecs People who ruled over Central Mexico from approximately 900 to 1200

tribute Payment made to a conqueror

AFTER YOU READ

Terms and Names

A. Write the name or term in each blank that best completes the meaning of the paragraph.

Mississippians

totems

pueblos

Anasazi

Iroquois

Several different Native American societies inhabited North America. One was the **1** _____, who occupied dry, desert lands of the Southwest. They built cliff dwellings and villages made up of apartment-like units called **2** _____. In lands near the Mississippi River, people called **3** _____ built a city called Cahokia that was the center of their culture. Among the Eastern tribes was a woodland group of tribes called the **4** _____. Although each of the Native American societies was distinct, all shared some characteristics. Among these was the use of **5** _____, symbols of a group's or clan's identity.

B. Write the letter of the name or term next to the description that explains it best.

a. obsidian

b. quipu

c. glyph

d. mita

e. codex

_____ **1.** Requirement for all Incan subjects to work for the state a certain number of days each year

_____ **2.** Arrangement of knotted strings on a cord, used by the Inca to record numerical information

_____ **3.** Picture symbol used as part of a writing system

_____ **4.** Book with bark-paper pages; one of three surviving ancient Maya books

_____ **5.** Hard, volcanic glass used by early peoples to make sharp weapons

AFTER YOU READ (cont.)   *CHAPTER 16* People and Empires in
                                              the Americas

Main Ideas

1. Explain who the Anasazi were and what their homes were like.

_____

_____

_____

2. How was Maya society organized?

_____

_____

_____

_____

3. How did the Aztecs build an empire?

_____

_____

_____

_____

4. How did the Incan Empire grow?

_____

_____

_____

_____

5. What steps did the Inca take to unify the different peoples of their empire?

_____

_____

_____

Thinking Critically

Answer the following questions on a separate sheet of paper.

1. Explain this statement and give examples: Maya cultural advances were connected to their religious beliefs.

2. Were the Aztecs good engineers? Explain your answer.

CHAPTER 17 Section 1 (pages 471–479)

Italy: Birthplace of the Renaissance

BEFORE YOU READ

In the prologue, you read about the development of democratic ideas.

In this section, you will begin your in-depth reading of modern history starting with the Renaissance.

AS YOU READ

Use this chart to take notes on important changes that occurred during the Renaissance in Italy.

CHANGES IN VALUES	CHANGES IN ART	CHANGES IN LITERATURE
Humanism—new focus on human potential and achievements		

Italy's Advantages (pages 471–472)

Why did the Renaissance begin in Italy?

The years 1300 to 1600 saw a rebirth of learning and culture in Europe called the **Renaissance**. This rebirth spread north from Italy. It began there for three reasons. First, Italy had several important cities. Cities were places where people exchanged ideas. Second, these cities included a class of *merchants* and bankers who were becoming wealthy and powerful. This class strongly believed in the idea of individual achievement. Third, Italian artists and scholars were inspired by the ruined buildings and other reminders of *classical* Rome.

1. What are three reasons why the Renaissance began in Italy?

_____

_____

Classical and Worldly Values (pages 472–473)

What new values did people hold?

The new interest in the classical past led to an important value in Renaissance culture—**humanism**. This was a deep interest in what people have already achieved as well as what they could achieve in the future. Scholars did not try to connect classical writings to Christian teaching. Instead, they tried to understand them on their own terms.

In the Middle Ages, the emphasis had been mostly on *spiritual* values. Renaissance thinkers stressed **secular** ideas. These ideas centered on the things of the world. One way that powerful or wealthy people showed this interest in worldly things was by paying artists, writers, and musicians to create beautiful works of art. Wealthy people who supported artists were known as **patrons.**

People tried to show that they could master many fields of study or work. Someone who succeeded in many fields was admired greatly. The artist Leonardo da Vinci was an example of this ideal. He was a painter, a scientist, and an inventor. Men were expected to be charming, witty, well educated, well mannered, athletic, and self-controlled. Women were expected to have many accomplishments, too. But women were not to show them in public.

2. What are secular ideas?

_____

_____

_____

The Renaissance Revolutionizes Art (pages 474–475)

How did art change during the Renaissance?

Renaissance artists sometimes used new methods. *Sculptors* made figures more *realistic* than those from the Middle Ages. Painters used **perspective** to create the illusion that their paintings were *three-dimensional*. The subject of artwork changed

also. Art in the Middle Ages was mostly religious. Renaissance artists reproduced other views of life. Michelangelo showed great skill as an architect, a sculptor, and a painter.

3. How did the methods and subjects in art change?

_____

_____

_____

Renaissance Writers Change Literature (pages 475–477)

How did literature change during the Renaissance?

Renaissance writers also achieved greatness. Several wrote in the **vernacular**. This means they wrote in their native languages. It was a change from the Middle Ages, when most writing was done in Latin. Writers also changed their subject matter. They began to express their own thoughts and feelings. Sometimes they gave a detailed look at an individual. Dante and others wrote poetry, letters, and stories that were more realistic. Niccoló Machiavelli took a new approach to understanding government. He focused on telling rulers how to expand their power. He believed rulers should do what was politically effective, even if it was not morally right.

4. What did Renaissance writers write about?

_____

_____

_____

The Northern Renaissance

TERMS AND NAMES

Utopia An ideal place

William Shakespeare Famous Renaissance writer

Johann Gutenberg German craftsman who developed the printing press

BEFORE YOU READ

In the last section, you read how the Renaissance began in Italy.

In this section, you will learn how Renaissance ideas spread in northern Europe.

AS YOU READ

Use the web below to show what happened during the northern Renaissance.

Ideas came from Italy and spread to northern Europe

THE NORTHERN RENAISSANCE

The Northern Renaissance Begins (page 480)

Why was the time right for the northern Renaissance to begin?

By 1450, the *bubonic plague* had ended in northern Europe. Also, the Hundred Years' War between France and England was ending. This allowed new ideas from Italy to spread to northern Europe. They were quickly adopted. Here, too,

rulers and merchants used their money to sponsor artists. But the northern Renaissance had a difference. Educated people combined classical learning with interest in religious ideas.

1. How was the northern Renaissance different from the Renaissance in Italy?

_____

_____

Artistic Ideas Spread (pages 480–481)

What ideas about art developed in northern Europe?

The new ideas of Italian art moved to the north, where artists began to use them. Major artists appeared in parts of Germany, France, Belgium, and the Netherlands. Dürer painted religious subjects and realistic *landscapes.* Holbein, Van Eyck, and Bruegel painted lifelike portraits and scenes of *peasant* life. They revealed much about the times. They began to use *oil-based paints.* Oils became very popular, and their use spread to Italy.

2. What did northern European artists paint?

_____

_____

_____

Northern Writers Try to Reform Society; The Elizabethan Age

(pages 482–483)

What did northern writers write?

Writers of the northern Renaissance combined humanism with a deep Christian faith. They urged reforms in the Church. They tried to make people more devoted to God. They also wanted society to be more fair. In England, Thomas More wrote a book about **Utopia**, an imaginary ideal society where greed, war, and conflict do not exist.

William Shakespeare is often called the greatest playwright of all time. His plays showed a brilliant command of the English language. They also show a deep understanding of people and how they interact with one another.

3. Who were two of the most famous writers of the northern Renaissance?

_____

_____

_____

Printing Spreads Renaissance Ideas; The Legacy of the Renaissance (pages 484–485)

Why was the printing press such an important development?

One reason that learning spread so rapidly during the Renaissance was the invention of *movable type.* The Chinese had invented the process of carving characters onto wooden blocks. They then arranged them in words, inked the blocks, and pressed them against paper to print pages.

In 1440, a German, **Johann Gutenberg**, used this same practice to invent his printing press. He produced his first book—the Gutenberg Bible—in 1455 on this press. The technology then spread rapidly. By 1500, presses in Europe had printed nearly 10 million books.

Printing made it easier to make many copies of a book. As a result, written works became available far and wide. Books were printed in English, French, Spanish, Italian, or German. More people began to read. The Bible was a popular book. After reading the Bible, some people formed new ideas about Christianity. These ideas were different from the official teachings of the Church.

The Renaissance prompted changes in both art and society. Artists and writers portrayed people in more realistic ways and celebrated individual achievement. In a larger sense, the Renaissance opened up a world of new ideas to people and led them to examine and question things more closely.

4. What effects did the printing press have on northern European life?

_____

_____

_____

Luther Leads the Reformation

TERMS AND NAMES

indulgence Release from punishments due for a sin

Reformation 16th-century movement for religious reform, leading to the founding of new Christian churches

Lutheran Member of a Protestant church founded on the teachings of Martin Luther

Protestant Member of a Christian church founded on the principles of the Reformation

Peace of Augsburg Agreement in 1555 declaring that the religion of each German state would be decided by its ruler

annul Cancel or put an end to

Anglican Relating to the Church of England

BEFORE YOU READ

In the last section, you saw how the Renaissance spread to northern Europe.

In this section, you will see how Renaissance ideas helped bring about the Reformation.

AS YOU READ

Use the chart below to take notes on the responses to Luther's challenge.

BATTLE/POLITICAL ISSUE	EFFECT
Responses to Luther's Challenge	The Pope threatens Luther with excommunication.

Causes of the Reformation

(pages 488–489)

Why was the Church criticized?

By 1500, the influence of the Church on the lives of people had weakened. Some people resented paying taxes to support the Church in Rome. Others sharply criticized the Church for some of its practices. Popes seemed more concerned with luxury and political power than with spiritual matters. The lower *clergy* had faults, too. Many local priests lacked education and were not able to teach people. Some lived immoral lives.

Reformers urged the Church to change its ways to become more spiritual and humble. Christian humanists such as Erasmus and Thomas More added their voices to calls for change. In the early 1500s, the calls grew louder.

1. **What kinds of changes did Church critics want to make?**

_____

_____

_____

Luther Challenges the Church
(page 489)

How did the Reformation begin?

In 1517, a German monk named Martin Luther protested the actions of a Church official. That person was selling **indulgences**. An indulgence was a kind of forgiveness. By paying money to the Church, people thought they could win *salvation*.

Luther challenged this practice and others. He posted a written protest on the door of a castle church. His words were printed and spread throughout Germany. This was the beginning of the **Reformation**, a movement for reform that led to the founding of new Christian churches.

2. What role did Martin Luther play in the Reformation?

_____

_____

The Response to Luther (pages 490–492)

What effects did Luther's protest have?

Pope Leo X punished Luther for his views, but he refused to change them. Holy Roman Emperor Charles V, a strong Catholic, called Luther an outlaw. Luther's books were burned. But it was too late. Many of his ideas were already being practiced. The **Lutheran** Church started around 1522.

In 1524, *peasants* in Germany hoped to use Luther's ideas about Christian freedom to change society. They demanded an end to serfdom—a condition like slavery. When it was not granted, they revolted. Luther disagreed with this *revolt*. German princes killed thousands in putting the revolt down.

Some *nobles* supported Luther's ideas. They saw a chance to weaken the emperor's power over them. Other German princes joined forces against Luther's supporters. They signed an agreement to remain loyal to the pope and the emperor. Supporters of Luther's ideas *protested* this agreement. They were called the Protestants. Eventually, the term **Protestant** meant Christians who belonged to non-Catholic churches.

War broke out between Catholic and Protestant forces in Germany. It finally ended in 1555 with the **Peace of Augsburg**. This treaty granted each prince the right to decide whether his subjects would be Catholic or Protestant.

3. Why did Luther's ideas lead to war?

_____

_____

England Becomes Protestant
(pages 492–494)

How did England become Protestant?

The Catholic Church faced another challenge to its power in England. Henry VIII, the king, was married to a Spanish princess. She gave birth to a daughter. England had never had a female ruler. Henry feared a civil war would start if he had no son. He believed his wife was too old to have another child. He tried to get the pope to **annul**, or put an end to, the marriage so he could remarry. The pope refused.

To remarry, Henry had to get out of the Catholic church. In 1534, Henry had *Parliament* pass laws that created the Church of England. These laws made the king or queen, not the pope, head of the Church of England. Henry no longer had to obey the pope. Henry remarried five times. His only son was from his third wife.

One of Henry's daughters, Elizabeth, became queen in 1558. She finished creating a separate English church. The new church was called **Anglican**. It had some practices that would appeal to both Protestants and Catholics. In this way, Elizabeth hoped to end religious conflict.

4. What role did Henry VIII play in creating the Church of England?

_____

_____

The Reformation Continues

BEFORE YOU READ

In the last section, you read how the Reformation began.
In this section, you will learn how it developed and spread.

AS YOU READ

Use the chart below to take notes on the reforms that occurred as the Reformation continued.

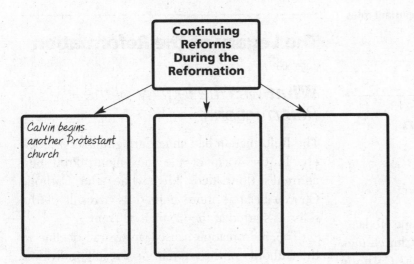

Continuing Reforms During the Reformation

Calvin begins another Protestant church

TERMS AND NAMES

predestination Doctrine that God has decided all things beforehand, including which people will be saved

Calvinism Religious teachings based on the ideas of the reformer John Calvin

theocracy Government controlled by religious leaders

Presbyterian Member of a Protestant church governed by elders and founded by John Knox

Anabaptist Member of a Protestant group during the Reformation who believed only adults should be baptized. Also believed that church and state should be separate

Catholic Reformation 16th-century Catholic reform movement in response to Protestant Reformation

Jesuits Members of the Society of Jesus, a Roman Catholic religious order founded by Ignatius of Loyola

Council of Trent Meeting of Roman Catholic leaders to rule on doctrines criticized by the Protestant reformers

Calvin Continues the Reformation (pages 495–496)

What did Calvin teach?

Protestantism arose elsewhere in the 1530s. This time under the leadership of John Calvin. Calvin wrote an important book that gave structure to Protestant beliefs. He taught that people are sinful by nature. He also taught **predestination,** the idea that God determines beforehand who will be saved. The religion based on Calvin's teachings is called **Calvinism.**

Calvin created a **theocracy** in Geneva, Switzerland. It was government run by religious leaders. It had strict rules of behavior that required people to live religious lives. Anyone who preached

different religious ideas might be burned at the stake.

A preacher named John Knox was impressed by Calvin's high moral ideals. Knox put these ideas into practice in Scotland. This was beginning of the **Presbyterian** Church. Others in Holland, France, and Switzerland adopted Calvin's ideas as well. In France, his followers were called Huguenots. Conflict between them and Catholics often turned into violence. In 1572, mobs killed about 12,000 Huguenots.

1. What is Calvinism?

_____

_____

Other Protestant Reformers

(pages 496–498)

What other reformers were important during the Reformation?

Another new Protestant group was the **Anabaptists.** They preached that people should be baptized into the faith as adults. Anabaptists also taught that the church and state should be separate. In addition, they refused to fight in wars.

Many women played key roles in the Reformation. They included Marguerite of Navarre. She protected John Calvin from being killed for his beliefs. Katherina von Bora was the wife of Martin Luther. She supported an equal role for women in marriage.

2. Who were two women who played important roles in the Reformation?

_____

_____

_____

The Catholic Reformation

(pages 498–499)

What was the Catholic Reformation?

Protestant churches grew all over Europe. To keep Catholic believers loyal, the Catholic Church took steps to change itself. This was called the **Catholic Reformation.**

One Catholic reformer was a Spanish noble named Ignatius. He founded a new group in the Church based on deep devotion to Jesus. Members of this group, called the **Jesuits,** started schools across Europe. They sent missionaries to convert people to Catholicism. In addition, they tried to stop the spread of Protestant faiths in Europe.

Two popes of the 1500s helped bring about changes in the Church. Pope Paul III set up a kind of court called the Inquisition. It was charged with finding, trying, and punishing people who broke the rules of the Church. He also called a meeting of church leaders, the **Council of Trent.** The council, which met in 1545, passed these *doctrines:*

- the Church's interpretation of the Bible was final
- Christians needed good works as well as faith to win salvation
- the Bible and the Church had equal authority in setting out Christian beliefs
- indulgences were valid expressions of faith

The next pope, Paul IV, put these doctrines into practice. These actions helped revive the Church. They also allowed it to survive the challenge of the Protestants.

3. What happened at the Council of Trent?

_____

_____

The Legacy of the Reformation

(page 500)

What was the legacy of the Reformation?

The Reformation had an enduring impact on society. In the wake of the movement, Protestant churches flourished. Meanwhile, the Catholic Church became more unified as a result of the reforms started at the Council of Trent.

The Reformation caused an overall decline in the authority of the church. As a result, individual monarchs and states gained greater power. This in turn led to the development of modern nation-states.

Women thought that their status in society might improve as a result of the Reformation. However, this did not happen. Women were still mainly limited to the concerns of home and family.

4. What was the result of the declining authority of the church?

_____

_____

Name _____ Date _____

Glossary — CHAPTER 17 European Renaissance and Reformation

bubonic plague Deadly disease that spread across Europe and Asia in the mid-14th century, killing millions of people

classical Related to ancient Greece and Rome and emphasizing ideas of order, balance, and harmony

clergy Religious officials

doctrines Principles; statements of policy

landscapes Pictures showing scenery or land forms

merchants Storekeepers and traders

movable type Printing blocks that did not have to be made one by one but could be moved into new positions and reused

nobles People of high rank

oil-based paints Paints that are made with oil; the oil dries slowly and allows for details, blending, and changes

Parliament Law-making body in England

peasant Related to poor or lower class people who worked the land

protested Actively disagreed

realistic Lifelike

revolt Uprising, rebellion

salvation Freedom from the effects of sin

sculptors People who create works of art by carving

spiritual Sacred; related to religion

three-dimensional Having length, width, and height; giving a sense of depth

AFTER YOU READ

Terms and Names

A. Fill in the blank with the name or term that best completes the paragraph.

Presbyterian

Anabaptists

Anglican

Lutheran

Reformation

Protestant

In Germany, Martin Luther began a movement for religious change called the **1** _____. He and his followers began a separate religious group called the **2** _____ Church. In England, Elizabeth founded and headed the **3** _____ church. In Scotland, John Knox established yet another branch of the **4** _____ faith. His church was the **5** _____ Church. Other Protestant reformers included the **6** _____, who believed in separation of church and state.

B. Write the letter of the name or term next to the description that best explains it.

a. Jesuits

b. secular

c. Calvinism

d. Peace of Augsburg

e. patrons

f. indulgence

g. Utopia

h. humanism

i. predestination

j. vernacular

_____ **1.** Focus on human potential and achievements

_____ **2.** An agreement in 1555 declaring that the religion of each German state would be decided by its ruler

_____ **3.** Concerned with worldly rather than spiritual matters

_____ **4.** Doctrine that God has decided all things beforehand, including which people will be eternally saved

_____ **5.** Use of native language instead of classical Latin

_____ **6.** Body of religious teachings based on the ideas of the reformer John Calvin

_____ **7.** Members of the Society of Jesus, a Roman Catholic religious order founded by Ignatius of Loyola

_____ **8.** Imaginary land described in a book by Thomas More; this word now means an ideal place

_____ **9.** People who financially supported artists

_____ **10.** Release from punishments due for a sin

AFTER YOU READ (continued)   *CHAPTER 17* European Renaissance and Reformation

Main Ideas

1. What changes in the arts occurred during the Italian Renaissance?

_____

_____

2. What changes in learning and the arts occurred during the northern Renaissance?

_____

_____

_____

3. What changes in the Christian Church did Martin Luther bring about?

_____

_____

_____

4. How did the Reformation in Germany change German political life?

_____

_____

_____

5. Why and how did the Church change in England?

_____

_____

_____

Thinking Critically

Answer the following questions on a separate sheet of paper.

1. How did the northern Renaissance differ from the Italian Renaissance?

2. Which leader—Henry VIII or Luther—do you think had a greater impact? Explain why.

The Ottomans Build a Vast Empire

TERMS AND NAMES

ghazis Warriors for Islam

Osman Successful ghazi who built a small state in Anatolia

sultans Rulers of Muslim states

Timur the Lame Conqueror of Persia and Russia

Mehmed II Conqueror who made Istanbul his capital

Suleyman the Lawgiver Ruler who brought Ottoman Empire to its height

devshirme Policy for creating the sultan's army

janissary Soldier slave drawn from conquered Christian territories

BEFORE YOU READ

In the last chapter, you read about changes in Europe during 1300-1600.

In this section, you will read about the rise of the Ottoman Empire during the same period.

AS YOU READ

Use the time line below to take notes on the major events in the history of the Ottoman Empire.

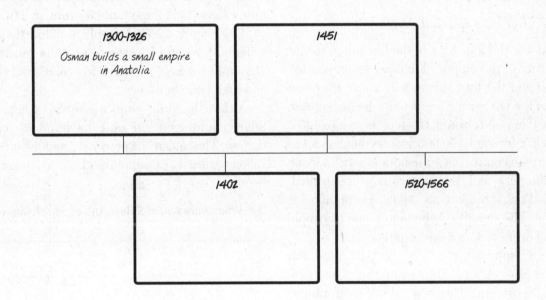

1300-1326
Osman builds a small empire in Anatolia

1451

1402

1520-1566

Turks Move into Byzantium

(pages 507–508)

How did the Ottoman Empire begin?

In 1300, the world of the eastern Mediterranean was also changing. The Byzantine Empire was fading. The Seljuk Turk state had been destroyed. Anatolia, the area of modern Turkey, was now inhabited by groups of *nomadic* Turks. They saw themselves as *ghazis*, or Muslim warriors for *Islam*. They raided the lands where non-Muslims lived.

The most successful ghazi was **Osman.** Western Europeans thought his name was Othman. They called his followers Ottomans. Between 1300 and 1326, Osman built a strong but small kingdom in *Anatolia*. Leaders who came after Osman called themselves **sultans,** or "ones with power." They extended the kingdom by buying land. They also formed *alliances* with other chieftains and conquered everyone they could.

The Ottomans ruled in a kindly way. Muslims had to serve in the army but paid no taxes. Non-Muslims paid tax but did not serve in the army. Many joined *Islam* just to avoid the tax. Most people adjusted easily to their new rule.

One warrior did not. He was **Timur the Lame**. He conquered Russia and Persia. In 1402, he defeated the Ottoman forces and captured the sultan and took him to Samarkand in a cage.

1. Who were the Ottomans?

_____

_____

_____

Powerful Sultans Spur Dramatic Expansion (pages 508–509)

How *did the empire grow?*

In Anatolia, the four sons of the last sultan fought for control of the empire. Mehmed I won control. His son and the four sultans who came after him brought the Ottoman Empire to its greatest power. One of them—**Mehmed II**—took power in 1451. He built a force of 100,000 foot soldiers and 125 ships to gain control of Constantinople. In 1453, he took the city and the waterway it controlled. Mehmed made the city his capital. He renamed it Istanbul. The rebuilt city became home to people from all over the Ottoman Empire.

Other emperors used *conquest* to make the empire grow. After 1514, Selim the Grim took Persia, Syria, and Palestine. He then captured Arabia, took the Muslim holy cities of Medina and Mecca, and gained control of Egypt.

2. Who was Mehmed II?

_____

_____

_____

_____

Suleyman the Lawgiver; The Empire Declines Slowly (pages 510–511)

Why *was Suleyman the Lawgiver a great leader?*

Suleyman I took power in 1520 and ruled for 46 years. He brought the Ottoman Empire to its greatest size and most impressive achievements. He conquered parts of southeastern Europe. He won control of the entire eastern Mediterranean Sea and took North Africa as far west as Tripoli.

Suleyman revised the laws of the empire. His people called him **Suleyman the Lawgiver.** Suleyman ruled his empire with a highly structured government. Thousands of slaves served the royal family. The policy of making people slaves was called **devshirme.** The **janissaries** were an enslaved group of soldiers. They were Christians taken as children and made slaves. They were trained as soldiers and fought fiercely for the sultan. Other slaves held important government jobs.

The empire allowed people to follow their own religion. Jews and Christians were not mistreated. His empire was also known for great works of art and many fine buildings.

Although the empire lasted long after Suleyman, it spent the next few hundred years in *decline.* That means its power slipped. None of the sultans were as accomplished as Suleyman had been.

3. What were two of Suleyman's accomplishments?

_____

_____

_____

_____

Cultural Blending

Case Study: The Safavid Empire

BEFORE YOU READ

In the last section, you read about the Ottomans.

In this section, you will learn about the development of another empire, the Safavid.

AS YOU READ

Use the chart below to show three of the long-lasting effects of the Safavid Empire.

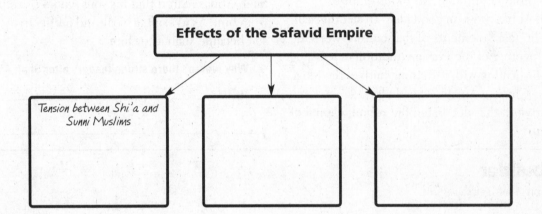

Effects of the Safavid Empire

Tension between Shi'a and Sunni Muslims

TERMS AND NAMES

Safavid Member of a Shi'a Muslim group that built an empire in Persia

Isma'il Safavid warrior who seized most of what is now Iran

shah Persian title meaning king

Shah Abbas Leader during the Safavid golden age

Esfahan Capital city of the Safavid Empire

Patterns of Cultural Blending
(pages 512–513)

What is cultural blending?

Throughout history, different peoples have lived together. Their cultures have influenced one another. Often these people have blended one culture with another. This can happen because of migration, trade, conquest, or pursuit of religious freedom or conversion.

Cultural blending results in changes in society. Some results of cultural blending are changes in language, religion, styles of government, or arts and architecture.

Societies that are able to benefit from cultural blending are open to new ways. They are willing to adapt and change.

1. What are the four causes of cultural blending?

_____

_____

The Safavids Build a Shi'a Empire (pages 513–514)

How did the Safavids rise to power?

Cultural blending took place in the Safavid Empire of Persia. The **Safavids** were members of the *Shi'a*, a branch of Islam. The major group of Muslims, the *Sunnis*, *persecuted* the Shi'a for their views. The Safavids feared the Sunni Muslims. They decided to build a strong army to protect themselves.

In 1499, a 14-year-old leader named **Isma'il** led this army to conquer Iran. He took the traditional Persian title of **shah**, or king, and made *Shi'a* the religion of the new empire. He destroyed Baghdad's Sunni population. Ottoman Turk rulers—who were Sunni Muslims—in turn killed all the Shi'a that they met. This conflict between the two groups of Muslims continues today.

2. Why are the Shi'a and Sunni Muslims enemies?

A Safavid Golden Age

Who was Shah Abbas?

The Safavids reached their height in the late 1500s under **Shah Abbas.** He created two armies that were loyal to him and him alone. He also gave new weapons to the army to make them better fighters. He got rid of *corrupt* officials in the government. He also brought gifted artists to his empire.

Shah Abbas drew on good ideas from other cultures. The main elements of that culture were the joining together of the Persian tradition of learning and sophistication with the strong faith of the Shi'a. He used Chinese artists. They helped create gorgeous artwork that decorated the rebuilt capital of **Esfahan**.

Under Shah Abbas, the Safavids enjoyed good relations with nations of Europe. The demand for Persian rugs increased greatly in Europe. In this period, rug-making, which had been a local craft in Persia, became a major industry for the country.

3. What were four reforms made by Shah Abbas?

The Dynasty Declines Quickly

(page 515)

Why did the Safavids lose power?

Like the Ottoman Empire, the Safavid Empire began to decline soon after it had reached its greatest height. Shah Abbas had killed or injured his most talented sons—just as Suleyman had done. Shah Abbas feared that his sons would seize power from him. As a result, a weak and ineffective grandson became shah after him.

4. Why weren't there strong leaders after Shah Abbas?

Skillbuilder

Use the chart to answer the questions.

1. Determining Main Ideas What are two reasons for interaction?

2. Recognizing Effects What are some results of cultural interaction?

Cultural Blending			
Location	**Interacting Cultures**	**Reason for Interaction**	**Some Results of Interaction**
India—1000 B.C.	Aryan and Dravidian Indian Arab, African, Indian	Migration	Vedic culture, forerunner of Hinduism
East Africa—A.D. 700	Islamic, Christian	Trade, religious conversion	New trade language, Swahili
Russia—A.D. 1000	Christian and Slavic	Religious conversion	Eastern Christianity, Russian identity
Mexico—A.D. 1500	Spanish and Aztec	Conquest	Mestizo culture, Mexican Catholicism
United States—A.D. 1900	European, Asian, Caribbean	Migration, religious freedom	Cultural diversity

The Mughal Empire in India

TERMS AND NAMES

Babur Founder of the Mughal Empire

Mughal One of the nomads who invaded the Indian subcontinent and established a powerful empire there

Akbar Mughal ruler with a genius for cultural blending, military conquest, and art

Sikh Nonviolent religious group that became the enemy of the Mughals

Shah Jahan Mughal ruler who built Taj Mahal

Taj Mahal Tomb built by Shah Jahan for his wife

Aurangzeb Last important Mughal ruler

BEFORE YOU READ

In the last section, you learn about how the Safavids established an empire in what is present-day Iran.

In this section, you will learn about the establishment of the Mughal Empire in what is now India.

AS YOU READ

Use the web diagram below to take notes. In each circle, write the name of one important Mughal ruler. Also write two or three words that identify each person or name a major accomplishment or problem of his rule.

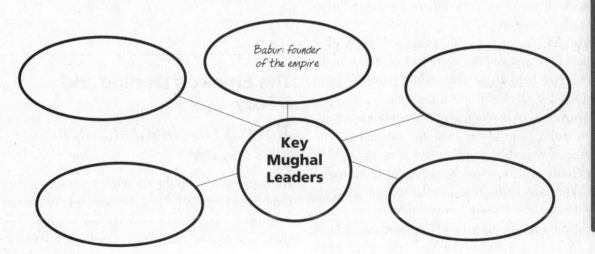

Babur: founder of the empire

Key Mughal Leaders

Early History of the Mughal Empire (page 516)

How did the Mughal Empire begin?

Starting in the 600s, India went through a long, unsettled period. Nomads from central Asia invaded the area and created many small kingdoms. In the 700s, Muslims arrived on the scene. This began a long history of fighting with the *Hindus* who had lived in India for centuries.

After about 300 years, a group of Muslim Turks conquered a region around the city of Delhi. They set up a new empire there. They treated the Hindus in their area as conquered peoples. Their rule was brought to an end in 1398.

A little over a hundred years later, a new leader named **Babur** raised an army and began to win large parts of India. He had many talents. He was a lover of poetry and gardens. He was also an excellent general. His empire was called the **Mughal** Empire because he and his families were related to the Mongols.

1. Who was Babur?

_____

_____

The Golden Age of Akbar

(pages 517–518)

Who was Akbar?

Babur's grandson was **Akbar**. His name means "Greatest One." He ruled with great wisdom and fairness for almost 40 years.

Akbar was a Muslim. However, he believed strongly that people should be allowed to follow the religion they choose. Both Hindus and Muslims worked in the government. He hired people in his government based on their ability and not their religion.

Akbar ruled fairly. He ended the tax that Hindu pilgrims had to pay. He also ended the tax that all non-Muslims had to pay. To raise money, he taxed people on a percentage of the food they grew. This made it easier for peasants to pay the tax. His land policy was less wise. He gave much land to government officials. However, when they died he took it back. As a result, workers did not see any point in caring for the land.

He had a strong, well-equipped army that helped him win and keep control of more lands. His empire held about 100 million people—more than lived in all of Europe at the time.

During Akbar's reign, his policy of blending different cultures produced two new languages. The languages were blends of several languages. One was *Hindi*, which is widely spoken in India today. The other was *Urdu*. It is now the official language of Pakistan. The empire became famous for its art, literature, and architecture. The best example of this art was small, highly detailed, colorful pictures called miniatures. He also sponsored the building of a new capital city.

2. What are some examples of Akbar's policy of fair rule?

_____

_____

Akbar's Successors (pages 518–521)

Who ruled after Akbar?

After Akbar's death in 1605, his son Jahangir, took control of the empire. During his reign, the real power was his wife, Nur Jahan. She plotted with one son to overthrow another son. She had a bitter political battle with the **Sikhs**, members of a separate, nonviolent religion. That group became the target of attacks by the government.

The next ruler was **Shah Jahan**. He too chose not to follow Akbar's policy of religious toleration. Shah Jahan was a great *patron* of the arts and built many beautiful buildings. One was the famous **Taj Mahal,** a tomb for his wife. His ambitious building plans required high taxes, though. People suffered under his rule.

His son **Aurangzeb** ruled for almost 50 years. He made the empire grow once again with new conquests. His rule also brought new problems. He was a *devout* Muslim, and he punished Hindus and destroyed their temples. This led to a rebellion that took part of his empire. At the same time, the Sikhs won control of another part of the empire.

3. How did Aurangzeb deal with Hindus?

_____

_____

The Empire's Decline and Decay (page 521)

How did the Mughal Empire lose its power?

Aurangzeb used up the empire's resources. People did not feel loyalty to him. As the power of the state weakened, the power of local lords grew. Soon there was only a patchwork of independent states. There continued to be a Mughal emperor, but he was only a *figurehead*, not a ruler with any real power. As the Mughal empire was rising and falling, Western traders were building power. They arrived in India just before Babur did. Shah Jahan let the English build a trading fort in Madras. Aurangzeb handed them the port of Bombay. This gave India's next conquerors a foothold in India.

4. How did the Mughal Empire change after Akbar?

_____

_____

Glossary · CHAPTER 18 The Muslim World Expands

alliances Partnerships

Anatolia Southwest Asian peninsula now occupied by the Asian part of Turkey—also called Asia Minor

conquest Act of conquering, defeating, or taking over

corrupt Having few or no moral values, or having moral values that are unsound

decline Gradual loss of power

devout Devoted to religion or religious duties

figurehead Ruler without real power

Hindi Blend of Persian and local languages still spoken in India

Hindus People who practice the Hindu religion, the main religion of India

Islam Religion that developed in Arabia in the 7th century

nomadic Moving from place to place

patron Sponsor or supporter

persecuted Caused to suffer because of beliefs

Shi'a Branch of Islam

Sunni Branch of Islam

Urdu Mixture of Arabic, Persian, and Hindi; the official language of Pakistan

AFTER YOU READ

Terms and Names

A. Write the name or term in each blank that best completes the meaning of the paragraph.

Suleyman the Lawgiver

Timur the Lame

Osman

ghazi

Mehmed II

The Ottoman Empire began when a successful **1** _____ built a small state in Anatolia. This warrior's name was **2** _____. The name Ottoman comes from his name. The rise of the Ottoman Empire was interrupted by a warrior named **3** _____. He conquered Persia and Russia. After that time, strong rulers brought power back to the Ottoman Empire. When **4** _____ conquered Constantinople, he opened the city to new citizens of many religions and backgrounds. Although his accomplishments were great, the peak achievement of the Ottoman Empire occurred under **5** _____. He brought a highly structured social organization and many cultural achievements to the Ottomans.

B. Write the letter of the name or term next to the description that explains it best.

a. Babur

b. Isma'il

c. Esfahan

d. Akbar

e. Aurangzeb

_____ **1.** Safavid leader who seized most of what is now Iran

_____ **2.** Capital city of the Safavid Empire under Shah Abbas

_____ **3.** Mughal emperor who drained the empire of its resources while the power of local lords grew

_____ **4.** Founder of the Mughal Empire

_____ **5.** Muslim Mughal leader who defended religious freedom and blended many cultures

AFTER YOU READ (continued) *CHAPTER 18* The Muslim World Expands

Main Ideas

1. How did the Ottomans come to power?

_____

_____

_____

2. How did Suleyman the Lawgiver use slaves in his government?

_____

_____

_____

3. Where does cultural blending take place?

_____

_____

_____

4. Why did the Safavid Empire decline?

_____

_____

_____

5. What were four of Akbar's great accomplishments?

_____

_____

_____

Thinking Critically

Answer the following questions on a separate sheet of paper.

1. How were cultures blended during the Safavid Empire?

2. How did the leaders who came after Akbar contribute to the end of the Mughal empire?

CHAPTER 19 Section 1 (pages 529–535)

Europeans Explore the East

TERMS AND NAMES

Bartolomeu Dias Portuguese explorer who rounded the tip of Africa

Prince Henry Portuguese supporter of exploration

Vasco da Gama Explorer who gave Portugal a direct sea route to India

Treaty of Tordesillas Treaty between Spain and Portugal dividing newly discovered lands between them

Dutch East India Company Dutch company that established and directed trade throughout Asia

BEFORE YOU READ

In the last chapter, you read about empire building in Asia.

In this section, you will learn why and how Europeans began an age of exploration.

AS YOU READ

Use the time line below to take notes on important events in European exploration.

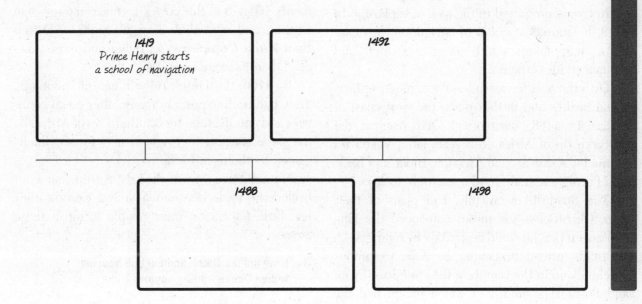

1419
Prince Henry starts a school of navigation

1492

1488

1498

For "God, Glory, and Gold"

(pages 529–530)

Why did Europeans begin to explore new lands?

For many centuries, Europeans did not have much contact with people from other lands. That changed in the 1400s. Europeans hoped to gain new sources of wealth. By exploring the seas, traders hoped to find new, faster routes to Asia—the source of spices and luxury goods. Another reason for exploration was spreading Christianity to new lands.

Bartolomeu Dias, an early Portuguese explorer, explained his motives: "to serve God and His Majesty, to give light to those who were in darkness and to grow rich as all men desire to do."

Advances in technology made these voyages possible. A new kind of ship, the *caravel*, was stronger than earlier ships. It had triangle-shaped sails that allowed it to sail against the wind. Ships could now travel far out into the ocean. The magnetic compass allowed sea captains to stay on course better.

1. What were the two main reasons for European exploration?

_____

_____

_____

Portugal Leads the Way; Spain Also Makes Claims

(pages 530–533)

How did Portugal lead the way in exploration?

The first nation to develop and use the caravel and the magnetic compass was Portugal. **Prince Henry** was committed to the idea of exploring. In 1419, he started a school of *navigation*. Sea captains, mapmakers, and navigators met and exchanged ideas there.

Over the next few decades, Portuguese captains sailed farther and farther down the west coast of Africa. In 1488, Bartolomeu Dias reached the southern tip of Africa. Ten years later, **Vasco da Gama** led a ship around Africa, to India, and back. The Portuguese had found a sea route to Asia.

The Spanish, meanwhile, had plans of their own. Christopher Columbus convinced the king and queen that he could reach Asia by sailing west. In 1492, instead of landing in Asia, Columbus touched land in the islands of the Americas. Spain and Portugal argued over which nation had the rights to the land that Columbus had claimed. In 1494, they signed the **Treaty of Tordesillas**. It divided the world into two areas. Portugal won the right to control the eastern parts—including Africa, India, and other parts of Asia. Spain got the western parts—including most of the Americas.

2. How did Spain and Portugal solve their differences over claims to new lands?

_____

_____

Trading Empires in the Indian Ocean (pages 533–535)

Who established trading empires in the Indian Ocean?

Portugal moved quickly to make the new Indian Ocean route pay off. Through military might, Portugal gained power over islands that were rich in desirable spices. They were called the Spice Islands. Spices now cost Europeans one-fifth of what they had cost before, while still making Portugal very wealthy.

Other European nations joined in this trade. In the 1600s, the English and Dutch entered the East Indies. They quickly broke Portuguese power in the area. Then both nations set up an East India Company to control Asian trade. These companies were more than businesses. They were like governments. They had the power to make money, sign treaties, and raise their own armies. The **Dutch East India Company** was richer and more powerful than England's company.

By 1700, the Dutch ruled much of Indonesia. They had trading posts in many other Asian countries and commanded the southern tip of Africa. At the same time, both England and France finally gained footholds in India.

Nevertheless, even though Europeans controlled the trade between Asia and Europe, they had little *impact* on most people living in these areas.

3. How did the Dutch and English become Indian Ocean trading powers ?

_____

_____

_____

China Limits European Contacts

BEFORE YOU READ

In the last section, you read about European exploration in the East.

In this section, you will read about China's reactions to the world around it.

AS YOU READ

Use the chart below to show important developments in the Ming Dynasty and the Qing Dynasty.

TERMS AND NAMES

Hongwu Commander of the rebel army that drove the Mongols out of China in 1368

Ming Dynasty Chinese dynasty that ruled from 1368 to 1644

Yonglo Ming ruler; son of Hongwu

Zheng He Muslim admiral who led seven voyages of exploration during the Ming Dynasty

Manchus People from Manchuria

Qing Dynasty Chinese dynasty that followed the Ming Dynasty and was begun by the Manchus

Kangxi Powerful Manchu emperor of the Qing Dynasty

MING DYNASTY	QING DYNASTY
Hongwu becomes the first emperor.	

China Under the Powerful Ming Dynasty (pages 536–539)

What occurred during the Ming Dynasty?

Mongol rule in China ended in 1368 when **Hongwu** led a *rebel* army that took control of the country. He declared himself the first emperor of the **Ming Dynasty**, which was to last for almost 300 years. Hongwu began his rule by increasing the amount of food produced and improving the government. Later he grew suspicious and untrusting. He caused the deaths of many people whom he suspected of plotting against him.

His son **Yonglo** continued his better policies. He also launched a major effort at making contact with other Asian peoples. Beginning in 1405, an admiral named **Zheng He** led several voyages to Southeast Asia, India, Arabia, and Africa. Wherever he went, he gave away gifts to show Chinese superiority.

Eventually the Chinese changed their position on foreign trade. They began to isolate themselves. China allowed Europeans to trade officially at only three ports, but illegal trade took place all along the coast. Europeans wanted Chinese silk and ceramics, and they paid silver for them. Manufacturing never grew very large in China, however. The

Confucian ideas that shaped Chinese thinking said that farming was a better way of life, so manufacturing was heavily taxed. *Missionaries* entered China at this time, bringing both Christianity and technology.

1. How was China influenced by foreigners during the Ming Dynasty?

_____

_____

_____

_____

Manchus Found the Qing Dynasty (pages 539–540)

How did China change during the Qing Dynasty?

The Ming Dynasty lost power because the government could not solve several problems. **Manchus**, people who came from a land north of China called Manchuria, took control of the country in 1644. They started the **Qing Dynasty**. Two important emperors were **Kangxi** and his grandson Qian-long. They brought China to its largest size, increased its wealth, and sponsored an increase in artistic production.

The Chinese insisted that Europeans had to follow certain rules in order to continue trading with them. These rules include trading only at special ports and paying fees. The Dutch were willing to do so, and they carried on the largest share of trade with China. The British, though, did not agree to following these rules.

At the same time, a feeling of national pride was rising in Korea, which had long been *dominated* by China.

2. Why was trade a problem during the Qing Dynasty?

_____

_____

_____

_____

Life in Ming and Qing China

(page 541)

What was life like in China under the Ming and Qing?

In China, the production of rice and the long period of peace gave the people better lives. In the 1600s and 1700s, the number of people in China almost doubled. The huge majority of these people were farmers. Because of the use of fertilizer and better *irrigation*, they could grow more food. The level of nutrition improved. This caused the population to grow.

In Chinese families, sons were valued over daughters. It was believed that only sons could carry out family religious duties and tend to the family farm. For that reason, many infant girls were killed, and adult women had few rights.

The invasions by the foreigners from Manchuria and the pressure from European traders bothered the Chinese. They tried to preserve their traditions and their isolation. Artists created books and paintings that showed traditional Chinese values and ideas. Plays about Chinese history and heroes were popular. They helped to unify the Chinese people.

3. Which parts of society improved during this time, and which continued to be the same?

_____

_____

_____

_____

CHAPTER 19 Section 3 (pages 542–547)

Japan Returns to Isolation

TERMS AND NAMES

daimyo Warrior-chieftains

Oda Nobunaga Daimyo who hoped to control all of Japan and seized Kyoto

Toyotomi Hideyoshi Daimyo who took control of almost all of Japan

Tokugawa Shogunate Dynasty that ruled Japan from 1603 to 1868

kabuki Type of Japanese theate

haiku Type of Japanese poetry

BEFORE YOU READ

In the last section, you saw how the Chinese reacted to foreigners.

In this section, you will read about civil war in Japan and its effects.

AS YOU READ

Use the chart below to show some ways in which Japan changed after it was unified

```
                    Japan Is Unified
        ┌──────────┬──────────┴──────────┬──────────┐
        │          │                     │          │
     political  economic             cultural     social
  new system of rule—
  Tokugawa Shogunate
```

A New Feudalism Under Strong Leaders (pages 542–544)

Why were warriors fighting in Japan?

From 1467 to 1568, Japan entered a long, dark period of civil war. Powerful warriors took control of large areas of land. They were called **daimyo**. They became the most important powers in the country. The daimyo fought each other constantly to gain more land for themselves.

In 1568, one of the daimyo, **Oda Nobunaga**, took control of Kyoto. It was the site of the emperor's capital. Another general, **Toyotomi Hideyoshi**, continued the work of bringing all of Japan under one rule. Using military conquest and clever *diplomacy*, he won that goal in 1590. He failed in his effort to capture Korea, however.

The work of *unifying* Japan was completed by Tokugawa Ieyasu. He became the *shogun*, or sole ruler. He moved the capital of Japan to a small fishing village named Edo. Later, it grew to become the city of Tokyo.

While all of Japan was ruled by Tokugawa, the daimyo still held much power in their lands. Tokugawa solved that problem by forcing them to follow his orders. Tokugawa died in 1616. All of the shoguns to follow him were from his family. They maintained a strong central government in Japan. This system of rule, called the **Tokugawa Shogunate**, lasted until 1867.

1. Which three leaders helped bring Japan under one rule?

_____

_____

Life in Tokugawa Japan (page 544)

How was Tokugawa society organized?

The new government brought about a long period of peace and prosperity for most people. Peasant farmers suffered greatly during this time, however. They worked long and hard on the farms and paid heavy taxes. Many left the countryside to move to the cities. By the mid-1700s, Edo had more than a million people. It was perhaps the largest city in the world. Women found more opportunities for work in this and other cities than they had in the country.

A *traditional* culture thrived. It preferred ceremonial dramas, stories of ancient warriors, and paintings of classical scenes. However, in cities, new styles emerged. Townspeople attended **kabuki,** dramas of urban life. They hung woodblock prints of city scenes in their homes. They also read **haiku**, poetry that presents images instead of expressing ideas.

2. What kinds of old and new culture were found in the cities?

_____

_____

Contact Between Europe and Japan; The Closed Country Policy (pages 545–547)

Who came to Japan?

In 1543, Europeans began to arrive in Japan. The Portuguese were first. In the beginning, Japanese merchants and the daimyo welcomed them. They even welcomed the Christian missionaries who came after 1549. Some missionaries scorned traditional Japanese beliefs. They also got involved in local politics. Tokugawa became worried. In 1612, he banned Christianity from the country. Christians were persecuted. Over the next 20 years or so, Japan managed to rid the country of all Christians. This was part of a larger plan to protect the country from European influence.

In 1639, leaders sealed Japan's borders except for one port city. It was open to only the Chinese and the Dutch. The Tokugawa shoguns controlled that port city, so they had tight control over all foreign contact. For the next 200 years, Japan remained closed to just about all European contact.

3. Why did the Japanese seal almost all of their borders?

_____

_____

JAPANESE SOCIETY

Emperor
Held highest rank in society
but had no political power

Daimyo
Large landowners

Shogun
Actual ruler

Samurai   Warriors
Loyal to Daimyo and Shogun

Peasants
Four-fifths of
the population

Artisans
Craftspeople
such as artists
and blacksmiths

Merchants
Low status but gradually gained influence

Skillbuilder

Use the illustration to answer these questions.

1. What three people or groups of people controlled Japanese society?

_____

_____

2. What was the relationship of the samurai to the other classes in Japanese society?

_____

_____

Glossary   CHAPTER 19   An Age of Exploration and Isolation

caravel Strong sailing ship designed in the 1400s

Confucian Related to Confucius, who taught principles of social order, harmony, and good government

diplomacy Work of keeping up relations between nations

dominated Ruled over or had great power over

irrigation Method of bringing water to crops

missionaries People who bring religious ideas to new places

navigation Finding one's way at sea

rebel Oppose the government by force

shogun Supreme military commander who ruled in the name of the emperor

traditional Based on what has been done in the past

unifying Bringing together under one rule

AFTER YOU READ

Names and Terms

A. Write the name or term in each blank that best completes the meaning of the paragraph.

Kangxi

Yonglo

Hongwu

Zheng He

Manchus

In China, the great Ming Dynasty began when **1** _____ led a rebel army to victory over the Mongols. He made some good changes in China that improved the government and led to the production of more food. His son, **2** _____, continued his better policies. Among other things, he sent the Muslim admiral **3** _____ on journeys of exploration. The power of the Ming Dynasty eventually declined, however. People from Manchuria known as **4** _____ took over. They established the Qing Dynasty. The emperor **5** _____ was one of its most important rulers.

B. Write the letter of the name or term next to the description that explains it best.

a. haiku

b. Treaty of Tordesillas

c. Vasco da Gama

d. Bartolomeu Dias

e. daimyo

____ **1.** Led voyage around Africa, to India, and back to Portugal

____ **2.** Warrior-chieftains

____ **3.** Led first voyage to reach the southern tip of Africa

____ **4.** Poetry that presents images

____ **5.** Agreement between Portugal and Spain that divided the world into two areas

AFTER YOU READ (cont.) *CHAP. 19* An Age of Exploration and Isolation

Main Ideas

1. Who led the way in European exploration, and why?

_____

_____

_____

2. What countries established trading empires in the Indian Ocean?

_____

_____

_____

3. How did the Ming Dynasty come to an end?

_____

_____

_____

4. What was Toyotomi Hideyoshi's greatest accomplishment?

_____

_____

_____

5. How did the Japanese react to the arrival of foreigners?

_____

_____

_____

Thinking Critically

Answer the following questions on a separate sheet of paper.

1. Why did the Europeans begin to explore overseas, and what technological advances made this possible?

2. What factors led to the growth of the Chinese population?

Name _____ Date _____

Spain Builds an American Empire

BEFORE YOU READ

In the last chapter, you read about European exploration in the East.

In this section, you will study the Spanish and Portuguese exploration of the Americas.

AS YOU READ

Use the web below to show some of the results of Spanish conquest.

TERMS AND NAMES

Christopher Columbus Italian explorer who landed in the Americas

colony Land controlled by another nation

Hernando Cortés Conquistador who defeated the Aztec

conquistadors Spanish explorers in the Americas

Francisco Pizarro Conquistador who defeated the Inca

Atahualpa Last Incan emperor

mestizo Person with mixed Spanish and Native American blood

encomienda System of mining and farming using natives as slave labor

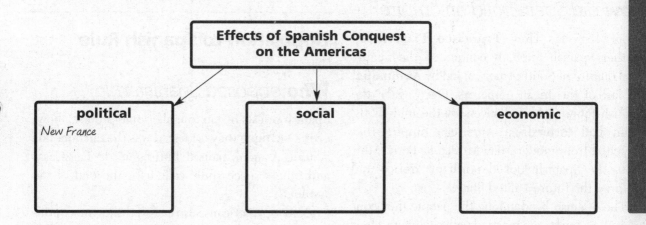

Effects of Spanish Conquest on the Americas

political
New France

social

economic

The Voyage of Columbus

(pages 553–554)

How *did the voyage of Columbus change the Americas?*

In 1492, **Christopher Columbus**, an Italian sailor, led a voyage for Spain. He sailed west hoping to reach Asia. Instead, he landed in the Americas. Columbus thought that he had reached the East Indies in Asia. He misnamed the natives he met there, calling them Indians. He claimed the land for Spain. From then on, Spain began to create **colonies**. Colonies are lands controlled by another nation.

In 1500, a Portuguese explorer claimed Brazil. In 1501, Amerigo Vespucci explored the eastern coast of South America. He said that these lands were a new world. Soon after, a mapmaker showed the lands as a separate continent. He named them America after Vespucci.

Other voyages gave Europeans more knowledge about the world. Balboa reached the Pacific Ocean. Ferdinand Magellan sailed completely around the world.

1. Which voyages gave Europeans new knowledge of the world?

_____

_____

_____

Spanish Conquests in Mexico

(pages 554–556)

Why did Spain conquer the Aztecs?

Hernando Cortés was one of the Spanish **conquistadors**, or conquerors. In the 16th century, they began to explore the lands of the Americas. They were seeking great riches. In 1519, Cortés came to Mexico and defeated the powerful *Aztec Empire* led by Montezuma II.

2. What was the main goal of Cortéz in his conquests?

_____

_____

Spanish Conquests in Peru

(pages 556–557)

How did Spain build an empire?

About 15 years later, **Francisco Pizarro** led another Spanish force. It conquered the mighty *Inca Empire* of South America, led by **Atahualpa,** the last of the Incan emperors. Once again, the Spanish found gold and silver. By the mid-1500s, Spain had formed an American empire that stretched from modern-day Mexico to Peru. After 1540, the Spanish looked north of Mexico and explored the future United States.

The Spanish lived among the people they conquered. Spanish men married native women. Their children and *descendants* were called **mestizo**—people with mixed Spanish and Native American blood. The Spanish also formed large farms and mines that used natives as slave labor. This system was known as *encomienda.*

One large area of the Americas—Brazil—was the *possession* of Portugal. In the 1830s, colonists began to settle there. Colonists built huge farms called *plantations* to grow sugar, which was in demand in Europe.

3. Give two examples of conquistadors and explain what they did.

_____

_____

Spain's Influence Expands

(page 558)

Where did Spain hope to gain more power?

Soon Spain began to want even more power in the Americas. It started to look at land that is now part of the United States. Explorers like Coronado led expeditions to the area. Catholic priests went along.

4. What area did Coronado explore?

_____

_____

Opposition to Spanish Rule

(page 559)

Who opposed Spanish rule?

Spanish priests began to make some protests, however. One thing they criticized was the encomienda system. A monk named Bartolomé de Las Casas and others successfully called for the end of the system.

Native Americans also resisted new or continued Spanish rule. One of the most serious *rebellions* occurred in New Mexico. A Pueblo leader named Popé led a well-organized effort. It involved about 17,000 warriors and drove the Spanish back into New Spain for 12 years.

5. What challenges to their power did the Spanish face?

_____

_____

Name _____ Date _____

European Nations Settle North America

BEFORE YOU READ

In the last chapter, you read about Spanish conquests.

In this section, you will see how other nations competed for power in North America.

AS YOU READ

Use the web below to show different claims in North America.

TERMS AND NAMES

New France Area of the Americas explored and claimed by France

Jamestown First permanent settlement in America

Pilgrims Group of English people who founded a colony in Plymouth

Puritans People who did not agree with the practices of the Church of England

New Netherland Dutch colony begun in modern New York City

French and Indian War War between Britain and France over land in North America

Metacom Native American leader who led an attack on the villages of Massachusetts; also called King Philip

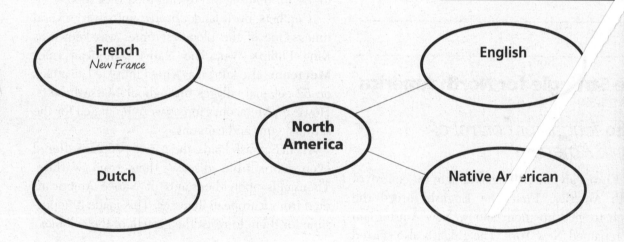

Competing Claims in North America (pages 561–562)

What new colonies were formed in North America?

In the early 1500s, the French began to explore North America. Jacques Cartier discovered and named the St. Lawrence River. He then followed it to the site of what is now Montreal. In 1608, Samuel de Champlain sailed as far as modern-day Quebec. In the next 100 years, the French explored and claimed the area around the Great Lakes and the Mississippi River all the way to its mouth at the Gulf of Mexico. The area became

known as **New France**. The main activity in this colony was trade in beaver fur.

1. What was the main economic activity in New France?

_____

_____

The English Arrive in North America (pages 562–563)

Why did the English settle in Massachusetts?

The English also began to colonize North America. The first permanent settlement was at **Jamestown**, in modern Virginia, in 1607. The colony struggled at first. Many settlers died from disease, hunger, or war with the native peoples. Soon, farmers began to grow tobacco to meet the high demand for it in Europe.

In 1620, a group known as **Pilgrims** founded a second English colony in Plymouth, in Massachusetts. These settlers and others who followed were deeply religious people who did not agree with the practices of the Church of England. They were called **Puritans**.

Meanwhile, the Dutch also started a new colony. They settled in the location of modern New York City and called it **New Netherland**. Like the French, they traded fur. The colony became known as a home to people of many different cultures. Europeans also took possession of many islands of the Caribbean. There they built tobacco and sugar plantations that used enslaved Africans as workers.

2. **In which two places did English colonists first settle?**

_____

_____

The Struggle for North America
(pages 563–564)

Who fought for control of North America?

The European powers began to fight for control of North America. First, the English forced the Dutch to give up their colony. New Amsterdam was renamed New York. The English also started other colonies along the Atlantic coast, from New Hampshire to Georgia. These English colonists interfered with the French settlers in Canada.

The British and the French clashed over the Ohio Valley in 1754. The fight was called the **French and Indian War**. When it ended in 1763, France was forced to give up all its land in North America to England.

3. **How did England gain land from the French?**

_____

_____

_____

Native Americans Respond
(pages 564–565)

How did native peoples respond to the colonists?

The native peoples responded to the colonists in many different ways. Many worked closely with the French and Dutch, joining in the fur trade and benefiting from it. Those who lived near the English, though, had stormier relations with colonists. More than just trade, the English were interested in settling the land and farming it. This was land that Native Americans would not be able to use for hunting or growing their own food.

Conflicts over land *erupted* into war several times. One of the bloodiest times was known as King Philip's War. The Native American ruler **Metacom** (also known as King Philip) led an attack on 52 colonial villages throughout Massachusetts. However, Metacom's forces were no match for the settlers' guns and cannons.

As in Spanish lands, the native peoples suffered even more from disease than from warfare. Thousands upon thousands of Native Americans died from European illnesses. This made it impossible for them to resist the growth of the colonies.

4. **Why did Native Americans lose their way of life?**

_____

_____

CHAPTER 20 Section 3 (pages 566–570)

The Atlantic Slave Trade

BEFORE YOU READ

In the last section, you saw how different European nations settled in North America.

In this section, you will read about the slave trade that brought Africans to the Americas.

AS YOU READ

Use the chart below to take notes on the triangular trade system.

TERMS AND NAMES

Atlantic slave trade Buying and selling of Africans for work in the Americas

triangular trade European trade between the Americas, Africa, and Europe involving slaves and other goods

middle passage Voyage that brought captured Africans to the West Indies and the Americas

Who traded?	What was traded?	Where were goods sent?
Spanish, Portuguese, and others		

Triangular trade

The Causes of African Slavery

(pages 566–567)

What *was the Atlantic slave trade?*

Slavery has had a long history in Africa and in the world. For most of that history in Africa, though, large numbers of people had not been enslaved. That changed in the 600s, when Muslim traders started to take many slaves to Southwest Asia.

Most worked as servants, and they did have certain rights. Also, the sons and daughters of slaves were considered to be free. The European slave trade that began in the 1500s was larger. The enslaved Africans also were treated far more harshly.

In the Americas, Europeans first used Native Americans to work farms and mines. When the native peoples began dying from disease, the Europeans brought in Africans. The buying and selling of Africans for work in the Americas became known as the **Atlantic slave trade**. From 1500 to 1870, when the slave trade in the Americas finally ended, about 9.5 million Africans had been *imported* as slaves.

The Spanish first began the practice of bringing Africans to the Americas. However, the Portuguese increased the demand for slaves. They were looking for workers for their sugar plantations in Brazil.

1. Why were slaves brought to the Americas?

_____

_____

Slavery Spreads Throughout the Americas (pages 567–568)

What sorts of plantations existed in the Americas?

Other European colonies also brought slaves to work on tobacco, sugar, and coffee plantations. About 400,000 slaves were brought to the English colonies in North America. Their population had increased to about 2 million in 1830.

Many African rulers joined in the slave trade. They captured people inland and brought them to the coast to sell to European traders.

2. How did some African rulers participate in the slave trade?

_____

_____

A Forced Journey (page 568–569)

What kinds of trade included human beings?

Africans taken to the Americas were part of a **triangular trade** between Europe, Africa, and the Americas. European ships brought manufactured goods to Africa, trading them for people. They carried Africans across the Atlantic to the Americas, where they were sold into slavery. The traders then bought sugar, coffee, and tobacco to bring back to Europe.

Another triangle involved ships sailing from the northern English colonies in North America. They carried rum to Africa, people to the West Indies, and sugar and molasses back to the colonies to make more rum.

The part of the voyage that brought people to the Americas was called the **middle passage**. It was harsh and cruel. People were crammed into ships, beaten, and given little food. About 20 percent of the people on these ships died.

3. What was the triangular trade?

_____

_____

Slavery in the Americas; Consequences of the Slave Trade (pages 569–570)

What was life like for the slaves?

Life on the plantations was harsh as well. People were sold to the highest bidder. They worked from dawn to dusk in the fields. They lived in small huts and had little food and clothing. Africans kept alive their traditional music and beliefs to try to maintain their spirits. Sometimes they rebelled. From North America to Brazil, from 1522 to the 1800s, there were small-scale slave revolts.

The Atlantic slave trade had a huge impact on both Africa and the Americas. In Africa many cultures lost generations of members. Africans began fighting Africans over the control of the slave trade.

The Africans' labor helped build the Americas. They brought skills and culture too. Many of the nations of the Americas have mixed race populations.

4. How did Africans change the Americas?

_____

_____

The Columbian Exchange and Global Trade

TERMS AND NAMES

Columbian Exchange Global transfer of foods, plants, and animals during the colonization of the Americas

capitalism Economic system based on private ownership and the investment of wealth for profit

joint-stock company Company in which people pooled their wealth for a common purpose

mercantilism Economic policy of increasing wealth and power by obtaining large amounts of gold and silver and selling more goods than are bought

favorable balance of trade Condition resulting from selling more goods than are bought

BEFORE YOU READ

In the last section, you read about the slave trade.

In this section, you will learn about other kinds of trade.

AS YOU READ

Use the chart below to take notes on the Columbian Exchange.

COLUMBIAN EXCHANGE	
Leaving the Americas	**Arriving in the Americas**
tomatoes, corn, potatoes	

The Columbian Exchange

(pages 571–573)

What was the Columbian Exchange?

There was constant movement of people and products from Europe and Africa to the Americas. The large-scale transfer of foods, plants, and animals was called the **Columbian Exchange**. Important foods such as corn and potatoes were taken from the Americas to Europe, Africa, and Asia.

Some foods moved from the Old World to the New. Bananas, black-eyed peas, and yams were taken from Africa to the Americas. Cattle, pigs, and horses had never been seen in the Americas until the Europeans brought them. Deadly illnesses also moved to the Americas. They killed a large part of the Native American population.

1. What did the Columbian Exchange take from the Americas, and what did it bring?

_____

_____

_____

Global Trade (pages 573–574)

How did business change?

The settling of the Americas and the growth of trade started an economic revolution. This revolution led to a new set of business practices still followed today. One was the rise of an economic system called **capitalism**. It is based on *private ownership* of property and the right of a business to earn a profit on money it has invested.

Another new business idea was the **joint-stock company**. In this type of company, many investors pool their money to start a business and share in the profits.

2. What is capitalism?

_____

_____

The Growth of Mercantilism
(pages 574–575)

Why were colonies important in mercantilism?

During the Commercial Revolution, European governments began to follow an idea called **mercantilism**. According to this theory, a country's power depended on its wealth. Getting more gold and silver increased a country's wealth. So did selling more goods than it bought. Selling more than it bought would result in a **favorable balance of trade.** Colonies played an important role because they provided goods that could be sold in trade.

The American colonies changed European society. Merchants grew wealthy and powerful. Towns and cities grew larger. Still, most people lived in the countryside, farmed for a living, and were poor.

3. Why were colonies important to European mercantilism?

_____

_____

Glossary   CHAPTER 20 The Atlantic World

Aztec Empire Great empire in the Valley of Mexico that had strong religious beliefs and a powerful army

descendants People who are offspring or ancestors of one family group

erupted Broke out

imported Brought into one country from another

Inca Empire Largest empire ever in the Americas, located in the Andes

plantations Large farms usually devoted to a single crop

possession Land owned by another country

private ownership Ownership by individuals instead of by groups or governments

rebellions Uprisings against the current government

AFTER YOU READ

Names and Terms

A. Write the name or term in each blank that best completes the meaning of the paragraph.

Puritans

Pilgrims

New France

New Netherland

Jamestown

colony

The first permanent **1** _____ to be established in what is now the United States was at **2** _____. Not long after a group of **3** _____ crossed the ocean and started a colony at Plymouth. They were followed by other **4** _____ who also settled in what is now Massachusetts. Settled by the English, these colonies were a kind of "New England." The empire established by France in America was called **5** _____. The empire established by the Dutch in America was called **6** _____.

B. Write the letter of the name or term that matches the description.

a. mercantilism

b. capitalism

c. middle passage

d. favorable balance of trade

e. Atlantic slave trade

_____ **1.** Buying and selling of Africans for work in the Americas

_____ **2.** Economic condition reached by selling more than is bought

_____ **3.** Economic system that encourages people to make a profit

_____ **4.** Economic policy that said a country's power depended mainly on its wealth

_____ **5.** Voyage of captured Africans to the Americas

AFTER YOU READ (continued) **CHAPTER 20** The Atlantic World

Main Ideas

1. Why did the French and British fight for control of North America, and what happened?

_____

_____

_____

2. How did Native Americans react to the colonists?

_____

_____

_____

3. Describe the middle passage of the triangular trade.

_____

_____

_____

4. What was traded in the Columbian Exchange?

_____

_____

_____

5. Name three new business practices of global trade.

_____

_____

_____

Thinking Critically

Answer the following questions on a separate sheet of paper.

1. How did Spanish conquests forever change the Americas?

2. Discuss the ways the lives of Africans and Native Americans were altered by the European conquest of the Americas.

Spain's Empire and European Absolutism

BEFORE YOU READ

In the last chapter, you read about Europe's new relationship to the Americas.

In this section, you will learn about changes occurring in Europe in the 1500s and 1600s.

AS YOU READ

Use the chart below to record reasons for change in Spain in the 16th century.

CAUSES	EFFECT
Inflation and unfair taxes hurt the poor	Spain's economy declines

A Powerful Spanish Empire

(pages 589–591)

How did Spain's power increase and then decrease?

Charles V of Spain ruled the Holy Roman Empire and other European countries. In 1556, he left the throne and split his holdings. His brother Ferdinand received Austria and the Holy Roman Empire. His son, **Philip II**, got Spain and its colonies.

Philip II *expanded* his holdings by taking control of Portugal when the king of Portugal, his uncle,

died without an heir. Philip also got its global territories in Africa, India, and the East Indies. When he tried to invade England in 1588, though, he failed. The defeat made Spain weaker. However, Spain still seemed strong because of the wealth—gold and silver—that flowed in from its colonies in the Americas.

1. Who was Philip II?

_____

_____

Golden Age of Spanish Art and Literature (pages 591–592)

How did works from the golden age of Spanish art and literature reflect the values and attitudes of the period?

Spain's great wealth allowed monarchs and nobles to become patrons of artists. Two of the greatest artists of the 16th and 17th century were El Greco and Diego Velásquez. El Greco's work reflected the faith of Spain during this period. The paintings of Velásquez reflected the pride of the Spanish monarchy.

In literature, Miguel de Cervantes wrote *Don Quixote de la Mancha,* which ushered in the birth of the modern European novel. The novel tells the story of a Spanish nobleman who reads too many books about heroic knights.

2. Who were some of the artists and writers of Spain's golden age?

_____

_____

The Spanish Empire Weakens (pages 592–593)

What weakened the Spanish Empire?

Spain's new wealth led to some serious problems. The prices of goods constantly rose. Unfair taxes kept the poor from building up any wealth of their own. As prices rose, Spaniards bought more goods from other lands. To finance their wars, Spanish kings had to borrow money from banks in foreign countries. The silver from the colonies began to flow to Spain's enemies.

In the middle of these troubles, Spain lost land. Seven *provinces* of the Spanish Netherlands rose in protest against high taxes and attempts to crush Protestantism in the Netherlands. These seven provinces were Protestant, whereas Spain was strongly Catholic. In 1579, they declared their independence from Spain and became the United Provinces of the Netherlands. The ten southern provinces (present-day Belgium) were Catholic and remained under Spanish control.

3. Why did Spain lose its power?

_____

_____

The Independent Dutch Prosper (pages 593–594)

Why did the Dutch prosper?

The United Provinces of the Netherlands was different from other European states of the time. It was a republic, not a kingdom. Each province had a leader elected by the people.

The Dutch also practiced *religious tolerance,* letting people worship as they wished. Dutch merchants established a trading empire. They had the largest fleet of merchant ships in the world. They were also the most important bankers in Europe.

4. Give two reasons for the success of the Dutch in trading.

_____

_____

Absolutism in Europe (pages 594–595)

What is absolutism?

Though he lost his Dutch possessions, Philip continued to hold tight control over Spain. He wanted to control the lives of his people. Philip and others who ruled in the same way were called **absolute monarchs**. They believed in holding all power. They also believed in **divine right**. This is the idea that a ruler receives the right to rule from God.

Widespread unrest in Europe in the 17th century led to an increase in absolute rule, or **absolutism,** and its restrictions. Absolute rulers used their increased power to impose order. They wanted to free themselves from the limitations imposed by the nobility and government bodies.

5. What did absolute monarchs believe?

_____

_____

CHAPTER 21 Section 2 (pages 596–602)

The Reign of Louis XIV

TERMS AND NAMES

Edict of Nantes Order that gave Huguenots the right to live in peace in Catholic France

Cardinal Richelieu Chief minister of France who reduced the power of the nobles

skepticism Belief that nothing could be known for certain

Louis XIV French king who was an absolute ruler

intendant Official of the French government

Jean Baptiste Colbert Chief Minister of Finance under Louis XIV

War of the Spanish Succession War fought by other European nations against France and Spain when those two states tried to unite their thrones

BEFORE YOU READ

In the last section, you were introduced to the idea of absolutism.

In this section, you will read about absolute power in France.

AS YOU READ

Use the time line below to show important events in France.

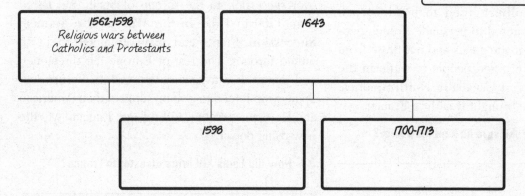

| 1562-1598 |
| Religious wars between Catholics and Protestants |

| 1643 |

| 1598 |

| 1700-1713 |

Religious Wars and Power Struggles; Writers Turn Toward Skepticism (pages 596–598)

What changes were occurring in France?

France was torn by eight religious wars between Catholics and Protestants from 1562 to 1598.

In 1589, a Protestant prince, Henry of Navarre, became King Henry IV. In 1593, he changed religions. He became a Catholic to please the majority of his people. In 1598, he issued an order called the **Edict of Nantes**. It gave Huguenots—French Protestants—the right to live in peace and have their own churches in some cities.

Henry rebuilt the French economy and brought peace to the land. He was followed by his son,

Louis XIII, a weak king. However, Louis had a very capable chief minister, **Cardinal Richelieu**. Richelieu ruled the land for Louis and increased the power of the crown.

The cardinal ordered the Huguenots not to build walls around their cities. He also said nobles had to destroy their castles. As a result, Protestants and nobles could not hide within walls to *defy* the king's power. Richelieu used people from the middle class—not nobles—to work in his government. That also reduced the power of the nobles.

French thinkers had reacted to the religious wars with horror. They developed a new philosophy called **skepticism**. Nothing could be known for certain, they argued. Doubting old ideas was the first step to learning the truth, they said.

1. How did the monarchy get stronger in France?

_____

_____

Louis XIV Comes to Power
(pages 598–599)

How did Louis XIV rule?

In 1643, **Louis XIV** became king at the age of about five. Cardinal Mazarin, who succeeded Richelieu as minister, ruled for Louis until he was 22. Louis became a powerful ruler, who had total control of France. He was determined to never let nobles challenge him.

He kept the nobles out of his government. He gave more power to government officials called **intendants** and made sure that they answered only to him. He also worked hard to increase the wealth of France. His chief minister of finance, **Jean Baptiste Colbert**, tried to build French industry. Colbert wanted to persuade French people to buy French-made goods and not those from other countries. He urged people to settle in the new French colony of Canada in North America. The fur trade there brought wealth to France.

2. How did Louis make sure he kept his power?

_____

_____

The Sun King's Grand Style; Louis Fights Disastrous Wars
(pages 599–602)

What changes did Louis make?

Louis enjoyed a life of luxury at his court. He built a huge and beautiful palace at Versailles near Paris. He also made sure that nobles had to depend on his favor to advance in society.

Louis made France the most powerful nation in Europe. France had a larger population and a bigger army than any other country. However, Louis made some mistakes that later proved costly. After winning some wars against neighboring countries, he became bolder and tried to seize more land. Other nations allied to stop France in the late 1680s. The high cost of these wars combined with poor harvests to produce problems at home in France.

The final war fought in Louis's time was fought over *succession* to the throne of Spain and lasted from 1700 to 1713. In this **War of the Spanish Succession,** France and Spain attempted to set up united thrones. The rest of Europe felt threatened and joined in war against them. Both France and Spain were forced to give up some of their American and European colonies to England. England was the new rising power.

3. How did Louis XIV bring disaster to France?

_____

_____

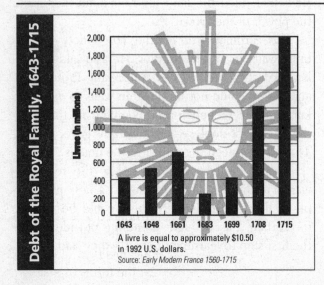

Debt of the Royal Family, 1643-1715

Livre (in millions)

2,000
1,800
1,600
1,400
1,200
1,000
800
600
400
200
0

1643 1648 1661 1683 1699 1708 1715

A livre is equal to approximately $10.50 in 1992 U.S. dollars.
Source: *Early Modern France 1560-1715*

Skillbuilder
Use the graph to answer these questions.

1. What is the general trend shown in this graph?

_____

_____

2. What was the difference in the debt, in millions of livres, between 1683 and 1715?

_____

_____

Central European Monarchs Clash

TERMS AND NAMES

Thirty Years' War Conflict over religion, territory, and power among European ruling families

Maria Theresa Empress of Austria whose main enemy was Prussia

Frederick the Great Leader of Prussia who sought to increase its territory

Seven Years' War Conflict from 1756 to 1763 in which the forces of Britain and Prussia battled those of Austria, France, Russia, and other countries.

BEFORE YOU READ

In the last section, you read how absolute power grew in France.

In this section, you will learn about absolutism in Austria and Prussia.

AS YOU READ

Use the time line below to take notes on key events in Central Europe.

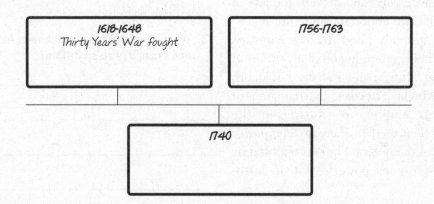

1618-1648
Thirty Years' War fought

1756-1763

1740

The Thirty Years' War (pages 603–604)

What caused the Thirty Years' War?

Germany had suffered from religious wars that ended in 1555. Rulers of each German state agreed that they would decide whether their lands would be Catholic or Protestant. Relations between sides became tense over the next decades. Then in 1618, a new war broke out and lasted for 30 terrible years. It was called the **Thirty Years' War**.

During the first half of the war, Catholic forces led by Ferdinand, the Holy Roman Emperor, won. However, Germany suffered because he allowed his large army to *loot* towns. Then the Protestant king of Sweden, Gustavus Adolphus, won several battles against him.

In the last years of the war, France helped the Protestants. Although France was a Catholic nation, Richelieu feared the growing power of the Hapsburg family, which was headed by Frederick.

The Thirty Years' War ended in 1648 with the Peace of Westphalia. It had been a disaster for Germany. About 4 million people had died, and the economy was in ruins. It took Germany two centuries to recover.

The peace treaty weakened the power of Austria and Spain. But it made France stronger. The French gained German territory. The treaty also made German princes independent of the Holy Roman Emperor. It ended religious wars in Europe. Lastly, the treaty introduced a new way of negotiating peace—a method still used today. All states involved in the fighting meet to settle the problems of a war and decide the terms of peace.

1. What were three results of the Thirty Years' War?

_____

_____

_____

_____

States Form in Central Europe

(page 605)

Who ruled Austria?

The formation of strong states took place slowly in central Europe. The economies there were less developed than in western Europe. Most people were still peasants. This region had not built an economy based on cities and commercialism. Nobles enjoyed great influence. This helped them keep the serfs on the land and prevent the rise of strong rulers. Still, two important states arose.

The Hapsburg family ruled Austria, Hungary, and Bohemia. Their empire linked many different peoples—Czechs, Hungarians, Italians, Croatians, and Germans. **Maria Theresa**, the daughter of Charles VI, was empress of Austria in the mid–1700s. She managed to increase her power and reduce that of the nobles. She was opposed by the kings of Prussia, a new powerful state in northern Germany.

2. Who were the Hapsburgs?

_____

_____

_____

_____

Prussia Challenges Austria

(pages 606–607)

What was Prussia?

Like Austria, Prussia rose to power in the late 1600s. Like the Hapsburgs of Austria, Prussia's ruling family, the Hohenzollerns, also had ambitions.

Prussia was a strong state that gave much power to its large, well-trained army. In 1740, **Frederick the Great** of Prussia invaded one of Maria Theresa's lands. Austria fought hard to keep the territory, but lost. Still, in fighting the War of the Austrian Succession, Maria Theresa managed to keep the rest of her empire *intact*.

The two sides fought again, beginning in 1756. In the **Seven Years' War**, Austria abandoned Britain, its old *ally*, for France and Russia. Prussia joined with Britain. The Prussians and British won. In that victory, Britain gained economic domination of India.

3. What effect did fighting between Austria and Prussia have on Britain?

_____

_____

_____

_____

CHAPTER 21 Section 4 (pages 608–611)

Absolute Rulers of Russia

TERMS AND NAMES

Ivan the Terrible Ruler who added lands to Russia, gave it a code of laws, and also used his secret police to execute "traitors"

boyar Russian noble who owned land

Peter the Great Important leader of Russia who started westernization

westernization Use of western Europe as a model of change

BEFORE YOU READ

In the last section, you read how Austria and Prussia became strong states.

In this section, you will learn how Russia developed into a powerful state.

AS YOU READ

Use the chart below to take notes on the changes made in Russia by Peter the Great.

```
              Peter the Great's Changes

  political        social        cultural        economic
Increased power of the
cz-ar
```

The First Czar (pages 608–609)

Who was Ivan the Terrible?

Ivan III had begun centralizing the Russian government. His son, Vasily, continued the work of adding territory to the growing Russian state. Ivan's grandson, Ivan IV, was called **Ivan the Terrible**. He came to the throne in 1533, when he was three years old.

At first, landowning nobles, known as **boyars**, tried to control Ivan. Eventually, he ruled successfully on his own. He added lands to Russia and gave the country a code of laws. After his wife, Anastasia, died, however, his rule turned harsh. He used secret police to hunt down enemies and kill them. Ivan even murdered his oldest son.

A few years after he died, Russian nobles met to name a new ruler. They chose Michael Romanov, the grandnephew of Ivan the Terrible's wife. He began the Romanov dynasty, which ruled Russia for about 300 years.

1. What good and bad did Ivan the Terrible do?

_____

_____

Peter the Great Comes to Power (page 609)

Who was Peter the Great?

The Romanovs restored order to Russia. In the late 1600s, Peter I came to power. He was called **Peter the Great** because he was one of Russia's greatest reformers. He began an intense program of trying to modernize Russia. He also continued the trend of increasing the czar's power.

When Peter came to power, Russia was still a land of boyars and serfs. Serfdom lasted much longer in Russia than it did in western Europe. It continued into the mid–1800s.

When a Russian landowner sold a piece of land, he sold the serfs with it. Landowners could give away serfs as presents or to pay debts. It was also against the law for serfs to run away from their owners.

Most boyars knew little of western Europe. But Peter admired the nations of western Europe. He traveled in Europe to learn about new technology and ways of working. It was the first time a czar traveled in the West.

2. **Why did Peter the Great visit Europe?**

_____

_____

_____

_____

Peter Rules Absolutely (pages 610–611)

What changes did *Peter the Great make?*

Peter the Great wanted Russia to be the equal of the countries of western Europe. He wanted

Russia to be strong both in its military and in its trade.

To meet these goals, Peter changed Russia. His first steps were to increase his powers, so he could force people to make the changes he wanted. He put the Russian Orthodox Church under his control. He reduced the power of nobles. He built up the army and made it better trained.

Peter also changed Russia through **westernization**. He took several steps to make Russia more western. He brought in potatoes as a new food, began Russia's first newspaper, gave more social status to women, and told the nobles to adopt Western clothes. He promoted education.

Peter also knew Russia needed a seaport that would make it easier to travel to the west. He fought a long war with Sweden to gain land along the shores of the Baltic Sea. There he built a grand new capital city, St. Petersburg. By the time of Peter's death in 1725, Russia was an important power in Europe.

3. **How did Peter the Great increase his power?**

_____

_____

_____

_____

CHAPTER 21 Section 5 (pages 614–617)

Parliament Limits the English Monarchy

BEFORE YOU READ

In the last section, you saw how power was becoming more absolute in Russia.

In this section, you will see how the power of the monarch was challenged and weakened in England.

AS YOU READ

Use the time line below to take notes on key changes in the government of England.

TERMS AND NAMES

Charles I King of England who was executed

English Civil War War fought from 1642 to 1649 between the Royalists, or Cavaliers, and the Puritan supporters of Parliament

Oliver Cromwell Leader of the Puritans

Restoration Period after the monarchy was restored in England

habeas corpus Law giving prisoners the right to obtain a document saying that the prisoner cannot go to jail without being brought before a judge

Glorious Revolution Bloodless overthrow of King James II

constitutional monarchy Government in which laws limit the monarch's power

cabinet A group of government ministers that was a link between the monarch and Parliament

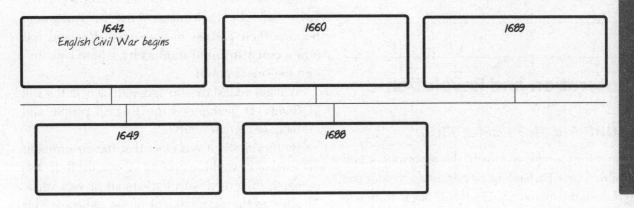

1642 English Civil War begins	1660	1689

1649	1688

Monarchs Defy Parliament

(page 614)

Why was there tension between the monarchy and Parliament?

When Queen Elizabeth I died, her cousin James, king of Scotland, became king of England. The reign of James I began a long series of struggles between king and Parliament. They fought over money. James's religious policies also angered the Puritans in Parliament. They wanted to reform the Church of England to remove any Catholic practices. James was not willing to make these changes.

During the reign of his son, **Charles I**, there was continued conflict between king and Parliament. Parliament forced Charles to sign the Petition of Right in 1628. By signing, Charles agreed that the king had to answer to Parliament. But he then *dissolved* Parliament and tried to raise money without it. This went directly against the Petition of Right.

1. How did Charles I make Parliament angry?

_____

_____

_____

English Civil War (pages 615–616)

Who fought the English Civil War?

When Charles tried to force Presbyterian Scots to follow the Anglican Church, Scotland threatened to invade England. Charles needed money to fight. When Charles called a new Parliament to get money, it quickly passed laws to limit his power. Charles responded by trying to arrest its leaders.

Soon England was fighting a civil war. Charles and his Royalists were opposed by the supporters of Parliament. Many of Parliament's supporters were Puritans.

The **English Civil War** lasted from 1642 to 1649. Under the leadership of **Oliver Cromwell,** the forces of the Puritans won. They tried and executed Charles for *treason* against Parliament. This was the first time a king had faced a public trial and execution. Cromwell became a military dictator, ruling until 1658. He crushed a rebellion in Ireland and tried to reform society at home.

2. **What happened as a result of the English Civil War?**

_____

_____

Restoration and Revolution
(page 616)

What was the Restoration?

Soon after Cromwell's death, the government collapsed. A new Parliament asked Charles's older son to restore the monarchy. Charles II began to rule in 1660. The period of his rule is called the **Restoration.**

Charles II's reign was calm. Parliament passed an important guarantee of freedom called **habeas corpus.** It gave every prisoner the right to get an order to be brought before a judge. The judge would then decide whether the prisoner should be tried or set free. This kept monarchs from putting people in jail just for opposing them. It also meant that people would not stay in jail forever without a trial.

After Charles II's death in 1685, his brother became King James II. His pro-Catholic policies angered and worried the English. They feared that he would restore Catholicism. Finally, in 1688, seven members of Parliament contacted James's older daughter, Mary, and her husband, William of Orange, prince of the Netherlands. Both were Protestants. The members of Parliament wanted William and Mary to replace James II on the throne. James was forced to flee to France. When that took place, the bloodless revolution was called the **Glorious Revolution.**

3. **Why did the Glorious Revolution take place?**

_____

_____

Limits on Monarch's Power
(page 617)

How was the power of the monarchy decreased in England?

William and Mary agreed to rule according to the laws made by Parliament. That is, Parliament became their partner in governing. England was now a **constitutional monarchy,** where laws limited the ruler's power.

William and Mary also agreed to accept the Bill of Rights. It guaranteed the English people and Parliament certain rights.

By the 1700's, it was clear that the government of England would come to a standstill if the monarch disagreed with Parliament or vice versa. This led to the development of the **cabinet**. This group of government ministers became the first link between the monarch and the majority in Parliament.

4. **What three changes gave Parliament more power in England?**

_____

_____

Name _____ Date _____

absolutism Condition that occurs when a ruler has absolute, or total, power

ally State associated with another state because it has signed a treaty or formed an alliance

defy Go against

dissolved Broken up

expanded Made bigger

intact Whole

loot Rob places that have been conquered or have experienced other disasters

provinces Political divisions, like states

religious tolerance Acceptance of more than one set of religious beliefs

succession Order in which people follow one another to the throne

treason Action to betray or overthrow government

AFTER YOU READ

Names and Terms

A. Write the name or term in each blank that best completes the meaning of the paragraph.

Glorious Revolution

English Civil War

Oliver Cromwell

Charles I

Restoration

The **1** _____ was fought from 1642 to 1649. The Puritans who supported Parliament were led by **2** _____ . They fought against the Royalists who supported **3** _____ . Although the Puritans won the war, their power did not last long. When Charles II came to the throne, the **4** _____ began. Nevertheless, the very next king to take power was overthrown. The bloodless overthrow of James II is known as the **5** _____ .

B. Write the letter of the name or term next to the description that explains it best.

a. Maria Theresa

b. Jean Baptiste Colbert

c. Frederick the Great

d. Peter the Great

e. Cardinal Richelieu

_____ **1.** Louis XIV's minister of finance

_____ **2.** Minister of France with enormous power

_____ **3.** Leader who westernized Russia

_____ **4.** Leader of Austria

_____ **5.** Leader of Prussia

AFTER YOU READ (cont.)   *CHAPTER 21*   Absolute Monarchs in Europe

Main Ideas

1. How did Spain lose some of its power?

_____

_____

_____

2. What kind of ruler was Louis XIV?

_____

_____

_____

3. How did the Thirty Years' War affect Germany?

_____

_____

_____

4. What did Peter the Great do to change Russia?

_____

_____

_____

5. How is a constitutional monarchy different from an absolute monarchy?

_____

_____

_____

Thinking Critically

Answer the following questions on a separate sheet of paper.

1. How did Richelieu and Louis XIV increase the power of the French king?

2. What are some of the events that led to the development of a constitutional monarchy in England?

CHAPTER 22 Section 1 (pages 623–628)

The Scientific Revolution

BEFORE YOU READ

In the last chapter, you learned about wars and political changes in Europe.

In this section, you will read how the Enlightenment transformed Europe and helped lead to the American Revolution.

AS YOU READ

Use the web diagram below to record important events that occurred during the Scientific Revolution.

TERMS AND NAMES

Scientific Revolution New way of thinking about the natural world based on careful observation and a willingness to question

heliocentric theory Theory that the sun is at the center of the universe

geocentric theory View which held that the earth was the center of the universe

Galileo Galilei Scientist who was forced by the Catholic Church to take back scientific ideas that disagreed with the church's view

scientific method logical procedure for gathering and ___ting ideas

Isaac Newton Scie__st who discovered laws of m__ion and gravity

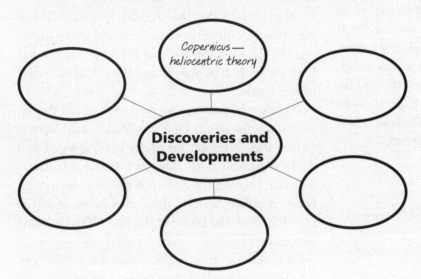

Copernicus—heliocentric theory

Discoveries and Developments

The Roots of Modern Science

(pages 623–624)

How did modern science begin?

During the Middle Ages, few scholars questioned beliefs that had been long held. Europeans based their ideas on what ancient Greeks and Romans believed or on the Bible. People still thought that the earth was the center of the universe. They believed that the sun, moon, other planets, and stars moved around it.

In the mid-1500s, attitudes began to change. Scholars started what is called the **Scientific Revolution**. It was a new way of thinking about the natural world. It was based on careful observation and the willingness to question old beliefs. European voyages of exploration helped to bring about the Scientific Revolution. When Europeans explored new lands, they saw plants and animals that ancient writers had never seen. These discoveries led to new courses of study in the universities of Europe.

1. What was the Scientific Revolution?

_____

_____

_____

A Revolutionary Model of the Universe (pages 624–625)

How did new ideas change accepted thinking in astronomy?

The first challenge to accepted thinking in science came in *astronomy*. In the early 1500s, Nicolaus Copernicus, a Polish astronomer, studied the stars and planets. He developed a **heliocentric theory.** Heliocentric meant sun-centered. It said that earth, like all the other planets, revolved around the sun. Copernicus did not publish his findings until just before his death. He had been afraid that his ideas would be attacked. They went against the long-accepted **geocentric theory.** This theory held that the earth was at the center of the universe. In the early 1600s, Johannes Kepler used mathematics to prove that Copernicus's basic idea was correct.

An Italian scientist—**Galileo Galilei**—made several discoveries that also undercut ancient ideas. He made one of the first telescopes and used it to study the planets. He found that Jupiter had moons, the sun had spots, and Earth's moon was rough. Some of his ideas about the earth, the sun, and the planets went against the teaching of the Catholic Church. Church authorities forced Galileo to take back his statements. Still, his ideas spread.

2. **What old belief about the universe did the new discoveries destroy?**

_____

_____

_____

The Scientific Method (pages 625–626)

Why was the scientific method an important development?

Interest in science led to a new approach, the **scientific method**. With this method, scientists ask a question based on something they have seen in the physical world. They form a *hypothesis*, or an attempt to answer the question. Then they test the hypothesis by making experiments or checking other facts. Finally, they change the hypothesis if needed.

The English writer Francis Bacon helped create this new approach to knowledge. He said scientists should base their thinking on what they can observe and test. The French mathematician René Descartes also influenced the use of the scientific method. His thinking was based on logic and mathematics.

3. **What thinkers helped advance the use of the scientific method?**

_____

_____

_____

Newton Explains the Law of Gravity; The Scientific Revolution Spreads (pages 626–628)

What scientific discoveries were made?

In the mid-1600s, the English scientist **Isaac Newton** described the *law of gravity*. Using mathematics, Newton showed that the same force ruled both the motion of planets and the action of bodies on the earth.

Other scientists made new tools to study the world around them. One invented a microscope. Others invented tools for understanding weather.

Doctors also made advances. One made drawings that showed the different parts of the human body. Another learned how the heart pumped blood through the body. In the late 1700s, Edward Jenner first used the process called *vaccination* to prevent disease. By giving a person the germs from a cattle disease called cowpox, he helped that person avoid getting the more serious human disease of smallpox.

Scientists made progress in chemistry as well. One questioned the old idea that things were made of only four elements—earth, air, fire, and water. He and other scientists were able to separate oxygen from air.

4. **How did the science of medicine change?**

_____

_____

_____

The Enlightenment in Europe

TERMS AND NAMES

Enlightenment Age of Reason

social contract According to Thomas Hobbes, an agreement people make with government

John Locke Philosopher who wrote about government

philosophes Social critics in France

Voltaire Writer who fought for tolerance, reason, freedom of religious belief, and freedom of speech

Montesquieu French writer concerned with government and political liberty

Rousseau Enlightenment thinker who championed freedom

Mary Wollstonecraft Author who wrote about women's rights

BEFORE YOU READ

In the last section, you read how the Scientific Revolution began in Europe.

In this section, you will learn how the Enlightenment began in Europe.

AS YOU READ

Use the chart below to take notes on important Enlightenment ideas.

THINKER	IDEA
Hobbes	social contract between people and government

Two Views on Government
(pages 629–630)

What were the views of Hobbes and Locke?

The **Enlightenment** was an *intellectual* movement. Enlightenment thinkers tried to apply reason and the scientific method to laws that shaped human actions. They hoped to build a society founded on ideas of the Scientific Revolution. Two English writers—Thomas Hobbes and John Locke—were important to this movement. They came to very different conclusions about government and human nature.

Hobbes wrote that there would be a war of "every man against every man" if there were no government. To avoid this war, Hobbes said, people formed a **social contract**. It was an agreement between people and their government. People gave up their rights to the government so they could live in a safe and orderly way. The best government, he said, is that of a strong king who can force all people to obey.

John Locke believed that people have three natural rights. They are life, liberty, and property. The purpose of government is to protect these rights. When it fails to do so, he said, people have a right to overthrow the government.

1. How were Hobbes's and Locke's views different?

The Philosophes Advocate Reason (pages 630–632)

Who were the philosophes?

French thinkers called **philosophes** had five main beliefs: (1) thinkers can find the truth by using reason; (2) what is natural is good and reasonable, and human actions are shaped by natural laws; (3) acting according to nature can bring happiness; (4) by taking a scientific view, people and society can make progress and advance to a better life; and (5) by using reason, people can gain freedom.

The most brilliant of the philosophes was the writer **Voltaire**. He fought for tolerance, reason, freedom of religious belief, and freedom of speech. Baron de **Montesquieu** wrote about separation of powers—dividing power among the separate branches of government. The third great philosophe was Jean Jacques **Rousseau**. He wrote in favor of human freedom. He wanted a society in which all people were equal. Cesare Beccaria was an Italian philosphe. He spoke out against *abuses* of justice.

2. Name the types of freedoms that Enlightenment thinkers championed.

Women and the Enlightenment; Legacy of the Enlightenment (pages 633–634)

What were Enlightenment views about individuals?

Many Enlightenment thinkers held traditional views about women's place in society. They wanted equal rights for all men but paid no attention to the fact that women did not have such rights. Some women protested this unfair situation. "If all men are born free," stated British writer **Mary Wollstonecraft**, "how is it that all women are born slaves?"

Enlightenment ideas strongly influenced the American and French Revolutions. Enlightenment thinkers also helped spread the idea of progress. By using reason, they said, it is possible to make society better. Enlightenment thinkers helped make the world less religious and more worldly. They also stressed the importance of the individual.

3. Explain the influence of Enlightenment ideas.

Major Ideas of the Enlightenment		
Idea	**Thinker**	**Impact**
Natural rights—life, liberty, property	Locke	Fundamental to U.S. Declaration of Independence
Separation of powers	Montesquieu	France, United States, Latin American nations use separation of powers in new constitutions
Freedom of thought and expression	Voltaire	Guaranteed in U.S. Bill of Rights and French Declaration of the Rights of Man and Citizen; European monarchs reduce or eliminate censorship
Abolishment of torture	Beccaria	Guaranteed in U.S. Bill of Rights; torture outlawed or reduced in nations of Europe and the Americas
Religious freedom	Voltaire	Guaranteed in U.S. Bill of Rights and French Declaration of the Rights of Man and Citizen; European monarchs reduce persecution
Women's equality	Wollstonecraft	Women's rights groups form in Europe and North America

Skillbuilder

Use the chart to answer these questions.

1. Which Enlightenment thinkers influenced the United States government?

2. Which Enlightenment ideas are in the United States Bill of Rights?

The Enlightenment Spreads

BEFORE YOU READ

In the last section, you read how Enlightenment ideas began.

In this section, you will learn about the spread of these ideas.

AS YOU READ

Use the chart below to take notes on how Enlightenment ideas were spread.

Enlightenment Ideas Spread

general knowledge	art and architecture	literature	music
The Encyclopedia gathers all known knowledge.			

A World of Ideas (page 636)

How did ideas spread from individual to individual?

In the 1700s, Paris was the cultural center of Europe. People came there from other countries to hear the new ideas of the Enlightenment. Writers and artists held social gatherings called **salons**. A woman named Marie-Thérèse Geoffrin became famous for hosting these discussions.

Geoffrin also supplied the money for one of the major projects of the Enlightenment. With her funds, Denis Diderot and other thinkers wrote and published a huge set of books called the *Encyclopedia*. Their aim was to gather all that was known about the world. The French government and officials in the Catholic Church did not like many of the ideas that were published in the *Encyclopedia*. They banned the books at first. Later, however, they changed their minds.

The ideas of the Enlightenment were spread throughout Europe by works like the *Encyclopedia* and through meetings in homes. The ideas also spread to the growing middle class. This group was becoming wealthy but had less social status than nobles. They also had very little political power. Ideas about equality sounded good to them.

1. Why were salons important?

_____

_____

_____

New Artistic Styles (page 637)

How did art and literature change?

The arts—painting, architecture, music, and literature—moved in new directions in the late 1700s. They used Enlightenment ideas of order and reason.

Earlier European painting had been very grand and highly decorated. It was a style known as **baroque**. Now styles began to change. A new simpler, yet elegant, style of painting and architecture developed. This style borrowed ideas and themes from Classical Greece and Rome. That is the reason it was called **neoclassical.**

In music, the style of the period is called classical. Three important composers of the time were Franz Joseph Haydn, Wolfgang Amadeus Mozart, and Ludwig von Beethoven. They composed music that was elegant and original. New musical forms were developed, including the sonata and the symphony.

In literature, the novel became popular. This new form presented long stories with twisting plots. It explored the thoughts and feelings of characters. A number of European authors, including women, began writing novels. These books were popular with the middle-class. They liked entertaining stories in everyday language.

2. What new styles and forms appeared in art, music, and literature?

_____

_____

_____

Enlightenment and Monarchy
(pages 638–639)

Who were the enlightened despots?

Some Enlightenment thinkers believed that the best form of government was a monarchy. In it, a ruler respected people's rights. These thinkers tried to influence rulers to rule fairly. Rulers who followed Enlightenment ideas in part but were unwilling to give up much power were called **enlightened despots**.

Frederick the Great of Prussia was an enlightened despot. He gave his people religious freedom and improved schooling. He also *reformed* the justice system. However, he did nothing to end *serfdom*, which made peasants slaves to the wealthy landowners. Joseph II of Austria did end serfdom. Once he died, though, the nobles who owned the lands were able to undo this reform.

Catherine the Great of Russia was another of the rulers influenced by Enlightenment ideas. She tried to reform Russia's laws but met resistance. She had hoped to end serfdom. But a bloody peasants' revolt persuaded her to change her mind. Instead, she gave the nobles even more power over serfs. Catherine did manage to gain new land for Russia. Russia, Prussia, and Austria agreed to divide Poland among themselves. As a result, Poland disappeared as a separate nation for almost 150 years.

3. In what way was Frederick the Great typical of an enlightened despot?

_____

_____

_____

CHAPTER 22 Section 4 (pages 640–645)

The American Revolution

BEFORE YOU READ

In the last section, you read about the spread of Enlightenment ideas in Europe.

In this section, you will learn how Enlightenment ideas influenced the American Revolution.

AS YOU READ

Use the web below to take notes on the influence of the Enlightenment on the early United States.

TERMS AND NAMES

Declaration of Independence Document declaring American independence from Britain

Thomas Jefferson Author of the Declaration of Independence

checks and balances System in which each branch of government checks, or limits, the power of the other two branches

federal system System of government in which power is divided between the national and state governments

Bill of Rights First ten amendments to the U.S. Constitution; protections of basic rights for individuals

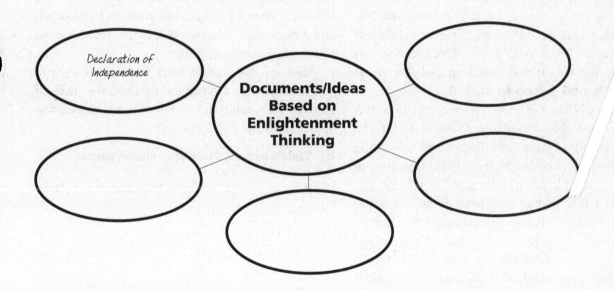

Web diagram: central oval labeled "Documents/Ideas Based on Enlightenment Thinking" connected to surrounding ovals, one labeled "Declaration of Independence".

Britain and Its American Colonies (page 640)

How were the colonies governed?

The British colonies in North America grew in population and wealth during the 1700s. Population went from about 250,000 in 1700 to 2,150,000 in 1770. Economically, they prospered on trade with the nations of Europe. The 13 colonies also had a kind of self-government. People in the colonies began to see themselves less and less as British subjects. Still, Parliament passed laws that governed the colonies. One set of laws banned trade with any nation other than Britain.

1. How did the colonists' image of themselves clash with their status as colonists?

_____

_____

Americans Win Independence
(pages 641–643)

What caused Britain and America to grow apart?

The high cost of the French and Indian War led Parliament to pass laws that put taxes on the colonists. The colonists became very angry. They had never before paid taxes directly to the British government. They said that the taxes *violated* their rights. Since Parliament had no members from the colonies, they said, Parliament had no right to tax them.

The colonists met the first tax, passed in 1765, with a *boycott* of British goods. Their refusal to buy British products was very effective. It forced Parliament to *repeal* the law.

Over the next decade, the colonists and Britain grew further apart. Some colonists wanted to push the colonies to independence. They took actions that caused Britain to act harshly. Eventually, the conflict led to war. Representatives of the colonies met in a congress and formed an army. In July 1776, they announced that they were independent of Britain. They issued the **Declaration of Independence**. It was based on Enlightenment ideas. **Thomas Jefferson** wrote it.

From 1775 to 1781, the colonies and the British fought a war in North America. The colonists had a poorly equipped army, and Britain was one of the most powerful nations in the world. However, in the end, the colonies won their independence.

The British people grew tired of the cost of the war and pushed Parliament to agree to a peace. The Americans were also helped greatly by aid from France. In 1783, the two sides signed a treaty. In it, Britain recognized the independent United States of America.

2. Name some of the steps that led to the American Revolution.

_____

_____

_____

_____

Americans Create a Republic
(pages 644–645)

What are some fundamental ideas in the U.S. Constitution?

The 13 states formed a new government under the Article of Confederation. This government was very weak. States held all the power and the central government had little. This proved unworkable. In 1787, American leaders met again. They wrote a new framework of government.

The Constitution of the United States drew on many Enlightenment ideas. It used Montesquieu's idea of separation of powers into three branches of government. Through a system of **checks and balances**, each branch was able to prevent other branches from abusing their power. The Constitution also set up a **federal system**. Under this system, power was divided between national and state governments.

The Constitution also used Locke's idea of putting power in the hands of the people. It used Voltaire's ideas to protect the right to free speech and freedom of religion. It used Beccaria's ideas about a fair system of justice.

Many of these rights were ensured in a set of additions to the Constitution called the **Bill of Rights.** The inclusion of a bill of rights helped win approval for the Constitution.

3. Explain how the Constitution divides power.

_____

_____

_____

_____

Glossary   CHAPTER 22 Enlightenment and Revolution

abuses Improper uses, misuses

astronomy Study of the universe beyond the earth

boycott Organized refusal to buy a certain good or participate in a certain action

hypothesis Attempt to answer a question that needs to be proven or disproven

intellectual Related to thinking or to the mind

law of gravity Idea linking motion in the heavens with motion on the Earth and based on the principle that every object attracts every other object

reformed Changed for the better

repeal Take back a law

serfdom State or condition of using workers as slaves

vaccination Introduction of weakened or killed viruses or bacteria into the body to protect against a specific disease

violated Went against

AFTER YOU READ

Terms and Names

A. Write the term or name in each blank that best completes the meaning of the paragraph.

Isaac Newton

heliocentric theory

Scientific Revolution

geocentric theory

Galileo Galilei

    Many thinkers contributed to the significant changes in scientific thinking known as the **1** _____. In astronomy, Nicolaus Copernicus first developed the idea that the earth revolved around the sun. This became known as the **2** _____. It refuted the earth-centered view of the universe, know as the **3** _____. A great pioneer in science at this time was **4** _____. He described the law of gravity. Another significant figure was **5** _____, who ended up having to recant his theories before a papal court.

B. Write the letter of the name or term next to the description that explains it best.

a. Mary Wollstonecraft

b. John Locke

c. Montesquieu

d. Thomas Jefferson

e. Voltaire

____ **1.** Philosopher who said people have natural rights

____ **2.** Thinker known for ideas about separation of powers

____ **3.** Writer who championed freedom of speech and freedom of religion

____ **4.** Writer who championed women's rights

____ **5.** Author of the Declaration of Independence

AFTER YOU READ (cont.) *CHAPTER 22* Enlightenment and Revolution

Main Ideas

1. How did European exploration help lead the way to the Scientific Revolution?

_____

_____

_____

2. Who were the philosophes, and what did they believe in?

_____

_____

_____

3. What was one of Montesquieu's key ideas about government?

_____

_____

_____

4. How did the arts change as a result of the Enlightenment?

_____

_____

_____

5. How did the government of the United States reflect Enlightenment ideas?

_____

_____

_____

Thinking Critically

Answer the following questions on a separate sheet of paper.

1. How was the Scientific Revolution related to the Enlightenment?

2. How did monarchs react to Enlightenment ideas?

The French Revolution Begins

BEFORE YOU READ

In the last chapter, you read about the Enlightenment and the American Revolution.

In this section, you will learn about the beginning of the French Revolution.

AS YOU READ

Use this chart to take notes on the causes and effects of the early stages of the French Revolution.

TERMS AND NAMES

Old Regime System of feudalism

estate Social class of people

Louis XVI Weak king who came to French throne in 1774

Marie Antoinette Unpopular queen; wife of Louis XVI

Estates-General Assembly of representatives from all three estates

National Assembly French congress established by representatives of the Third Estate

Tennis Court Oath Promise made by Third Estate representatives to draw up a new constitution

Great Fear Wave of panic

Causes

Old regime—society unequal

Dawn of the Revolution

Effects

The Old Order (pages 651–652)

How was French society unequal?

In the 1700s, France was the leading country of Europe. It was the center of the new ideas of the Enlightenment. However, beneath the surface there were major problems. Soon the nation would be torn by a violent revolution.

One problem was that people were not treated equally in French society. A political and social system called the **Old Regime** remained in place. The French were divided into three classes, or **estates.** The *First Estate* consisted of the Roman Catholic clergy. The *Second Estate* was made up of nobles. Only about 2 percent of the people belonged to these two estates. Yet they owned 20 percent of the land. They had easy lives.

Everybody else belonged to the *Third Estate.* This huge group included three types of people:

- the *bourgeoisie*—mostly well-off merchants and skilled workers who lacked the status of nobles
- city workers—cooks, servants, and others who were poorly paid and often out of work
- peasants—farm workers, making up more than 80 percent of the French people

Members of the Third Estate were angry. They had few rights. They paid up to half of their income in taxes, while the rich paid almost none.

1. What were the three classes of French society?

_____

_____

_____

The Forces of Change (pages 652–653)

Why were the French ready for the revolution?

Three factors led to revolution. First, the Enlightenment spread the idea that everyone should be equal. The powerless people in the Third Estate liked that. Second, the French economy was failing. High taxes kept profits low, and food supplies were short. The government owed money. Third, King **Louis XVI** was a weak leader. His wife, **Marie Antoinette,** was unpopular. She was from Austria, France's long-time enemy, and was noted for her extravagant spending.

In the 1780s, France was deep in debt. Louis tried to tax the nobles. Instead, they forced the king to call a meeting of the **Estates-General,** an assembly of *delegates* of the three estates.

2. What three factors led to revolution?

_____

_____

_____

Dawn of the Revolution (pages 654–655)

How did the Revolution begin?

The meeting of the Estates-General began in May 1789 with arguments over how to count votes. In the past, each estate had cast one vote. The Third Estate now wanted each delegate to have a vote. The king and the other estates did not agree to the plan because the Third Estate was larger and would have more votes.

The Third Estate then broke with the others and met separately. In June 1789, its delegates voted to rename themselves the **National Assembly.** They claimed to represent all the people. This was the beginning of *representative government* for France.

At one point, the members of the Third Estate found themselves locked out of their meeting. They broke down a door leading to a tennis court. Then they promised to stay there until they made a new constitution. This promise was called the **Tennis Court Oath.**

Louis tried to make peace. He ordered the clergy and nobles to join the National Assembly. However, trouble erupted. Rumors flew that foreign soldiers were going to attack French citizens. On July 14, an angry crowd captured the *Bastille,* a Paris prison. The *mob* wanted to get gunpowder for their weapons in order to defend the city.

3. Why did the National Assembly form?

_____

_____

_____

A Great Fear Sweeps France (page 655)

What was the Great Fear?

A wave of violence called the **Great Fear** swept the country. Peasants broke into and burned nobles' houses. They tore up documents that had forced them to pay fees to the nobles. Late in 1789, a mob of women marched from Paris to the king's palace at *Versailles.* They were angry about high bread prices and demanded that the king come to Paris. They hoped he would end hunger in the city. The king and queen left Versailles, never to return.

4. What happened during the Great Fear?

_____

_____

_____

CHAPTER 23   Section 2 (pages 656–662)

Revolution Brings Reform and Terror

BEFORE YOU READ

In the last section, you read how the French Revolution began.

In this section, you will learn what course it took and where it led.

AS YOU READ

Use the time line below to take notes on major events.

TERMS AND NAMES

Legislative Assembly Assembly that replaced the National Assembly in 1791

émigrés Nobles and others who left France during the peasant uprisings and who hoped to come back to restore the old system

sans-culottes Radical group of Parisian wage-earners

Jacobin Member of the Jacobin Club, a radical political organization

guillotine Machine for beheading people

Maximilien Robespierre Revolutionary leader who tried to wipe out every trace of France's past monarchy and nobility

Reign of Terror Period of Robespierre's rule

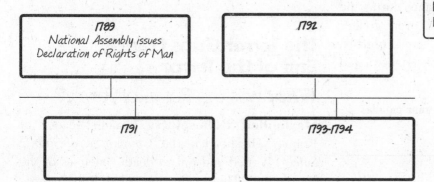

1789
National Assembly issues Declaration of Rights of Man

1792

1791

1793-1794

The Assembly Reforms France
(pages 656–657)

What reforms resulted from the revolution?

In August 1789, the National Assembly took steps to change France. It made a revolutionary statement called the *Declaration of the Rights of Man*. One new law ended all the special rights that members of the First and Second Estates had enjoyed. Another law gave all French men equal rights. Though women did not get these rights, it was a bold step. Other laws gave the state power over the Catholic Church.

The new laws about the church divided people who had supported the Revolution. Catholic peas-
ants remained loyal to the church. They were angry that the church would be part of the state. Thereafter, many of them opposed the Revolution's reforms.

For months, the assembly worked on plans for a new government. During this time, Louis was fearful for his safety. One night, he and his family tried to escape the country. They were caught, brought back to Paris, and placed under guard. This escape attempt made the king and queen more unpopular. It also increased the power of his enemies.

1. What new laws came into being?

_____

_____

_____

Divisions Develop (pages 657–658)

What groups called for different kinds of changes?

In the fall of 1791, the assembly drew up a new constitution. It took away most of the king's power. The assembly then turned over its power to a new assembly, the **Legislative Assembly.**

This new assembly soon divided into groups. *Radicals* wanted sweeping changes in the way government was run. Moderates wanted some changes in government, but not as many as the radicals. *Conservatives* upheld the idea of a limited monarchy and wanted few changes in government.

There were groups outside the Legislative Assembly who wanted to influence the government, too. One group wanted an end to revolutionary changes. This group included the **émigrés,** nobles and others who had fled France during the uprisings. Another group wanted even greater changes. This group included the **sans-culottes.** These wage-earners and small shopkeepers wanted a greater voice in government.

2. In what ways did the émigrés and sans-culottes have opposite goals?

_____

_____

War and Execution
(pages 658–660)

What caused the French people to take extreme measures?

At the same time, France faced serious trouble on its borders. Kings in other countries feared that revolution would spread to their lands. They wanted to use force to restore control of France to Louis XVI. Soon foreign soldiers were marching toward Paris. Many people thought that the king and queen were ready to help the enemy. Angry French citizens imprisoned them. Many nobles were killed in other mob actions.

The government took strong steps to meet the danger from foreign troops. It took away all the king's powers. In 1792, the National Convention—another new government—was formed. **Jacobins,** members of a radical political club, soon took control of this new government. They declared Louis a common citizen. He was then tried for treason and convicted. Like many others, the king was beheaded by a machine called the **guillotine.** The National Convention also ordered thousands of French people into the army.

3. What happened to the king?

_____

_____

The Terror Grips France; End of the Terror (pages 660–661)

What was the Reign of Terror?

Maximilien Robespierre became leader of France. He headed the *Committee of Public Safety.* It tried and put to death "enemies of the Revolution." Thousands were killed. Robespierre's rule, which began in 1793, was called the **Reign of Terror.** It ended in July 1794, when Robespierre himself was put to death.

The French people were tired of the killing and the unrest. They wanted a return to order. Moderate leaders drafted a new, less revolutionary plan of government.

4. Where did the Reign of Terror lead?

_____

_____

Napoleon Forges an Empire

BEFORE YOU READ

In the last section, you read about the Revolution's extremes, including the Reign of Terror.

In this section, you will learn how Napoleon grabbed power and brought order to France.

AS YOU READ

Use the time line below to take notes on Napoleon's changing power.

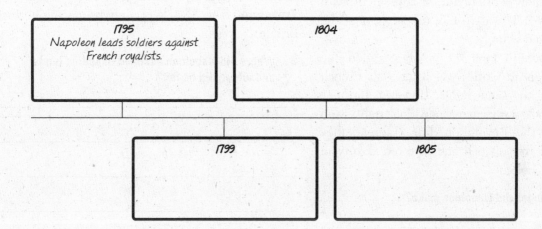

1795
Napoleon leads soldiers against French royalists.

1804

1799

1805

Napoleon Seizes Power
(pages 663–664)

How did Napoleon rise to power?

Napoleon Bonaparte was born in 1769 on the Mediterranean island of Corsica. When he was nine years old, his parents sent him to military school. In 1785, he finished school and became an artillery officer. When the revolution broke out, Napoleon joined the army of the new government.

In 1795, Napoleon led soldiers against French *royalists* who were attacking the National Convention. For this, he was thought of as the savior of the French republic.

By 1799, the unsettled French government had lost the people's support. In a bold move, Napoleon used troops to seize control of the government. This was a **coup d'état**, or a sudden takeover of power. Napoleon then assumed dictatorial powers.

1. How did Napoleon get control of the government?

_____

_____

_____

Napoleon Rules France (pages 664–665)

How did Napoleon use the Revolution's ideas in his government?

Napoleon pretended to be the rightfully elected leader of France. In 1800, a **plebiscite,** or vote of the people, was held to approve a new constitution. The people voted for it overwhelmingly, and Napoleon took power as first consul.

Napoleon made several changes that were meant to build on the Revolution's good ideas:

1. He made tax collection more fair and orderly. As a result, the government could count on a steady supply of money.
2. He removed dishonest government workers.
3. He started **lycées**—new public schools for ordinary citizens.
4. He gave the church back some of its power. He signed a **concordat,** or agreement, with the pope. This gave him the support of the organized church.
5. He wrote a new set of laws, called the **Napoleonic Code,** which gave all French citizens the same rights. However, the new laws took away many individual rights won during the Revolution. For example, they limited free speech and restored slavery in French colonies.

2. What changes did Napoleon make?

_____

_____

_____

_____

Napoleon Creates an Empire
(pages 665–667)

What goals did Napoleon have beyond France's borders?

Napoleon had hoped to make his empire larger in both Europe and the New World. In 1801, he had sent soldiers to retake the island of present-day Haiti. Slaves in that colony had seized power during a civil war. But his troops failed. Napoleon then gave up on his New World plans. In 1803, he sold the largest part of France's North American land— the huge Louisiana Territory—to the United States.

Napoleon had been stopped in the Americas. So he then moved to add to his power in Europe. In 1804, he made himself *emperor* of France. He took control of the Austrian Netherlands, parts of Italy, and Switzerland. Napoleon's only loss during this time was to the British navy in the **Battle of Trafalgar.** This loss kept him from conquering Britain.

3. Where did Napoleon succeed in adding lands, and where did he fail?

_____

_____

_____

_____

_____

Napoleon's Empire Collapses

BEFORE YOU READ

In the last section, you read how Napoleon built his power. In this section, you learn why he lost it.

AS YOU READ

Use the chart below to take notes on mistakes Napoleon made.

TERMS AND NAMES

blockade Forced closing of ports

Continental System Napoleon's policy of preventing trade and communication between Great Britain and other European nations

guerrilla Spanish peasant fighter

Peninsular War War that Napoleon fought in Spain

scorched-earth policy Policy of burning fields and slaughtering livestock so that enemy troops would find nothing to eat

Waterloo Battle in Belgium that was Napoleon's final defeat

Hundred Days Napoleon's last bid for power, which ended at Waterloo

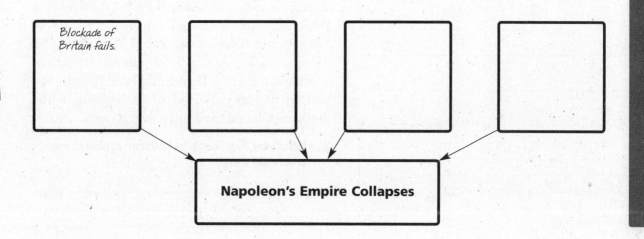

Blockade of Britain fails.

Napoleon's Empire Collapses

Napoleon's Costly Mistakes

(pages 668–670)

What mistakes did Napoleon make abroad?

Napoleon's own personality posed a threat to his empire. His love of power pushed him to expand his empire. His efforts to extend French rule led to his empire's collapse.

Napoleon made three costly mistakes. His first mistake was caused by his desire to crush Britain. He wanted to hurt the British economy. So in 1806 he ordered a **blockade.** This was an effort to stop

all trade between Britain and the other European nations. Napoleon called this policy the **Continental System.** It was supposed to make continental Europe more self-sufficient.

The effort failed because some Europeans secretly brought in British goods. At the same time, the British put their own blockade around Europe. Because the British navy was so strong, it worked well. Soon the French economy, along with others on the European continent, weakened.

Napoleon's second mistake was to make his brother king of Spain in 1808. The Spanish people were loyal to their own king. With help from

Britain, bands of peasant fighters called **guerrillas** fought Napoleon for five years. Napoleon lost 300,000 troops during this **Peninsular War.** (The war gets its name from the Iberian Peninsula on which Spain is located.)

Napoleon's third mistake was perhaps his worst. In 1812, he tried to conquer Russia, far to the east. He entered Russia with more than 400,000 soldiers. As the Russians retreated, however, they followed a **scorched-earth policy.** They burned their fields and killed their livestock so Napoleon's armies could not eat what they left behind.

Although the French got as far as Moscow, winter was coming. Napoleon was forced to order his soldiers to head back. On the way home, bitter cold, hunger, and Russian attacks killed thousands. Thousands more *deserted*. By the time Napoleon's army left Russian territory, only 10,000 of his soldiers were able to fight.

1. **What happened to Napoleon in Russia?**

_____

_____

_____

_____

_____

Napoleon's Downfall (pages 670–671)

What other defeats did Napoleon suffer?

Other leaders saw that Napoleon was now weaker. Britain, Russia, Prussia, Sweden, and Austria joined forces and attacked France. Napoleon was defeated at the Battle of Leipzig, in Germany, in 1813. In 1814, Napoleon gave up his throne and was exiled, or sent away, to the tiny island of Elba off the Italian coast.

Louis XVIII took the throne in Paris. But he quickly became unpopular. The peasants feared the new king would undo the land reforms of the Revolution.

News of Louis XVIII's trouble was all Napoleon needed to try to regain his empire. In March 1815, he escaped from Elba and boldly returned to France. He took power and raised another army.

The rest of the European powers raised armies to fight against Napoleon. Led by the Duke of Wellington, they defeated Napoleon in his final battle near a Belgian town called **Waterloo.** This defeat ended Napoleon's last attempt at power, which was called the **Hundred Days.** He was then sent to the far-off island of St. Helena in the southern Atlantic Ocean. He died there in 1821.

2. **What was Napoleon's last attempt at power, and where did it end?**

_____

_____

_____

_____

CHAPTER 23 Section 5 (pages 672–675)

The Congress of Vienna

TERMS AND NAMES

Congress of Vienna Meetings in Vienna for the purpose of restoring order to Europe

Klemens von Metternich Key leader at the Congress of Vienna

balance of power Condition in which no one country becomes a threat to the other

legitimacy Bringing back to power the kings that Napoleon had driven out

Holy Alliance League formed by Russia, Austria, and Prussia

Concert of Europe Series of alliances to help prevent revolution

BEFORE YOU READ

In the last section, you saw how Napoleon's empire collapsed.

In this section, you will learn how the rest of Europe reacted to both the French Revolution and Napoleon's rise and fall.

AS YOU READ

Use the chart below to take notes on the ways that leaders and people of other nations were affected by the ideas and results of the French Revolution.

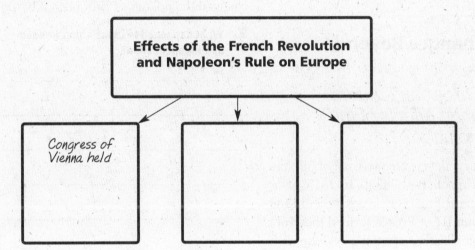

Effects of the French Revolution and Napoleon's Rule on Europe

Congress of Vienna held

Metternich's Plans for Europe
(pages 672–673)

What was the Congress of Vienna?

In 1814, leaders of many nations met to draw up a peace plan for Europe. This series of meetings was called the **Congress of Vienna.** The most important person at the Congress of Vienna was the foreign minister of Austria, **Klemens von Metternich.** He shaped the peace conditions that were finally accepted.

Metternich had three goals at the congress. First, he wanted to make sure that the French would not attack another country again. Second, he wanted a **balance of power** in which no one nation was strong enough to threaten other nations. Third, he wanted **legitimacy.** This meant restoring monarchs to the thrones they had before Napoleon's conquests. The other leaders agreed with Metternich's ideas.

Metternich achieved his first goal when the congress strengthened the small nations that surrounded France. Meanwhile, France was not punished too severely. It remained independent and kept some overseas possessions. This helped achieve Metternich's second goal to create a balance of power.

The congress also worked to fulfill Metternich's third goal. Many rulers were returned to power in states throughout Europe, including France.

The Congress of Vienna created very successful peace agreements. None of the great powers fought against one another 40 years. Some did not fight in a war for the rest of the century.

1. What three goals did Metternich have?

_____

_____

_____

_____

Political Changes Beyond Vienna (pages 673–675)

How did European leaders respond to the effects of the French Revolution?

Many European rulers were nervous about the effects of the French Revolution. In 1815, Czar Alexander, Emperor Francis I of Austria, and King Frederick William III of Prussia formed the **Holy Alliance.** Other alliances created by Metternich

were called the **Concert of Europe.** The idea of these alliances was for nations to help one another if revolution came.

Across Europe, conservatives held control of European governments. Conservatives were people who opposed the ideals of the French Revolution. They also usually supported the rights and powers of royalty. They did not encourage individual liberties. They did not want any calls for equal rights.

But many other people still believed in the ideals of the French Revolution. They thought that all people should be equal and share in power. Later they would again fight for these rights.

People in the Americas also felt the desire for freedom. Spanish colonies in the Americas revolted against the restored Spanish king. Many colonies won independence from Spain. National feeling grew in Europe, too. Soon people in areas such as Italy, Germany, and Greece would rebel and form new nations. The French Revolution had changed the politics of Europe and beyond.

2. What happened to ideas about freedom and independence?

_____

_____

_____

_____

_____

Name _____ Date _____

Bastille Paris prison

bourgeoisie Well-off merchants and skilled workers

Committee of Public Safety Committee led by Robespierre that tried "enemies of the Revolution" and had them executed

conservatives Those favoring established or traditional ways of governing

Declaration of the Rights of Man Revolutionary statement guaranteeing rights such as liberty and property

delegates Representatives

deserted Left without permission; ran away

emperor Absolute ruler

First Estate Class made up of Roman Catholic clergy

mob Unpredictable crowd that acts as a single body

radicals Revolutionaries; people with extreme political views

representative government Government in which lawmakers represent the will of the people

royalists Supporters of the monarchy

Second Estate Class made up of nobles

stability Order; safety and security

Third Estate All merchants, skilled workers, city workers, and peasants

Versailles Site of the extremely luxurious palace of the kings of France

AFTER YOU READ

Terms and Names

A. Write the name or term in each blank that best completes the meaning of the paragraph.

National Assembly

Estates-General

Tennis Court Oath

Old Regime

estates

Before the revolution in France, a system known as the **1** _____ was in place. In this system, the French were divided into three **2** _____. These groups were unequal. In 1789, the king called these groups together in the **3** _____. Shortly after, the lowest of these groups renamed itself the **4** _____. Members of this gathering took the **5** _____, pledging not to leave until they had written a new constitution.

B. Write the letter of the name or term next to the description that explains it best.

a. Jacobins

b. Continental System

c. Congress of Vienna

d. Concert of Europe

e. Hundred Days

_____ **1.** Napoleon's policy of cutting Britain off from the rest of Europe

_____ **2.** Napoleon's last attempt at power

_____ **3.** Members of a radical political organization, such as Jean-Paul Marat and Georges Danton

_____ **4.** Series of alliances to protect European nations against revolutions

_____ **5.** Meeting of European nations to decide the fate of Europe after Napoleon

AFTER YOU READ (cont.)   CHAPTER 23   The French Revolution and Napoleon

Main Ideas

1. What problems led to the French Revolution?

_____

_____

_____

2. What happened during Robespierre's reign in France?

_____

_____

_____

3. What did Napoleon do to bring back order in France?

_____

_____

_____

4. What costly mistakes did Napoleon make in Spain and Russia?

_____

_____

_____

5. What important ideas did Metternich bring to the Congress of Vienna?

_____

_____

_____

Thinking Critically

Answer the following questions on a separate piece of paper.

1. In what ways did the revolution in France create divisions instead of uniting people in a common goal?

2. Why did Napoleon's empire collapse?

Latin American Peoples Win Independence

BEFORE YOU READ

In the last section, you read about revolution and the Congress of Vienna.

In this section, you will learn how Latin American countries got their independence.

AS YOU READ

Use the time line below to take notes on when each country got its independence.

TERMS AND NAMES

peninsulares Latin Americans born in Spain

creoles Spaniards born in Latin America

mulattos Africans or people of mixed European and African ancestry

Simón Bolívar Leader of Venezuelan independence movement

José de San Martín Leader who helped win independence for Chile and Argentina

Miguel Hidalgo Priest who began the revolt against Spanish rule in Mexico

José Morelos Leader of the Mexican revolt after Hidalgo was defeated

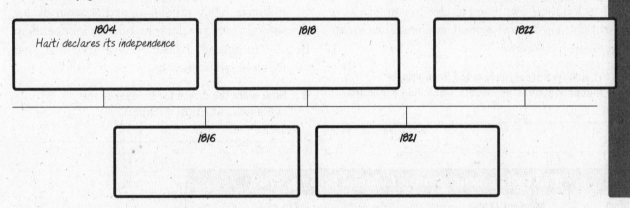

1804
Haiti declares its independence

1818

1822

1816

1821

Colonial Society Divided (pages 681–682)

What classes existed in Latin American society?

In Latin America, society was divided into six classes of people. ***Peninsulares***—those born in Spain—were at the top. Next were **creoles,** or Spaniards who had been born in Latin America. Below them were *mestizos*. Mestizos had mixed European and Indian ancestry. Next were **mulattos,** with mixed European and African ancestry, and then Africans. At the bottom were Indians.

1. **Which groups of society were of European ancestry?**

_____

_____

Revolutions in the Americas

(page 682)

Where in Latin America was independence first declared?

In the early 1800s, colonial peoples in Latin America fought for independence. The French colony of Saint Domingue was the first Latin American colony to fight for independence.

Almost all of the people who lived in the French colony were slaves of African origin. In 1791, about 100,000 of them rose in revolt. Toussaint L'Ouverture, a former slave, became their leader. In 1802 Napoleon sent troops to the island to end the rebellion. They failed. In 1804, the colony declared its independence as Haiti.

2. **How did Haiti become independent?**

_____

_____

Creoles Lead Independence

(pages 682–684)

Why did Creoles want independence?

Creoles felt that they were not treated fairly. This bad feeling boiled over when Napoleon overthrew the king of Spain and named his own brother as king. Creoles in Latin America had no loyalty to the new king. They revolted. Even after the old king was restored, they did not give up their fight for freedom.

Two leaders pushed much of South America to independence. **Simón Bolívar** was a writer, fighter, and political thinker. He survived defeats and *exile* to help win independence for Venezuela in 1821. **José de San Martín** helped win independence for Argentina in 1816 and Chile in 1818. Bolívar led their combined armies to a great victory in 1824. This victory gained independence for all the Spanish colonies.

3. Which two great leaders led the fights for independence in Venezuela, Chile, and Argentina?

_____

Mexico Ends Spanish Rule; Brazil's Royal Liberator (pages 685–686)

How did Mexico and Brazil achieve independence?

In Mexico, mestizos and Indians led the fight for independence. In 1810, **Miguel Hidalgo,** a village priest, called for a revolt against Spanish rule. Creoles united with the Spanish government to put down this revolt by the lower classes.

Hidalgo lost, but Padre **José María Morelos** took over leadership of the rebels. Fighting continued until 1815, when the creoles won.

After a revolution in Spain put a new government to power, the creoles joined with the other groups fighting for independence. In 1821, Mexico won its independence. In 1823, the region of Central America separated itself from Mexico.

In Brazil, 8,000 creoles signed a paper asking the son of Portugal's king to rule an independent Brazil. He agreed. Brazil became free that year through a bloodless revolt.

4. How were the drives for independence in Mexico and Brazil different?

_____

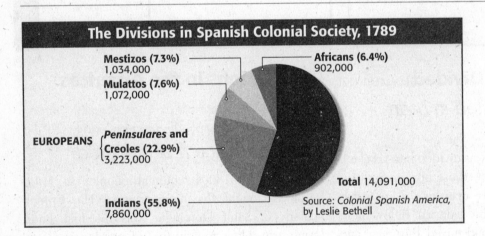

The Divisions in Spanish Colonial Society, 1789

Mestizos (7.3%) 1,034,000

Mulattos (7.6%) 1,072,000

EUROPEANS *Peninsulares* and Creoles (22.9%) 3,223,000

Africans (6.4%) 902,000

Indians (55.8%) 7,860,000

Total 14,091,000

Source: *Colonial Spanish America,* by Leslie Bethell

Skillbuilder

Use the chart above to answer these questions.

1. Comparing What were the largest and smallest groups in society?

_____

2. Comparing How many more Indians were in Spanish society than Africans?

_____

228 CHAPTER 24   SECTION 1

Europe Faces Revolutions

BEFORE YOU READ

In the last section, you read about Latin American independence movements.

In this section, you will learn about revolutions in Europe.

AS YOU READ

Use the web below to show changes that occurred in Europe at this time.

> **TERMS AND NAMES**
>
> **conservative** People who supported the monarchy
>
> **liberal** People who wanted to give more power to elected legislatures
>
> **radical** People who wanted to end the rule by kings and give full voting rights to all people
>
> **nationalism** Belief that a person's loyalty belongs to the nation itself instead of to the nation's ruler
>
> **nation-state** Country with its own independent government
>
> **the Balkans** Region including all or part of present-day Greece, Albania, Bulgaria, Romania, Turkey, and former Yugoslavia
>
> **Louis-Napoleon** Winner of the presidential election in France in 1848; later emperor
>
> **Alexander II** Ruler of Russia who freed the serfs

```
    Greece                France
 Wins self-rule
 from the Ottomans
                                           Russia

             Changes in
              Europe
```

Clash of Philosophies; Nationalism Develops (pages 687–689)

What forces and peoples struggled for power?

There was a power struggle in Europe in the first half of the 1800s. Three forces were involved. **Conservatives** wanted to continue to support the kings who had ruled these lands for many centuries. These were nobles and other people who owned large amounts of property. **Liberals** wanted to give more power to elected *legislatures*. They were typically middle-class merchants and business people. They wanted to limit voting rights to people who were educated and owned property. **Radicals** wanted the end of rule by kings and full voting rights for all people.

At the same time, another movement arose in Europe—**nationalism.** This was the belief that a person's loyalty should go not to the country's ruler but to the nation itself. When the nation also had its own independent government, it became a **nation-state.** Nationalists thought that people with a common language and culture were a nation. And they had the right to their own government. These ideas grew out of the French Revolution.

1. What different goals did conservatives, liberals, and radicals have?

_____

_____

_____

_____

Nationalists Challenge Conservative Power (pages 689–690)

What changes were occurring in Western Europe?

The first people to win self-rule during this period were the Greeks. Greece had been part of the Ottoman Empire for centuries. The Ottomans controlled most of **the Balkans.** That region includes most of modern Greece, Albania, Bulgaria, Romania, Turkey, and the former Yugoslavia. In 1821, the Greeks revolted against Turkish rule. The Greeks won their independence by 1830.

Other revolts broke out in other parts of Europe. In 1830, the Belgians declared their independence from rule by the Dutch. Nationalists began a long struggle to *unify* all of Italy. The Poles revolted against Russian rule. Conservatives managed to put down these rebellions. However, new ones broke out again in 1848 among Hungarians and Czechs. Once again, they were put down forcibly.

2. What groups challenged conservative rule?

_____

_____

Radicals Change France (page 690)

Why did French radicals lose?

Events differed in France. Riots in 1830 forced the king to *flee*, and a new king was put in his place. Another revolt broke out in 1848. The king was overthrown and a republic established. However, the radicals who had won this victory began arguing. They differed over how much France should be changed. Some wanted only political changes. Others wanted social and economic changes that would help the poor.

When these forces began to fight in the streets, the French gave up on the radical program. They introduced a new government. It had a legislature and a strong president. The new president was **Louis-Napoleon,** Napoleon Bonaparte's nephew. He later named himself emperor of France. He built railroads and helped industry. The economy got better and more people had jobs.

3. What did Louis-Napoleon accomplish for France?

_____

_____

Reform in Russia (pages 690–691)

How did Alexander II change Russia?

In the early 1800s, Russia still did not have an industrial economy. The biggest problem was that serfdom still existed there. Peasants were bound to the nobles whose land they worked. Russia's rulers were reluctant to free the serfs, though. They feared they would lose the support of the nobles.

A new ruler of Russia, **Alexander II,** decided to free the serfs. Though it seemed bold, Alexander's move went only part way. Nobles kept half their land and were paid for the other half that went to the peasants. The former serfs were not given the land. They had to pay for it. This debt kept them still tied to the land. The *czar's* efforts to make changes ended when he was assassinated in 1881. Alexander III, the new czar, brought back tight control over the country. He also moved to make the economy more industrial.

4. What major reform was made in Russia at this time?

_____

_____

_____

Nationalism

Case Study: Italy and Germany

BEFORE YOU READ

In the last section, you read about revolutions and reform in western Europe.

In this section, you will learn about nationalism.

AS YOU READ

Use a chart like the one below to take notes on the effects of nationalism.

Divided Empires

Austrian Empire

Effects of Nationalism

Unified Nations

Nationalism: A Force for Unity or Disunity (pages 692–693)

What is nationalism?

Nationalists thought that many factors linked people to one another. First was nationality, or a common *ethnic* ancestry. Shared language, culture, history, and religion were also seen as ties that connected people. People sharing these traits were thought to have the right to a land they could call their own. Groups with their own government were called nation-states.

Leaders began to see that this feeling could be a powerful force for uniting a people. The French Revolution was a prime example of this. However,

nationalism could also be a force to rip apart empires. This happened in three empires in Europe.

1. What shared characteristics can unite people and create a strong national feeling?

_____

_____

Nationalism Shakes Aging Empires (page 693)

Why did nationalism divide empires?

Feelings of nationalism threatened to break apart three aging empires. The Austrian Empire was forced to split in two parts—Austria and Hungary. In Russia, harsh rule and a policy called **Russification** that forced other peoples to adopt Russian ways helped produce a revolution in 1917. This revolution overthrew the czar. Like the other two, the Ottoman Empire broke apart around the time of World War I.

2. What three empires were torn apart by nationalism?

_____

_____

Cavour Unites Italy (page 694)

How did nationalism unite Italy?

Italians used national feeling to build a nation, not destroy an empire. Large parts of Italy were ruled by the kings of Austria and Spain. Nationalists tried to unite the nation in 1848. But the revolt was beaten down. Hopes rested with the Italian king of the state of Piedmont-Sardinia. His chief minister was Count **Camillo di Cavour.** Cavour worked to expand the king's control over other areas of the north.

Meanwhile, **Giuseppe Garibaldi** led an army of patriots that won control of southern areas. Garibaldi put the areas he conquered under control of the Italian king. In 1866, the area around Venice was added to the king's control. By 1870, the king completed the uniting of Italy.

3. Who helped unify Italy?

Bismarck Unites Germany; A Shift in Power (page 695)

How was Germany united?

Germany had also been divided into many different states for many centuries. Since 1815, 39 states had joined in a league called the German Confederation. Prussia and Austria-Hungary controlled this group. Over time, Prussia rose to become more powerful. Leading this move was prime minister **Otto von Bismarck.** He was supported by wealthy landowners called **Junkers.** Bismarck was a master of **realpolitik**—tough power politics.

Bismarck worked to create a new **confederation** of German states. Prussia controlled it. To win the loyalty of German areas in the south, he purposefully angered a weak France so that it would declare war on Prussia. Prussia won the Franco-Prussian War in 1871. The war with France gave the southern German states a nationalistic feeling. They joined the other states in naming the king of Prussia as emperor, or **kaiser,** of a strong united Germany.

These events changed the balance of power in Europe. Germany and Britain were the strongest powers, followed by France. Austria, Russia, and Italy were all even weaker.

4. What was the result of the defeat of France and the uniting of Germany?

_____

_____

Types of Nationalist Movements		
Type	**Characteristics**	**Examples**
Unification	• Mergers of politically divided but culturally similar lands	• 19th century Germany • 19th century Italy
Separation	• Culturally distinct group resists being added to a state or tries to break away	• Greeks in the Ottoman Empire • French-speaking Canadians
State-building	• Culturally distinct groups form into a new state by accepting a single culture	• The United States • Turkey

Skillbuilder

Use the chart to answer the questions.

1. Categorizing
Which type of nationalism movement occurred in the United States?

_____

2. Drawing Conclusions
Which type of nationalist movement is a force for disunity?

_____

Revolutions in the Arts

TERMS AND NAMES

romanticism Movement in art and ideas that focused on nature and the thoughts and feelings of individuals

realism Movement in art that tried to show life as it really was

impressionism Style of art using light and light-filled colors to produce an "impression"

BEFORE YOU READ

In the last section, you read how political borders changed in Europe.

In this section, you will learn about changes in the arts in Europe.

AS YOU READ

Use the chart below to show new movements in the arts.

MOVEMENT	DEFINITION	AUTHORS/COMPOSERS
romanticism	Focus on nature; focus on thoughts and feelings	William Wordsworth, Beethoven

The Romantic Movement
(pages 698–699)

What is romanticism?

In the early 1800s, the Enlightenment gradually gave way to another movement, called **romanticism.** This movement in art and ideas focused on nature and on the thoughts and feelings of individuals. Gone was the idea that reason and order were good things. Romantic thinkers valued feeling, not reason, and nature, not society. Romantic thinkers held idealized views of the past as simpler, better times. They val-

ued the common people. As a result, they enjoyed folk stories, songs, and traditions. They also supported calls for democracy. However, not all romantic artists and thinkers supported all of these ideas.

Romantic writers had different themes. During the first half of the 19th century, the Grimm brothers collected German folk tales. They also created a German dictionary and worked on German grammar. These works celebrated being German long before there was a united German nation. Other writers wrote about strong individuals. Some wrote about beauty and nature.

Germany produced one of the greatest early Romantic writers. Johann Wolfgang von Goethe wrote *The Sorrows of Young Werther*. It was a story about a young man who kills himself after he falls in love with a married woman.

British Romantic poets William Wordsworth and Samuel Taylor Coleridge honored nature as the source of truth and beauty. A type of horror story called a *Gothic novel* became popular. Novels such as Mary Shelley's *Frankenstein* were tales about good and evil.

Romanticism was important in music as well. Composers wrote music to appeal to the hearts and souls of listeners. Ludwig van Beethoven, a German, was the foremost of these composers. Romanticism made music a popular art form.

1. What did Romantic thinkers and artists value?

_____

_____

_____

_____

The Shift to Realism in the Arts

(pages 700–701)

What is realism?

In the middle 1800s, the *grim* realities of industrial life made the dreams of romanticism seem silly. A new movement arose—**realism**. Artists and writers tried to show life as it really was. They used their art to protest unfair social conditions. French writer Emile Zola's books revealed harsh working

conditions for the poor. They led to new laws aimed at helping those people. In England, Charles Dickens wrote many novels that showed how poor people suffered in the new industrial economy.

A new device, the camera, was developed in this period. Photographers used cameras to capture realistic images on film.

2. For what purposes did writers use realism?

_____

_____

_____

_____

Impressionists React Against Realism (page 701)

What is impressionism?

In the 1860s, Parisian painters reacted against the realistic style. This new art style—**impressionism**—used light and light-filled colors to produce an impression of a subject or moment in time. Impressionist artists like Claude Monet and Pierre-Auguste Renoir glorified the delights of the life of the rising middle class in their paintings. Composers created music that set a mood by using different music structures, instruments, or patterns.

3. What was the focus of Impressionist art and music?

_____

_____

Name _____ Date _____

Glossary CHAPTER 24 Nationalist Revolutions Sweep the West

confederation Group that joins together for a common purpose

czar Emperor of Russia

ethnic Related to a religious, racial, national, or cultural group

exile State of being sent away from one's own country

flee Run away

Gothic novel Stories filled with fear, violence, or supernatural events

grim Harsh; hard to bear

legislatures Law-making bodies

mestizos People with mixed European and Indian ancestry

turmoil Disorder or confusion

unify Unite; create one country out of separate states or other political divisions

AFTER YOU READ

Terms and Names

A. Write the name or term in each blank that best completes the meaning of the paragraph.

Camillo di Cavour

Giuseppe Garibaldi

the Balkans

nationalism

nation-state

In Europe, feelings of **1** _____ were developing. People no longer felt loyal to a king, queen, or other ruler. Instead, they felt loyal to their own particular country, group, or **2** _____. These feelings led to fights for self-rule by the Greeks. They had been part of a large region controlled by the Ottomans called **3** _____. Feelings of national pride and a desire for unity also helped **4** _____ bring together the northern part of Italy. These same feelings helped **5**_____ unite the southern part of Italy.

B. Write the letter of the name or term next to the description that explains it best.

a. Otto von Bismarck

b. Miguel Hidalgo

c. José de San Martín

d. Louis-Napoleon

e. Simón Bolívar

____ **1.** Emperor of France

____ **2.** Liberator of Chile and Argentina

____ **3.** Liberator of Venezuela

____ **4.** Prussian leader

____ **5.** Priest who began the Mexican revolution

Main Ideas

1. How was society divided in Spanish colonies in the Americas?

_____

_____

_____

2. How did Mexico end Spanish rule?

_____

_____

_____

3. Why was nationalism a force for change in Europe?

_____

_____

_____

4. How did Otto von Bismarck unite Germany?

_____

_____

_____

5. What new artistic movements began in Europe at this time?

_____

_____

_____

Thinking Critically

Answer the following questions on a separate sheet of paper.

1. Explain how the result of German unification was different than that of Italian unification.

2. Why do you think realism replaced romanticism?

CHAPTER 25 Section 1 (pages 717–722)

The Beginnings of Industrialization

BEFORE YOU READ

In the last section, you read about romanticism and realism in the arts.

In this section, you will read about the beginning of the Industrial Revolution.

AS YOU READ

Use this chart to take notes on important developments and conditions that led to industrialization.

TERMS AND NAMES

Industrial Revolution Great increase in machine production that began in England in the 18th century

enclosure Large closed-in field for farming

crop rotation Planting a different crop in a different field each year

industrialization Process of developing machine production of goods

factors of production Conditions needed to produce goods and services

factory Building where goods are made

entrepreneur Person who organizes, manages, and takes on the financial risk of a business enterprise

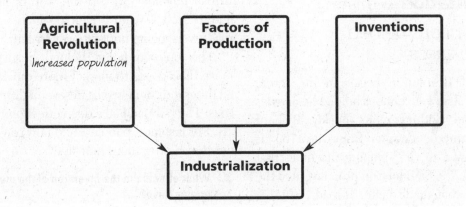

Agricultural Revolution — Increased population

Factors of Production

Inventions

Industrialization

Industrial Revolution Begins in Britain (pages 717–718)

How did the Industrial Revolution begin?

The **Industrial Revolution** was the great increase in production that began in England during the 18th century. Before the Industrial Revolution, people made most goods by hand. By the middle of the 1700s, more and more goods were made by machines.

The Industrial Revolution began with an *agricultural revolution*. In the early 1700s, large landowners in Britain bought much of the land that had been owned by poorer farmers. The landown-

ers collected these lands into large fields closed-in by fences or hedges. These fields were called **enclosures.** Many of the poor farmers who lost their lands became *tenant farmers*. Others gave up farming and moved to the cities.

New farm methods made farmers more productive. For example, Jethro Tull invented a seed drill that made planting more efficient. Farmers also practiced **crop rotation.** Crop rotation is the practice of planting a different crop in a different field each year.

The increase in farm *output* made more food available. People enjoyed better diets. The population of Britain grew. Fewer farmers were needed to grow food. More people began to make goods other than food. The growth in the number of people in cities to work in factories helped create the Industrial Revolution.

For several reasons, Britain was the first country to industrialize. **Industrialization** is the process of developing machine production of goods.

Great Britain had all the resources needed for industrialization. These resources included coal, water, iron ore, rivers, harbors, and banks. Britain also had all the **factors of production** that the Industrial Revolution required. These factors of production included land, labor (workers), and capital (wealth).

1. Why was Britain the first country to industrialize?

_____

_____

Inventions Spur Industrialization (pages 718–720)

What inventions helped change business?

The Industrial Revolution began in the *textile* industry. Several new inventions helped businesses make cloth and clothing more quickly. Richard Arkwright invented the water frame in 1769. It used water power to run spinning machines that made yarn. In 1779, Samuel Compton invented the spinning mule that made better thread. In 1787, Edmund Cartwright developed the power loom. The power loom was a machine that sped up the cloth-making process.

These new inventions were large and expensive machines. Business owners built large **factories** to house and run these machines. These factories were built near rivers because these machines needed water-power to run them.

2. How was the textile industry changed by the new inventions?

_____

_____

Improvements in Transportation; The Railway Age Begins (pages 721–722)

The invention of the steam engine in 1705 brought in a new source of power. The steam engine used fire to heat water and produce steam. The power of the steam drove the engine. Eventually steam-driven engines were used to run factories.

At the same time, improvements were being made in transportation. Robert Fulton, an American, invented the first steam-driven boat. This invention allowed people to send goods more quickly over rivers and canals.

Starting in the 1820s, steam brought a new burst of industrial growth. George Stephenson, a British engineer, set up the world's first railroad line. It used a steam-driven locomotive. Soon, railroads were being built all over Britain.

The railroad *boom* helped business owners move their goods to market more quickly. It created thousands of new jobs in several different industries. The railroad had a deep effect on British society. For instance, people could now travel throughout the country more quickly.

3. What effects did the invention of the steam engine have?

_____

_____

_____

Name _____ Date _____

Industrialization Case Study: Manchester

TERMS AND NAMES

urbanization City building and the movement of people to cities

middle class A social class of skilled workers, professionals, business people, and wealthy farmers

BEFORE YOU READ

In the last section, you saw how the Industrial Revolution began.

In this section, you will read about some of its effects.

AS YOU READ

Use the chart below to record the effects of industrialization.

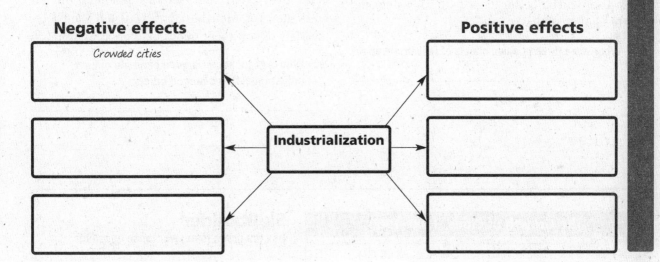

Negative effects

Crowded cities

Positive effects

Industrialization

Industrialization Changes Life

(pages 723–725)

How did industrialization change people's ways of life?

Industrialization brought many changes to the British people. More people could use coal to heat their homes, eat better food, and wear better clothing.

Another change was **urbanization**—city building and the movement of people to cities. For centuries, most people in Europe had lived in the country. By the 1800s, more and more people lived in cities, where they had come to find jobs.

Living conditions were bad in crowded cities. Many people could not find good housing, schools,

or police protection. Filth, garbage, and sickness were part of life in the *slums*. A person in a city could expect to live 17 years. In the countryside, a person could expect to live 38 years.

Working conditions were also bad. The average worker spent 14 hours a day on the job, 6 days a week. Many workers were killed or seriously injured in accidents.

1. What were major changes in living conditions and working conditions?

_____

_____

_____

Class Tensions Grow; Positive Effects of the Industrial Revolution (pages 725–726)

Who were the members of the middle class?

Some people's lives were improved in the new economy. The Industrial Revolution created new wealth for the **middle class,** which included skilled workers, professionals, business people, and wealthy farmers. People in the middle class enjoyed comfortable lives in pleasant homes. This class began to grow in size. Some people grew wealthier than the nobles who had been in control for many centuries.

The Industrial Revolution had many good effects. It created wealth. It created jobs for workers and over time helped many of them live better lives. It produced better diets, better housing, and better clothing at lower prices.

2. What were three positive effects of industrialization?

_____

_____

The Mills of Manchester (pages 726–728)

What changes occurred in Manchester?

The English city of Manchester is a good example of how industrialization changed society. Rapid growth made the city crowded and filthy. The factory owners risked their money and worked long hours to make their businesses grow. In return, they enjoyed huge profits and built huge houses. The workers also worked long hours, but had few benefits. Many of these workers were children, some only six years old. The British government did not limit the use of children as workers until 1819.

The large amount of industry in Manchester caused environmental problems. Coal smoke and cloth dyes from the factories polluted the air and water. Yet, Manchester also created many jobs, a variety of consumer goods, and great wealth.

3. Why is Manchester a good example of how industrialization changed cities?

_____

_____

_____

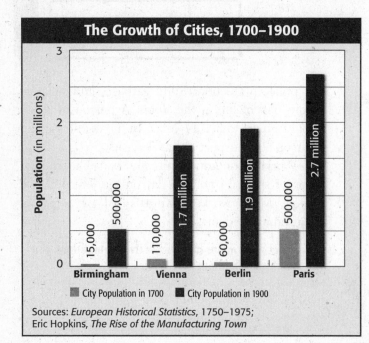

The Growth of Cities, 1700–1900

Population (in millions)

Birmingham: 15,000 / 500,000
Vienna: 110,000 / 1.7 million
Berlin: 60,000 / 1.9 million
Paris: 500,000 / 2.7 million

■ City Population in 1700   ■ City Population in 1900

Sources: *European Historical Statistics*, 1750–1975;
Eric Hopkins, *The Rise of the Manufacturing Town*

Skillbuilder

Use the graph to answer these questions.

1. How many years does this data cover?

_____

_____

2. What was the rate of growth in Birmingham from 1700 to 1900?

_____

_____

CHAPTER 25 Section 3 (pages 729–733)

Industrialization Spreads

TERMS AND NAMES

stock Right of ownership in a company called a corporation

corporation Business owned by stockholders who share in its profits but are not responsible for its debts

BEFORE YOU READ

In the last section, you read about some of the effects of industrialization.

In this section, you will see how industrialization spread to other nations.

AS YOU READ

Use the chart below to take notes on how, where, and why industrialization began in other countries.

```
                    ┌──────────────────┐
                    │    Spread of     │
                    │ Industrialization│
                    └──────────────────┘
```

United States	Belgium	Germany	France
Begins in Northeast in textile industry			

Industrial Development in the United States (pages 729–731)

How did industrialization begin in the United States?

Other countries began to industrialize after Great Britain. The United States was one of the first. Like Britain, the United States had a great deal of coal and water to create power. There was also plenty of iron. In addition, the immigrants that came to the United States created a large supply of workers.

The United States also benefited from conflict with Britain. During the War of 1812, Britain stopped shipping goods to the United States. As a result, American industries began to make many of the goods that Americans wanted.

In the United States, industrialization began in the textile industry. In 1789, Samuel Slater, a British worker, brought the secret of Britain's textile machines to North America. Slater built a machine to spin thread.

In 1813, a group of Massachusetts investors built textile factories in Waltham, Massachusetts. Just a few years later they built even more factories in the Massachusetts town of Lowell. Thousands of workers, mostly young girls, came to these towns to work in the factories.

American industry first grew in the Northeast. In the last decades of the 1800s, industrial growth spread to other areas of the nation. This boom was fueled by large supplies of coal, oil, and iron. New inventions, including the electric light, also helped. As in Britain, railroad building was also a big part of American industrial growth.

Businesses needed huge sums of money to do big projects. To raise money, companies sold **stock.** Stocks are shares of ownership in a company. All those who held stock were part owners of the company. This form of business organization is called a **corporation.**

1. How did industrialization begin in the United States?

_____

_____

_____

Continental Europe Industrializes (pages 731–732)

Where did industrialization begin in Continental Europe?

Industrial growth also spread from England to the European continent. Belgium was the first to industrialize. It was rich in iron and coal and had good waterways.

Germany was divided politically until the late 1800s. As a result, it did not develop much industry at first. However, the Ruhr Valley in Western Germany was rich in coal. The Ruhr Valley eventually became a leading industrial region.

Across Europe, small areas began to change to the new industries. Industrial growth did not occur in France until after 1830. It was helped by the

government's construction of a large network of railroads. Some countries, such as Austria-Hungary and Spain, faced transportation problems that held them back from industrializing.

2. Which nations industrialized first, and why?

_____

_____

_____

The Impact of Industrialization
(page 733)

How did industrialization change the world?

The Industrial Revolution changed the world. Countries that industrialized gained more wealth and power than those that did not. The countries of Europe soon began to take advantage of lands in Africa and Asia.

The Europeans wanted to use these lands as sources of *raw materials* for their factories. European merchants saw the people on other continents as little more than markets for European goods. The European nations took control of the lands in many areas of the world outside of Europe. This practice is called *imperialism.*

The Industrial Revolution that took place in the 1700s and 1800s changed life forever in the countries that industrialized. Problems caused by industrialization led to movements for social reform.

3. How did industrialization lead to imperialism?

_____

_____

_____

Name _____ Date _____

Reforming the Industrial World

BEFORE YOU READ

In the last section, you saw how industrialization spread to different nations.

In this section, you will learn about new ideas and reforms.

AS YOU READ

Fill in the web below with the major ideas and changes you read about.

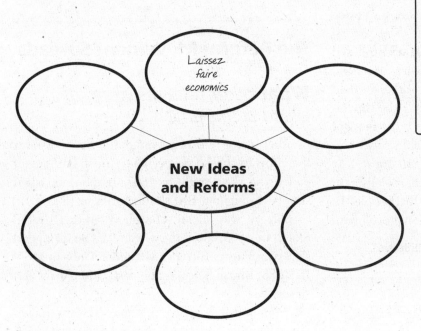

Laissez faire economics

New Ideas and Reforms

The Philosophers of Industrialization (pages 734–735)

What is capitalism?

Industrialization led to new ways of thinking about society. Some economists thought that the government should leave business owners alone. Their view is called **laissez faire.**

Adam Smith argued that governments should not put limits on business. He believed this freedom would help a nation's economy grow. He and others, including British economists Thomas

Malthus and David Ricardo, supported a system called **capitalism.** In a capitalist economy, people invest their money in businesses to make a profit. Smith and the others believed that society would benefit over time from this system. Supporters of laissez faire opposed laws to protect workers.

1. How does capitalism work?

_____

_____

_____

_____

Rise of Socialism; Marxism; Radical Socialism (pages 735–738)

What is socialism?

Other thinkers challenged capitalist ideas. One group was called the utilitarians. According to **utilitarianism,** an idea or practice is good only if it is useful. The utilitarians thought it was unfair that workers should work so hard for such little pay and live in such poor conditions. They thought the government should work to end great differences in wealth among people.

Some thinkers wanted society as a whole to own businesses. This way a few people would not grow wealthy at the expense of everyone else. Instead, all people would enjoy the benefits of increased production. This view—called **socialism**—grew out of a belief in progress and a concern for justice and fairness.

A German thinker named **Karl Marx** proposed a form of socialism that became known as *Marxism.* He said that factory owners and workers would struggle for power. Over time, he said, the capitalist system would destroy itself. The great mass of workers would rebel against the wealthy few.

Marx wrote *The Communist Manifesto.* It described **communism,** a form of socialism in which production is controlled by the people. In the early 1900s, these ideas would bring revolution.

2. How are capitalism and socialism different?

_____

_____

_____

Labor Unions and Reform Laws

(pages 738–739)

How did workers take action to improve their lives?

While thinkers discussed these different ideas, workers fought to improve their lives. Many workers joined **unions.** A union is a group of workers that tries to bargain with employers for better pay and better working conditions.

When employers *resisted* these efforts, the workers went on **strike,** or refused to work. British and American workers struggled for a long time to win the right to form unions. By the late 1800s, workers in both countries had made some progress.

The British Parliament and reformers in the United States also tried to fix other social problems. Britain passed laws to limit how much work women and children could do. Groups in the United States pushed for similar laws.

3. How did both the government and workers themselves try to improve workers' lives?

_____

_____

_____

The Reform Movement Spreads

(pages 739–740)

What other reforms were taking place at this time?

Another major reform movement of the 1800s was the effort to *abolish* slavery. The British Parliament ended the slave trade in 1807. It then abolished slavery throughout British territories in 1833.

Slavery was finally abolished in the United States in 1865, after the Civil War. Spain ended slavery in Puerto Rico in 1873 and in Cuba in 1886. In 1888 Brazil became the last country to *ban* slavery.

Women were active in many reform movements. As they fought for the end of slavery, many women began to fight for equal rights for women. The movement for equality began in the United States in 1848. In 1888, women from around the world formed a group dedicated to this cause.

Reformers took on other projects as well. Some pushed for—and won—improved education. Others tried to improve conditions in prisons.

4. Name two major reform movements of the 1800s.

_____

_____

_____

Glossary

abolish To end

agricultural revolution Changes that led to great increases in the amount of food farmers produced

ban To forbid

boom A time of increased activity, wealth, and prosperity

economists People who study the ways that goods are made, sold, and bought

imperialism Actions or policies by which one country controls another

Marxism Form of socialism proposed by Karl Marx

output Amount of something produced or manufactured

raw materials Materials used in factories to create goods

resisted Worked against

slums Areas of poverty and poor housing

stock Shares of ownership in a company

tenant farmers Farmers who work land rented from someone else

textile Related to cloth or clothing

AFTER YOU READ

Terms and Names

A. Write the term or name in each blank that best completes the meaning of the paragraph.

Karl Marx

Adam Smith

socialism

capitalism

laissez faire

A great economic thinker who believed in free markets was **1** _____. He also supported a policy of leaving businesses alone to run the economy. This philosophy is called **2** _____. Ideas like this are part of a larger economic system called **3** _____. Another great economic and social thinker was **4** _____. He described an economic and government system called communism. This system is a form of **5** _____.

B. Write the letter of the name or term next to the description that explains it best.

a. industrialization

b. urbanization

c. corporation

d. utilitarianism

e. factors of production

____ **1.** Process of developing machine production of goods

____ **2.** Belief that an idea or thing is only as good as it is useful

____ **3.** Resources needed to produce goods and services

____ **4.** Business owned by stockholders

____ **5.** City building and movement of people to cities

AFTER YOU READ (continued)   *CHAPTER 25* The Industrial Revolution

Main Ideas

1. What was the agricultural revolution, and what caused it?

_____

_____

_____

2. What inventions played a key role in the early development of the Industrial Revolution?

_____

_____

_____

3. How did the Industrial Revolution change cities?

_____

_____

_____

4. Name two countries in which industrialization got an early start. Explain why.

_____

_____

_____

5. What were three of the most important social reforms that followed the Industrial Revolution?

_____

_____

_____

Thinking Critically

Answer the following questions on a separate sheet of paper.

1. Discuss the major negative effects of industrialization on society.

2. How did the Industrial Revolution affect economic thought?

Democratic Reform and Activism

TERMS AND NAMES

suffrage Right to vote

Chartist movement Movement in England to give the right to vote to more people and to obtain other rights

Queen Victoria Leader of Britain when democratic changes were occurring

Third Republic Government formed in France after Napoleon III was exiled

Dreyfus affair Events surrounding the framing of a Jewish officer in the French army

anti-Semitism Prejudice against Jews

Zionism Movement to establish a separate homeland in Palestine for the Jews

BEFORE YOU READ

In the last section, you read about the Industrial Revolution.

In this section, you will read about democratic reforms in Great Britain and France.

AS YOU READ

Use the time line below to take notes on key events in Britain and France.

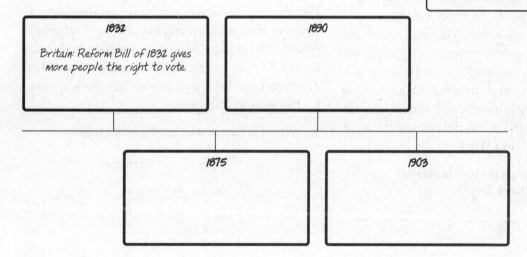

1832	1890
Britain: Reform Bill of 1832 gives more people the right to vote.	

1875	1903

Britain Enacts Reforms (pages 747–748)

How did Britain become more democratic?

Since the 1600s, Britain's government had been a constitutional monarchy. A king or queen ruled the country, but the elected legislature—Parliament—held the real power.

Still, very few people could vote for members of Parliament. Only men who owned property—about five percent of the population—had the right to vote. That situation changed in the 1800s. The *Reform Bill of 1832* was the first step. Middle-class

people across England protested the fact that they could not vote. Worried by revolutions sweeping Europe, Parliament passed the Reform Bill. This law gave **suffrage,** the right to vote, to many in the middle class.

Those who still could not vote began the **Chartist Movement.** They wanted the vote and other rights. They presented their demands to Parliament in The People's Charter of 1838. Although they did not get what they wanted at first, over time their demands became law.

The leader of England during all these changes was **Queen Victoria.** She was queen for 64 years.

She performed her duties wisely and capably, but during her reign Parliament gained more power. The era that she was queen is known as the Victorian Age.

1. How did power shift in Britain in the 1800s?

_____

_____

_____

_____

Women Get the Vote (page 749)

How did women campaign for the right to vote?

By 1890, a few countries had given the right to vote to all men. But none gave the right to vote to all women. In the 1800s, women in the United States and Britain campaigned peacefully for the vote.

In 1903, a group called the Women's Social and Political Union began a stronger campaign for women's suffrage in Britain. This campaign included rallies, parades, and demonstrations during speeches of government officials. But women in Britain and the United States did not win the right to vote until after World War I.

2. When did women get the right to vote in Britain and the United States?

_____

_____

_____

France and Democracy (pages 749–750)

What was the Dreyfus affair?

The road to democracy in France was rocky. France lost a war with Prussia. The National Assembly met to decide on a new government. Finally, in 1875, a new government—the **Third Republic**—was formed. It lasted over 60 years. They were years marked by fighting between many political parties.

In the 1860s, French society was divided over the case of an army officer named Alfred Dreyfus. Dreyfus was accused of being a traitor. The charge was made mainly because Dreyfus was a Jew. Many people believed the charge was true. Dreyfus was found guilty. The issue became known as the **Dreyfus affair.** A few years later, evidence showed that Dreyfus had been *framed.* He was later declared innocent.

The Dreyfus affair revealed **anti-Semitism,** or *prejudice* against Jews, in Europe. In Eastern Europe, anti-Semitism was bad. The Russian government even allowed organized attacks on Jewish villages. From the 1880s on, many Jews fled to the United States. In the 1890s, a movement called **Zionism** began. Its goal was a separate homeland for the Jews in Palestine.

3. Where in Europe was anti-Semitism found?

_____

_____

_____

_____

Self-Rule for British Colonies

TERMS AND NAMES

dominion Nation in the British Empire allowed to govern its own domestic affairs

Maori Polynesian people who settled in New Zealand

Aborigine Native people of Australia

penal colony Place where convicts are sent to serve their sentences as an alternative to prison

home rule Local control over domestic affairs

Irish Republican Army Unofficial military force seeking independence

BEFORE YOU READ

In the last section, you read about democracy and prejudice in Britain, France, and other parts of Europe.

In this section, you will read about the fight for self-rule in British colonies.

AS YOU READ

Use the web below to show struggles for self-rule and their results.

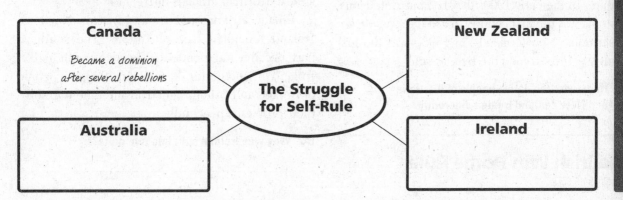

Canada — Became a dominion after several rebellions

Australia

The Struggle for Self-Rule

New Zealand

Ireland

Canada Struggles for Self-Rule
(pages 751–752)

How was the dominion of Canada formed?

Britain had colonies all over the world. Three of them—Canada, Australia, and New Zealand—were settled by colonists from Europe. Over time, the people in these colonies wanted to control their own governments.

The white settlers of Canada were split into two groups. One group included French-speaking Catholics that lived in the colony. Britain had won Canada from France in 1763. The other group was English-speaking and mostly Protestant. The two groups did not get along. In 1791, Britain split the colony into two *provinces*. Each colony had its own government.

But the French-speaking people were not happy with British rule. After several rebellions, the British Parliament put the two provinces back together under one government. Other smaller colonies were added to create the Dominion of Canada. As a **dominion,** Canada had the right to make all laws concerning its own affairs. But Parliament kept the right to control Canadian relations with other countries. By 1871, Canada stretched all the way from the Atlantic Ocean to the Pacific Ocean.

1. Why does Canada today contain both French-speaking and English-speaking people?

_____

_____

_____

Australia and New Zealand

(pages 752–753)

How were Australia and New Zealand settled?

New Zealand became part of the British Empire in 1769. Britain claimed Australia in 1770. Australia was a **penal colony.** The first settlers there were convicted criminals. The **Aborigines,** as Europeans later called the native people of Australia, were *nomadic.* They fished and hunted.

The settlement of New Zealand went slowly because the British government recognized that the native people—the **Maori**—had rights to the land. By the 1840s, though, the number of British settlers in New Zealand was growing.

During the 1850s, Australia and New Zealand became self-governing. But they stayed in the British Empire. In the early 1900s they became dominions. Australia was the first country to use the *secret ballot* in elections. New Zealand—in 1893—was the first country to give women the right to vote.

2. How were the native people of Australia and New Zealand treated differently?

_____

_____

The Irish Win Home Rule

(pages 754–755)

Why did the British hesitate to give Ireland independence?

Irish self-rule took a long time to achieve. The Irish opposed English rule from its start in the 1100s.

Religious conflict also divided the Catholic Irish and the small group of English Protestants who lived in the north.

In the 1840s, the Irish suffered a terrible famine. Many died of starvation and disease. Others lost their land. Millions of Irish people emigrated, or left Ireland. Most went to the United States or Britain.

In the late 1800s, some Irish pushed for complete independence. Most argued for **home rule**—the right to govern internal affairs. The British government opposed this move. They were afraid that the Catholic majority would treat harshly the Protestants in the north. In 1914, Parliament enacted a home rule bill for the southern part of Ireland. When World War I delayed its *enactment,* Irish *nationalists* rebelled. **The Irish Republican Army,** a military force seeking independence, attacked British officials in Ireland.

Finally, Britain split Ireland in two. Northern Ireland remained part of Britain. The southern part became independent. Violence continued in Ireland off and on for decades. In 1998, the people of Ireland and Britain signed an agreement to solve their problems peacefully.

3. Why was Ireland split into two parts?

_____

_____

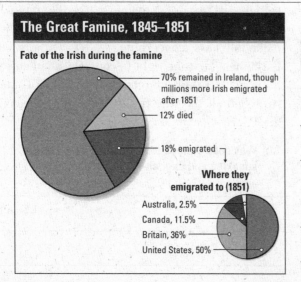

The Great Famine, 1845–1851

Fate of the Irish during the famine

70% remained in Ireland, though millions more Irish emigrated after 1851

12% died

18% emigrated

Where they emigrated to (1851)

Australia, 2.5%
Canada, 11.5%
Britain, 36%
United States, 50%

Skillbuilder

Use the pie graphs to answer these questions.

1. What percentage of the Irish emigrated at this time?

_____

_____

2. To what two countries did most Irish go?

_____

_____

War and Expansion in the United States

BEFORE YOU READ

In the last section, you read about the struggle for self-rule in British colonies.

In this section, you will read about changes in the United States during the same time period.

AS YOU READ

Use the time line below to take notes on changes that caused the United States to change or to grow in area and numbers.

TERMS AND NAMES

manifest destiny Belief that the United States would rule the land from the Atlantic Ocean to the Pacific Ocean

Abraham Lincoln 16th president of the United States

secede To leave the nation

U.S. Civil War War fought between the North and South from 1861–1865

Emancipation Proclamation 1863 proclamation to free the slaves in the Confederate states

segregation Separation by race

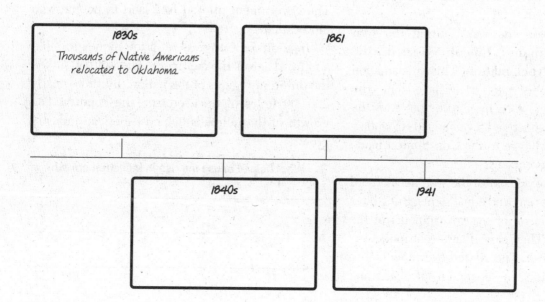

1830s
Thousands of Native Americans relocated to Oklahoma.

1861

1840s

1941

Americans Move West (pages 758–759)

What was manifest destiny?

The United States expanded across North America and fought a bloody civil war. In the early 1800s the nation grew in size. It bought a huge piece of land from France in the Louisiana Purchase. It won a war with Mexico in the 1840s, and gained even more land.

Many believed in **manifest destiny**—the belief that the United States would control land from the Atlantic Ocean to the Pacific. As white settlers moved farther west, Native Americans suffered. In the 1830s, thousands of Native Americans were forced to move from their homes in the East to the present state of Oklahoma.

The growth of the nation raised serious questions. The Southern states used slave labor to grow crops such as cotton. People in the South hoped to extend slavery to the Western lands. But many Northerners believed that slavery was wrong and should be ended.

1. What problems did the movement westward bring?

_____

_____

_____

Civil War Tests Democracy
(pages 759–761)

Why was the Civil War fought?

The struggle over slavery led to the **U.S. Civil War.** The Southern states **seceded,** or pulled out of, the *Union*. The Southerners formed their own nation known as the *Confederate States of America*. War broke out after Confederate forces fired on a Union fort in 1861. The fighting lasted four years.

The North won the war. During the war, President **Abraham Lincoln** issued the **Emancipation Proclamation.** This proclamation declared that the people enslaved in the Confederate states were free. After the war, the Constitution was amended, or changed, to outlaw slavery. Another change to the Constitution made African Americans citizens.

In the first few years after the war, newly freed African Americans enjoyed equal rights. But whites soon regained control of the governments of the Southern states. They passed laws that took away the rights of blacks. The white governments also set up **segregation,** or separation, of blacks and whites. African Americans have continued to fight for equality since then.

2. What changes came about as a result of the Civil War?

_____

_____

_____

The Postwar Economy
(page 761)

What happened after the war?

After the Civil War, the nation experienced quick industrial growth. A sharp rise in *immigration* from Europe and Asia helped cause this growth. By 1914, more than 20 million people had come to the United States.

Many of these new citizens moved to the West. The government offered free land to people who moved there.

In addition, Congress set aside money to build a railroad across the continent. The railroad linked the different regions of the nation. By 1900, nearly 200,000 miles of track crossed the country. The growth of the railroads helped American industry grow.

3. What helped cause the rise in industrial growth?

_____

_____

_____

Name _____ Date _____

Nineteenth-Century Progress

BEFORE YOU READ

In the last section, you read about political change in the United States.

In this section, you will learn about progress in science and other fields.

AS YOU READ

Use the web below to take notes on the changes that occurred during the nineteenth century.

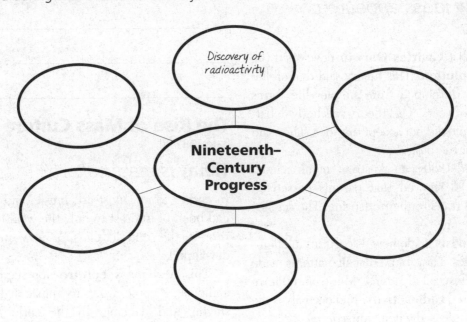

Discovery of radioactivity

Nineteenth–Century Progress

Inventions Make Life Easier

(pages 762–764)

How did inventions change ways of life?

In the late 1800s, new inventions changed how people lived. Inventors around the world worked to make new machines. Thomas Edison received *patents* on more than 1,000 inventions. Among them were the electric light bulb and phonograph. Alexander Graham Bell invented the telephone. Guglielmo Marconi created the first radio.

There were changes in transportation, too. Henry Ford made the car affordable to ordinary people. He had a factory with an **assembly line.** It allowed him to build cheap cars. These cars were affordable for ordinary people. In 1903, the Wright brothers flew the first motor-powered airplane flight. Soon there was an aircraft industry.

1. What were three important inventions during this period?

_____

_____

New Ideas in Medicine (page 764)

What new ideas appeared in medicine?

Until the mid-1800s, no one knew about germs. French scientist Louis Pasteur discovered that microscopic animals could live in food. Pasteur called these tiny creatures *bacteria*. Scientists such as Joseph Lister soon realized that bacteria could cause disease.

2. What relevance did Pasteur's ideas have to the treatment of disease?

_____

_____

New Ideas in Science (pages 765–766)

What new ideas appeared in science?

English scientist **Charles Darwin** developed the **theory of evolution.** This theory said that all life on earth had developed from simpler life forms over millions of years. This theory was hotly debated. Many people did not accept this idea. They said it went against the bible.

In the mid-1880s, an Austrian monk named Gregor Mendel showed that parents passed on their personal traits to their offspring. The science of genetics began.

Other scientists made new discoveries in chemistry and physics. They found that all matter is made of tiny particles called atoms. Marie and Pierre Curie discovered **radioactivity.** Radioactivity is the energy that is released when atoms *decay*.

3. Tell what each of the following discovered or developed: Charles Darwin, Gregor Mendel, Marie and Pierre Curie.

_____

_____

_____

_____

Social Sciences Explore Behavior (page 766)

What is psychology?

In the late 1800s, some thinkers began to study the human mind. This new social science was called **psychology.** The Russian scientist Ivan Pavlov conducted a series of experiments. These experiments convinced him that people responded to certain situations because of how they were trained.

Sigmund Freud, an Austrian doctor, argued that a person's actions are shaped by forces in the *subconscious* mind. These views shocked many. They seemed to overturn the idea that people could use their reason to build better lives.

4. What did Freud reveal about the mind?

_____

_____

_____

_____

The Rise of Mass Culture
(pages 766–767)

What is mass culture?

In earlier times, most art, music, and the theater had been of interest to only the wealthy. With the rise of the middle class, a new mass culture developed.

This new **mass culture** appealed to a wide audience. People went to music halls to enjoy singing and dancing. In the early 1900s, they watched the first silent movies. People also enjoyed sporting events, both as participants and as spectators.

5. What new forms of entertainment became popular?

_____

_____

_____

_____

Glossary
CHAPTER 26   An Age of Democracy and Progress

amended Changed

bacteria Microscopic organisms; germs

Confederate States of America Name taken by the states that seceded from the Union leading to the U.S. Civil War

decay Break down

enactment Officially becoming law

exile Absence from one's country

framed Made to appear guilty or assume the guilt for a crime one

has not committed

immigration Movement into a country

nationalists People who are loyal to a particular nation or group of people

nomadic Without a fixed home

patents Inventor's rights to make, use, and sell his or her inventions

prejudice Unfair attitudes or beliefs, often aimed at a specific group

provinces Political divisions similar to states

Reform Bill of 1832 Bill that gave some members of the middle class in Britain the right to vote

secret ballots Method of voting in privacy

subconscious Part of the mind below the conscious

Union Name for the United States, often used in reference to the U.S. Civil War

AFTER YOU READ

Terms and Names

A. Write the name or term in the blank that best completes the meaning of the paragraph.

theory of evolution

mass culture

radioactivity

psychology

assembly line

One of the greatest developments in mass production occurred in the nineteenth century. This development was the use of the **1** _____. Another important development in the nineteenth century was the discovery of **2** _____ by Marie and Pierre Curie. Darwin's **3** _____ stated that all life on earth developed from simpler forms of life. Freud made great contributions in the field of **4** _____ . At this time, a new **5** _____ also developed. It produced art and entertainment that appealed to a large audience.

B. Write the letter of the name or term next to the description that explains it best.

a. suffrage

b. anti-Semitism

c. Zionism

d. segregation

e. Third Republic

_____ **1.** Separation of races

_____ **2.** Government in France established in 1875

_____ **3.** Prejudice against Jews

_____ **4.** Right to vote

_____ **5.** Movement to create a separate homeland for Jews in Palestine

AFTER YOU READ (cont.) *CHAPTER* **26** An Age of Democracy and Progress

Main Ideas

1. How was the Chartist movement related to suffrage?

_____

_____

_____

2. Why was the Dreyfus affair significant?

_____

_____

_____

3. What problems did Ireland face in its struggle for home rule?

_____

_____

_____

4. How did the lives of African Americans change after the U.S. Civil War? How did they stay the same?

_____

_____

_____

5. How did new inventions change transportation?

_____

_____

_____

Thinking Critically

Answer the following questions on a separate sheet of paper.

1. How were the struggles for self-rule in Canada, Australia, and New Zealand alike?

2. Why were the ideas of Darwin and Freud hard for so many people to accept?

CHAPTER 27 Section 1 (pages 773–778)

The Scramble for Africa

BEFORE YOU READ

In the last section, you read about movements for democracy and self-rule.

In this section, you will learn about imperialism in Africa.

AS YOU READ

Use the chart below to take notes on the reasons why Europeans created overseas empires.

TERMS AND NAMES

imperialism Control by a strong nation over a weaker nation

racism Belief that one race is superior to others

Social Darwinism Use of Charles Darwin's ideas about evolution to explain human societies

Berlin Conference Meeting at which Europeans agreed on rules for colonizing Africa

Shaka Zulu chief who created a large centralized state

Boer Dutch colonist in South Africa

Boer War War between the British and the Boers

Economic	Political	Cultural
Sell goods to new markets		

↓ ↓ ↓

Imperialism

Africa Before European Domination; Forces Driving Imperialism (pages 773–775)

Why did imperialism begin in the 1800s?

In the early 1800s, Europeans controlled a few areas along the coast of Africa. By the mid-1800s, Europeans were expanding their control to new lands. This policy is called **imperialism.**

There were four basic reasons for imperialism. The first reason for imperialism had to do with money. Europeans wanted colonies to provide raw materials for their factories. The Europeans also wanted to sell their goods in their new colonies.

National pride was a second reason for imperialism. Some nations wanted to gain colonies to show their national strength.

Racism was a third reason for imperialism. Racism is the belief that one race is better than others. Many Europeans believed that whites were better than other races.

Racism is related to Social Darwinism. **Social Darwinism** is the use of Charles Darwin's ideas about evolution to explain human societies. One of Darwin's ideas was "survival of the fittest." This idea was that the fittest, or strongest, species would survive. Weak species would not survive.

People who believed in Social Darwinism argued that fit people and nations survived. They also believed that weak people and nations would not survive.

Christian *missionaries* also supported imperialism. They thought that European rule would end the slave trade. The missionaries also wanted to *convert* the people of other continents to Christianity.

Europeans began to take lands in Africa for these reasons. Technology helped the Europeans succeed. The African peoples were divided. It was hard for them to resist European advances.

1. What are four reasons for imperialism?

_____

_____

_____

_____

The Division of Africa (pages 775–776)

How did European nations claim African lands?

The *"scramble for Africa"* began in the 1880s. Diamonds were discovered in South Africa in 1867. Gold was discovered there in 1886. Europeans became more interested in the continent.

The European nations did not want to fight over the land. They met at the **Berlin Conference** in 1884–85. They agreed that any nation could claim any part of Africa by telling the others and by showing that it had control of the area. Europeans quickly grabbed land. By 1914, only Liberia and Ethiopia were free from European control.

2. What was the purpose of the Berlin Conference?

_____

_____

_____

_____

_____

Three Groups Clash over South Africa (pages 776–778)

What groups fought over South Africa?

In South Africa, three groups struggled over the land. In the early 1800s, the *Zulu* chief **Shaka** fought to win more land. Shaka's successors were not able to keep his kingdom intact. The Zulu land was taken over by the British in 1887.

Meanwhile, the British took control of the Dutch colony on the southern coast. Thousands of Dutch settlers, called **Boers,** moved north to escape the British. This movement is known as the Great Trek. The Boers fought the Zulus whose land they were entering.

At the end of the century, Boers fought a vicious war against the British called the **Boer War.** The Boers lost this war. The Boers then joined the British-run Union of South Africa.

3. Who were the Boers, and whom did they fight?

_____

_____

_____

_____

_____

Imperialism
Case Study: Nigeria

TERMS AND NAMES

paternalism Governing in a "parental" way by providing for needs but not giving rights

assimilation Absorbing colonized people into the culture of the imperialist nation

Menelik II Leader of Ethiopian resistance

BEFORE YOU READ

In the last section, you learned about the reasons for imperialism.

In this section, you will read about how the colonies were controlled.

AS YOU READ

Use the chart below to contrast direct and indirect rule.

DIRECT RULE	INDIRECT RULE
Colonizers controlled colonial affairs	Local powers controlled daily matters

A New Period of Imperialism; A British Colony (pages 779–782)

What forms and methods did imperialist nations use to control their colonies?

Each imperial power had goals for its colonies. Imperialist nations had four forms of control: *colony, protectorate, sphere of influence,* and *economic imperialism.*

A colony is an area ruled by a foreign government. A protectorate runs its own daily affairs, but is controlled by an imperialist nation. A sphere of influence is an area where an imperialist nation has exclusive economic rights. Economic imperialism

refers to a situation where an independent nation is controlled by foreign businesses rather than foreign governments.

Imperialist nations also developed two basic methods to manage their colonies. France and other European nations used *direct control.* They felt native peoples could not handle the tough job of running a country. Instead, the imperialist power governed. This policy was called **paternalism.** The French also had a policy of **assimilation.** All colonial institutions were patterned after French institutions. The French hoped that the native peoples would learn French ways.

Britain used *indirect control.* In this system, local rulers had power over daily matters. There were also councils of native people and government officials. These councils were supposed to help native people learn to govern themselves in the British method. When the United States began to colonize, it also used the indirect method of control.

Britain tried to rule Nigeria through indirect control. The British let local chiefs manage their areas. The system did not always work. The local chiefs in some regions of Nigeria resented having their power limited by the British.

1. What forms and methods did imperialists use to control and manage colonies?

African Resistance (pages 782–784)

How *did Africans resist imperialism?*

Some Africans resisted imperialism. People in Algeria fought against the French for almost 50 years. In German East Africa, thousands of Africans died when they tried to use magic to fight German machine guns.

Only Ethiopia resisted the Europeans successfully. There, Emperor **Menelik II** played one European country against another. In 1896, he used European weapons to defeat an Italian army.

2. Who resisted imperialism in Africa, and what were the results?

The Legacy of Colonial Rule
(page 784)

How *did colonial rule affect Africa?*

Africans enjoyed some benefits from *colonial rule*. European governments reduced local conflicts. The Europeans also brought Africa deeper into the world economy. Railroads, dams, and telephone and telegraph lines were built.

But imperialism mostly caused damage. Africans lost control over much of their land. Many African traditions were destroyed. People were forced out of their homes. Many were made to work in bad conditions. The boundaries that Europeans drew had no relation to *ethnic* divisions in Africa. These boundaries caused problems when the colonies became independent nations.

3. What were three benefits and three problems of colonial rule?

Forms of Imperialism	Definitions
Colony	A country or a territory governed internally by a foreign power
Protectorate	A country or territory with its own internal government but under the control of an outside power
Sphere of Influence	An area in which an outside power claims exclusive investment or trading privileges
Economic Imperialism	An independent but less-developed nation controlled by private business interests rather than other governments

Skillbuilder
Use the chart to answer these questions.

1. Under which type of imperialism is the local government most independent?

---

2. What is the difference between a sphere of influence and economic imperialism?

Europeans Claim Muslim Lands

TERMS AND NAMES

geopolitics Interest in or taking of land for its location or products

Crimean War Conflict in which the Ottoman Empire halted Russian expansion near the Black Sea

Suez Canal Human-made waterway connecting the Red and Mediterranean Seas

BEFORE YOU READ

In the last section, you read about imperialism in Africa.

In this section, you will learn about imperialism in Muslim lands.

AS YOU READ

Use the web below to take notes on how other countries took control of Muslim holdings in these lands.

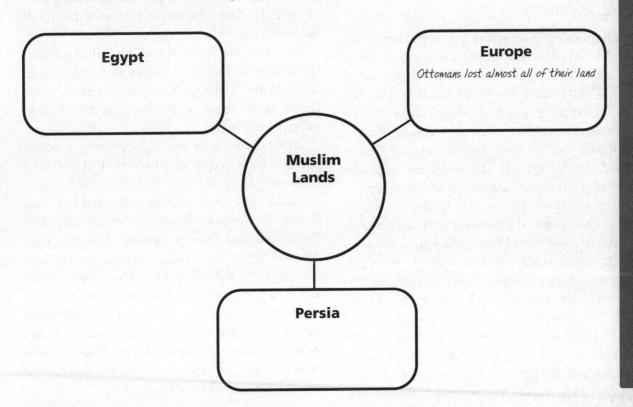

Egypt

Europe
Ottomans lost almost all of their land

Muslim Lands

Persia

Ottoman Empire Loses Power
(page 786)

When *did the Ottoman Empire become weak?*

The Ottoman Empire was based in modern Turkey. But it controlled lands in Eastern Europe, North Africa, and Southwest Asia.

This empire lasted for hundreds of years, but by the 1800s, it was weak. The ruling party broke up into quarreling factions. Corruption and theft caused financial chaos. The Ottomans had once embraced modern technologies but now were falling behind the Europeans.

Nationalism began to stir among people in the empire. In 1830, Greece won its independence and

Serbia won the right to govern itself. European nations eyed what remained of the empire hungrily.

1. What happened when the Ottoman Empire weakened?

_____

_____

_____

_____

Europeans Grab Territory
(pages 786–788)

Where did Europeans grab territory?

Geopolitics is the interest in or taking of land for its location or products. It played an important role in the fall of the Ottoman Empire. Russia hoped to win control of the Black Sea so it could ship grain into the Mediterranean Sea. Russia fought a war with the Ottomans in the 1850s called the **Crimean War.**

Russia lost the war when Britain and France joined on the side of the Ottomans. Still, the Ottomans later lost almost all of their land in Europe and parts of Africa. Muslim leaders, seeing this decline, decided to modernize their countries.

Russia also fought Great Britain in a war known as the "Great Game." Russia sought to extend its empire and gain access to India, one of Britain's most valuable colonies. The British defended India and also attempted to spread its empire beyond India's borders. Much of the war was fought in the independent Muslim kingdom of Afghanistan. After decades of fighting, both countries withdrew and agreed to respect Afghanistan's independence.

2. Why did Russia engage in the Crimean War and the Great Game?

_____

_____

_____

_____

Egypt Initiates Reforms; Persia Pressured to Change (pages 788–790)

What measures did Muslim countries take to avoid imperialist domination?

Some Muslim leaders tried to adopt reforms to block European control of their lands. In Egypt, Muhammad Ali broke away from Ottoman control. He reformed the army and the economy. Ali's grandson continued to modernize the empire. He joined with the French in building the **Suez Canal.** It connected the Mediterranean to the Red Sea.

The canal was extremely expensive to build. Egypt quickly found that it could not afford to repay the money it owed. The British took control of the canal. Later the British took over the rest of the country as well.

In Persia, the Russians and the British competed for control. Russia wanted to use Persia to gain access to the Persian Gulf and Indian Ocean. Twice Russia forced Persia to give up territories through military victories.

Britain wanted to use Afghanistan as a buffer between India and Russia. In 1857, Britain forced Persia to give up all claims to Afghanistan.

In the early 1900s, oil was discovered in Persia. A British company signed an agreement with Persia's ruler to develop these oil fields. Persians rebelled against their ruler, who was corrupt, and the growing influence of Europeans. Then Russia and Britain stepped in and took control of the land.

In Muslim lands, the Europeans gained control by using economic imperialism and creating spheres of influence. Some Muslim countries tried to modernize. But these efforts came too late to prevent Europeans from taking over.

3. What happened in Egypt and in Persia?

_____

_____

_____

_____

British Imperialism in India

TERMS AND NAMES

sepoy Indian soldier under British command

"jewel in the crown" Term referring to India as the most valuable of all British colonies

Sepoy Mutiny Uprising of Indian soldiers against the British

Raj British rule over India from 1757 to 1947.

BEFORE YOU READ

In the last section, you saw how Europeans grabbed Muslim lands.

In this section, you will read about British control of India.

AS YOU READ

Use the chart below to take notes on the causes of the nationalist movement in India.

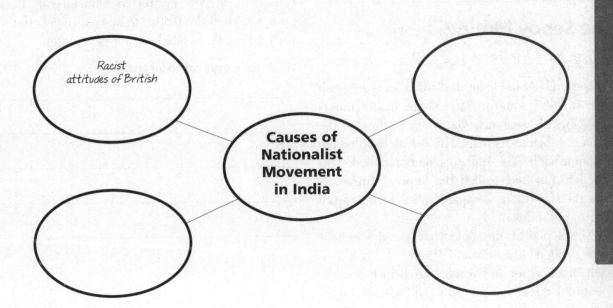

Racist attitudes of British

Causes of Nationalist Movement in India

British Expand Control over India

(pages 791–795)

How did British rule affect India?

The Mughal Empire of India fell into decline in the early 1700s. By the mid-1700s, the British East India Company was the most important power in India. The company held huge amounts of land. The company even had its own army. This army was led by British officers. It was staffed by **sepoys,** Indian soldiers.

India was the main supplier of raw materials for Britain. The British called India the **"jewel in the crown"** because it was Britain's most valuable colony.

India enjoyed some benefits from British rule. India's rail system was the third largest in the world. The railroad helped make India's economy more modern. The British made other improvements, too. They built telephone and telegraph lines, dams, bridges, and canals. They also improved *sanitation* and public health and built schools.

But British rule also caused problems. A great deal of wealth flowed from India to Britain. Indian industry died out because of British trade laws. Many farmers and villages could no longer feed themselves because they were forced to grow cash crops. India suffered famines in the late 1800s. In addition, most British officials had *racist* attitudes that threatened Indian culture.

1. What problems did British rule bring?

_____

_____

_____

_____

The Sepoy Mutiny (pages 793–794)

Why did Indians rebel?

By the mid-1800s, many Indians resented British rule. In 1857, some Indian soldiers heard rumors about British weapons. The rumors offended the Indians' religious feelings. The British handled the situation badly. The Indian soldiers rebelled. This rebellion has been called the **Sepoy Mutiny.** It took the East India Company and British troops a year to put it down.

The Sepoy Mutiny failed because the Indians were divided. Muslims and Hindus did not trust each other. After the revolt, the British government took direct control of British India. The term **Raj** refers to British rule over India from 1757 to 1947.

2. What was the Sepoy Mutiny?

_____

_____

_____

Nationalism Surfaces in India

(page 795)

What were the goals of the Indian nationalist movement?

Indians also resisted British control in other ways. Leaders such as Ram Mohun Roy urged changes in traditional Indian practices. He wanted to make Indian society more modern and to free India of foreign control.

Nationalist feelings also started to grow in India. Indians resented the British discrimination against them. Indians were barred from the best jobs in the Indian Civil Service. British workers were paid more than Indian workers doing the same job.

Indians formed two groups—the Indian National Congress and the Muslim League. Both groups pushed the British to make changes. In the early 1900s, they called for self-government.

3. What groups called for change?

_____

_____

_____

_____

_____

Imperialism in Southeast Asia

BEFORE YOU READ

In the last section, you saw how the Indians reacted to imperialism.

In this section, you will read about imperialism in Southeast Asia.

AS YOU READ

Use the web below to show the various lands controlled by each Western nation.

> ### TERMS AND NAMES
>
> **Pacific Rim** Southeast Asian mainland and islands along the rim of the Pacific Ocean
>
> **King Mongkut** King who helped Siam modernize
>
> **Emilio Aguinaldo** Leader of Filipino nationalists
>
> **annexation** Adding of territory
>
> **Queen Liliuokalani** Last Hawaiian ruler of Hawaii

```
        Dutch                              Americans
      Indonesia
                         Southeast
                           Asia
        British                              French
```

European Powers Invade the Pacific Rim (pages 796–799)

Which Western powers grabbed land in Southeast Asia?

European nations also grabbed land in the **Pacific Rim,** Southeast Asia and the islands on the edge of the Pacific Ocean. The lands of Southeast Asia were perfect for plantation agriculture. Sugar, coffee, cocoa, rubber, coconuts, bananas, and pineapples were important products.

The Dutch controlled Indonesia. Many of the Dutch who moved to Indonesia thought of Indonesia as their home. They set up a class system that kept the Dutch at the top. Wealthy and edu-

cated Indonesians came next. Plantation workers were at the bottom. The Dutch forced farmers to use one-fifth of their land for export crops.

The British took the port of Singapore plus Malaysia and Burma (modern Myanmar). They used Singapore as a base for trade. It became one of the world's busiest ports. The British encouraged the Chinese to move to Malaysia. The Malaysians have become a minority in their own country. Tension between the Malays and the Chinese remains to this day.

France grabbed Indochina (modern Laos, Cambodia, and Vietnam). The French ruled Indochina directly and tried to push French culture on the Indochinese. The French did not encourage industry. Rice became a major crop. Although the Vietnamese grew more rice than before, they ate less of it because so much rice was sent out of the region. This problem set the stage for Vietnamese resistance to French rule.

Colonialism brought some features of modern life to these regions. But economic change benefited Europeans more than the local people. Even so, schooling, health, and sanitation were improved. Millions of people migrated to new regions of Southeast Asia. The mix of cultures did not always go smoothly. Even today, some conflict between groups results from this period.

1. What major problems did colonialism bring?

_____

_____

_____

_____

Siam Remains Independent
(page 708)

How *did imperialism affect Siam?*

One land—*Siam* (modern Thailand)—stayed independent. Siam was surrounded by lands taken by the French and British. The French and British did not want the other to control Siam. The Siamese kings played the French and British against one another to remain free of both nations.

King Mongkut and his son modernized Siam. They started schools and reformed the government. They also built railroads and telegraph lines and ended slavery. These changes happened with little social turmoil.

2. How did Siam confront imperialism?

_____

_____

_____

U.S. Imperialism in the Pacific Islands (pages 798–799)

What *lands did the United States acquire?*

In the late 1800s, the United States also began to seek colonies. After the Spanish-American War in 1898, the United States took control of Puerto Rico, Guam, and the Philippine Islands.

Filipino nationalists led by **Emilio Aguinaldo** fought against the Americans for their freedom. The United States defeated the rebels but promised to give the Philippines self-rule later. In the meantime, American businesses took advantage of Filipino workers.

American businessmen grew wealthy from sugar plantations in Hawaii. But they wanted to make more money. They also asked for the **annexation,** or addition, of Hawaii to the United States. That way they would get more money when they sold sugar in the United States. The American businessmen had a great deal of power in Hawaii.

In the 1890s, **Queen Liliuokalani** tried to regain control of her country for the Hawaiian people. The American businessmen overthrew her. They declared a republic. In 1898, it became a territory of the United States.

3. What happened in the Philippines?

_____

_____

_____

_____

Glossary CHAPTER 27 The Age of Imperialism

colonial rule Control of one nation by another

colony Area governed by a foreign power

convert To change religion

direct control System of completely governing a colony

economic imperialism Area controlled by private businesses rather than by a foreign government

ethnic Related to one particular group or race of people

Filipino Person from the Philippine Islands

indirect control System of running a colony in which local rulers have some power

missionaries People who spread the message of their religion

protectorate Area with its own government under the control of a foreign power

racist Belief that one race is superior to another race

sanitation Cleanliness; measures taken to create a clean or healthy environment

scramble for Africa European grab for African land that began in the 1880s

Siam Old name for what is now modern Thailand

sphere of influence Area claimed as the exclusive investment or trading realm of a foreign power

Zulu Member of a large nation in southeastern Africa

AFTER YOU READ

Terms and Names

A. Write the name or term in each blank that best matches the description.

racism

Social Darwinism

paternalism

imperialism

assimilation

1. _____ Control over a weak nation by a stronger nation

2. _____ Belief that one race is superior to others

3. _____ Use of the theory of evolution to explain human societies

4. _____ Governing in a "parental" way by providing for needs but not giving rights

5. _____ Absorbing colonized people into the culture of the imperialist nation

B. Write the letter of the name next to the description that explains it best.

a. Menelik II

b. Shaka

c. Emilio Aguinaldo

d. King Mongkut

e. Queen Liliuokalani

____ **1.** Leader who modernized Siam

____ **2.** Ruler of Hawaii

____ **3.** Leader of Filipino nationalists

____ **4.** Zulu chief who created a large state

____ **5.** Leader of Ethiopian resistance

AFTER YOU READ (continued)   *CHAPTER 27* The Age of Imperialism

Main Ideas

1. Explain what happened in the scramble for Africa. Tell which nations remained independent.

_____

_____

_____

2. Explain why indirect control of Nigeria did not work.

_____

_____

_____

3. Why was the Crimean War fought, and what happened?

_____

_____

_____

4. How did Indians rebel against British power?

_____

_____

_____

5. In what way was Siam different from other countries of Southeast Asia?

_____

_____

_____

Thinking Critically
Answer the following questions on a separate sheet of paper.

1. Explain the relationship between these terms: Raj and "jewel in the crown."

2. What was similar and what was different about U.S. imperialism in the Philippines and in Hawaii?

China Resists Outside Influence

BEFORE YOU READ

In the last section, you read about imperialism in Asia.

In this section, you will see how China dealt with foreign influence.

AS YOU READ

Use the chart below to take notes on events that occurred in China.

TERMS AND NAMES

Opium War War between Britain and China over the opium trade

extraterritorial rights Rights of foreign residents to follow the laws of their own government rather than those of the host country

Taiping Rebellion Rebellion against the Qing Dynasty

sphere of influence Area in which a foreign nation controls trade and investment

Open Door Policy Policy proposed by the United States giving all nations equal opportunities to trade in China

Boxer Rebellion Rebellion aimed at ending foreign influence in China

CAUSE	EFFECT ON CHINA
British bring opium to China	

China and the West

(pages 805–806)

Was China able to resist foreign influence?

In the late 1700s, China had a strong farming economy based on growing rice. Other crops, such as peanuts, helped to feed its large population. The Chinese made silk, cotton, and ceramics. Mines produced salt, tin, silver, and iron. China needed nothing from the outside world.

China limited its trade with European powers. All goods shipped to China had to come through one port. Britain bought so much Chinese tea that it was eager to find something that the Chinese

would want in large quantities. In the early 1800s, the British began shipping *opium,* a dangerous drug, to China. The opium came mostly from India. The Chinese tried to make the British stop.

As a result of the **Opium War** that followed, the British took possession of Hong Kong. Later, the United States and European nations won **extraterritorial rights** and the right to trade in five ports. The Chinese resented these treaties but could not stop them.

1. What happened as a result of the Opium War?

_____

_____

_____

Growing Internal Problems

(pages 806–807)

What problems did China face?

China had *internal* problems as well. The population had grown quickly. When rains were too light or too heavy, millions starved. The Chinese government was weak and too corrupt to solve its problems.

A leader arose who hoped to save China. His name was Hong Xiuquan, and he led the **Taiping Rebellion.** More than one million peasants joined his army. The rebels won control of large parts of the south. The government needed 14 years to put down this rebellion. The fighting destroyed much farmland. At least 20 million people died.

2. What was the Taiping Rebellion?

_____

_____

_____

Foreign Influence Grows

(pages 807–808)

What was the official attitude toward reform?

In the late 1800s, one person ruled China—the Dowager Empress Cixi. She supported a few reforms in education, civil service, and the military. Despite her efforts to bring change, China continued to face problems.

Other countries were well aware of China's weakness, and they took advantage of the situation. Throughout the late 1800s, many foreign nations won a **sphere of influence** in China. A sphere of influence is a region in which a foreign nation controls trade and investment.

The United States opposed these spheres of influence. Americans urged an **Open Door Policy**, in which all powers had equal *access* to Chinese markets. The Europeans agreed. This policy did not help China, however. Although it was not a colony or group of colonies, China was *dominated* by foreign powers.

3. How did foreigners begin to gain control over China?

_____

_____

_____

An Upsurge in Chinese Nationalism

(pages 808–809)

What actions resulted from growing nationalism?

Humiliated by their loss of power, many Chinese wanted strong reforms. In 1898, the young Emperor Guangxu, Cixi's nephew, tried to put in place broader reforms.

Conservatives didn't like this. The retired Empress Cixi had him arrested and she took back control of the government. China had lost a chance for reform.

Some Chinese peasants and workers formed the Society of Harmonious Fists, known as the Boxers. They wanted to get rid of all Western influence. That included any Chinese who had accepted Western culture or the Christian religion. At the start of the **Boxer Rebellion** in early 1900, Boxers surrounded Beijing's European section. After many weeks, they were driven out by a *multinational* army.

Cixi finally began to allow major reforms. But change came slowly. In 1908, Chinese officials said that China would become a *constitutional monarchy* by 1917. However, *unrest* soon returned.

4. What was the Boxer Rebellion?

_____

_____

Modernization in Japan

BEFORE YOU READ

In the last section, you read about foreign influence in China.

In this section, you will learn about the steps taken by Japan to modernize.

AS YOU READ

Use the chart below to take notes on how Japan's power increased at home and abroad.

```
               Growing Japanese Power

  Asks foreigners to
  give up special
  rights in Japan
```

Japan Ends Its Isolation (paged 810–811)

How did isolation end in Japan?

From the early 1600s to the mid-1800s, Japan traded with China and the Dutch and had diplomatic contact with Korea. But beyond that, Japan was largely isolated. British, French, Russian, and American officials tried to convince the Japanese to open up. But the Japanese repeatedly refused.

That situation changed in 1853 when American steamships with cannons entered Japanese waters. The next year, Japan and the United States signed the **Treaty of Kanagawa.** It agreed to open Japan

to trade with America. Soon afterwards, Japan made similar deals with European nations.

Many Japanese were upset with the *shogun,* the military dictator, who had agreed to these new treaties. The Emperor Mutsuhito got their support and managed to overthrow the shogun. For the first time in centuries, the emperor ruled Japan directly. He reigned for 45 years, from 1867 to 1912. This period is called the **Meiji era.** The name *Meiji* means "enlightened rule."

The emperor wanted to modernize Japan. He sent government officials to Europe and the United States. From what they saw, they shaped a new Japan. They modeled the government after the strong central government of Germany. They patterned the army after Germany's and the navy after Britain's. They adapted the American system of schooling for all children.

The emperor also supported changes to Japan's economy. The country mined coal and built railroads and factories. In just a few years, Japan's economy was as modern as any in the world.

1. What steps did Emperor Mutsuhito take to modernize Japan?

_____

_____

_____

_____

Imperial Japan
(pages 811–813)

How did Japan increase its influence in Asia?

By 1890, Japan had the strongest military in Asia. It asked foreigners to give up their special rights in Japan. The European nations agreed. Japan felt equal to the Western nations.

Japan became more imperialistic as its power grew. When China broke an agreement not to send armies into Korea, Japan went to war. It drove

China out of Korea and gained Taiwan and some other islands as new colonies. In 1904, Japan and Russia fought the **Russo–Japanese War** over China's Manchurian territory. Japan surprised the world by defeating a larger power that was supposed to be stronger.

The next year, Japan attacked Korea. Japan made Korea a protectorate. Japanese officials took more and more power away from the Korean government. The Korean king was unable to get help for his government from other countries. By 1910, Japan achieved **annexation** of Korea.

The Japanese were harsh rulers. They shut down Korean newspapers. They allowed only Japanese history and language to be taught. They took land from Korean farmers and gave it to Japanese settlers. They built factories run by Japanese only. Koreans were not allowed to start new businesses. Koreans resented these actions. They began a nationalist movement and protested against Japanese rule.

2. How did Japan expand its empire to Korea?

_____

_____

_____

_____

_____

U.S. Economic Imperialism

BEFORE YOU READ

In the last section, you saw how Japan increased its power and became an imperialist nation.

In this section, you will read about U.S. economic imperialism in Latin America.

AS YOU READ

Use the chart below to take notes on the causes and effects of U.S. imperialism.

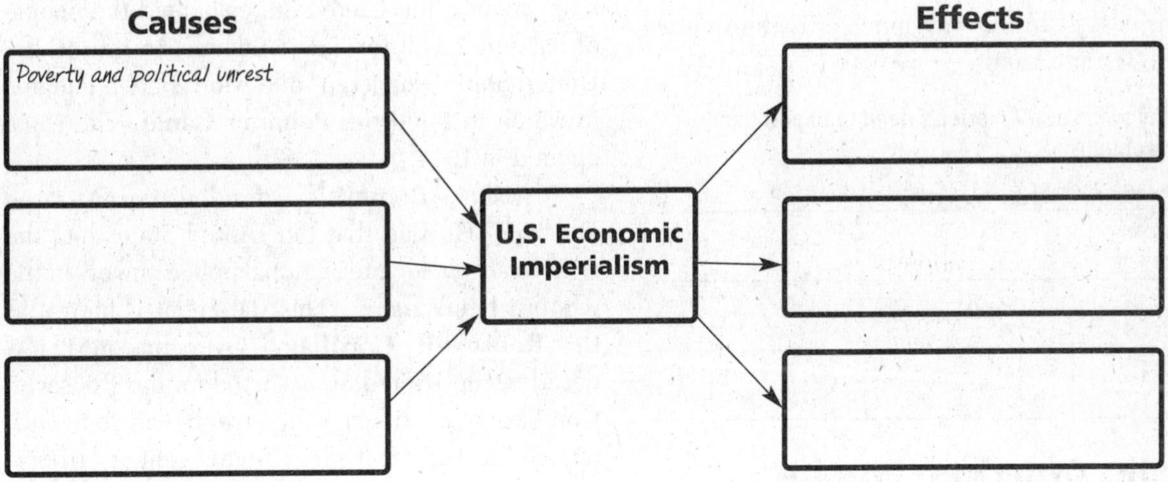

TERMS AND NAMES

caudillo Military dictator

Monroe Doctrine U.S. statement of opposition to European influence in the Americas

José Martí Cuban writer who fought for Cuban independence

Spanish–American War War fought between the United States and Spain in 1898, in which the Americans supported the Cuban fight for independence

Panama Canal Man-made waterway connecting the Atlantic and Pacific Oceans

Roosevelt Corollary Statement that the United States had the right to exercise "police power" in the Western Hemisphere

---

Causes

Poverty and political unrest

→ **U.S. Economic Imperialism** →

Effects

Latin America After Independence (pages 816–817)

What *conditions existed among the new nations of Latin America?*

In the early 1800s, the new nations of Latin America had serious problems. Most people were poor laborers. They worked on farms for large landowners who took advantage of them.

Another problem was political unrest. Local military leaders who wanted power ruled Latin American nations as **caudillos,** or military dicta-

tors. Landowners kept the caudillos in power. The landowners refused to give power to the mass of poor people. Only people with property could vote.

Sometimes reformers did take office. But they never lasted long. When their reforms threatened the power of the wealthy too much, a dictator would rise and remove them from office.

1. **What problems did the people in the new nations of Latin America face?**

_____

_____

Economies Grow Under Foreign Influence (pages 817–818)

What nations controlled Latin American economies?

Spain's trade laws in Latin America ended when Spain lost control of those lands. The new countries could now trade with any nation. Britain and the United States became the chief trading partners. Businesses in these nations soon dominated Latin American economies.

The Latin American economies depended on exports. Other countries benefited from trade with Latin America more than the Latin Americans did.

Latin America did not develop its own manufacturing industries. It had to *import* manufactured goods. These goods cost more than what was earned from exports.

In addition, Latin American countries often borrowed money from foreign banks. When they could not repay the loans, lenders took control of the businesses. In this way, much of Latin America fell into foreign hands.

2. Why was Latin America's need to import goods a problem?

_____

_____

_____

_____

A Latin American Empire

(pages 818–819, 821)

How did the United States gain Latin American territories?

In 1823, President James Monroe issued the **Monroe Doctrine.** It warned European nations against interfering in the American continents. The United States did not really enforce this policy until the end of the century.

In the 1890s, the people of Cuba were fighting for their independence from Spain. The writer **José Martí** was one of them. American businesses had economic interests on the island. Also, Spain had placed Cuban civilians in *concentration camps.* This upset many Americans. For these reasons, the United States fought against Spain in the **Spanish–American War.**

The United States won the war and gained several new territories. The United States put a military government in place in Cuba. This step made many Cubans angry at the United States.

Into the early part of the 20th century, ships traveling from the east to the west coast had to go around the southern tip of South America. This took many weeks. Americans wanted to find a quicker route. They hoped to build a canal across Panama.

President Roosevelt offered $10 million to Colombia—to which Panama belonged—for the right to build this canal. When Colombia asked for more money, the United States helped the people of Panama revolt for independence. In return, the United States won a ten-mile-wide zone in Panama in which to build the **Panama Canal.** The canal opened in 1914.

In 1904, Roosevelt extended the Monroe Doctrine. He said that the United States had the right to act as "an international police power" in the western hemisphere. This statement is known as the **Roosevelt Corollary.** Over the next few decades, the United States acted on the Roosevelt Corollary many times. When trouble arose in various countries, the United States sent its troops. Sometimes they stayed for many years.

3. How did the United States win a zone in Panama for a canal?

_____

_____

_____

_____

CHAPTER 28 Section 4 (pages 822–827)

Turmoil and Change in Mexico

TERMS AND NAMES

Antonio López de Santa Anna Leader in Mexico's fight for independence

Benito Juárez Leader of *La Reforma*

La Reforma Movement in Mexico aimed at achieving land reform, better education, and other goals

Porfirio Díaz Dictator who came to power after Juárez

Francisco Madero Enemy of Díaz who believed in democracy

"Pancho" Villa Popular leader of the Mexican revolution

Emiliano Zapata Leader of a powerful revolutionary army

BEFORE YOU READ

In the last section, you read about U.S. economic imperialism in Latin America.

In this section, you will read about revolution and reform in Mexico.

AS YOU READ

Use the time line below to take notes on the reforms and key events of the Mexican Revolution.

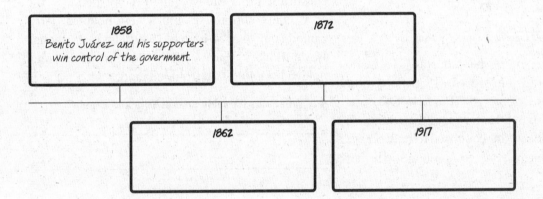

1858
Benito Juárez and his supporters win control of the government.

1872

1862

1917

Santa Anna and the Mexican War (pages 822–823)

Who was Santa Anna?

Antonio López de Santa Anna was a leading figure in the early history of independent Mexico. He fought for Mexican independence from Spain in 1821. He fought against Spain again in 1829 when Spain tried to recapture Mexico. He served as Mexico's president four times.

But in the 1830s, Santa Anna was unable to stop Texas from winning independence from Mexico. In the 1840s, the United States annexed Texas. This angered many Mexicans.

When a border dispute between Mexico and Texas turned into armed conflict, the United States invaded Mexico. Santa Anna led his nation's army and was defeated. Mexico surrendered huge amounts of land to the United States.

1. **What losses did Mexicans suffer under Santa Anna?**

_____

_____

_____

Juárez and *La Reforma* (pages 823–825)

What was La Reforma?

Another important leader of the middle 1800s was **Benito Juárez.** Juárez wanted to improve conditions for the poor in Mexico. He led a movement called *La Reforma*—"the reform." *La Reforma* aimed to break the power of the large landowners and give more schooling to the poor. Juárez and his supporters won control of the government in 1858.

But conservatives who opposed *La Reforma* did not give up. They plotted with France to retake Mexico. In 1862, Napoleon III of France sent an army that captured the country in 18 months. Napoleon III named a European noble as emperor. But Juárez and his followers kept fighting. Five years later, they drove the French from Mexican soil and executed the emperor.

2. How did conservatives oppose *La Reforma?*

_____

_____

Porfirio Díaz and "Order and Progress" (pages 825–826)

Who was Porfirio Díaz?

Juárez again pressed for his reforms. He made some progress but died in office in 1872. Soon after he died, a new leader emerged. **Porfirio Díaz** was a leader in Mexican politics for more than 30 years. Díaz brought order to the country. He ended raids by bandits and brought some economic growth, but

he limited political freedom. A leader named **Francisco Madero** called for the overthrow of Díaz.

3. What were the benefits and drawbacks of Díaz's rule?

_____

_____

Revolution and Civil War
(pages 826–827)

Who were Villa and Zapata?

In the early 1900s, calls for reform got louder. Francisco **"Pancho" Villa** and **Emiliano Zapata** called for better lives for the poor. They raised armies and forced Díaz to step down. But political unrest continued. For many years, leaders struggled for power. In 1917, Mexico adopted a new constitution that survived all of the turmoil.

Conflict continued until a new political party gained control of Mexico in 1929. The Institutional Revolutionary Party (PRI) brought peace and political *stability* to a troubled land.

4. What was the main goal of Villa and Zapata?

_____

_____

Glossary

CHAPTER 28 Transformations Around the Globe

access Means of getting in

Boxers Chinese people who fought against foreign influence in China

concentration camps Places where people are held, usually for being political enemies

conservatives People who do not want change

constitutional monarchy Government in which royal power is limited by the law

dominated Controlled

exports Goods sold to another country

humiliated To have lost pride, dignity, or self-respect

import To buy a good from another country

internal Inside a country

isolated Cut off from other nations

multinational Made up of people from many nations

opium A dangerous drug that the British exported to China from India

plotted Made a secret plan

shogun Japanese military ruler

stability Order; freedom from constant change

unrest Political change and dissatisfaction

AFTER YOU READ

Terms and Names

A. Write the name or term in each blank that best completes the meaning of the paragraph.

"Pancho" Villa

Emiliano Zapata

Antonio López de Santa Anna

Benito Juárez

Porfirio Díaz

One of the most important leaders in early Mexican history is **1** _____. He helped fight for Mexican independence from Spain. **2** _____ was the leader of *La Reforma,* a Mexican reform movement. Many of the reforms he established were undone by **3** _____, who brought order to the country but also limited freedom. A far more popular leader was **4** _____. Along with **5** _____, he helped the poor fight for better lives.

B. Write the letter of the name or term next to the description that explains it best.

a. Open Door Policy

b. Treaty of Kanagawa

c. Roosevelt Corollary

d. Boxer Rebellion

e. Taiping Rebellion

____ **1.** Policy that gave all nations an opportunity to trade in China

____ **2.** Agreement to open two Japanese ports to American ships

____ **3.** Uprising against foreign influence in China

____ **4.** Revolt against the Qing Dynasty

____ **5.** Addition to the Monroe Doctrine

AFTER YOU READ (cont.) *CHAP. 28* Transformations Around the Globe

Main Ideas

1. Why did the Taiping Rebellion occur?

_____

_____

_____

2. Who was Cixi?

_____

_____

_____

3. What occurred in Japan during the Meiji Era?

_____

_____

_____

4. In what ways did the United States both help and hurt the Cuban people?

_____

_____

_____

5. What are three reforms made by the Mexican constitution of 1917?

_____

_____

_____

Thinking Critically

Answer the following questions on a separate sheet of paper.

1. Describe how Japan acted on its feelings of pride and strength in the late 1800s.

2. What did Juárez, Villa, and Zapata have in common?

Marching Toward War

BEFORE YOU READ

In the last chapter, you read about political changes around the globe.

In this section, you will learn about the First World War.

AS YOU READ

Use this chart to take notes on the causes of World War I.

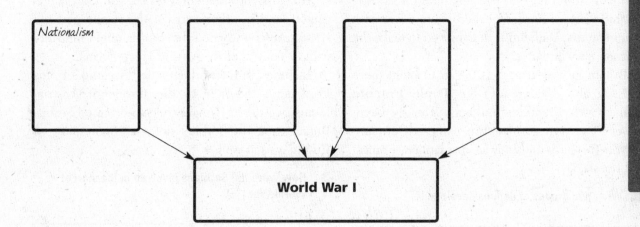

TERMS AND NAMES

militarism Glorifying war and preparing for it

Triple Alliance Military agreement between Germany, Austria-Hungary, and Italy

Kaiser Wilhelm II Emperor of Germany

Triple Entente Military agreement among Britain, France, and Russia

Rising Tensions in Europe
(pages 841–842)

Why didn't peace last in Europe?

Many people in Europe had joined groups to work for peace. However, developments would soon lead Europe into war.

One of those developments was *nationalism*—a deep feeling of attachment to one's own nation. This force helped *unify* the people of a country. It also created competition between countries.

By 1900, six nations were *rivals* for power in Europe. These nations, called the *Great Powers*, were Germany, Austria-Hungary, Great Britain, Russia, Italy, and France. They competed economically, and they competed for neighboring land.

Imperialism was another force that helped lead to war. France and Germany were each seeking to control of parts of Africa. They almost came to war twice in the early 1900s. Mistrust was a huge problem.

The third factor leading to war was a growing arms race. Each country in Europe—except Great Britain—built a large army. Glorifying war and preparing for it is called **militarism**.

1. What were three factors leading to war?

_____

_____

_____

Tangled Alliances (pages 842–843)

What caused countries to fear one another?

Growing *rivalries* led the nations to make military *alliances*. Prussia's chancellor, Otto von Bismarck, feared that France would want revenge for its defeat in the Franco-Prussian War. He set out to *isolate* France. In 1879, he formed a **Triple Alliance** with Austria-Hungary and Italy. He also signed a treaty with Russia.

Kaiser Wilhelm II of Germany did not want to share power with Bismarck. He forced Bismarck to resign and followed his own foreign policy. He let the agreement with Russia end. Russia soon allied itself with France. This alliance meant that Germany would have to fight enemies on its eastern and western borders if there were a war with either country. Wilhelm II then moved to make the German navy larger.

Britain grew alarmed. It began to build more ships. It also entered into the **Triple Entente** alliance with France and Russia. The six Great Powers had now formed two camps—Germany, Austria-Hungary, and Italy against Britain, France, and Russia.

2. What two groups of nations developed?

_____

_____

_____

_____

Crisis in the Balkans (pages 843–844)

What part did the Balkans play in the increasing tensions?

Meanwhile, trouble was brewing in the Balkans, in southeastern Europe. The Ottoman Empire controlled this area. But it was breaking apart. Both Austria-Hungary and Russia wanted some of this land.

The kingdom of Serbia was also in this region. It wanted to bring other Slavic peoples who lived in the Balkans under its control. In 1908, Austria-Hungary seized Bosnia and Herzegovina. These lands had Slavic peoples. This action angered the Serbs. However, their Russian allies were unwilling to support them, and they backed down.

By 1914, the situation was different. Serbia had gained land in other parts of the region and felt strong. Austria worried that Serbia might interfere with its control of Bosnia and Herzegovina.

In June 1914, a Serbian killed Archduke Franz Ferdinand, the *heir* to the throne of Austria-Hungary. Austria-Hungary declared war on Serbia. Russia came to Serbia's defense. Soon most of Europe was at war.

3. How were the Serbians involved in the start of World War I?

_____

_____

_____

Europe Plunges into War

TERMS AND NAMES

Schlieffen Plan Germany's plan for winning the war on two fronts

Allies Great Britain, France, Russia, and other nations who fought on their side

Central Powers Germany, Austria-Hungary, and other nations who fought on their side

trench warfare Fighting from trenches dug in the battlefield

Western Front Region of northern France where much fighting took place

Eastern Front Region along German-Russian border where much fighting took place

BEFORE YOU READ

In the last section, you read how World War I began.

In this section, you will learn the details of this costly and tragic war.

AS YOU READ

Use the chart below to compare and contrast the Western Front and the Eastern Front. Include who fought, where they fought, and how they fought.

WESTERN FRONT	EASTERN FRONT
Area in France	

The Great War Begins (page 845)

How did so many nations become involved?

The system of alliances turned the war between Austria-Hungary and Serbia into a wider war. Russia moved against Austria-Hungary. It figured that Germany would support Austria-Hungary. So it moved troops against Germany as well. Germany declared war on Russia. Soon after, it also declared war on Russia's ally, France.

Germany had a plan for winning the war on two fronts. This was the **Schlieffen Plan**. It called for a rapid push through France, a quick defeat of that nation, and a turn to face Russia in the east. To capture France quickly, Germany moved through Belgium. Belgium was a neutral country. Britain was outraged by Germany's action. It declared war on Germany. France, Britain, and Russia were called the **Allies**. They were later joined by Italy, which broke with Germany and Austria-Hungary. Bulgaria and the Ottoman Empire joined Germany and Austria-Hungary. They were called the **Central Powers**.

1. Who were the Allies and Central Powers?

_____

_____

_____

_____

A Bloody Stalemate (pages 846–848)

What kind of warfare was used?

After the German army moved almost to Paris, French defenses strengthened and stopped them in September 1914. Both sides became bogged down in a bloody conflict. Soldiers dug deep *trenches* into the ground. **Trench warfare** began.

When soldiers left the trenches to storm enemy lines, they faced powerful weapons. Machine guns, tanks, poison gas, and larger pieces of *artillery* killed hundreds of thousands of soldiers. This was how the war was fought in France, which was called the **Western Front.**

2. What was the war like on the Western Front?

_____

_____

_____

_____

The Battle on the Eastern Front
(pages 848–849)

What happened on the Eastern Front?

The war on the **Eastern Front** showed more movement at first—but it was equally *destructive*. Russian armies attacked both Germany and Austria-Hungary. They had some early success but were driven back in both places. One reason was that Russia did not have a fully industrial economy. It could not keep troops supplied.

Still, Russia had a huge population and could send millions to war. The large Russian army provided a constant threat to Germany. This threat prevented Germany from putting its full resources against the Allies in the west.

3. What weaknesses and strengths did Russia have?

_____

_____

_____

_____

A Global Conflict

BEFORE YOU READ

In the last section, you read how the war was fought in Europe.

In this section, you will learn how the war affected the world.

AS YOU READ

Use the chart below to take notes on the effects of World War I around the world and on the home fronts.

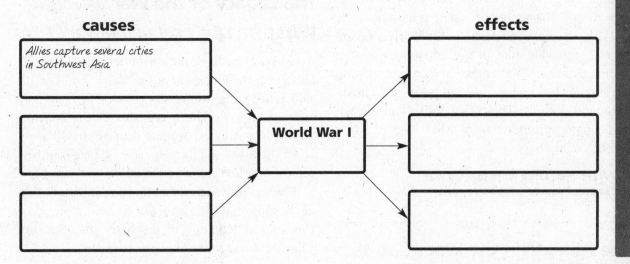

causes

Allies capture several cities in Southwest Asia.

World War I

effects

War Affects the World (pages 851–853)

What other areas of the world were involved?

The Allies hoped to take a part of the Ottoman Empire called the Dardanelles. The attack failed with great loss of life. A more successful operation was headed by a British officer named T. E. Lawrence. He helped lead an Arab revolt against Ottoman rule. As a result, the Allies were able to capture several important cities in Southwest Asia.

Japan took German colonies in China and the Pacific Ocean. The Allies also captured three of the four German colonies in Africa.

The British had used their strong navy to block all supplies from reaching Germany. The Germans

responded by increasing their submarine attacks on ships bringing food and supplies to the Allies. They used **unrestricted submarine warfare**. This meant sinking any ship without warning in the waters around Great Britain.

When American ships were sunk and lives were lost, the American people grew angry. Then the British intercepted a secret message from Germany to Mexico. This message asked México to ally itself with Germany. In return, Germany offered to help Mexico regain land lost to the United States in the 1840s. In April 1917, Congress declared war on Germany.

1. What areas outside of Europe were affected by the war?

_____

_____

War Affects the Home Front

(pages 853–854)

What happened on the home fronts?

By 1917, the war had already killed millions. It had drastically changed the lives of millions more—people at home as well as soldiers. This "Great War," as it was called, was a **total war**. It demanded all the resources of the countries that fought it.

Governments took control of factories. It told them what to produce and how much of it to make. Governments also used **rationing**. This limited how much food and other goods people could buy and hold. That way armies in the field would have the supplies they needed. Governments used **propaganda** to get support for the war. They also took steps to stop *dissent*, or opposition to the war.

With so many men in the military, women played a growing role in the economies of the countries at war. They worked in factories, offices, and shops. They built planes and tanks, grew food, and made clothing. These changes had an impact on people's attitudes toward what kind of work women could do.

2. **What were three ways that the war affected people's day-to-day lives?**

_____

_____

The Allies Win the War (pages 854–855)

Why did the Allies win?

In 1917, the United States entered the war. And Russia left it. Suffering during the war chipped away at the Russian people's support for the *czar*. In March, he stepped down. The new government hoped to continue fighting the war, but the Russian armies refused. Just months later, a new revolution broke out. Communists seized Russia's government. They quickly made a treaty with Germany and gave up huge amounts of land in return for peace.

In March 1918, Germany tried one final attack. Once again, the German army nearly reached Paris. But the soldiers were tired, and supplies were short. The Allies—now with fresh American troops—drove the Germans back.

Bulgaria and the Ottoman Empire surrendered. In October, a revolution overthrew the emperor of Austria-Hungary. In November, Kaiser Wilhelm II was forced to step down in Germany. The new government signed an **armistice**, an agreement to stop fighting. On November 11, 1918, Europe was finally at peace.

3. **What were the final problems that Germany and Austria-Hungary faced?**

_____

The Legacy of the War (page 855–856)

What was the cost of the war?

World War I had a devastating effect on the world. About 8.5 million soldiers had died. Another 21 million had been wounded. Countless civilians had suffered as well. The economies of the warring nations had suffered serious damage, too. Farms were destroyed, and factories ruined. One estimate said the war had caused $338 billion in damage.

The war also had an emotional cost. People felt all the suffering did not seem to have a purpose. The art and literature of the years after the war reflected a new sense of hopelessness.

4. **Name one political, economic, and emotional cost of the war.**

_____

_____

_____

_____

_____

A Flawed Peace

BEFORE YOU READ

In the last section, you read how World War I spread and finally ended.

In this section, you will learn about the harsh peace that followed.

AS YOU READ

Use the web below to take notes on the Treaty of Versailles.

TERMS AND NAMES

Woodrow Wilson President who proposed the Fourteen Points and represented the United States at Versailles

Georges Clemenceau France's premier and delegate at Versailles

Fourteen Points Plan for a just and lasting peace

self-determination Allowing people to decide for themselves about what kind of government they want

Treaty of Versailles Agreement at the end of World War I between Germany and the Allied Powers

League of Nations International group with the goal of keeping peace among nations

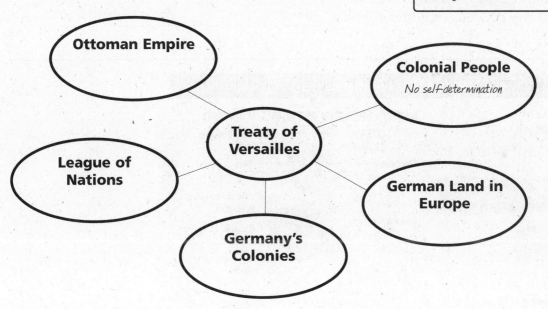

Ottoman Empire

Colonial People
No self-determination

Treaty of Versailles

League of Nations

German Land in Europe

Germany's Colonies

The Allies Meet and Debate
(pages 858–859)

What decisions were made at Versailles?

Many nations sent delegates to the peace talks in Paris. The main leaders were **Woodrow Wilson** of the United States, **Georges Clemenceau** of France, and David Lloyd George of Britain. Germany and its allies and Russia were not present.

Wilson pushed for his peace plan called the **Fourteen Points**. He wanted to end secret treaties

and alliances and give people **self-determination,** the right to form their own nation. He also hoped to set up a world organization that would police the actions of nations and prevent future wars.

Britain and especially France had different views. They had suffered greatly in the war. They wanted to punish Germany. After long debates, the leaders finally agreed on a peace settlement. It was called the **Treaty of Versailles** and was signed in June 1919.

The treaty called for a **League of Nations—** the world organization that Wilson wanted. It would include 32 nations. The United States,

Britain, France, Japan, and Italy would make up the leadership. Germany and Russia were left out of the League. The treaty took away German land in Europe and took away its colonies in Africa and the Pacific. Limits were placed on the size of Germany's armed forces. Finally, Germany was given complete blame for the war. That meant it would have to make payments to the Allies for the damage caused.

1. How did the Treaty of Versailles affect Germany?

_____

_____

_____

A Troubled Treaty (pages 859–861)

Who opposed the treaty?

Germany's former colonies were given to the Allies to govern until they decided which were ready for independence. Poland, Czechoslovakia, and Yugoslavia were all declared independent. Finland, Estonia, Latvia, and Lithuania—once part of Russia—were made independent nations as well. The treaty also broke up the Ottoman Empire. The Ottomans kept control only of Turkey.

The treaty did not make a lasting peace. The United States Senate never approved the treaty or joined the League of Nations. Germans bitterly resented the treaty because placed all the blame for the war on them. Colonial peoples in Africa and Asia were angry because the treaty did not make them independent. Japan and Italy were also upset by getting few *territorial* gains.

2. Which groups opposed the treaty and why?

_____

_____

_____

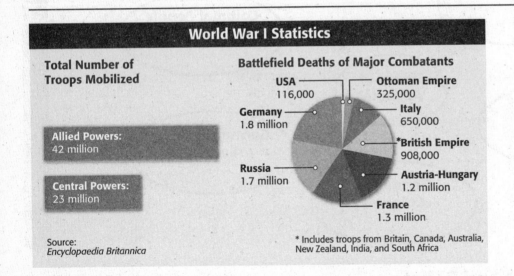

World War I Statistics

Total Number of Troops Mobilized

Allied Powers: 42 million

Central Powers: 23 million

Source: *Encyclopaedia Britannica*

Battlefield Deaths of Major Combatants

USA 116,000
Germany 1.8 million
Russia 1.7 million
Ottoman Empire 325,000
Italy 650,000
*British Empire 908,000
Austria-Hungary 1.2 million
France 1.3 million

* Includes troops from Britain, Canada, Australia, New Zealand, India, and South Africa

Skillbuilder

Use the graph to answer the questions.

1. Which country suffered the most battlefield deaths? Which country suffered the least?

_____

2. Based on the graph, why did the Allies appear to have an advantage in the war?

_____

Glossary

alliances Agreements to help other countries in a military way

artillery Large guns, cannons

czar Ruler of Russia

destructive Causing negative effects, including death and ruin

dissent Disagreement

Great Powers Germany, Austria-Hungary, Great Britain, Russia, Italy, and France

heir Person who inherits; next in line

intercepted Took or received something intended for someone else

isolate Set apart; cut off

legacy Results; lasting effects

nationalism Feeling of attachment to one's own nation

rival One who tries to be better or do better than another

rivalries Competitions

territorial Related to territories; related to colonies or other imperialist holdings

trenches Long, deep holes in the ground dug for protection from enemy fire

unify Bring together as one

AFTER YOU READ

Terms and Names

A. Write the name or term in each blank that best completes the meaning of the paragraph.

Western front

Eastern front

total war

trench warfare

rationing

World War I was a **1** _____. Nations used all their resources to fight it. At home, people were faced with **2** _____. This reserved needed materials for the military. On the battlefield, fighting was brutal. Soldiers used **3** _____ in northern France. This area was known as the **4** _____. On the **5** _____, a bloody war was fought between the Germans, Serbs, and Russians.

B. Write the letter of the name or term next to the description that explains it best.

a. Fourteen Points

b. Allies

c. Central Powers

d. Triple Alliance

e. Triple Entente

____ **1.** Agreement among Germany, Austria-Hungary, and Italy

____ **2.** British alliance with France and Russia

____ **3.** Great Britain, France, Russia, and other nations that fought on their side

____ **4.** Germany, Austria-Hungary, and other nations that fought on their side

____ **5.** Plan for achieving peace

Main Ideas

1. How did imperialism help lead to World War I?

_____

_____

_____

2. What did the Schlieffen Plan involve?

_____

_____

_____

3. How did America get involved in the war?

_____

_____

_____

4. How did the war help lead to revolution in Russia?

_____

_____

_____

5. What was Wilson's plan for peace, and what did it involve?

_____

_____

_____

Thinking Critically

Answer the following questions on a separate sheet of paper.

1. Explain why this war can be called "a truly global conflict."

2. Discuss the weaknesses of the Treaty of Versailles.

Revolutions in Russia

TERMS AND NAMES

proletariat The workers

Bolsheviks Group of revolutionaries led by Lenin

Lenin Leader of the Bolsheviks and first ruler of the Soviet Union

Rasputin Eccentric monk assassinated because of his corrupt influence on the Russian royal family

provisional government Temporary government led by Alexander Kerensky

soviet Local governing council

Communist Party A political party practicing the ideas of Karl Marx and Lenin

Joseph Stalin Revolutionary leader who took control of the Communist Party after Lenin

BEFORE YOU READ

In the last chapter, you read about World War I.

In this section, you will learn about the revolutions in Russia that occurred at the same time.

AS YOU READ

Use the time line below to take notes on key events in Russia's history just before, during, and after the revolutions.

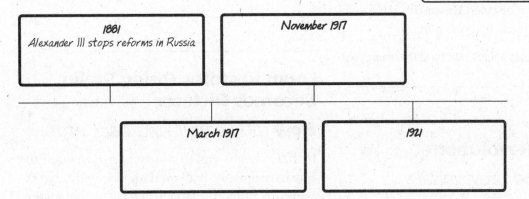

1881
Alexander III stops reforms in Russia

November 1917

March 1917

1921

Czars Resist Change (page 867)

How did Alexander III rule?

In 1881 *Czar* Alexander II was killed by *radical* students. When a new czar, Alexander III, took control of the Russian government, reforms stopped. He cracked down on anyone who seemed to threaten his government. He also mistreated all non-Russian peoples who lived within the Russian empire, especially Jews. Nicholas II, the son of Alexander III, continued his father's firm rule.

1. How did Alexander and Nicholas rule?

_____

_____

Russia Industrializes (page 868)

What changes did industrialization cause?

Russia started a buildup of industry. It quickly became a leading producer of steel. Russia also built the Trans-Siberian Railway—the longest continuous rail line in the world.

Although there was progress, working conditions were poor, wages were low, and children were forced to work. Workers grew angry. Revolutionary groups wanted to overthrow the government. Some followed the teachings of Karl Marx. One group—the **Bolsheviks**—was led by **Lenin**. He fled Russia a few years later to await a better time to put forth his ideas.

2. Who were the Bolsheviks?

_____

_____

Crises at Home and Abroad
(pages 868–869)

What crises did Russia face?

In early 1905, the Russian army killed hundreds of hungry workers who had peacefully gathered to ask for relief. Strikes spread in protest. Nicholas was forced to allow some reforms to take place. He approved the creation of the Duma, Russia's first parliament.

The suffering caused by World War I was the final blow against the czar's rule. As the war worsened, the czar lost control of Russia. Soldiers refused to fight, prices shot sky high, and people starved. Meanwhile, his wife fell under the influence of an odd monk named **Rasputin**. He spread *corruption* throughout the government.

3. What developments helped lead up to the revolution?

_____

_____

The March Revolution (pages 869–870)

What was the provisional government?

In March 1917, the czar was forced to step down. A year later, he and his family were *executed*. A **provisional government** led by Alexander Kerensky was formed.

Kerensky hoped to keep Russia in the war. The decision cost him the support of soldiers who no longer wanted to fight. He also lost the support of workers and peasants who wanted an end to food shortages. Across the country, these forces formed local councils called **soviets**. In some cities, the soviets had more real power than the government. In the middle of all this change, Lenin returned to Russia.

4. How did Kerensky lose support?

_____

_____

The Bolshevik Revolution
(pages 870–872)

Who led the Bolshevik Revolution?

Lenin's slogan "Peace, Land, and Bread" was soon taken up by many people. In November 1917, armed workers took control of government offices. Kerensky's power came to an end.

To win the peasants' support, Lenin ordered all farmland be given to them. Workers were given control of the factories. Soon, Lenin agreed to a peace treaty with Germany. It gave away large amounts of Russian land, but it ended the war. Then, forces opposed to Lenin's revolution tried to defeat the Bolshevik army. The civil war lasted two years. The fighting and the famine that followed killed 15 million Russians. In the end, Lenin's Red Army won.

5. Who fought the civil war?

_____

_____

Lenin Restores Order; Stalin Becomes Dictator (pages 872–873)

How did Lenin bring back order?

In 1921, Lenin started a new plan to rebuild the Russian economy. It allowed for some private ownership of property. He also changed the government to form a new nation—the Soviet Union. It would be run by the leaders of the **Communist Party.** By the late 1920s, the Soviet economy had recovered. Farms and factories were producing as much as they had before World War I. After Lenin's death **Joseph Stalin** took power.

6. What changes did Lenin make?

_____

_____

Case Study: Stalinist Russia

TERMS AND NAMES

totalitarianism Government that has total control over people's lives

Great Purge Arrest, exile, or killing of thousands of suspected enemies of the Communist Party

command economy Economy in which the government makes all the economic decisions

Five-Year Plans Plans to develop the Soviet Union's economy

collective farm Large, government-owned farm

BEFORE YOU READ

In the last section, you learned about the factors leading to revolution in Russia.

In this section, you will read about the totalitarian government that resulted.

AS YOU READ

Use the web below to show what Stalin's totalitarian state was like.

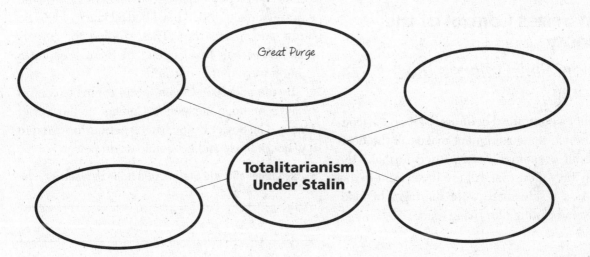

A Government of Total Control

(pages 874–876)

What is totalitarianism?

The term **totalitarianism** describes a government that takes control of almost all parts of people's lives. A very powerful leader leads this type of government. Usually the leader brings security to the nation. The government stays in power by using different ways to keep control.

The weapons of totalitarianism include using police terror. Police may spy on people, use brutal force, or even murder them. The government might also control schools and use them to mold students' minds. Another weapon is *propaganda*.

This is false information that is spread by the government to make people believe the government is working for their best interests. At other times the government will censor, that is block, certain information from becoming public.

Totalitarian rulers might also choose some people to persecute. The group may be blamed for things that go wrong in the country. Often these are people from a certain ethnic group or religion. They may be forced to live in certain areas or have rules that apply only to them.

1. What are two weapons of totalitarianism?

_____

_____

Stalin Builds a Totalitarian State

(pages 877–878)

How did Stalin control the country?

Stalin kept tight control on the Soviet Union. He did this by creating a powerful secret police. In the mid-1930s, he turned against enemies—both real and imagined—within the Communist Party. Thousands were arrested. Many were sent to exile or killed. This was known as the **Great Purge.**

Stalin also used propaganda to keep control. He controlled newspapers, radio, and other sources of information. He also used the arts to promote his ideas. Stalin's government also moved against religion. Churches were destroyed. Church leaders were killed or sent into exile.

2. Who died in the Great Purge?

_____

_____

Stalin Seizes Control of the Economy (pages 877–878)

How did Stalin change the economy?

Stalin built a **command economy.** This is an economy in which the government makes all the decisions about economic life. He tried to make the economy fully industrial. All resources went to this effort. As a result, there were shortages of food, housing, and clothing for many years.

Stalin also began a farming revolution. The government took control of people's farms. It put them together into large, government-owned farms called **collective farms.** Wealthy peasants called kulaks resisted. Millions were killed, and millions more were exiled to Siberia. Stalin got farm output to rise by using these brutal methods.

3. How did Stalin's economic changes result in suffering?

_____

_____

Daily Life under Stalin; Total Control Achieved (pages 878–879)

How did Stalin change Soviet society?

Stalin completely changed Soviet society. Women enjoyed equal rights. They filled all kinds of jobs on farms and in factories. They studied for careers that before had been closed to them. People in general were more educated.

By the mid-1930s Stalin was in complete control of all economic and political affairs in the Soviet Union. The Soviet Union had been transformed into a major political and economic world power.

4. What benefits did Stalin's rule bring to women?

_____

_____

Imperial China Collapses

BEFORE YOU READ

In the last section, you read about totalitarianism in the Soviet Union.

In this section, you will learn about the overthrow of the Qing dynasty and the beginnings of the Communist party in China.

AS YOU READ

Use the time line below to take notes on the changes that occurred in China in the early decades of the 20th century.

TERMS AND NAMES

Sun Yixian One of the first leaders of the Kuomintang; "father of modern China"

Kuomintang Nationalist Party of China that overthrew the Qing Dynasty

May Fourth Movement Chinese nationalist protest against China's fate as decided by the Treaty of Versailles

Mao Zedong Leader of the Communist revolution in China

Jiang Jieshi Leader of the Chinese Nationalist Party

Long March Escape of Communists to safety after being surrounded by Nationalist forces

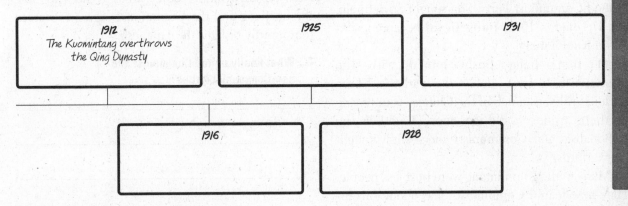

1912	1925	1931
The Kuomintang overthrows the Qing Dynasty		

1916	1928

Nationalists Overthrow Qing Dynasty (pages 882–883)

Who was Sun Yixian?

The early 20th century was a time of change in China. Many Chinese resented the great control that foreign nations had over their economy. Some wanted to modernize China. They hoped it could regain power.

One of the leaders of this push was **Sun Yixian**. His group was called the **Kuomintang,** or Nationalist Party. In 1912, he led a revolt that overthrew the Qing Dynasty. A republic was established, and he was made the president.

Sun wanted political and economic rights for all Chinese people. He also wanted an end to the foreign control of China. But Sun did not have the support of the military. Six weeks later, he turned over his presidency to Yuan Shikai, a powerful general. Yuan became a military dictator. After he died in 1916, civil war broke out. The people suffered terribly from famine and brutal attacks.

China's leaders hoped to win the support of the Allies during World War I. They declared war on Germany. When the war ended, though, they were disappointed. The Treaty of Versailles did not give China freedom from foreign influence. It only changed masters. The parts of China that had been controlled by Germany were handed over to Japan.

Angry Chinese protested during the **May Fourth Movement.** Protesters included **Mao Zedong.** He later became the leader of China's Communist revolution.

1. What did China's Nationalists want?

_____

_____

_____

_____

The Communist Party in China
(pages 883–884)

What happened to the Communist Party?

In the 1920s, revolutionaries began to look to Marxism and the Russian Revolution for a solution to China's problems. Meanwhile, Sun Yixian became disappointed in the Western democracies. They refused to support his struggling government. He decided to become allies with the newly formed Communist Party. Sun sought Soviet help, too. He died in 1925. **Jiang Jieshi** became leader of the Kuomintang.

At first, Jiang Jieshi joined with the Communists to try to defeat the warlords. These warlords ruled as much of the Chinese countryside as their armies could conquer. Together the Nationalists and Communists successfully fought the warlords.

Many in the Kuomintang were business people. They now feared Communist ideas about government control of economic life. In 1927, Jiang began fighting the Communists. The Communists were forced into hiding. In 1928, Jiang became president of China. Soon China was torn by a civil war between the remaining Communists and Jiang's forces.

2. What role did Jiang Jieshi play in creating the civil war?

_____

_____

_____

_____

Civil War Rages in China
(pages 884–886)

Who fought the civil war?

Jiang had promised democracy and political rights to all Chinese. But his government had become less democratic and more corrupt. Nothing was done to improve the life of the rural peasants. Many of them gave their support to the Chinese Communist Party.

Communist leader, Mao Zedong, built an army of peasants. In 1933, Jiang's army surrounded them. But the Communists got away. They began the famous **Long March** of 6,000 miles to the north. Thousands died. The Communists settled in caves in Northwest China.

At the same time, China had other problems. In 1931, Japan *invaded* the part of China called Manchuria. Japan took control there and six years later began invading other areas. With this new threat, Jiang and the Communists agreed to unite temporarily to fight the Japanese.

3. What finally united Communist and non-Communist forces?

_____

_____

_____

_____

Nationalism in India and Southwest Asia

TERMS AND NAMES

Rowlatt Acts Laws to prevent Indians from protesting British actions

Amritsar Massacre The slaughter of Indians by the British

Mohandas K. Gandhi Leader of the movement for Indian independence from Britain

civil disobedience Disobeying the law for the purpose of achieving some higher goal

Salt March A march to the sea to protest British salt tax

Mustafa Kemal Leader of Turkish nationalists who overthrew the last Ottoman sultan

BEFORE YOU READ

In the last section, you read about nationalism and civil war in China.

In this section, you will learn about nationalism in India and Southwest Asia.

AS YOU READ

Use the chart below to take notes on how nationalism brought change.

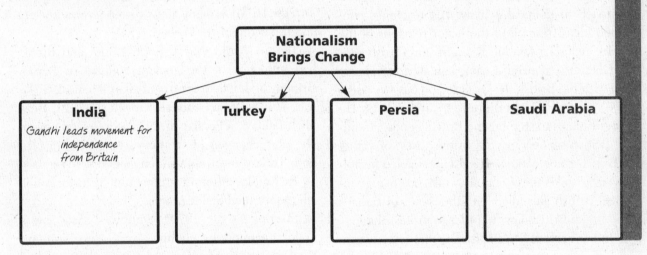

Nationalism Brings Change

India — *Gandhi leads movement for independence from Britain*

Turkey

Persia

Saudi Arabia

Indian Nationalism Grows

(pages 887–888)

Why did feelings of nationalism increase?

Many Indians grew angry at British *domination* of Indian life. Indian nationalism had been growing since the mid-1800s. Some Indians joined the Congress Party or the Muslim League. These were two groups that worked toward independence

More than one million Indians served in the British army in World War I. The British promised to make changes to the government of India. These changes would give the Indian people greater control of their own nation. After the war, though,

returning Indian soldiers were once again treated as second-class citizens. Reforms were not made. When Indians protested, the British Parliament passed the **Rowlatt Acts** that allowed protesters to be jailed without a trial. Western-educated Indians believed this to be a violation of their rights.

About 10,000 Indians gathered at the city of Amritsar to protest this act in the spring of 1919. The British had also *banned* such public meetings. But the crowd was mostly unaware of that fact. British troops fired on the crowd. Several hundred protesters were killed. The **Amritsar Massacre** sparked further protests. Almost overnight millions of Indians changed from loyal British subjects to revolutionaries and nationalists.

1. What were three reasons for the increase of Indian nationalism?

_____

_____

_____

_____

2. How did Indians use nonviolence to achieve their goals?

_____

_____

_____

_____

Gandhi's Tactics of Nonviolence; Great Britain Grants Limited Self-Rule (pages 888–889)

What were Gandhi's ideas about nonviolence?

Mohandas K. Gandhi became the leader of India's protest movement. He had attended law school in England. He had a deeply religious approach to political activity. His teachings contained ideas from all of the major religions of the world, including Hinduism, Islam, and Christianity.

Ghandi organized a campaign of *noncooperation* with the British. It was based on passive resistance, or **civil disobedience,** to unjust laws. He asked Indians to stop buying British goods, attending British schools, paying British taxes, or voting in British-run elections. He also persuaded his followers to take these actions while not using violence. British jails filled with thousands of Indians who broke British laws in order to protest them.

Indians resented a British law that forced them to buy salt only from the government. Gandhi organized a huge march to the sea to make salt by evaporating sea water. This action was called the **Salt March.**

Soon afterward, some demonstrators planned another march. They went to the place where the British government made salt. They wanted to close this site down. The British violently broke up the march. A news story about the event was published everywhere. It helped Ghandi's independence movement gain worldwide support. In 1935, the British finally gave in. They passed a law that allowed local Indian self-government.

Nationalism Spreads to Southwest Asia (pages 890–891)

What countries in Southwest Asia experienced great changes?

Other changes took place in Southwest Asia. **Mustafa Kemal**, a military commander, led nationalists in overthrowing the last Ottoman sultan. Kemal became the leader of a new republic in Turkey. He took many steps to modernize society and the economy in Turkey.

Before World War I, both Britain and Russia had influence in the ancient country of Persia. Britain tried to take control of all of Persia after the war. This led to a nationalist revolt. In 1921, Reza Shah Pahlavi, a Persian army officer, seized power. He later changed his country's name to Iran. In both Turkey and Iran, women gained new rights.

In Arabia, different groups united to form one kingdom called Saudi Arabia.

Starting in the 1920s, Southwest Asia saw a major economic change and development. Western companies discovered large reserves of oil in several countries in this area. Oil brought huge sums of money to these countries. Western nations tried to gain power in the region so they could get some of this wealth.

3. What new countries were formed in Southwest Asia?

_____

_____

_____

_____

_____

Glossary

banned Made a law or ruling against

corruption Dishonesty; failure to act in the best interests of others

czar Ruler of Russia

domination Control

executed Killed

invaded Entered a country with the goal of taking it over

noncooperation Failure to obey rules and laws

propaganda Information or material used to advance a cause; persuasion for a political purpose

radical Those who favor completely new ways of doing things

Siberia Place of punishment in Russia

slogan Saying

AFTER YOU READ

Terms and Names

A. Write the name or term in each blank that best completes the meaning of the paragraph.

soviets

Duma

Lenin

Bolsheviks

provisional government

In the early 1900s, a group of revolutionaries called **1** _____ came into being in Russia. Their leader was **2** _____ . A few years later, the czar created a parliamentary body called the **3** _____ . Still, this was not sufficient change for the revolutionaries. In March 1917, the czar stepped down. A **4** _____ was set up. It was led by Alexander Kerensky. Revolutionaries formed groups called **5** _____ . These were local councils that gained a great deal of decision-making power.

B. Write the letter of the name or term next to the description that explains it best.

a. Kuomintang

b. Long March

c. totalitarian

d. civil disobedience

e. command economy

____ **1.** Escape of Communist forces in China

____ **2.** Noncooperation with the government to resist unfair laws

____ **3.** A style of government with complete control of the lives of its citizens

____ **4.** Economic system in which the government makes all decisions

____ **5.** Nationalist party of China

AFTER YOU READ (cont.) *CHAPTER 30* Revolution and Nationalism

Main Ideas

1. How did revolution lead to civil war in Russia?

_____

_____

_____

2. How did Stalin gain total control of the Soviet Union?

_____

_____

_____

3. Why did Chinese nationalists overthrow the Qing Dynasty?

_____

_____

_____

4. What is the significance of the Salt March in Indian history?

_____

_____

_____

5. What role did Mustafa Kemal play in Turkish history?

_____

_____

_____

Thinking Critically

Answer the following questions on a separate sheet of paper.

1. How was Stalin's control of the economy typical of totalitarianism?

2. How did the Treaty of Versailles add to China's problems?

CHAPTER 31 Section 1 (pages 897–901)

Postwar Uncertainty

BEFORE YOU READ

In the last chapter, you read about nationalism and revolution.

In this section, you will learn how new ideas changed old ways of thinking.

AS YOU READ

Use the web diagram below to take notes on changes in the postwar period.

TERMS AND NAMES

Albert Einstein Scientist who developed the theory of relativity

theory of relativity Idea that as moving objects approach the speed of light, space and time become relative

Sigmund Freud Physician who exposed the workings of the unconscious mind

existentialism Philosophy that says each person must make meaning in a world that has no universal meaning

Friedrich Nietzsche German philosopher who dismissed reason, democracy, and progress as empty ideas

surrealism Art movement in which a dreamlike world, outside of reality, is portrayed or evoked

jazz Lively, loose form of popular music developed in the United States

Charles Lindbergh First person to fly alone across the Atlantic

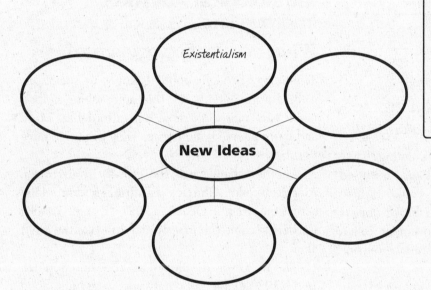

A New Revolution in Science
(page 897)

How did Einstein and Freud challenge old ideas?

Two thinkers developed *radical* new ideas that challenged old ways of thinking. **Albert Einstein** completely changed *physics* with his ideas about space, time, matter, and energy. He said that as moving objects neared the speed of light, space and time became relative. That means they change. His idea is the **theory of relativity**.

Sigmund Freud changed the way people thought about the human mind. He said that much of human behavior was *irrational*—due to urges and desires buried in the unconscious mind of each person. At first, people did not want to accept Freud's ideas. Eventually, they gained wide influence.

1. What were Einstein's and Freud's new ideas?

_____

_____

Literature in the 1920s (pages 898–899)

How did writers and philosophers of the 1920s reflect society's concerns?

Many philosophers lost faith in reason and progress after they looked at the destruction caused by

World War I. One group developed the idea known as existentialism. **Existentialism** argues that there is no universal meaning to the world. Each person must give life meaning through his or her own actions.

These thinkers had been influenced by **Friedrich Nietzsche**. Nietzsche was a German philosopher of the late 1800s. He said that reason, democracy, and progress were empty ideas. He urged people to adopt the values of pride and strength.

Some authors, like Franz Kafka, wrote about the horrors of modern life. His novels put people in threatening situations that they could not understand or escape.

2. What is existentialism?

_____

_____

Revolution in the Arts (page 899)

How was painting of this time different from traditional painting?

Artists rebelled against traditional painting. They did not recreate realistic objects. Paul Klee used bold colors and *distorted* lines. Pablo Picasso founded a style called *cubism* that broke objects into geometric shapes. An art movement called **surrealism** showed a dreamlike existence outside reality.

Composers created a new style of music. Some, like Igor Stravinsky, used unusual rhythms or harsh, rather than pleasing, sounds. African-American musicians in the United States developed a lively, loose form of popular music called **jazz**.

3. What two new styles arose in the visual arts?

_____

_____

Society Challenges Convention
(page 900)

How did society change?

Society changed after World War I as well. Young people experimented with modern values. Women set aside earlier forms of dress, wearing new styles that were looser and shorter. Many women also began to work in new careers.

4. In what ways was society more open?

_____

_____

_____

Technological Advances Improve Life (pages 900–901)

What new technology arose?

Technology brought about changes to society as well. Improvements to the automobile helped make cars more desirable and affordable. More and more people bought cars. They began to move to suburbs.

Another change was the growth in air travel. American pilot **Charles Lindbergh** flew alone across the Atlantic Ocean in 1927. In 1932, Amelia Earhart became the first woman to make the flight alone.

The radio was developed and became popular. In the 1920s, large radio networks were built. Soon millions of people were entertained by radios in their homes. Millions more went to movie theaters to watch motion pictures.

5. What major changes came about in travel and entertainment?

_____

_____

CHAPTER 31 Section 2 (pages 904–909)

A Worldwide Depression

BEFORE YOU READ

In the last section, you read about new ideas in the postwar world.

In this section, you will learn about economic crisis and worldwide depression.

AS YOU READ

Use the web below to record causes and effects of the Great Depression.

Causes

Boom hid economic problems

The Great Depression

Effects

TERMS AND NAMES

coalition government Temporary alliance of several political parties

Weimar Republic Government of Germany after World War I

Great Depression Severe economic downturn that followed the collapse of the U.S. stock market in 1929

Franklin D. Roosevelt President of the United States during the Depression

New Deal Roosevelt's program for creating jobs and improving the American economy

---

Postwar Europe; The Weimar Republic (pages 904–906)

What problems did Europe face after the war?

After the war, European countries were in bad political and economic shape. Even nations that had democratic governments for many years experienced problems. They had so many political parties that no one party could rule alone. Sometimes a **coalition government** had to be formed. This was an alliance of several political parties. In addi-

tion, governments lasted for such a short time that it was hard to develop policies.

The situation was the worst in Germany. The people felt little loyalty to the government. Germany's government, the **Weimar Republic**, was very weak. Prices rose sharply, and money lost its value. Later, American bank loans helped the German economy recover.

World nations also took steps to try to make sure there would be lasting peace. France and Germany promised never to attack one another. Most countries of the world signed a treaty in which they *pledged* not to go to war. There was no way to enforce the treaty, however.

1. Why was the postwar situation in Germany especially bad?

_____

_____

_____

Financial Collapse; The Great Depression (pages 906–908)

Where and how did the Great Depression begin?

The economy of the United States enjoyed a *boom* in the 1920s. But this growth hid problems. Consumers were unable to buy all the goods produced. When their purchases slowed, factories slowed production. Farmers faced falling food prices and slow sales. They were unable to repay loans and lost their farms. In 1929, stock prices in the United States plunged. The **Great Depression** had begun.

The depression affected other countries. Nations raised *tariffs*—taxes on goods imported from other countries—to keep import prices high. They hoped to increase sales by local companies. Unfortunately, trade between nations dropped, and unemployment shot up in many countries. The world suffered.

2. What caused the Great Depression?

_____

_____

The World Confronts the Crisis
(pages 908–909)

How did various countries meet this crisis?

Each country met the economic crisis in its own way. In Britain, a new multiparty government took over. It took steps that slowly improved the economy and cut unemployment.

In France, the political situation was worse. After several governments lost support, *moderates* and *socialists* combined to form a government. It passed laws to help workers, but companies raised prices to cover their labor costs. Unemployment remained high.

In Sweden, Norway, and Denmark, the governments played active roles in the economy. They taxed people with jobs to have money to pay benefits to people without jobs. The governments also created jobs by hiring out-of-work people to build roads and buildings.

In the United States, **Franklin D. Roosevelt** began a program called the **New Deal**. The government spent large amounts of money on constructing roads, dams, bridges, airports, and buildings. This effort created jobs for millions. Businesses and farmers also got help from the government. The American economy got better, but the *recovery* was slow.

3. How did the United States meet the crisis?

_____

_____

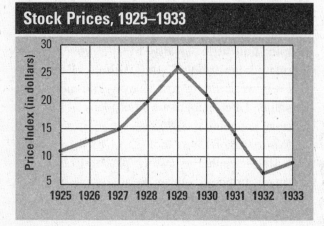

Stock Prices, 1925–1933

Skillbuilder
Use the graph to answer the questions.

1. How did the average price per stock share change between 1925 and 1929?

_____

_____

2. How did the average price per share change between 1929 and 1932?

_____

_____

Fascism Rises in Europe

TERMS AND NAMES

fascism Political movement based on nationalism that gives power to a dictator and takes away individual rights

Benito Mussolini Fascist leader of Italy

Adolf Hitler Fascist leader of Germany

Nazism German brand of fascism

Mein Kampf Book by Hitler outlining his beliefs and goals for Germany

lebensraum Living space

BEFORE YOU READ

In the last section, you read about the Great Depression.

In this section, you will learn about the rise of fascism in Europe during troubled economic times.

AS YOU READ

Use the web diagram below to show characteristics and examples of fascism.

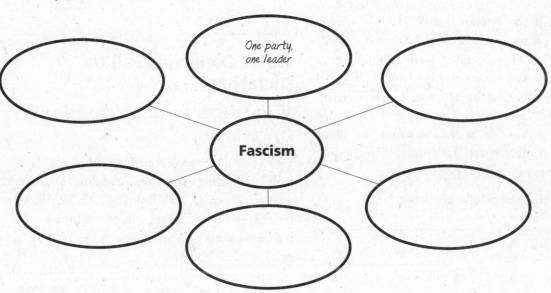

Fascism's Rise in Italy (pages 910–911)

Why did fascism arise in Italy?

The economic crisis of the Great Depression led to the loss of democracy in some countries. In these nations, millions of people turned to strong rulers to try to solve their economic problems. Such leaders followed a set of beliefs called **fascism**. Fascist leaders were very nationalistic. They believed in authority and built powerful military forces. Fascist governments were controlled by one party, and that party was ruled by one leader. The leader was the nation's *dictator*. Fascist governments did not let their people have individual rights.

Fascism arose in Italy. It started there because people were angry that they did not get more territory in the treaty that ended World War I. Also, inflation and unemployment were big problems. **Benito Mussolini** came to power by promising to help the economy and build the armed forces. He used armed *thugs* to threaten political opponents. The king of Italy decided Mussolini was the best hope to save his dynasty and let him lead the government.

Mussolini became Il Duce, or the leader, of Italy. He outlawed all political parties except fascism. He tried to control the economy and outlawed strikes.

1. What did Mussolini promise the Italians?

_____

_____

_____

_____

Hitler Rises to Power in Germany (pages 911–912)

How did Hitler gain control of Germany?

Another Fascist came to power in Germany. **Adolf Hitler** was the leader of the Nazi party. The German brand of fascism was called **Nazism.** He tried to take control of the government of Germany in 1923, but the attempt failed. He was sent to prison. In prison, Hitler wrote a book that summarized his ideas. It was called *Mein Kampf.* Hitler believed that Germans were superior to all other people. He said that the Treaty of Versailles treated Germany unfairly. He also said that a crowded Germany needed more *lebensraum*, or living space. To get that space, he promised to conquer the lands of eastern Europe and Russia.

2. What were some of Hitler's beliefs?

_____

_____

_____

Hitler Becomes Chancellor

(pages 912–914)

What did Hitler do when he became Germany's leader?

When the depression hit Germany, the country was in terrible shape. Hitler was named leader of the German government. Soon, he took the powers of a dictator. He became Germany's führer, or leader.

Those who opposed him were arrested. His economic program gave work to millions but took away their rights to organize into unions or to strike. He took control of all areas of life. He burned books that went against Nazi ideas. He forced children to join Nazi groups.

Hitler also attacked Germany's Jews. Laws took away their rights. In November 1938, mobs attacked Jewish people and destroyed thousands of Jewish-owned buildings. This was the start of a process to eliminate the Jews from German life.

3. What changes did Hitler make?

_____

_____

_____

_____

Other Countries Fall to Dictators (page 914)

What other countries were ruled by dictators?

Fascist dictators took control in other countries as well, including Hungary, Poland, Yugoslavia, Albania, Bulgaria, and Romania. All had dictators or kings who ruled like dictators. Only Czechoslovakia remained as a democracy in eastern Europe.

Elsewhere in Europe, only in nations with strong democratic traditions—Britain, France and the Scandinavian countries—did democracy survive.

4. Why did democracy survive in some countries?

_____

_____

_____

_____

CHAPTER 31 Section 4 (pages 915–919)

Aggressors Invade Nations

BEFORE YOU READ

In the last section, you read about the rise of fascism.
In this section, you will learn about military actions that led to a second world war.

AS YOU READ

Use the time line below to show when and where aggression took place.

> **TERMS AND NAMES**
> **appeasement** Giving in to keep the peace
> **Axis Powers** Germany, Italy, and Japan
> **Francisco Franco** Spain's Fascist dictator
> **isolationism** Belief that political ties with other countries should be avoided
> **Third Reich** German empire
> **Munich Conference** Meeting of world powers in 1938 that allowed Hitler to take part of Czechoslovakia

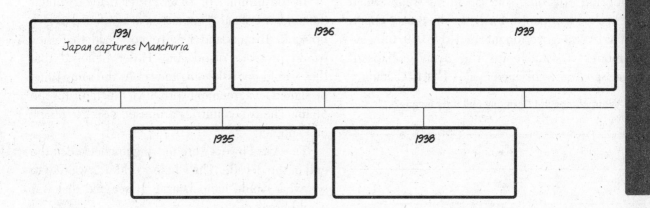

1931
Japan captures Manchuria

1936

1939

1935

1938

Japan Seeks an Empire (pages 915–916)

Why did Japan wish to expand?

Military leaders took control of Japan during the Great Depression. They wanted to solve the country's economic problems by foreign expansion.

In 1931, the Japanese army *invaded* Manchuria, a province of China. Manchuria was rich in coal and iron. These were valuable resources for the Japanese economy. Other countries spoke in protest in the League of Nations but did nothing else. Japan ignored the protests. In 1933, it pulled out of the League.

Four years later, Japan invaded China. The powerful Japanese army swept Chinese fighters aside. It killed tens of thousands of civilians and soldiers in the city of Nanjing. In spite of these losses, Chinese forces—both the nationalists of the

government and Communist rebels—continued to resist Japan.

1. What territories did Japan invade?

_____

_____

European Aggressors on the March (pages 916–917)

What European nations were aggressors?

Italy's Mussolini also wanted to expand. He dreamed of an Italian empire in Africa. In 1935 he ordered the invasion of Ethiopia. His troops won an easy victory. Haile Selassie, the emperor of Ethiopia, pleaded with the League of Nations to help. The League did nothing. By giving in to Mussolini in Africa, Britain and France hoped to keep the peace in Europe.

Hitler made moves also. He broke the Versailles Treaty by rebuilding Germany's army. In 1936, he sent troops into an area along the Rhine River between Germany and France that the treaty had forbidden the Germans to enter. The French and British again responded with **appeasement**—giving in to keep the peace.

The German movement into the Rhineland marked a turning point in the march toward war. Also in 1936, Hitler signed an alliance with Mussolini and with Japan. These three nations came to be called the **Axis Powers**.

In 1936, civil war broke out in Spain. The army, led by General **Francisco Franco,** revolted against a government run by liberals and socialists. Hitler and Mussolini sent aid to the army, which was backed by Spanish Fascists. The Soviet Union sent aid to the government. In early 1939, the government's resistance to the army collapsed. Francisco Franco became Spain's Fascist dictator.

2. What places did Germany and Italy invade?

_____

_____

_____

_____

Democratic Nations Try to Preserve Peace (pages 918–919)

Why did the world's democracies fail to stop the aggression?

At this time, many Americans resisted accepting the nation's new role as a world leader. They believed that the United States should follow a pol-

icy of **isolationism**. Isolationism was the belief that political ties with other countries should be avoided. This, it was thought, would keep the country out of another foreign war.

In March 1938, Hitler moved his troops into Austria. He made it part of the **Third Reich**, or German Empire. This action broke the Versailles Treaty again. France and Britain once more did nothing.

Later that year, Hitler demanded that Czechoslovakia give up a part of its land to Germany. Czechoslovakia refused. The **Munich Conference** was held in September 1938 to solve the problem. At this meeting Germany, France, Britain, and Italy agreed to allow the Germans to take the land. In return, Hitler promised to respect the new borders of Czechoslovakia. A few months later, however, he took the entire country.

In the summer of 1939, Hitler made a similar demand of Poland. That nation also refused to give up land. Britain and France now said that they would protect Poland. But Hitler believed that they would not risk going to war. At the same time, he signed an agreement with Soviet dictator Joseph Stalin. The two countries promised never to attack one another.

The Axis Powers were moving unchecked at the end of the decade. The whole world was waiting to see what would happen next. It seemed that war would break out.

3. What happened at the Munich Conference?

_____

_____

_____

_____

Glossary

boom Period of great economic growth

cubism Art style that portrayed objects in geometric shapes

dictator Ruler who has absolute authority

distorted Twisted; not in the usual shape

invaded Entered a country for the purpose of taking it over

irrational Not reasonable; not consciously thought out

moderates People who are not liberal (in favor of great change) or conservative (reluctant to change) but in the middle

physics Science of matter and energy

pledged Promised

radical Extreme; carried to the limit

recovery Economic growth following a depression or recession

socialists People who believed in socialist ideas, such as shared ownership of business

tariffs Taxes on goods imported from other countries

thugs People who carry out violent activities on someone else's orders

AFTER YOU READ

Terms and Names

A. Write the name or term in each blank that best completes the meaning of the paragraph.

theory of relativity

existentialism

Sigmund Freud

Friedrich Nietzsche

Albert Einstein

Postwar Europe produced many new thinkers. Among them was the scientist **1** _____. He offered new ideas about space, time, and matter. One of them was his **2** _____. Another important thinker of this time was a doctor who studied the mind. His name was **3** _____. He helped reveal the power of the unconscious mind. An important philosopher whose ideas greatly influenced thinkers of this era was **4** _____. Thinkers of this time developed a new philosophy. This philosophy, **5** _____, says that it is up to individuals to give meaning to a meaningless world.

B. Write the letter of the name or term next to the description that explains it best.

a. Weimar Republic

b. Third Reich

c. coalition government

d. fascism

e. *lebensraum*

_____ **1.** German empire

_____ **2.** Temporary alliance of several political parties

_____ **3.** living space

_____ **4.** Government of Germany after the first world war

_____ **5.** Political movement emphasizing loyalty to the state

AFTER YOU READ (continued) **CHAPTER 31** Years of Crisis

Main Ideas

1. How did technology change society after the war?

_____

_____

_____

2. Describe the programs of the New Deal.

_____

_____

_____

3. Name four of Hitler's actions that showed he was an absolute ruler, or dictator.

_____

_____

_____

4. What beliefs and goals did Hitler express in *Mein Kampf?*

_____

_____

_____

5. What were the policies of the United States when the Axis Powers were invading other lands?

_____

_____

_____

Thinking Critically

Answer the following questions on a separate sheet of paper.

1. What conditions in Europe helped give rise to the rule of dictators?

2. Why did the democracies of Europe fail to stop aggression?

Hitler's Lightning War

BEFORE YOU READ

In the last chapter, you read about actions that led up to World War II.

In this section, you will learn about the first years of the war in Europe.

AS YOU READ

Use the time line below to take notes on key events in the first two years of the war.

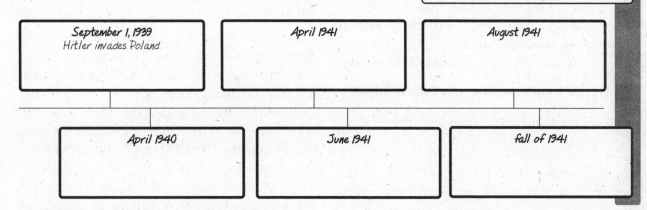

September 1, 1939
Hitler invades Poland

April 1941

August 1941

April 1940

June 1941

fall of 1941

Germany Sparks a New War in Europe (pages 925–926)

What caused Britain and France to declare war?

In 1939, Adolf Hitler decided to move on Poland. He had already conquered Austria and Czechoslovakia. When Hitler signed a **nonaggression pact** with Joseph Stalin of the Soviet Union, they agreed not to attack each other. Secretly, they also agreed to split Poland between them. This deal removed the threat of the Soviets attacking Germany from the east.

So, on September 1, the German army invaded Poland in a surprise attack. Using planes, tanks, and troops, it moved suddenly in a technique called **blitzkrieg**, or "lightning war." Britain and France

declared war, but Poland fell before they could help.

On September 17, after secret agreement with Hitler, Stalin invaded eastern Poland. Stalin then began annexing the regions covered in a second part of the agreement. Lithuania, Latvia, and Estonia fell without a struggle. However, Finland fought back. In March 1940, Finland was forced to surrender.

For seven months after Poland fell to the Germans, Europe was calm. France and Britain got their armies ready. They waited for Hitler's next move.

1. Why did Poland fall to the Germans so quickly?

_____

_____

_____

The Fall of France; The Battle of Britain (pages 926–928)

What happened when France and Britain were attacked?

Suddenly in April 1940, Hitler's armies invaded Denmark and Norway. Within two months, they also captured Belgium, the Netherlands, Luxembourg, and France. Part of the French army, led by **Charles de Gaulle**, escaped to Britain to remain free and continue the fight. By then, Italy's Benito Mussolini had joined Hitler's side.

Great Britain—now led by **Winston Churchill**—stood alone. The German air force began bombing Britain. It wanted to weaken the country. Germany was getting prepared to invade Britain. But the British air force fought back. It was helped by the recently developed radar. This was an electronic tracking system that warned of coming attacks. Also, the British had broken the German army's secret code. The **Battle of Britain** lasted many months. Unable to break British *defenses*, Hitler called off the attacks in May 1941.

2. Why did Germany fail to win the Battle of Britain?

_____

_____

_____

_____

The Mediterranean and the Eastern Front (pages 928–930)

What countries did Hitler invade?

Hitler then turned his attention to the east and to the Mediterranean. Germany sent troops under General **Erwin Rommel** to North Africa to help Italy fight the British. In April 1941, German armies quickly took control of Yugoslavia and Greece. In June, Hitler began a surprise invasion of the Soviet Union. The Red Army was the largest in the world. But it was not well-equipped or well-trained. The Germans quickly pushed deep into Soviet territory. The Red Army was forced to retreat.

To keep supplies out of German hands, the Red Army destroyed everything left behind. The

Germans were stopped from taking Leningrad in the north. They then turned on Moscow, the Soviet capital. A strong Soviet *counterattack*, combined with fierce Russian winter weather, forced the Germans back. Moscow had been saved, and the battle had cost the Germans 500,000 lives.

3. What happened when Germany invaded the Soviet Union?

_____

_____

_____

_____

The United States Aids its Allies (page 930)

How did the United States take sides?

The United States watched these events. Many Americans did not want to join in the war. President Roosevelt wanted to help the Allies, however. He asked Congress to allow Britain and France to buy American weapons. Soon, American ships were *escorting* British ships carrying guns bought from the United States. By the fall of 1941, U.S. ships had orders to fire on German submarines that threatened the ships. The United States and Germany were fighting an undeclared naval war.

Roosevelt met secretly with Churchill in August of 1941. Although the United States was not officially in the war, the two leaders issued a statement called the **Atlantic Charter**. It supported free trade and the right of people to form their own government.

4. Name two ways in which the United States supported the Allies.

_____

_____

_____

_____

CHAPTER 32 Section 2 (pages 931–935)

Japan's Pacific Campaign

BEFORE YOU READ

In the last section, you read about the war against Hitler in Europe.

In this section, you will learn about the war against Japan in the Pacific.

AS YOU READ

Use the chart below to record key events in the war in the Pacific.

TERMS AND NAMES

Isoroku Yamamoto Japanese admiral who decided that the U.S. fleet in Hawaii had to be destroyed

Pearl Harbor Navy base in Hawaii attacked by the Japanese

Battle of Midway Sea and air battle in which American forces defeated Japanese forces near Midway Island in the Pacific

Douglas MacArthur U.S. general who commanded Allied forces in the Pacific

Battle of Guadalcanal Six-month battle on the island of Guadalcanal in which American and Australian troops defeated Japanese defenders

	ACTION	RESULT
Pearl Harbor	Japanese bomb American fleet.	
Battle of the Coral Sea		
Battle of Midway		
Battle of Guadalcanal		

Surprise Attack on Pearl Harbor
(pages 931–932)

How did the United States fight Japan before declaring war?

The military leaders who ran the Japanese government also had plans to build an empire. Japan was overcrowded and did not have enough raw materials or oil.

The Japanese captured part of China in 1931. In 1937, they invaded the center of China. There they met strong *resistance*. Needing resources for this war, they decided to move into Southeast Asia.

The United States feared that Japanese control of this area would threaten U.S. holdings in the Pacific. Roosevelt gave military aid to China. He also cut off oil shipments to Japan.

Japanese Admiral **Isoroku Yamamoto** decided that the U.S. *fleet* in Hawaii had to be destroyed. On December 7, 1941, the Japanese navy began a surprise attack on the U.S. naval base at **Pearl Harbor** in Hawaii. In just two hours, Japanese planes sank or damaged a major part of the U.S. Pacific fleet—19 ships, including 8 battleships. The next day, Congress, at the request of President Roosevelt, declared war on Japan and its allies.

1. How did the United States respond to the Japanese attack on Pearl Harbor?

_____

_____

Japanese Victories (page 932)

What areas of Asia did the Japanese conquer between December 1941 and mid-1942?

The Japanese attack on Pearl Harbor was just one of many sudden strikes. Japan also captured Guam, Wake Island, and the Philippines from the United States. It took Indonesia from the Dutch and Hong Kong, Malaya, and Singapore from the British.

Japan then invaded Burma, located between India and China. Japan wanted to stop China from receiving supplies through Burma. Burma fell in May 1942. By that time, Japan had conquered more than 1 million square miles of land with about 150 million people.

Before these conquests, the Japanese had tried to win the support of Asians. They used the anti-colonial slogan "Asia for the Asians." After their victory, the Japanese made it clear that they had come as conquerers.

2. What countries lost territory to Japan early in the war?

_____

_____

_____

The Allies Strike Back; An Allied Offensive (pages 934–935)

How did the Allies strike back?

The Japanese seemed unbeatable after a string of victories. But the Allies wanted to strike back in the Pacific. In April 1942, the United States sent planes to drop bombs on Tokyo. The attack raised the *morale* of Americans. In May 1942, the Allies suffered heavy losses at the Battle of the Coral Sea. Still, they were able to stop the Japanese advance and save Australia.

The next month, the U.S. Navy scored an important victory near Midway Island in the central Pacific. In the **Battle of Midway**, Japan lost four aircraft carriers, the most important naval weapon in the war. The victory turned the tide of war against Japan.

The United States now went on the attack. General **Douglas MacArthur** did not want to invade the Japanese-held islands that were most strongly defended. He wanted to attack weaker ones. The first attack came on Guadalcanal, in the Solomon Islands in August. The Japanese were building an air base there. It took six months of fighting for U.S. and Australian troops to drive the Japanese off the island in the **Battle of Guadalcanal**. The Japanese abandoned the island in February 1943.

3. Name three Allied victories against Japan.

_____

_____

_____

_____

CHAPTER 32 Section 3 (pages 936–939)

The Holocaust

BEFORE YOU READ

In the last section, you read about the battles in the Pacific.

In this section, you will read about Hitler's "final solution" in Europe.

AS YOU READ

Use the web below to record important information about the Holocaust.

TERMS AND NAMES

Aryans Germanic peoples

Holocaust Systematic mass killing of Jews and other groups considered inferior by Nazis

Kristallnacht "Night of Broken Glass," when Nazis attacked Jews throughout Germany

ghettos Neighborhoods in which European Jews were forced to live

"Final Solution" Hitler's plan to kill as many Jews as possible

genocide Systematic killing of an entire people

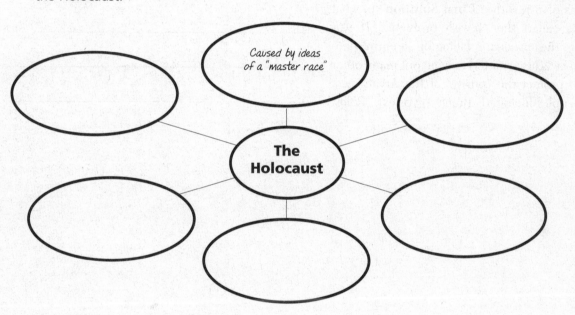

Caused by ideas of a "master race"

The Holocaust

The Holocaust Begins (pages 936–937)

What was the Holocaust?

Part of Hitler's new order for Europe included getting rid of "inferior" people. Hitler believed that the **Aryans**, or German peoples, were a "master race." He had a deep-seated hatred of people who were not German. He particularly hated Jews. This led to the **Holocaust**, the killing of millions of Jews and other civilians.

During the 1930s, Hitler passed laws that took away the rights of German Jews. One night in November 1938, Nazi mobs attacked Jews throughout Germany. They destroyed homes and businesses and killed or beat many people. This night became known as *Kristallnacht*, or "Night of Broken Glass."

Kristallnacht was a major step-up in the Nazi policy of *persecuting* the Jews. The future for the Jews in Germany looked grim. Thousands of Jews tried to leave Germany. Other countries accepted a large number but were unwilling to take all those who wished to leave.

Hitler ordered all Jews in Germany and his conquered lands to live in certain parts of cities called **ghettos**. The Nazis then sealed off the ghettos with barbed wire and stone walls. They wanted the Jews inside to starve or die of disease. Even under these horrible conditions, the Jews hung on.

1. How did the Holocaust begin?

_____

_____

_____

_____

The "Final Solution" (pages 937–939)

What was the "Final Solution"?

Hitler soon got tired of waiting for the Jews to starve or die of disease in the ghettos. He decided to take more direct action. He was going to kill as many Jews as possible.

Hitler's plan was the "**Final Solution**" to what the Nazis called the "Jewish problem." It was **genocide**, the *systematic* killing of an entire people. The Nazis also wanted to wipe out many other people to protect the "purity" of the Aryan race. These people included Roma (gypsies), Poles,

Russians, and those who were mentally or physically disabled. The Germans paid the most attention on Jews, however.

Thousands of Jews were shot to death by "killing squads." Millions were gathered and placed in *concentration camps*. These prisons used the *inmates* as slave workers. Many in the camps died of starvation or disease.

Starting in 1942, the Nazis built "death camps." At these camps, thousands of Jews were gassed to death in huge gas chambers. In the end, six million Jews were killed by the Nazis. Fewer than four million European Jews survived.

2. How was the "Final Solution" carried out?

_____

_____

_____

_____

The Allied Victory

BEFORE YOU READ

In the last section, you read about the Holocaust in Europe.

In this section, you will learn how the war was fought and brought to an end around the world.

AS YOU READ

Use the time line below to take notes on key events in the last three years of the war.

TERMS AND NAMES

Dwight D. Eisenhower American general who helped drive the Germans out of Africa

Battle of Stalingrad Battle during which the Red Army forced the Germans out of Stalingrad

D-Day Huge Allied invasion mounted to retake France from the Germans

Battle of the Bulge Final large-scale attack by German troops that was forced back by the Allies

kamikaze Japanese suicide pilots

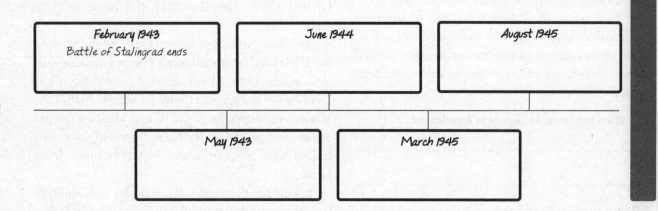

February 1943	June 1944	August 1945
Battle of Stalingrad ends		

May 1943	March 1945

The Tide Turns on Two Fronts
(pages 940–941)

Where did the tide of war turn in favor of the Allies?

In 1942, Roosevelt, Churchill, and Stalin planned the Allies' strategy. Stalin wanted Britain and the United States to open a second front against Germany to relieve the pressure on his armies. Stalin wanted the attack in France. Roosevelt and Churchill agreed to a second front but chose to attack German General Erwin Rommel in North Africa.

In late 1942, the British army led by General Bernard Montgomery drove the Germans out of Egypt and back to the west. Meanwhile, American troops under the command of General **Dwight D. Eisenhower** landed behind the Germans and began moving east. The Germans were finally forced out of Africa in May 1943.

At the same time, the Soviets gained a major victory as well. German troops had invaded the Soviet city of Stalingrad in 1942. The Red Army forced the Germans to surrender in February 1943, ending the **Battle of Stalingrad**.

American and British soldiers next invaded Italy and captured Sicily in August 1943. Mussolini was driven from power and the new Italian government surrendered. But Hitler did not want to give up Italy. His army fought there until 1945.

1. What major victories did the Allies win?

_____

_____

The Allied Home Fronts
(pages 941–943)

What problems did people face at home?

While the Allies continued to fight, people at home suffered. Some British and Soviet citizens died. In the United States, citizens faced shortages. Goods such as food, tires, gasoline, and clothing were in short supply. The government _rationed_ these items. It limited how much a person could have so there would be enough for the military.

Some Americans were even imprisoned. Bitter feelings against the Japanese became widespread. As a result, mistrust of Japanese Americans grew. The U.S. government took thousands of Japanese Americans who lived on the west coast and moved them to relocation camps in the western United States. Two-thirds of these people were American citizens.

2. What happened to Japanese Americans?

_____

_____

Victory in Europe (pages 943–945)

What were the final battles in Europe?

In early 1944, the Allies built a _massive_ force to retake France. In June, an invasion of thousands of ships, planes, and soldiers was launched. It was called **D-Day.** The invasion force suffered heavy losses but gained a foothold in northern France. A month later, Allied forces began to pour through German lines. In August, they marched in triumph into Paris. By September, they had driven the Germans out of France, Belgium, Luxembourg, and much of the Netherlands.

At the same time, the Soviets were pushing the Germans back in eastern Europe. In late 1944, Hitler ordered his army to make one final, large-scale attack in the west. In the **Battle of the Bulge,** it punched through Allied lines until an Allied counterattack forced it back to Germany. By late April 1945, Soviet troops surrounded Berlin, Hitler's headquarters. Five days later, he killed himself. A week later, the Germans surrendered. Roosevelt did not live to see this victory, however. He had died in early April. Harry Truman was now president.

3. Name three events that led directly to Germany's surrender.

_____

_____

Victory in the Pacific (pages 945–947)

What led to victory in the Pacific?

In the Pacific, the Allies began to move toward Japan in 1943. They landed troops in the Philippines in the fall of 1944. In the Battle of Leyte Gulf, in October 1944, the Japanese navy was crushed.

As American troops moved closer to Japan, they faced attacks by **kamikaze**. These Japanese suicide pilots sank Allied ships by crashing their bomb-filled planes into them. In March 1945, U.S. Marines captured the island of Iwo Jima, a _strategic_ Japanese stronghold. By June, they had won control of Okinawa, an island just 350 miles from Japan.

Japan was the next stop. But the U.S. military feared that an invasion of Japan would cost half a million Allied lives. In August, President Truman ordered that an atomic bomb be dropped on the city of Hiroshima to try to end the war quickly. A second bomb was dropped on Nagasaki three days later. Tens of thousands of Japanese died. Japan surrendered in September.

4. Name two events that led directly to Japan's surrender.

_____

_____

CHAPTER 32 Section 5 (pages 948–951)

Europe and Japan in Ruins

BEFORE YOU READ

In the last section, you read about how the war ended.

In this section, you will learn about the war's effects on Europe and Japan.

AS YOU READ

Use the chart below to take notes on the effects of the war on Europe and Japan.

```
          ┌──────────────────┐
          │   Effects of     │
          │  World War II    │
          └──────────────────┘
         ↙         ↓          ↘
┌──────────────┐ ┌──────────┐ ┌──────────┐
│  Economic    │ │ Political│ │  Social  │
│ Hundreds of  │ │          │ │          │
│ cities       │ │          │ │          │
│ destroyed    │ │          │ │          │
└──────────────┘ └──────────┘ └──────────┘
```

Devastation in Europe

(pages 948–949)

How did the war change Europe?

The war had left Europe in ruins. Almost 40 million people were dead. Hundreds of cities were reduced to rubble by constant bombing and shelling. The ground war had destroyed much of the countryside. *Displaced persons* from many nations were trying to get back home. Often there was no water, no electricity, and little food. Hunger was constant.

Agriculture had been disrupted. Most able-bodied men had served in the military, and the women had worked in war production. Few had remained to plant the fields. With factories destroyed or damaged, most people had no earnings to buy the food that was available. Also the small harvests did not reach the cities because the transportation system had been destroyed. Suffering continued for many years in Europe.

1. What conditions existed in Europe after World War II?

_____

_____

Postwar Governments and Politics (pages 949–950)

Who did the Europeans blame for the war?

Europeans often blamed their leaders for the war and its aftermath. Once Germany was defeated, some prewar governments—like those in Belgium,

Holland, Denmark, and Norway—returned quickly. In Germany, Italy, and France, the old fascist governments had disappeared. At first, the Communist parties grew strong in France and Italy. People who opposed Communism grew alarmed. They voted leaders from other parties into power. Communism lost its appeal when the economies of these lands improved.

During efforts to rebuild Europe, the Allies held the **Nuremberg Trials** in the German city of Nuremberg. There, captured Nazi leaders were charged with crimes against humanity. They were found guilty, and some were executed.

2. **What were the Nuremberg Trials?**

_____

_____

_____

Postwar Japan; Occupation Brings Deep Changes (pages 950–951)

What changes were made in Japan?

The defeat suffered by Japan in World War II had *devastated* that country. Two million lives had been lost. The country's major cities were in ruins.

The U.S. Army occupied Japan under the command of General MacArthur. He began a process of **demilitarization**, breaking down the Japanese armed forces. MacArthur also paid attention to **democratization,** or creating a government elected by the people. His first step was to write a new constitution. It gave all power to the Japanese people, who voted for members of a parliament that would rule the land. All Japanese over age 20—including women—were given the right to vote. In 1951, other nations finally signed a formal peace with Japan. A few months later, U.S. military occupation ended.

3. **How did the government of Japan change?**

_____

_____

_____

Glossary

concentration camp Camp where enemies of the government and other people are held against their will, often under brutal conditions

counterattack Attack made in response to an enemy's attack

defenses Weapons used against, or readiness for, attack

devastated Destroyed

displaced persons People driven from their homeland by war or internal upheaval

escorting Traveling with for the sake of protection

fleet Number of ships operating together under one command

inmates Prisoners

massive Huge

morale Spirit

persecuting Harassing with ill-treatment, especially because of race, religion, or beliefs

rationed Limited the amount a person could have

resistance Fighting back

strategic Important or essential to a plan of action

systematic Done according to a plan or system

AFTER YOU READ

Terms and Names

A. Write the name or term in each blank that best completes the meaning of the paragraph.

"Final Solution"

Aryans

ghettos

Kristallnacht

Holocaust

During World War II, Hitler began to carry out a plan of mass killing. This was called the **1** _____. Hitler aimed to kill those people who were not **2** _____, or Germanic. Most of the people he killed were Jews. One of his earliest attacks on Jews occurred on November 9, 1938. It has come to be known as **3** _____. Soon, Nazis began placing all the Jews in **4** _____, or separate neighborhoods. Then they began to carry out the plan for getting rid of them forever—the **5** _____.

B. Write the letter of the name next to the description that explains it best.

a. Charles de Gaulle

b. Winston Churchill

c. Battle of the Bulge

d. Douglas MacArthur

e. Battle of Midway

_____ **1.** Leader of the French government-in-exile

_____ **2.** Leader of Allied forces in the Pacific

_____ **3.** Air and sea battle fought in the Pacific

_____ **4.** Leader of Great Britain

_____ **5.** Large-scale offensive launched by the Germans late in 1944

Main Ideas

1. How was Hitler first stopped?

_____

_____

_____

2. What did Japan do in its effort to create a Pacific Empire?

_____

_____

_____

3. What groups were targeted by Hitler for the "Final Solution"?

_____

_____

_____

4. What types of suffering occurred on home fronts during the war?

_____

_____

_____

_____

5. How did the American occupation change Japan?

_____

_____

_____

Thinking Critically

Answer the following questions on a separate sheet of paper.

1. In what ways had the United States begun fighting World War II before it was attacked?

2. Explain and support this statement: Early Allied victories in the Pacific were extremely costly.

Cold War: Superpowers Face Off

BEFORE YOU READ

In the last section, you learned about the end of the Second World War.

In this section, you will learn about the international tensions that followed the war.

AS YOU READ

Use the chart below to take notes on causes and effects of the Cold War.

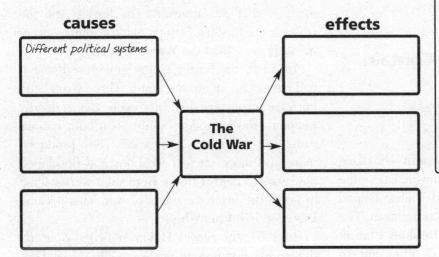

causes

Different political systems

The Cold War

effects

TERMS AND NAMES

United Nations World organization formed to prevent war

iron curtain Division between Eastern and Western Europe during the Cold War

containment Policy aimed at preventing the spread of communism

Truman Doctrine Policy of giving aid to countries threatened by communism

Marshall Plan Plan to give aid to European countries to help them recover from the war

Cold War State of tension and mistrust between the United States and the Soviet Union after World War II

NATO Military alliance including the United States, Canada, and several countries in Western Europe

Warsaw Pact Military alliance between the Soviet Union and the countries of Eastern Europe

brinkmanship Willingness on the part of the superpower to go to the brink, or edge, of war

Allies Become Enemies (pages 965–966)

What caused the Cold War?

The United States and the Soviet Union were allies during World War II. In February 1945, they agreed to divide Germany into separate zones. Each zone was occupied by the soldiers of one of the Allies. The Allies also helped form the **United Nations** (UN) in 1945. The UN pledged to prevent war.

The United States and the Soviet Union had important differences after the war. The United States suffered few casualties and was the richest nation in the world. The Soviet Union suffered enormous loss of life and damage to its cities.

There were also striking political differences. The United States wanted to create new markets for its goods. It also wanted to encourage democracy. The Soviet Union wanted to set up Communist governments and make sure it did not get attacked again from the west. These differences caused tensions between the two countries.

1. How did U.S. goals and Soviet goals differ after World War II?

_____

_____

_____

Eastern Europe's Iron Curtain

(page 967)

How did the Soviet Union gain control of Eastern Europe?

At the end of World War II, Soviet forces occupied lands along its western border. After the war, Stalin made sure Communist governments were in place in these lands: Albania, Bulgaria, Hungary, Czechoslovakia, Romania, Poland, and Yugoslavia. This divided Europe between East and West. Winston Churchill called this division the **"iron curtain."**

2. **What countries were separated from the West by the iron curtain?**

_____

_____

_____

United States Tries to Contain Soviets (pages 967–969)

How did the United States respond to communism?

Truman began a policy of **containment**—blocking the Soviets from spreading communism. Under the **Truman Doctrine,** the United States helped nations that were threatened by communism. The United States also adopted the **Marshall Plan** in 1947. This plan gave food and other aid to European countries to help them recover from the war.

In 1948, the Soviets and Americans *clashed* over Germany. France, Britain, and the United States agreed to pull their troops out of Germany. They let the three zones that they occupied unite. But the Soviets refused to leave their zone. Then they cut off all highway and train traffic into Berlin, which was deep within the Soviet zone. The United States and Britain responded with the *Berlin airlift.* They flew food and supplies into the city for 11 months. Finally, the Soviets lifted the *blockade.*

3. **What was the Berlin airlift?**

_____

_____

_____

Cold War Divides the World

(pages 969–971)

Why did tensions between the superpowers increase?

The struggle between the United States and the Soviet Union was called the **Cold War.** Many countries supported one superpower or the other.

The United States, Canada, and several countries in Western Europe formed the North Atlantic Treaty Organization (**NATO**). NATO was a military *alliance.* Each nation promised to defend any other member that was attacked. The Soviets and the countries of Eastern Europe made a similar agreement. It was called the **Warsaw Pact.**

In 1949, the Soviet Union announced that it had developed an atomic bomb. Three years later, both superpowers had an even more deadly weapon—the hydrogen bomb. Soon both nations were involved in an arms race. They produced more and more nuclear weapons and developed new ways to deliver them. Both sides were willing to go to the brink, or edge, of war. This became known as **brinkmanship.**

In 1957, the Soviet Union launched *Sputnik,* the world's first human-made satellite. Many people were shocked. Americans felt that the Soviets were far ahead in science and technology. The United States then began spending huge amounts of money to improve science education.

The U-2 incident brought more tension. The United States sent planes, called U-2 planes, to spy over Soviet territory. One was shot down in 1960.

4. **What are three developments or events that increased tensions during the Cold War?**

_____

_____

_____

Communists Take Power in China

BEFORE YOU READ

In the last section, you read about tensions between the superpowers.

In this section, you will read about civil war and the rise of communism in China.

AS YOU READ

Use the chart below to take notes on changes in China.

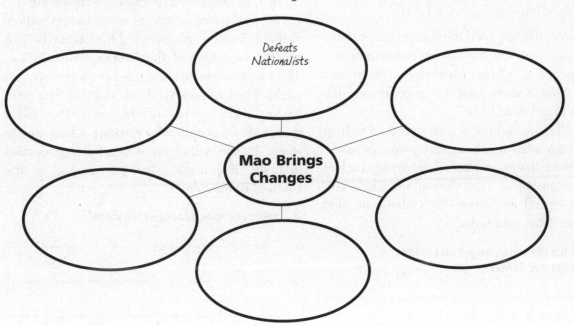

Defeats Nationalists

Mao Brings Changes

Communists vs. Nationalists

(pages 972–973)

Who fought the civil war?

Nationalists and Communists fought for control of China in the 1930s. During World War II, they joined forces to fight against the Japanese. The Communists, led by **Mao Zedong,** organized an army of peasants in northwestern China. From there they fought the Japanese in the northeast.

The Nationalists, led by **Jiang Jieshi,** controlled southwestern China. The Nationalists

were protected from the Japanese by mountains. The United States sent the Nationalists large amounts of money and supplies, but corrupt officers took much of it. The Nationalists built a large army, but they only fought a few battles against the Japanese.

After the Japanese surrendered, the Communists and Nationalists resumed their civil war. The war lasted from 1946 to 1949. The Communists won because their troops were well-trained in *guerrilla war.* They also enjoyed the backing of the peasants to whom they had promised land. In 1949, Jiang Jieshi and other Nationalist leaders fled to the island of Taiwan.

1. What two groups fought the civil war, and who led them?

_____

_____

_____

_____

_____

The Two Chinas Affect the Cold War (pages 973–974)

How did the two Chinas participate in the Cold War?

The United States helped the Nationalists set up a new government. The Nationalists called their land the Republic of China. Meanwhile, the Soviets helped Mao Zedong and his government, the People's Republic of China.

The Chinese and the Soviets promised to help defend each other if either country were attacked. The United States responded by trying to halt Soviet expansion in Asia. Communist China also tried to expand its power. The Chinese invaded Mongolia, Tibet, and India.

2. How did the superpowers take sides with the two Chinas?

_____

_____

_____

_____

_____

The Communists Transform China (pages 974–975)

How did Mao change China?

Mao set out to rebuild China. He seized land and gave it to the peasants. But he also forced the peasants—in groups of 200 to 300 households—to join *collective farms*, or **communes.** On these farms, the land belonged to the group. Mao also took control of China's industries. Under Mao's plan, production of industrial products went up.

With this success, Mao launched the "Great Leap Forward." He wanted to make the communes larger and more productive. The plan failed. People did not like strong government control. The government did not plan effectively. Between 1958 and 1961, famine killed millions.

In 1966, Mao tried to revive the revolution. He encouraged young people to revive the revolution. Students formed groups called **Red Guards.** This was the beginning of the **Cultural Revolution.** The Red Guards struck at teachers, scientists, and artists. They shut down schools and sent intellectuals to the country to work on farms. They killed thousands of people who resisted. China was in chaos. Factories shut down and farm production dropped. Eventually, Mao put an end to the Cultural Revolution.

3. What are three changes Mao made?

_____

_____

_____

_____

_____

Wars in Korea and Vietnam

BEFORE YOU READ

In the last section, you read about the civil war in China. In this section, you will read about wars in Korea and Vietnam.

AS YOU READ

Use the time line below to take notes on important events in Korea, Vietnam, and Cambodia.

TERMS AND NAMES

38th parallel Line that separated North Korea and South Korea

Douglas MacArthur Leader of United Nations forces during the Korean War

Ho Chi Minh Vietnamese nationalist who drove the French out of Vietnam and who led North Vietnam

domino theory Theory that nations were like a row of dominoes: if one fell to communism, the others would fall, too

Vietcong Communist rebels in South Vietnam who were supported by North Vietnam

Ngo Dinh Diem Leader of the anticommunist government of South Vietnam

Vietnamization Nixon's plan for gradually withdrawing U.S. troops from Vietnam and replacing them with South Vietnamese troops

Khmer Rouge Communist rebels who set up a brutal government in Cambodia

---

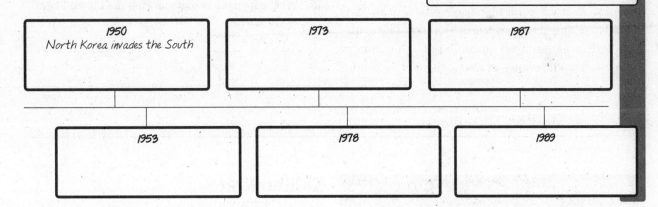

| 1950 North Korea invades the South | 1973 | 1987 |

| 1953 | 1978 | 1989 |

War in Korea (pages 976–978)

How was Korea divided?

When World War II ended, Korea became a divided nation. North of the **38th parallel,** a line that crosses Korea at 38 degrees north *latitude,* the Japanese surrendered to the Soviets. South of that line, the Japanese surrendered to the Allies.

As in Germany, two nations developed. The Soviet Union supported a Communist government in North Korea. The United States supported a non-Communist government in South Korea. On June 25, 1950, North Korea invaded South Korea. President Truman fought this move with help from the UN. The United States and other countries sent troops to assist South Korea. At first, the North Korean army captured almost all of South Korea.

Then the UN army made a bold *counterattack.* The attack was led by General **Douglas MacArthur.** In 1953, the two Koreas agreed to a *cease-fire.* The earlier boundary splitting North and South Korea remained the same.

North Korea had a Communist government. It had a strong army and tight government control, but it also had many economic problems. For more than 30 years, dictators ruled South Korea. But its economy grew, in part because it received U.S. aid. Free elections were held in South Korea after a new constitution was adopted in 1987.

1. **How did the Korean War change the way Korea was divided?**

_____

_____

War Breaks Out in Vietnam; The United States Get Involved; Postwar Southeast Asia (pages 978–981)

How did the United States get involved in Vietnam?

A nationalist named **Ho Chi Minh** drove the French out of Vietnam. This worried the United States because Ho had turned to the Communists for help. Many Americans thought if one country became Communist, others would also, like a row of dominoes. This idea is known as the **domino theory.** A peace conference split Vietnam in two, with Ho taking charge of North Vietnam. The country had a Communist government. Communist rebels—the **Vietcong**—stayed active in the South.

The non-Communist government of the South had been set up by the United States and France. Its leader was **Ngo Dinh Diem.** When his government was threatened by Communists, the United States began to send troops. When they could not win the war on the ground, they tried bombing. Many people in the United States came to oppose the war.

In the late 1960s, President Richard Nixon began a plan called **Vietnamization.** This plan called for a gradual pullout of U.S. troops. At the same time, the South Vietnamese increased their combat role. The last American troops left in 1973. Two years later, North Vietnam overran the South and made Vietnam one country again. Today, Vietnam remains Communist but is looking for other nations to invest in its economy.

Fighting in Vietnam spilled over into Vietnam's neighbor, Cambodia. Rebels there were known as the **Khmer Rouge.** They set up a brutal Communist government. The Khmer Rouge killed 2 million people. In 1978, the Vietnamese invaded the country. They overthrew the Khmer Rouge. Vietnam withdrew in 1989. In 1993, Cambodia held free elections for the first time.

2. **What happened in Vietnam after the United States withdrew?**

_____

_____

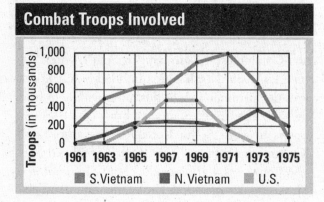

Combat Troops Involved

Troops (in thousands): 1,000 / 800 / 600 / 400 / 200 / 0

1961 1963 1965 1967 1969 1971 1973 1975

■ S.Vietnam ■ N.Vietnam ■ U.S.

Skillbuilder

Use the graph to answer these questions.

1. **In which year was the number of U.S. troops in Vietnam the highest?**

_____

2. **What is the greatest number of troops the South Vietnamese army had at one time?**

_____

The Cold War Divides the World

BEFORE YOU READ

In the last section, you read about wars in Korea and Vietnam.

In this section, you will learn about Cold War struggles in other parts of the world.

AS YOU READ

Use the chart below to take notes on Cold War conflicts.

COUNTRY	CONFLICT OR CHANGE
Cuba	Castro takes power

Fighting for the Third World

(pages 982–983)

How were developing nations affected by the Cold War?

After World War II, the world's nations were grouped into three "worlds." The First World included the United States and its allies. The Second World consisted of Communist nations led by the Soviet Union. The **Third World** was composed of developing nations in Africa, Asia, and Latin America.

Many Third World nations had serious problems. These problems were often due to a long history of colonialism. Some Third World nations faced *political unrest* that threatened the peace. Other problems included poverty and a lack of education and technology. Some of these countries tried to stay *neutral* in the Cold War. They met to form what they called a "third force." It consisted of **nonaligned nations,** or countries that did not take sides between the Soviets and Americans. Others actively sought American or Soviet aid.

1. What problems did Third World nations face?

_____

_____

_____

_____

Confrontations in Latin America

(pages 984–985)

What happened in Latin America?

In Cuba, the United States supported a dictator in the 1950s. In 1959, a young lawyer, **Fidel Castro,** led a successful revolt. Castro received aid from the Soviet Union. In 1962, the Soviets and Americans almost went to war over nuclear missiles that the Soviets placed in Cuba. The Soviets finally pulled the missiles out. Over time, the Cuban economy became more dependent on Soviet aid. When the Soviet Union collapsed in 1991, this aid stopped. It was a serious blow to Cuba's economy.

The United States had also backed a dictator, **Anastasio Somoza,** in Nicaragua. Somoza's government fell to Communist rebels in 1979. The rebels were led by **Daniel Ortega.** When the new government began helping leftist rebels in nearby El Salvador, the United States struck back. It began to support Nicaraguan rebels that wanted to overthrow the Communists. The civil war in Nicaragua lasted more than a decade. Finally, the different sides agreed to hold free elections.

2. Where did Communists gain power in Latin America?

_____

_____

_____

_____

Confrontations in the Middle East (pages 986–987)

What happened in Iran and Afghanistan?

The Middle East often saw conflict between those who wanted a more modern, Western-style society and those who wanted to follow traditional *Islam.* Such a struggle took place in Iran. In the 1950s, a group tried to take control of the government from Iran's ruler, **Shah Mohammed Reza Pahlavi.** The United States helped the Shah defeat them.

Over time, the Shah tried to weaken the influence of Islam in Iran. A Muslim leader, the **Ayatollah Ruholla Khomeini,** led a successful revolt. In 1979, the Shah was forced to leave the country. Khomeini made Islamic law the law of the land. He followed a foreign policy that was strongly against the United States. He also led his country in a long war against its neighbor Iraq.

The Soviets gained influence in Afghanistan after 1950. In the 1970s, Islamic rebels threatened the country's Communist government. The Soviets sent in troops to support the government. The United States felt its Middle East oil supplies were in danger and supported the rebels. In 1989, after a costly occupation, Soviet troops left Afghanistan.

3. How did Khomeini change Iran?

_____

_____

_____

_____

CHAPTER 33 Section 5 (pages 988–991)

The Cold War Thaws

BEFORE YOU READ

In the last section, you read about Cold War struggles around the world.

In this section, you will read about the major events of the Cold War from the 1950s to the 1980s.

AS YOU READ

Use the time line below to show key events that decreased or increased tensions between the superpowers.

TERMS AND NAMES

Nikita Khrushchev Leader of the Soviet Union after Stalin

Leonid Brezhnev Soviet leader after Khrushchev

John F. Kennedy President of the United States from 1961 to 1963

Lyndon Johnson President of the United States from 1963 to 1969

détente Policy to decrease tensions between the superpowers

Richard M. Nixon President of the United States from 1969 to 1974

SALT Talks to limit nuclear arms in the United States and the Soviet Union

Ronald Reagan President of the United States from 1981 to 1989

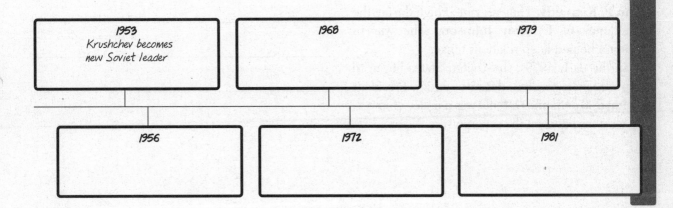

1953 Krushchev becomes new Soviet leader	1968	1979
1956	1972	1981

Soviet Policy in Eastern Europe and China (page 988)

How did the Soviets keep control over Eastern Europe?

Nikita Khrushchev became the Soviet leader after Stalin died in 1953. Krushchev began a process of "destalinization." This meant getting rid of Stalin's memory. Krushchev also believed that the Soviet Union should have "peaceful competition" with the capitalist nations.

In Eastern Europe, many people still resented Soviet rule. Eastern Europeans took part in protest movements against Soviet control. In 1956, protesters and the army overthrew the Communist government of Hungary. Khrushchev sent Soviet tanks to put the Communists back in power. In 1964, **Leonid Brezhnev** replaced Krushchev. When Czechoslovakians began to reform their Communist government in 1968, Brezhnev sent in tanks to stop them.

The Soviets did not have the same control over their larger neighbor, China. Although the Soviet Union and China enjoyed friendly relations at first, they gradually grew apart. The split became so wide that the Soviet Union and China sometimes fought along their border. The two nations now have a peaceful relationship.

1. In what two European countries did the Soviets put down revolts against Soviet control?

_____

_____

_____

_____

From Brinkmanship to Détente; The Collapse of Détente (pages 990–991)

Did tensions between the United States and the Soviet Union change?

Tensions between the Soviets and the United States had been very high during the presidency of **John F. Kennedy.** They remained high during the presidency of **Lyndon Johnson.** The war in Vietnam helped keep relations tense.

In the early 1970s, the United States began to follow a policy called **détente** under President **Richard M. Nixon.** Détente was a policy of lowering tensions between the superpowers. Nixon made visits to both Communist China and the Soviet Union. In 1972, he and Brezhnev held meetings called the Strategic Arms Limitations Talks (**SALT**). They signed a treaty to limit the number of nuclear missiles each country could have.

The United States retreated from détente when the Soviet Union invaded Afghanistan in 1979. In 1981, **Ronald Reagan,** a fierce anti-Communist, became president. He proposed a costly anti-missile defense system to protect America against Soviet missiles. It was never put into effect. But it remained a symbol of U.S. anti-Communist feelings.

The Soviets grew angry over American support for the rebels fighting against the Communists in Nicaragua. Tensions between the United States and the Soviet Union increased until 1985 when a new leader came to power in the Soviet Union.

2. Name two actions or events that got in the way of détente.

_____

_____

_____

_____

_____

Glossary   *CHAPTER 33* Restructuring the Postwar World

alliance Union of people, groups, or nations to achieve common goals

Berlin airlift Flying of food and supplies into West Berlin by Britain and the United States to break a Soviet blockade

blockade Act of cutting off one place from all others

brink Edge

cease-fire End to fighting

clashed Disagreed strongly

collective farms Large farms worked by many families

counterattack To make a return attack

fragile Delicate; easily broken

guerrilla war Warfare carried out by small, independent groups, often acting secretly in and around their own towns and villages

Islam Religion with a belief in one god that developed in Arabia

latitude A line that measures distance north or south from the earth's equator

neutral Not choosing sides between any particular nations or groups

political unrest State of conflict over the government, its leaders, or its laws

revive To bring back to life; to give new strength

AFTER YOU READ

Terms and Names

A. Write the name in each blank that best completes the meaning of the paragraph.

Leonid Brezhnev

Nikita Khrushchev

Fidel Castro

Shah Mohammed Reza Pahlavi

Ayatollah Ruholla Khomeini

  Some leaders have played a greater role in post-World War II politics than others. One of the first Cold War leaders that the United States feared was **1** _____, the leader of Cuba. A leader of Iran who also challenged the United States was **2** _____. He had taken power by overthrowing the pro-American leader, **3** _____. Soviet leaders during the Cold War included **4** _____, the leader of the Soviet Union after Stalin. They also included **5** _____, who sent tanks into Czechoslovakia in 1968.

B. Write the letter of the name or term next to the description that explains it best.

a. Truman Doctrine

b. Marshall Plan

c. containment

d. domino theory

e. Vietnamization

_____ **1.** Idea that the fall of one country to communism would lead other countries to become Communist

_____ **2.** Policy of giving aid to countries threatened by communism

_____ **3.** Gradual replacement of U.S. troops with South Vietnamese troops

_____ **4.** Plan that gave aid to European countries to help them recover from World War II

_____ **5.** Policy aimed at preventing the spread of communism

AFTER YOU READ (cont.) *CHAPTER 33* Restructuring the Postwar World

Main Ideas

1. Why did Truman start his policy of containment?

_____

_____

_____

2. Why did the Nationalists lose the Civil War in China?

_____

_____

_____

3. What changes did the Khmer Rouge bring to Cambodia?

_____

_____

_____

4. Describe what happened in Nicaragua after Anastasio Somoza fell from power.

_____

_____

_____

5. Explain when and how tensions between the superpowers decreased and when and how they increased again.

_____

_____

_____

Thinking Critically

Answer the following questions on a separate sheet of paper.

1. Discuss how disagreements between the United States and the Soviet Union after World War II led to the Cold War.

2. Explain the relationship of Ronald Reagan and Star Wars to détente.

The Indian Subcontinent Achieves Freedom

BEFORE YOU READ

In the last chapter, you read about the Cold War.

In this section, you will read about changes in India, Pakistan, and Sri Lanka.

AS YOU READ

Use the time line below to take notes on changes in India, Pakistan, and Sri Lanka.

TERMS AND NAMES

Congress Party Group consisting mostly of Hindus that led a campaign for India's independence

Muhammed Ali Jinnah Leader of the Muslim League

Muslim League Muslim group that led a campaign for India's independence

partition Division of India into two nations

Jawaharlal Nehru First prime minister of India

Indira Gandhi Daughter of Nehru who followed him as prime minister

Benazir Bhutto Former prime minister of Pakistan

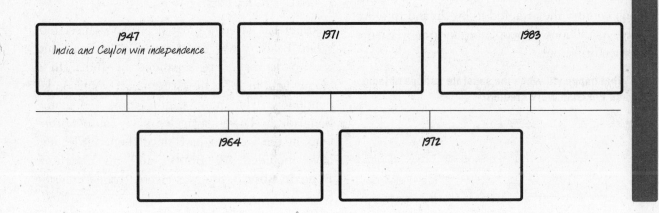

| 1947 India and Ceylon win independence | 1971 | 1983 |

| 1964 | 1972 |

A Movement Toward Independence (page 997)

***What** led to the movement for independence?*

Many Asians served in the armies of the colonial powers during World War II. The fight against the Nazis deepened Asians' desire for independence. Japanese victories over European powers early in the war made Asians believe that the colonial rulers could be defeated. In Europe, people began to doubt that it was right for nations to have colonies.

1. Name two things that increased Asian hopes for independence.

_____

_____

_____

Freedom Brings Turmoil (pages 998–999)

***What** divisions existed between Indian political groups?*

In the 1920s, Mohandas Gandhi led a movement for Indian independence. Two groups worked in this effort. The Indian National Congress, also called the **Congress Party,** said that it represented all of India. Most of its members were Hindu. **Muhammad Ali Jinnah** formed the **Muslim League** in 1906. He said that the Congress Party did not care for the rights of Indian Muslims. The British encouraged the division of Hindus and Muslims into two opposing groups. This division helped the British keep control of the country.

After World War II, Britain was ready for India to be independent. But the British did not know which people in India would take power. Riots broke out between the Hindus and Muslims throughout India.

Gandhi tried to end the violence. A Hindu extremist *assassinated* him for protecting Muslims. Lord Louis Mountbatten, the last British *viceroy* of India, also tried to stop the violence. He finally accepted the idea that **partition,** or the division of India into two nations, was necessary.

The British Parliament passed a law granting independence in July 1947. It created the separate Hindu and Muslim nations of India and Pakistan. The law gave people only one month to decide which country they wanted to live in and to move there. As millions of people began to move, more violence broke out.

2. **What happened when the separate nations of India and Pakistan were created?**

_____

_____

_____

_____

Modern India (pages 999–1000)

What problems has modern India faced?

Jawaharlal Nehru became the first prime minister of India. He led the country for 17 years.

India and Pakistan went to war over the state of Kashmir. Kashmir bordered both countries. It had a Hindu ruler and a large Muslim population. Conflict over Kashmir continues today.

Nehru tried to reform Indian society. He hoped to improve the status of the lower *castes* and of women. Shortly after he died in 1964, his daughter, **Indira Gandhi,** became prime minister. She took steps to increase food production. In 1984, she ordered an attack on Sikh rebels. A few months later, she was killed by Sikhs. She was followed by her son Rajiv Gandhi. He was later assassinated. *Separatist movements* continue to *disrupt* Indian society.

3. **Why does conflict continue in Kashmir?**

_____

_____

_____

_____

Pakistan Copes with Freedom; Bangladesh and Sri Lanka Struggle (pages 1001–1003)

How have new political divisions led to violence?

Pakistan has faced a great deal of violence, too. When Pakistan was first formed, it had east and west parts that were separated by India. In a bloody fight in 1971, the eastern part won its independence. The new nation took the name Bangladesh. Power struggles have caused problems in the western part since then. Its leaders have included Ali Bhutto and his daughter, **Benazir Bhutto.** She was elected prime minister twice.

Ceylon, an island on the southeastern coast of India, won its independence in 1947 as well. In 1972 it was renamed Sri Lanka. Since 1983, a Hindu minority on the island—the *Tamils*—have led a bloody fight to form a separate nation.

4. **Why has violence occurred in Pakistan?**

_____

_____

_____

Southeast Asian Nations Gain Independence

TERMS AND NAMES

Ferdinand Marcos Leader of the Philippines who was elected but ruled as a dictator

Corazón Aquino Woman who defeated Marcos in the elections of 1986

Aung San Suu Kyi Daughter of Aung San; winner of Nobel Prize for her fight for democracy in Burma

Sukarno Leader of Indonesian independence movement; first president of Indonesia

Suharto Leader who turned Indonesia into a police state

BEFORE YOU READ

In the last section, you read about independence and conflict in India.

In this section, you will read about independence and the challenges of self-rule in Southeast Asia.

AS YOU READ

Use the web below to show key people and events in each struggle for independence.

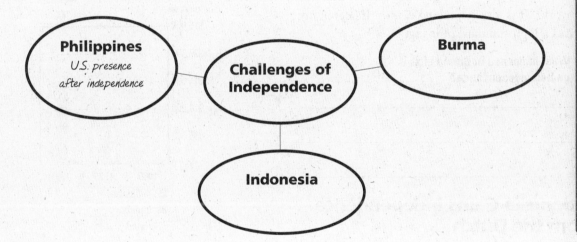

The Philippines Achieves Independence (pages 1004–1006)

***What** happened in the Philippines after it gained independence?*

In 1946, the United States gave the Philippines independence. The United States also promised money to help the Filipinos rebuild their economy. To win the aid, however, the Filipinos had to agree to a trade deal. For the next few decades, the United States kept naval and air bases on the islands. Many Filipinos wanted the bases closed. In 1991, the United States left the bases.

From 1966 to 1986, **Ferdinand Marcos** led the country. He was elected president but after a few years ruled as a dictator. He then harshly put down *dissent* and stole millions of dollars from the country. When he lost an election to **Corazón Aquino** in 1986, he refused to leave office. A large public outcry forced him to step down.

1. Who was Ferdinand Marcos?

_____

_____

British Colonies Gain Independence (pages 1006–1007)

Which Southeast Asian British colonies won independence?

Burma was the first British colony in Southeast Asia to become independent. Nationalist leader Aung San helped drive the British out of Burma. Burma changed its name to *Myanmar* in 1989. Since 1962, generals have ruled the country. Myanmar has been torn by conflict often. **Aung San Suu Kyi** won the Nobel Peace Prize in 1991 for her opposition to this military rule.

After World War II, the British moved back into the Malay peninsula. They tried to form a country there. But ethnic conflict between Malays and Chinese who lived in the area stopped them. In 1957, independence was given to Malaya, Singapore, and parts of two distant islands.

Singapore later declared independence as a city-state. Singapore is one of the busiest ports in the world. It is also a banking center. Its economy creates a high standard of living.

2. **What happened in Burma after it gained independence?**

_____

_____

_____

Indonesia Gains Independence from the Dutch (pages 1008–1009)

What challenges did Indonesia face?

Sukarno led an independence movement in Indonesia while Japan held that country. After World War II, he quickly declared an independent Indonesia. The Dutch at first tried to regain control over their former colony. But in 1949 they recognized Indonesia's independence.

Indonesia is spread out. It has 13,600 islands and includes people from 300 different groups that speak 250 different languages. It has been difficult for leaders to unite the nation. In 1967, a general named **Suharto** took control. He ruled until 1998. Many criticized him for taking over the island of

East Timor and for corruption in his government. In the late 1990s Indonesia faced severe economic problems.

3. **Why has governing Indonesia proven difficult?**

_____

_____

_____

_____

Comparing Economies

Gross Domestic Product is the dollar value of all goods and services produced within a country during one year. In this graph, the GDP is divided by the number of productive workers in each country. This results in the GDP per capita, or per person.

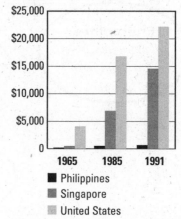

- ■ Philippines
- ■ Singapore
- ■ United States

Sources: *World Statistics in Brief* (1978) and *World Statistics Pocketbook* (1995), published by the United Nations.

Skillbuilder

Use the illustration to answer these questions.

1. **How does the rate of growth in the Philippines compare with that of Singapore?**

_____

2. **Given the trend on this graph, what might you expect to see in later years?**

_____

_____

CHAPTER 34 Section 3 (pages 1012–1016)

New Nations in Africa

BEFORE YOU READ

In the last section, you read about the struggle
for self-rule in Southeast Asian colonies.

In this section, you will read about new nations in Africa.

AS YOU READ

Use the web below to take notes on challenges
facing each nation after independence.

TERMS AND NAMES

Negritude movement African
movement after World War II to
celebrate African culture, heritage,
and values

Kwame Nkrumah Leader in the Gold
Coast independence movement

Jomo Kenyatta Nationalist who
helped lead Kenya to independence

Mobutu Sese Seko Ruler who took
control of the Congo in 1965 and
renamed it Zaire

Ahmed Ben Bella Leader of the FLN
who became the first president and
prime minister of Algeria

COUNTRY	CHALLENGES
Ghana	Military rule since 1981
Kenya	
Congo	
Algeria	
Angola	

Achieving Independence
(pages 1012–1013)

Why did independence movements increase after World War II?

During World War II, Africans fought as soldiers
along with Europeans. After the war, Africans
wanted independence. Many Africans took part in
the **Negritude movement.** The purpose of this
movement was to celebrate African culture, *heritage*, and values.

1. What was the Negritude movement?

_____

_____

Ghana Leads the Way; Fighting for Freedom (pages 1013–1015)

What challenges did newly independent nations face?

The British gave Africans a greater part in the colonial government of its Gold Coast colony. **Kwame
Nkrumah** led a movement to push Britain to act
more quickly. The effort succeeded. In 1957 the
Gold Coast colony became independent. The new
nation took the name Ghana.

Nkrumah had big plans for building the economy of Ghana. But these plans were very expensive.
Opposition grew. Finally, the army seized power in
1966. Ghana has been ruled by a military dictator
since 1981.

The strong leadership of nationalist **Jomo Kenyatta** helped Kenya achieve independence in 1963. An uprising of Africans called Mau Mau also helped. Mau Mau aimed at frightening the British settlers to leave. Kenyatta became president of the new nation. He tried to unite the many different people in his country. Kenya has faced violence and a weak economy in the 1990s.

A bloody conflict for independence took place in Algeria. About 1 million French settlers lived there. They were unwilling to give up their property or their control of the colonial government.

Violence broke out in 1945 and continued for many years. In 1954, the Algerian National Liberation Front, or FLN, announced its intention to fight for independence. In 1962, the French finally granted independence to Algeria.

Ahmed Ben Bella, a leader of the FLN, was the first prime minister and then the first president of Algeria. From 1965 until 1988, Algerians tried to *modernize* their country. These efforts failed.

An Islamic party won elections in 1991. But the government rejected the vote. Fighting between Islamic *militants* and the government continued through the 1990s.

2. **What problems did the new nations of Ghana and Kenya face?**

_____

_____

_____

Civil War in Congo and Angola
(pages 1015–1016)

What happened in the Congo after independence?

The Congo won its independence from Belgium in 1960. But the new nation was not well-prepared for self-rule. The Congo quickly fell into civil war.

In 1965, **Mobutu Sese Seko** took control. He renamed the country Zaire and ruled until 1997. Zaire had rich mineral resources. But Mobutu's harsh and corrupt rule made the country poor. He was overthrown in a coup in 1997. The country's name was changed back to the Congo.

The colonies of Portugal were the last to gain their independence. Portugal did nothing to prepare the people of Angola for self-rule. Three Angolan groups emerged in the 1960s that were determined to control the new government.

In the 1970s, the army of Portugal revolted against its government over the war in Angola. The troops left Angola without putting any group in charge. Angolans fought a long civil war. The war ended in 1989. But no strong government has formed yet.

3. **How did Mobutu rule the Congo?**

_____

_____

_____

Conflicts in the Middle East

TERMS AND NAMES

Anwar Sadat Egyptian leader who signed a peace agreement with Israel

Golda Meir Israeli prime minister at the time of the 1973 Arab–Israeli war

Camp David Accords Agreement in which Egypt recognized Israel as a nation and Israel gave the Sinai peninsula back to Egypt

Oslo Peace Accords Agreement aimed at giving Palestinians self-rule

PLO Palestinian Liberation Organization

Yasir Arafat Leader of the PLO

intifada Sustained rebellion by the Palestinians

BEFORE YOU READ

In the last section, you read about conflicts in the new nations of Africa.

In this section, you will learn about conflict in the Middle East.

AS YOU READ

Use the time line below to take notes on the conflicts and hopes for peace that followed the creation of the state of Israel.

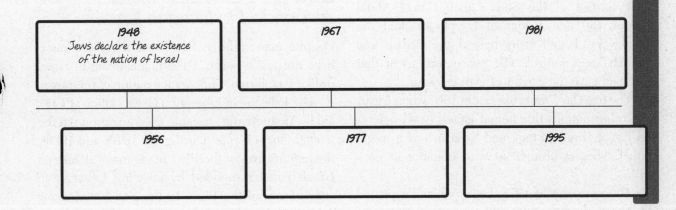

| 1948 Jews declare the existence of the nation of Israel | 1967 | 1981 |

| 1956 | 1977 | 1995 |

Israel Becomes a State

(pages 1017–1018)

How did Israel come into being?

The movement to settle Jews in *Palestine* began in the late 1800s and early 1900s. These Jews believed that Palestine belonged to them because it was their home 3,000 years ago. But Muslims had lived there for the last 1,300 years.

After World War I, Britain took control of the area. The British found that Jews and Muslims did not live together peacefully. In 1917, Britain said it supported the establishment of a Jewish national homeland in Palestine. This statement is known as the Balfour Declaration.

After World War II, the British left the area. The United Nations divided the land into two parts. One part was set aside for the *Palestinians*. The other part was set aside part for Jews.

Islamic countries voted against the plan. The Palestinians opposed it. Many countries backed the idea of a separate Jewish state. They wanted to help make up for the suffering Jews had experienced in World War II. On May 14, 1948, the

Jewish people in Palestine declared the existence of the Jewish state of Israel.

1. Why did the creation of Israel cause conflict?

_____

_____

Israel and the Arab States in Conflict (pages 1018–1019)

How did Arab states respond to the creation of Israel?

On May 15, 1948, six Islamic nations invaded Israel. Israel won the war in a few months with strong support from the United States. This war was the first of many Arab–Israeli wars.

Another war was started by the Suez Crisis. The crisis began in 1956 when a group of Egyptian army officers seized control of the government of Egypt from Britain. The British and French had kept control of the Suez Canal. Gamal Abdel Nasser, the new leader of Egypt, attacked the canal. The Israeli army helped the British and French keep control. The peace settlement that followed gave the canal to Egypt anyway.

The Six-Day War broke out in 1967 when Egypt and other nations threatened Israel. Israel defeated Egypt, Iran, Jordan, and Syria in just a week. Israel's success brought new areas under its control.

The next war, in 1973, began when Egypt, led by **Anwar Sadat,** and its allies launched a surprise attack. At first, Arab forces won some of the territory lost in 1967. Israel, led by its prime minister, **Golda Meir,** fought back and won control of much of the territory it had lost.

2. What did the Suez Crisis and Six-Day War have in common?

_____

_____

Efforts at Peace (pages 1020–1021)

What happened at Camp David?

In 1977, Egyptian leader Sadat signed a peace agreement with Israeli prime minister Menachem Begin. In this agreement, Israel gave the Sinai Peninsula back to Egypt. In return, Egypt recognized Israel as a nation. Egypt was the first Islamic country to give this recognition. This agreement became known as the **Camp David Accords.** It was the first signed agreement between Israel and an Arab country. This angered many Arabs. Sadat was assassinated in 1981.

3. What is significant about the Camp David Accords?

_____

_____

Peace Slips Away (pages 1022–1023)

How have the Palestinians responded to living in Israel?

Despite many efforts, Israel and the Palestinians have not made peace. Palestinians living in Israel dislike Israeli rule. They want a nation of their own.

The Palestinian Liberation Organization (**PLO**), led by **Yasir Arafat,** became a leading group in the struggle for self-rule. During the 1970s and 1980s, the military arm of the PLO made many attacks on Israel. Israel responded by invading Lebanon to attack bases of the PLO. In the late 1980s, many Palestinians in Israel began a revolt called the **intifada.** The intifada continued into the 1990s.

In the early 1990s, the two sides took steps toward peace. Israel agreed to give Palestinians control of an area called the Gaza Strip and of the town of Jericho. The agreement was known as the **Oslo Peace Accords.** The Israeli leader who signed this agreement, Yitzhak Rabin, was assassinated in 1995. He was killed by a Jewish *extremist* who opposed giving in to the Palestinians. In 2003, the two sides began working on a new peace plan pushed by U.S. leaders.

4. What is the state of Israeli–Arab relations today?

_____

_____

Central Asia Struggles

BEFORE YOU READ

In the last section, you read about conflicts in the Middle East.

In this section, you will learn how the nations of Central Asia have struggled to achieve freedom.

AS YOU READ

Use the time line below to take notes on key events in the history of Afghanistan.

TERMS AND NAMES

Transcaucasian Republics The nations of Armenia, Azerbaijan, and Georgia

Central Asian Republics The nations of Uzbekistan, Turkmenistan, Tajikistan, Kazakhstan, and Kyrgyzstan

mujahideen A group that fought against the Soviet-supported government in Afghanistan

Taliban A conservative Islamic group that controlled most of Afghanistan from 1998 to 2001.

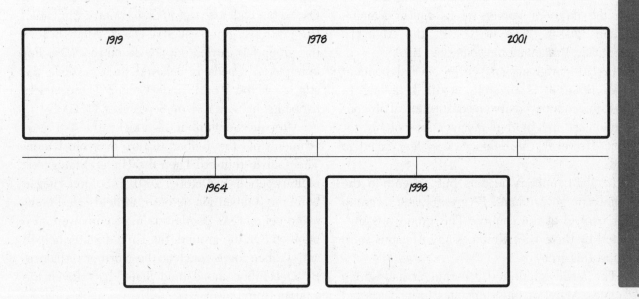

1919

1978

2001

1964

1998

Freedom Brings New Challenges (pages 1024–1025)

What challenges have the countries of Central Asia faced?

In 1991 the Soviet Union broke apart. As a result, the republics that it had conquered became fifteen independent states. These states include nine countries in Central Asia. One group of Central Asia States is known as the **Transcaucasian Republics.** The other group of states is called the **Central Asian Republics.**

Since independence, the countries of Central Asia have faced economic problems. These coun-

tries are some of the poorest in the world. They were helped economically by the Soviet Union. When they gained independence, they had a hard time standing on their own. In addition, economic practices during the Soviet era have created problems. For example, the Soviets made certain areas of Central Asia grow only one crop, such as cotton. Growing a single crop hurt the nations of Central Asia. They did not develop a balanced economy.

Central Asia is home to many different peoples. Some of these people have a history of hatred toward each other. When the Soviets ruled the region, they controlled these hatreds. However, after the Soviet Union broke apart, various groups began to fight. Some of these fights became regional wars.

1. Why have countries in Central Asia faced economic problems?

_____

_____

_____

Afghanistan and the World

(pages 1025–1027)

How has Afghanistan struggled for freedom?

Afghanistan had a long history of struggle. During the 1800s, both Russia and Britain wanted to control Afghanistan. Russia wanted to get to the Indian Ocean through Afghanistan. Britain wanted to protect the northern borders of its Indian Empire. Britain fought three wars with the Afghanis. Eventually, Britain left the country in 1919.

In 1919, Afghanistan became an independent nation. It set up a monarchy, or rule by a king. In 1964, the country created a constitution. This constitution set up a more democratic style of government. However, the democratic system failed to grow.

In 1973, military leaders put an end to the democratic government. Five years later, a group took control of the country. This group was supported by the Soviet Union. Many Afghanis were against this group.

The Soviet-supported government had strong enemies. Many of these enemies formed a rebel group known as the **mujahideen,** or holy warriors. The mujahideen fought strongly against the Soviet-supported government. The Soviet Union wanted to defeat the rebels in Afghanistan. To get this done, Soviet troops invaded Afghanistan in 1979. The Soviets greatly outnumbered the rebels. Despite this, the rebels were tough to beat. The two groups fought for 10 years. Eventually, the Soviet troops left the country.

After the Soviets left, various Afghan rebel troops began fighting each other for control of the country. By 1998, an Islamic group known as the **Taliban** controlled most of Afghanistan. Another rebel group, the Northern Alliance, held the northwest corner of the country.

The Taliban had an unusual understanding of the Islamic religion. Many other Muslims disagreed with this understanding. The Taliban believed that they should control nearly every part of Afghan life. Women were forbidden to go to school or hold jobs. The Taliban did not allow watching television and movies or listening to modern music. Punishment for disobeying the rules included whipping and execution.

The Taliban allowed terrorist groups to train in Afghanistan. They allowed terrorist leaders, such as Osama bin Laden, to stay in their country. Bin Laden led a terrorist group called al-Qaeda. Many believe this group has carried out attacks on the West. For example, Al-Qaeda is believed to have done the attacks on the World Trade Center. Those attacks happened in New York on September 11, 2001.

After the September 11 attacks, the U.S. government told the Taliban to turn over bin Laden. The Taliban refused. Then the United States took military action. In October 2001, U.S. forces began bombing Taliban air defense, airfields, and command centers. Al-Qaeda training camps were also bombed. On the ground, the United States helped anti-Taliban forces, such as the Northern Alliance. By December, the United States had driven the Taliban from power.

The Afghanis then created a new government. Hamid Karzai was the leader of this government.

2. What are some of the ways that the Taliban controlled Afghan society?

_____

_____

_____

Glossary   *CHAPTER 34*   The Colonies Become New Nations

assassinated Murdered for political reasons

castes Social groupings

disrupt Disturb; break apart

dissent Disagreement with the government

extremist A person who has extreme views on an issue

heritage Sense of the past of one's nation, culture, or family

intifada Uprising of the Palestinian people against Israeli rule

militants Aggressive people or parties

modernize To make something modern

Myanmar Name of Burma since 1989

Palestine Region of southwest Asia

Palestinians People from Palestine

separatist movement Movement by ethnic, religious, or other groups within a country to create a separate country

Tamils Hindu group in Sri Lanka that wants to form its own nation

viceroy Kind of governor or top government leader

AFTER YOU READ

Terms and Names

A. Write the name in each blank that best completes the meaning of the paragraph.

partition

Indira Gandhi

Muhammad Ali Jinnah

Benazir Bhutto

Jawaharlal Nehru

Important leaders in the history of India and Pakistan during the twentieth century include the leader of the Muslim league, **1** _____. He helped India fight for its independence. The first prime minister of India was **2** _____. India fought a war with Pakistan over Kashmir during his rule. His daughter, **3** _____, followed him in the role of prime minister. She, in turn, was followed to power by her son, Rajiv Gandhi. The **4** _____ of India led to the creation of Pakistan. One of the important leaders of Pakistan was **5** _____.

B. Write the letter of the name next to the description that explains it best.

a. Taliban

b. Kwame Nkrumah

c. Ahmed Ben Bella

d. Corazón Aquino

e. Mobutu Sese Seko

_____ **1.** Filipino leader who defeated Marcos in national elections

_____ **2.** Islamic group that ruled Afghanistan beginning in the late 1990s

_____ **3.** Leader who helped the Gold Coast gain independence

_____ **4.** Leader who took control of the Congo

_____ **5.** Leader of the Algerian National Liberation Front

Main Ideas

1. What role did the British play in the partition of India and the violence that followed?

_____

_____

_____

2. Describe the leadership of Ferdinand Marcos in the Philippines.

_____

_____

_____

_____

3. What problems has the Congo faced since gaining its independence?

_____

_____

_____

_____

4. Explain the events and significance of the Suez Crisis.

_____

_____

_____

_____

5. What events brought about the fall of the Taliban?

_____

_____

_____

_____

Thinking Critically

Answer the following questions on a separate sheet of paper.

1. Angola gained its independence in a unique way. How was it different from the way other African nations gained independence?

2. Describe how the Arab–Israeli conflict reaches far back in the past and why it could continue into the future.

Democracy

Case Study: Latin American Democracies

TERMS AND NAMES

Brasília Capital city of Brazil

land reform Breaking up large estates in order to give land to the landless

standard of living Quality of life as judged by the amount of goods people have

recession Decrease in the size of the economy

PRI Institutional Revolutionary Party, which has controlled Mexico for most of the century

BEFORE YOU READ

In the last section, you read about conflicts in the Middle East.

In this section, you will read about the struggles for democracy in Latin America.

AS YOU READ

Use the chart below to take notes on the challenges to democracy in Latin America.

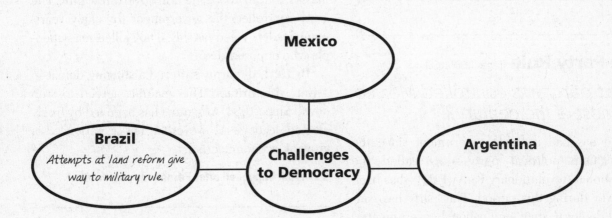

Mexico

Brazil — *Attempts at land reform give way to military rule.*

Challenges to Democracy

Argentina

Democracy As a Goal
(pages 1033–1034)

How does democracy work?

For democracy to work, several conditions must exist. There must be free and fair elections. There must also be more than one political party. The people of the country should have a good education. Then they can make informed choices. They should share a common culture. All must accept the idea that everyone has equal rights. Finally, there must be rule by law, not by power. Many nations in Latin America have had difficulty achieving democracy because all these factors are not present.

1. Name at least four factors needed to make democracy work.

_____

_____

Dictators and Democracy
(pages 1034–1036)

What challenges has Brazil faced?

After independence in 1822, Brazil started out as a monarchy. After 1930, a dictator ruled. But in 1956, Juscelino Kubitschek was elected president. He tried to improve the economy. He built a new capital city, **Brasília.** He supported **land reform.**

Land reform aimed at breaking up large estates and giving land to the peasants.

Landowners opposed land reform. They backed a group of army leaders who took power in 1964. The military ruled Brazil for 20 years. The country's economy grew. But the people had few rights. Eventually, their **standard of living** also fell. This means the quality of life, judged by the amount of goods people have, went down. By the 1980s a **recession**—a decrease in the size of the economy—hurt Brazil.

2. **What changes did land reform bring in Brazil?**

_____

_____

_____

_____

One-Party Rule (pages 1036–1038)

What party has controlled Mexico for most of the century?

Mexico has had a stable government since the 1920s. One political party—now called the Institutional Revolutionary Party (**PRI**)—has been in power during this period. This party has controlled the local, state, and national governments.

At times, the PRI acted harshly to stop any *dissent*. For example, in 1968 the government killed many people who took part in a demonstration for economic reform.

The PRI recently opened up the political system to candidates from other parties. In 1997, two opposition parties won many seats in the national legislature. They ended PRI control of that congress. Then, in 2000, Mexican voters ended 71 years of PRI rule by electing Vicente Fox as president.

3. **How has the PRI controlled Mexico?**

_____

_____

_____

_____

Political and Economic Disorder
(pages 1038–1039)

How has democracy grown in Argentina?

Argentina has also struggled toward democracy. In the 1940s and 1950s, Juan Perón was a popular dictator. He put in place many programs to benefit the masses. But in 1955, the army overthrew him. The army controlled the government for many years. Army leaders ruled harshly. They killed many people who opposed them.

In 1982, the army suffered a stinging defeat in a war with Britain. The generals agreed to step down. Since 1983, Argentina has been led by freely elected leaders. However, it has experienced a growing economic crisis.

4. **What happened after Perón was overthrown?**

_____

_____

_____

_____

CHAPTER 35 Section 2 (pages 1040–1045)

The Challenge of Democracy in Africa

BEFORE YOU READ

In the last section, you read about challenges to democracy in South America and Mexico.

In this section, you will read about struggles for democracy in Africa.

AS YOU READ

Use the chart below to take notes on the struggles for democracy in Nigeria and South Africa. Record key events and changes in government.

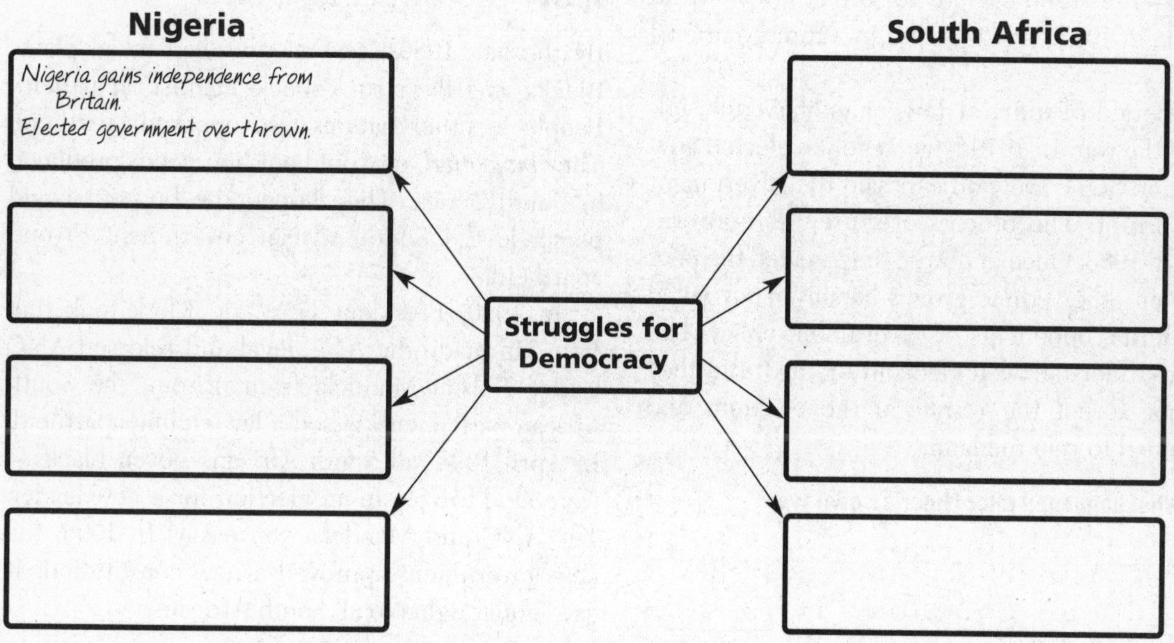

Nigeria

Nigeria gains independence from Britain.
Elected government overthrown.

South Africa

Struggles for Democracy

Colonial Rule Limits Democracy

(page 1040)·

What problems did colonial rule create?

African nations have had a hard time setting up democratic governments because of the effects of colonial rule. European powers made borders in Africa that paid no attention to ethnic groupings.

They put people who disliked each other in the same area. This practice caused conflict.

Also, the European nations never built up the economies of their colonies. Most of the colonies lacked a middle class or skilled workers. Both are needed for a strong democracy. When Britain and France gave their African colonies independence, they gave them democratic governments. But problems soon arose between rival groups.

1. Name three things that have slowed democracy in Africa.

_____

_____

_____

_____

Civil War in Nigeria; Nigeria's Nation-Building (pages 1041–1043)

What happened after Nigeria gained independence?

In 1960, Nigeria became independent from Britain. It adopted a federal system. In a **federal system,** power is shared between state governments and a central authority. But conflict broke out in just a few years. The people of one ethnic group—the Igbo—tried to break away from Nigeria in 1967. The Igbo lost in a three-year civil war.

A period of **martial law,** or military rule, followed the war. In 1979 Nigeria got an elected government. Some army officers said the government was corrupt, The officers overthrew the government in 1983. Once in power, they treated the people from other ethnic groups harshly. They jailed **dissidents,** opponents of government policy. The military rulers allowed elections in 1993. But they did not accept the results of the elections and continued to rule the land.

2. What happened after Nigeria's civil war?

_____

_____

_____

_____

South Africa Under Apartheid (page 1043)

What was apartheid?

In South Africa, the conflict was between races. A white minority ruled a black majority. In 1948, the whites put in place a policy called **apartheid**—the strict separation of blacks and whites. Black South Africans were denied many basic rights. Some joined together in a group called the *African National Congress* (ANC) to fight for their rights. The white government cracked down on the ANC. They put many ANC leaders in prison. **Nelson Mandela,** the leader of the ANC, was one of the people imprisoned.

3. Why was the African National Congress formed?

_____

_____

_____

_____

Struggle for Democracy
(pages 1044–1045)

How did apartheid end?

By the late 1980s, several riots had taken place. Blacks angrily struck back against apartheid. People in other nations also opposed apartheid. They *boycotted*, or would not buy, goods produced in South Africa. They hoped the boycott would persuade the South African government to end apartheid.

In 1990, President F. W. de Klerk took that step. He made the ANC legal and released ANC leader Nelson Mandela from prison. The South African parliament passed a law ending apartheid. In April 1994, all South Africans—even blacks— were able to vote in an election for a new leader. The ANC and Mandela won easily. In 1996, the new government approved a new constitution. It gave equal rights to all South Africans.

4. Why did F. W. de Klerk end apartheid?

_____

_____

_____

_____

CHAPTER 35 **Section 3** (pages 1046–1051)

The Collapse of the Soviet Union

BEFORE YOU READ

In the last section, you read about political conflicts in Africa.

In this section, you will read about the fall of the Soviet Union and the rise of Russia.

AS YOU READ

Use the time line below to take notes on key events leading up to and following the collapse of the Soviet Union.

TERMS AND NAMES

Politburo Ruling committee of the Communist Party

Mikhail Gorbachev Leader of the Soviet Union from 1985 to 1991

glasnost Gorbachev's policy of openness

perestroika Gorbachev's policy aimed at reforming the Soviet economy

Boris Yeltsin Political opponent of Gorbachev who became president of Russia

CIS Commonwealth of Independent States, a loose federation of former Soviet territories

"shock therapy" Yeltsin's plan for changing the Soviet economy

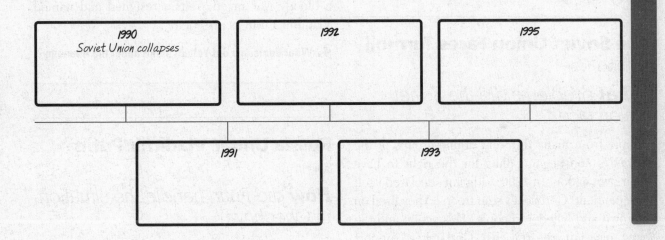

1990
Soviet Union collapses

1992

1995

1991

1993

Gorbachev Moves Toward Democracy (page 1046)

How did Gorbachev open up Soviet society?

During the 1960s and 1970s, the leaders of the Soviet Union kept tight control on society. Leonid Brezhnev and the **Politburo**—the ruling committee of the Communist Party—crushed all political dissent. In 1985, Communist Party leaders named **Mikhail Gorbachev** as the leader of the Soviet Union. He was the youngest Soviet leader since Joseph Stalin. He was expected to make minor reforms. But his reforms led to a revolution.

Gorbachev felt that Soviet society could not improve without the free flow of ideas. He started a policy called **glasnost,** or openness. He opened churches. He let political prisoners out of prison. He allowed books to be published that in the past had been *banned*.

1. What was Gorbachev's policy of glasnost?

_____

_____

_____

Reforming the Economy and Politics (page 1047)

What changes did Gorbachev make in the Soviet economy and politics?

Gorbachev began a policy called **perestroika,** or economic restructuring. It tried to improve the Soviet economy by lifting the tight control on all managers and workers.

In 1987, Gorbachev opened up the political system by allowing the Soviet people to elect representatives to a legislature.

Finally, Gorbachev changed Soviet foreign policy. He moved to end the arms race against the United States.

2. What was Gorbachev's policy of perestroika?

_____

_____

The Soviet Union Faces Turmoil

(pages 1048–1050)

What problems did the Soviet Union face?

People from many different ethnic groups in the Soviet Union began calling for the right to have their own nation. In 1990, Lithuania declared itself independent. Gorbachev sent troops. They fired on a crowd and killed 14 people. This action and the slow pace of reform cost Gorbachev support among the Soviet people.

Many people began to support **Boris Yeltsin.** Old-time Communists were becoming angry at Gorbachev. They thought his changes made the Soviet Union weaker. In August 1991, they tried to take control of the government. When the army refused to back the *coup* leaders, they gave up.

To strike back, the parliament voted to ban the party from any political activity. Meanwhile, more republics in the Soviet Union declared their independence. Russia and the 14 other republics each became independent states. Most of the republics then agreed to form the Commonwealth of Independent States, or **CIS,** a loose *federation* of former Soviet territories. By the end of 1991, the Soviet Union had ceased to exist.

3. Name three events that led up to the collapse of the Soviet Union.

_____

_____

Russia Under Boris Yeltsin (page 1050)

What happened when Gorbachev lost power?

After the coup failed, Gorbachev lost all power. Yeltsin became the most powerful Russian leader. As president of Russia, he faced many problems. He tried to change the economy. His economic plan was known as **"shock therapy."** This move toward capitalism caused suffering.

In addition, rebels in the small republic of Chechnya declared their independence from Russia. Yeltsin refused to allow it. He sent thousands of troops to put down the Chechen rebels. As a bloody war raged, Yeltsin resigned and named Vladimir Putin as president.

4. What decisions did Yeltsin make about the economy?

_____

_____

Russia Under Vladimir Putin

(page 1051)

How did Putin handle the situation in Chechnya?

Putin dealt harshly with the rebellion in Chechnya but the rebellion dragged on for years. Chechen rebels seized a theater in Moscow and more than 100 people died.

Economic troubles continued as Russia dealt with social upheaval caused by years of change and reform. Social problems included homeless children, domestic violence, and unemployment, as well as declines in population, standard of living, and life expectancy.

5. What were some of the signs of social distress in Russia?

_____

_____

Name _____ Date _____

Changes in Central and Eastern Europe

BEFORE YOU READ

In the last section, you read about the collapse of the Soviet Union.

In this section, you will read about the fall of communism and other changes in Central and Eastern Europe.

AS YOU READ

Use the web below to take notes on changes that occurred in Communist countries.

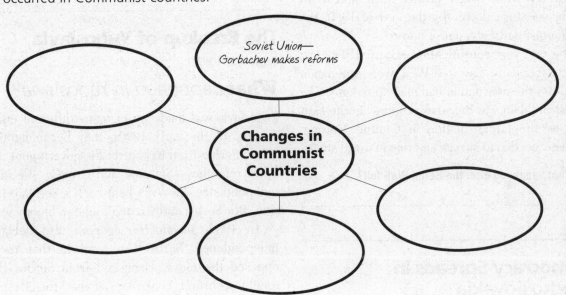

Soviet Union—Gorbachev makes reforms

Changes in Communist Countries

Poland and Hungary Reform

(pages 1052–1053)

How did Poland and Hungary change?

Gorbachev urged Communist leaders in Eastern Europe to change their policies but many of them resisted. Despite resistance from the old Communist leaders, the people of Eastern Europe wanted reform. Protest movements began to build.

In Poland, years of economic problems troubled the people. Polish workers organized a union

called **Solidarity.** Solidarity went on strike to get the government to recognize the union.

The government gave in to Solidarity's demands. But later, the government banned the union and threw **Lech Walesa,** the union's leader, in jail. This caused unrest. Finally, the government was forced to allow elections. The Polish people voted overwhelmingly against the Communists and for Solidarity. However, the Polish people became frustrated with how slow and painful the road to economic recovery and capitalism was. In 1995, they voted Walesa out of office and replaced him with Aleksander Kwasniewski as president.

Inspired by the Poles, leaders in Hungary started a reform movement. The reformers took over the Communist party. Then the party voted itself out of existence. In 1999, Hungary joined NATO as a full member.

1. What caused frustration and change in Poland?

_____

_____

Germany Reunifies (pages 1053–1054)

What changes occurred in Germany?

Change soon came to East Germany as well. Its leaders resisted at first. Then thousands of people across the country demanded free elections. Soon, the Berlin Wall, which divided East and West Berlin, was torn down. By the end of 1989, the Communist party was out of power.

The next year **reunification** occurred. The two parts of Germany, East and West, were one nation again. But the new nation had many problems. The biggest problem was the weak economy in the east. And, as the largest nation in Central Europe, Germany needed to face its new role in world affairs.

2. What happened after the Berlin Wall fell?

_____

_____

Democracy Spreads in Czechoslovakia (page 1055)

What happened in Czechoslovakia?

In Czechoslovakia, calls for reform took place. When the government cracked down on protesters, thousands of Czechs poured into the streets. One day hundreds of thousands of people gathered to protest in the nation's capital. The Communists agreed to give up power.

Reformers launched an economic reform program that caused a sharp rise in unemployment that especially hurt Slovakia, the republic occupying the eastern third of the country. In 1993, the country split into two separate nations: the Czech Republic and Slovakia. The economies of both slowly improved.

3. How did the government of Czechoslovakia change?

_____

Overthrow in Romania (pages 1055–1056)

What happened in Romania?

In Romania, Nicolae Ceausescu, the Communist dictator, ordered the army to shoot at protesters. This caused larger protests. The army then joined the people and fought against the secret police loyal to Ceausescu. He was captured and executed in 1989. General elections quickly followed and the new government reformed the economy.

Romania struggled with corruption and crime as it tried to improve the economy. The government made economic reforms to introduce capitalism.

4. How did the government of Romania change?

_____

The Breakup of Yugoslavia

(pages 1056–1058)

What happened in Yugoslavia?

Yugoslavia was made up of many different ethnic groups. In the early 1990s, they began fighting. When *Serbia* tried to control the government, two other republics—*Slovenia* and *Croatia*—declared independence. Slovenia beat back a Serbian invasion. But Serbia and Croatia fought a bloody war.

In 1992, *Bosnia-Herzegovina* also declared independence. Serbs who lived in that region opposed the move. Using aid from Serbia, they fought a brutal civil war against the Bosnian Muslims, the largest group in Bosnia. The Serbs used murder and other forms of brutality against the Muslims. This **ethnic cleansing** was intended to rid Bosnia of its Muslims. The United Nations helped create a peace agreement. .

In 1998, the Balkan region experienced violence again in Kosovo, a province in southern Serbia, which Serbian forces invaded in order to suppress an independence movement. A NATO bombing campaign forced Serbian leaders to withdraw their forces.

5. Who fought in the civil war in Yugoslavia?

_____

CHAPTER 35 Section 5 (pages 1059–1063)

China: Reform and Reaction

BEFORE YOU READ

In the last section, you read about the collapse of communism and other changes in Central and Eastern Europe.

In this section, you will learn about the recent history of China.

AS YOU READ

Use the time line below to take notes on the key events in recent Chinese history.

1966 Cultural Revolution begins	1989

1977	1997

TERMS AND NAMES

Zhou Enlai Chinese leader who worked with President Nixon to improve U.S.–Chinese relations

Deng Xiaoping Chinese leader after Zhou Enlai

Four Modernizations Goals of Deng Xiaoping that called for progress in agriculture, industry, defense, and science and technology

Tiananmen Square Square in the capital of Beijing; scene of a student demonstration and massacre

Hong Kong Island that became part of China again in 1997

The Legacy of Mao
(pages 1059–1060)

How did Mao change China?

Mao Zedong had tried to build a China on the ideas of equality, revolutionary spirit, and hard work. But his policies failed to create a strong economy. He reduced incentives for higher production. The Great Leap Forward helped cause an economic disaster.

During Mao's rule, China had little role in world affairs. **Zhou Enlai**, another Chinese leader, worried about this. He worked with U.S. President Richard Nixon to improve U.S.–Chinese relations.

1. How successful were Mao's economic programs?

_____

_____

China and the West (page 1060)

How did Deng Xiaoping change China?

After Mao and Zhou died in 1976, *moderates* took control of the government. The most powerful leader was **Deng Xiaoping.** He tried to modernize the economy. Deng had goals known as the **Four Modernizations.** These called for progress in agriculture, industry, defense, and science and technology. He ended farming communes and allowed farmers more to sell part of their produce for a profit. Farm production increased greatly.

Deng made similar changes to industry. People's incomes began to rise. They began to purchase appliances and other goods that were once scarce.

2. What were the results of Deng Xiaoping's changes?

_____

_____

_____

Massacre in Tiananmen Square

(pages 1061–1062)

What caused the protest at Tiananmen Square?

Deng's new plan caused problems. The gap between rich and poor grew wider, which caused unrest. Western political ideas spread throughout the country. In 1989, thousands of Chinese students gathered in **Tiananmen Square** in the capital of Beijing. They called for democracy and freedom. Deng responded by sending army troops and tanks to put down the rally. Thousands were killed or wounded. China has continued to stamp out protests since then.

3. What happened to the protesters at Tiananmen Square?

_____

_____

_____

China Enters the New Millennium (pages 1062–1063)

What happened to Hong Kong?

Another major issue for China was the status of **Hong Kong.** The island became part of China again in 1997 when the British gave it back after 155 years of colonial rule. China promised to respect Hong Kong's freedom for 50 years. But many worried that China would take away Hong Kong's freedoms.

4. Why do people worry about Hong Kong's new rule?

_____

_____

_____

China Beyond 2000 (page 1063)

What is the connection between political and economic reform in China?

Liberal economic reforms in China did not immediately lead to political reforms. China has been successful in reducing poverty, in part because it has been cautious in privatizing the economy. China managed to maintain economic growth in the early 21st century.

As economic and social conditions in China improve, the political situation may improve as well. An important sign of China's engagement with the world is its successful campaign to be chosen as the site for the 2008 Summer Olympics.

5. Which came first in China—political or economic reform?

_____

_____

_____

Glossary

African National Congress (ANC) Group that fought for the rights of black South Africans

banned Forbidden by law

Bosnia-Herzegovina Part of the former Yugoslavia in which Serbs fought a civil war with Muslims and where ethnic cleansing took place

boycotted Refused to buy

coup Sudden overthrow of government

Croatia Part of the former Yugoslavia that fought Serbia

dissent Political disagreement

federation A group with common interests

moderates People who are in the political middle

Serbia Part of the former Yugoslavia that wanted control of the government

Slovenia Part of the former Yugoslavia that fought back an invasion by Serbia

AFTER YOU READ

Terms and Names

A. Write the name or term in each blank that best completes the meaning of the paragraph.

dissidents

martial law

apartheid

reunification

land reform

Reform movements have had many different goals. A key goal in Brazil was **1** _____, which would make land ownership more equal. In South Africa, a key goal was the end of a strict separation of races called **2** _____. The struggle for democracy in East Germany led to the fall of the Berlin Wall. This change also led to the **3** _____ of Germany. The road to democracy can be rocky. Civil war and other power struggles can lead to **4** _____, or temporary military rule, as they did in Nigeria. Under this type of rule, opponents of government policy, **5** _____, are usually silenced.

B. Write the letter of the name or term next to the description that explains it best.

a. PRI

b. CIS

c. Four Modernizations

d. Solidarity

e. Politburo

_____ **1.** Ruling committee of the Communist party in the Soviet Union

_____ **2.** Polish labor union that worked for reform and led to the defeat of communism

_____ **3.** Loose federation of former Soviet territories

_____ **4.** Deng Xiaoping's goals for progress in China

_____ **5.** Political party that controlled Mexico for most of the 20th century

AFTER YOU READ (cont.)   *CHAPTER 35* Struggles for Democracy

Main Ideas

1. Name three similarities in the struggles for democracy in Argentina and Brazil.

_____

_____

_____

2. How did apartheid come to an end in South Africa?

_____

_____

_____

3. How did the spirit of reform under Gorbachev in the Soviet Union spill over into Eastern Europe?

_____

_____

_____

4. What caused the civil war in Yugoslavia?

_____

_____

_____

5. How did the events in Tiananmen Square affect the struggle for democracy in China?

_____

_____

_____

Thinking Critically

Answer the following questions on a separate sheet of paper.

1. Give two examples of nations that experienced setbacks in the struggle for democracy. Explain which factors were missing that are needed for democracy to succeed.

2. Compare and contrast Mao Zedong and Deng Xiaoping.

The Impact of Science and Technology

BEFORE YOU READ

In the last section, you read about struggles for democracy in China.

In this section, you will learn about recent changes in science and technology.

AS YOU READ

Use the chart below to take notes on recent developments and discoveries and their effects.

DEVELOPMENT/DISCOVERY	EFFECT
Satellites	Improved television broadcasts.

Exploring the Solar System and Beyond (pages 1071–1072)

How did competition give way to cooperation in space?

From the 1950s to the 1970s, the United States and Soviet Union took their Cold War rivalry to space. Each nation tried to be the first to reach the moon and beyond.

In the 1970s, the two nations began to cooperate in space exploration. In 1975, United States and Soviet spacecraft *docked*, or joined together, in space. Later, American and Soviet space missions included scientists from other countries. In the late 1990s, the United States, Russia, and 14 other nations began working together to build the **International Space Station.**

Some space missions did not include human crew members. Unmanned flights sent back pictures and information about other planets.

In 1990, the United States and European countries sent the Hubble Space Telescope into orbit around the earth. This satellite sent back *unprecedented* images of objects in space.

1. Give three examples of international cooperation in space.

_____

_____

_____

_____

Expanding Global Communications (pages 1072–1073)

How has technology changed communications?

Every day satellites are used to track the weather around the world. They are also used to search for minerals on the planet. Satellites allow television broadcasts to carry events live around the world.

Another advance in technology has been the computer. Computers have become more powerful since they were first invented. At the same time, they have gotten smaller in size. Consumer goods such as microwave ovens, telephones, and cars often include computer chips to keep them running.

Millions of people around the world use personal computers at work or at home. Many of these people are connected through the **Internet,** a worldwide computer network. The Internet allows people to get a great deal of information more quickly and easily than ever before. The Internet also allows people to communicate with one another.

2. How have computers changed everyday living?

_____

_____

_____

_____

Transforming Human Life
(pages 1073–1074)

How has new technology changed medicine?

New technology has changed medicine. *Lasers* allow doctors to perform surgery to fix problems in delicate areas, such as in the eye or the brain. New methods for making images of the body help doctors locate problems.

Research into genes has helped unlock the secrets of some diseases. **Genetic engineering** enables scientists to use genes in new ways. For example, scientists can develop plants with special traits. **Cloning** is part of genetic engineering. It is the creation of identical copies of *DNA*. Cloning can be used to produce plants and animals that are identical to the existing plants and animals. The application of this new understanding of genes has led to many developments in agriculture.

Scientists have made other advances in farming. In the **green revolution,** scientists have developed new strains of food crops to help farmers grow more food.

3. Why is genetic engineering an important development?

_____

_____

_____

_____

Global Economic Development

BEFORE YOU READ

In the last section, you read about changes in science and technology.

In this section, you will read about the new global economy.

AS YOU READ

Use the chart below to show the causes and effects of global economic development.

TERMS AND NAMES

developed nation Industrialized nation

emerging nation Nation that is still developing industry

global economy Economy linking the economies of many nations

free trade Absence of barriers that can block trade between countries

ozone layer Layer of atmosphere that blocks dangerous rays from the sun

sustainable growth Economic growth that meets current needs but conserves resources for the future

Causes

New technology

Global Economic Development

Effects

Technology Revolutionizes the World's Economy (pages 1075–1076)

How have the economies of the developed nations changed?

Technology has changed the world's economies. In the 1950s, scientists found new ways to make plastics, which came to be widely used. In recent years, industries have begun using robots to make products. These changes have required workers to have more and different skills than before.

In industrialized nations, or **developed nations,** there are more jobs in service and information industries. Manufacturing jobs began to grow more quickly in the **emerging nations** where wages are lower.

1. What types of jobs are on the increase in developed nations?

_____

_____

_____

Economic Globalization (pages 1076–1077)

Why is free trade important in a global economy?

A **global economy** continued to develop in the 1980s. Telephone and computer links connect banks and other financial companies around the world. *Multinational corporations* operate in many countries.

After World War II, many leaders believed that world economies would grow best if there were **free trade.** This means there would be no barriers to block goods from one country from entering another country. Many steps have been taken to put free trade in practice. In 1951, some nations in Europe joined together to create free trade. That group, now called the *European Union* (EU), has grown to become a powerful trading bloc.

The United States, Canada, and Mexico agreed to the North American Free Trade Agreement (NAFTA) in 1994. Another free trade zone was set up in Latin America. Similar groups are being put together in Africa and Asia.

In recent years, there has been considerable disagreement on the impact of the globalization of the economy. Supporters suggest that open, competitive markets and the free flow of goods, services, technology, and investments benefit all nations. Opponents charge that globalization has been a disaster for the poorest countries. Many, they suggest, are worse off today than they were in the past.

2. Name three steps that have been taken in the direction of free trade.

_____

_____

Impact of Global Development (pages 1079–1080)

How has the development of the global economy affected the use of energy and other resources?

Economic growth needs many resources. Manufacturing and trade both use huge amounts of energy. Oil has been a major source of this energy. Whenever the flow of oil has been threatened, the world's economies have suffered shocks.

In 1990, Iraq invaded Kuwait. This threatened the flow of Kuwaiti oil. Soon, the countries of the United Nations went to war against Iraq. This was known as the Gulf War.

Economic growth has also caused environmental problems. Burning coal and oil has polluted the air. It has also caused *acid rain* and contributed to global warming. The release of some chemicals into the air has weakened Earth's **ozone layer.** This layer of atmosphere blocks dangerous rays from the sun.

One new idea about growth involves sustainable development. **Sustainable growth** requires meeting current needs while *conserving* future resources.

3. What environmental problems have resulted from economic growth?

_____

_____

Name _____ Date _____

Global Security Issues

TERMS AND NAMES

proliferation spread

Universal Declaration of Human Rights 1948 United Nations statement of specific rights that all people should have

political dissent Difference of opinion over political issues

gender inequality Difference between men and women in terms of wealth and status

AIDS Acquired immune deficiency syndrome, a disease that attacks the immune system, leaving sufferers open to deadly infections

refugees People who leave their country to move to another to find safety

BEFORE YOU READ

In the last section, you read about the growth of the global economy.

In this section, you will read about challenges to global security.

AS YOU READ

Use the web below to take notes on threats to global security.

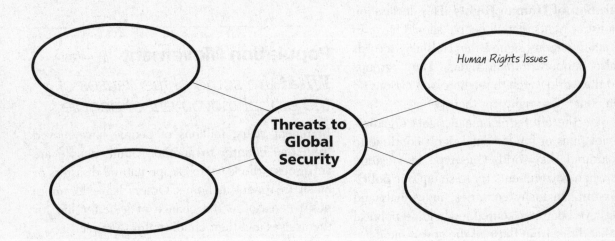

Issues of War and Peace

(pages 1082–1083)

How have nations worked together for global security?

After World War II, nations joined together to pursue global security. The United Nations (UN) was formed at the end of World War II to promote world peace. It now has more than 180 member nations. The UN provides a place for countries—or groups within countries—to share their views.

The UN can also send troops as a *peacekeeping force*. These soldiers—who come from member nations—try to stop violence from breaking out. UN peacekeepers have served in regions such as Asia and Africa.

Another approach to world peace has been to limit weapons of mass destruction. These include *nuclear weapons, chemical weapons*, and *biological weapons*. In 1968, many nations signed a Nuclear Non-Proliferation Treaty. The nations that signed the treaty agreed to prevent the **proliferation,** or spread, of nuclear weapons. In the 1990s, the United States and Russia agreed to destroy many of their nuclear weapons. In another treaty, many nations promised not to develop chemical or biological weapons.

Ethnic and religious differences are the sources of many world conflicts. Some of these conflicts have roots that reach back decades or, in a few cases, centuries. Governments and many international organizations, including the UN, are trying to find peaceful solutions to these conflicts.

1. Name two specific approaches toward collective security.

_____

_____

_____

Human Rights Issues (page 1084)

What efforts have been made to ensure human rights?

In 1948, the UN approved the **Universal Declaration of Human Rights**. This declaration gives a list of rights that all people should have. In 1975, many nations signed the Helsinki Accords that also support human rights. Many groups around the world watch to see how well nations do in protecting these rights for their people.

Despite the efforts of human rights organizations, violations of fundamental rights continue to occur around the world. One type of violation occurs when governments try to stamp out **political dissent.** In many countries, individuals and groups have been persecuted for holding political views that differ from those of the government.

In the past, women suffered considerable discrimination. However, a heightened awareness of human rights encouraged women to work to improve their lives. They pushed for new laws that gave them greater equality. Since the 1970s, women have made notable gains, especially in the areas of education and work. Even so, **gender inequality** still is an issue.

2. Name two events that have been important in the worldwide struggle for human rights.

_____

_____

_____

Health Issues (page 1085)

What is the greatest challenge to global health?

Recently, the enjoyment of a decent standard of health has become recognized as a basic human right. However, for many people across the world, poor health is still the norm. Perhaps the greatest global challenge to the attainment of good health is **AIDS,** or acquired immune deficiency syndrome. AIDS is a worldwide problem. However, Sub-Saharan Africa has suffered most from the epidemic. The disease has had devastating impact on the populations and economies of many countries in this region.

3. Which area of the world has been hardest hit by the AIDS epidemic?

_____

_____

Population Movement (page 1086)

What are some of the causes of the global movement of people?

In recent years, millions of people have moved from one country to another. Some people are **refugees,** who leave to escape natural disasters or harsh treatment at home. Others leave for more positive reasons—the chance of a better life for themselves and their children, for example.

While people have a right to leave, every country does not have to accept them. Sometimes these people have to live in crowded refugee camps. They suffer hunger and disease. They can also cause political problems for the country where they are held. However, immigrants also can bring many benefits to their new home.

4. What problems can result from the global movement of people?

_____

_____

_____

Terrorism
Case Study: September 11, 2001

TERMS AND NAMES

terrorism Use of violence against people or property to force changes in societies or governments

cyberterrorism Attacks on information systems for political reasons

Department of Homeland Security Department of the U.S. government that organizes the fight against terrorism in the United States.

USA Patriot Act Antiterrorism law that allowed the government certain rights to help chase and capture terrorists

BEFORE YOU READ

In the last section, you read about global security issues.

In this section, you will learn about terrorism and its effect on today's world.

AS YOU READ

Use a chart like the one below to take notes on the effects of terrorism.

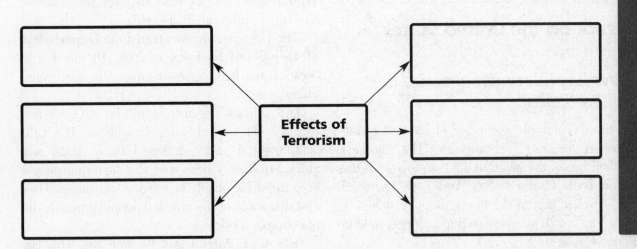

What Is Terrorism? (pages 1087–1088)

What motivates terrorists and what methods do they use?

Terrorism is the use of violence against people or property to force changes in societies or governments. The reasons for modern terrorism are many. Reasons include gaining independence, getting rid of foreigners, and changing society. In the late 20th century, another type of terrorist appeared. These terrorists wanted to destroy what they believed were the forces of evil.

Terrorists use violence to try to achieve their goals. Terrorists often use bombs and bullets. The targets of terrorist attacks usually are crowded places. Some terrorist groups have used biological and chemical weapons. Attacks on information systems such as computer networks are called **cyberterrorism.** These attacks are done for political reasons.

1. What types of weapons do terrorists use?

_____

_____

Terrorism Around the World
(pages 1088–1089)

How has terrorism affected the world?

In the Middle East, Palestinians and Israelis have argued for decades about land ownership. This argument has resulted in many terrorist acts. Often a Palestinian group does an act of terrorism. In response, the Israelis strike back. In Northern Ireland, the Irish Republican Army (IRA) has carried out terrorist acts for many years. The IRA want the British to give up control over Northern Ireland.

Many terrorist groups are found in East Asia. For example, a religious cult named Aum Shinrikyo wants to control Japan. In Africa, civil unrest and regional wars cause most terrorist acts. Narcoterrorism often happens in Latin America. Narcoterrorism is terrorism connected with the trade of illegal drugs.

2. **What has caused most of the terrorist activity in Africa?**

_____

_____

Attack on the United States

(pages 1090–1091)

How has terrorism affected the United States?

On the morning of September 11, 2001, 19 Arab terrorists *hijacked* four airliners. The hijackers crashed two of the jets into the twin towers of the World Trade Center in New York City. The third jet destroyed part of the Pentagon in Washington, D.C. The fourth plane crashed in an empty field in Pennsylvania.

As a result of the attacks, the twin towers fell to the ground within two hours. About 3,000 people died in all the attacks. The dead included more than 340 New York City firefighters and 60 police officers. They had rushed to the World Trade Center to help people in the buildings.

Before September 11, many Americans thought that terrorism was something that happened in other countries. After September 11, many Americans became afraid that terrorist attacks could happen to them.

A few days after September 11, letters containing the disease anthrax were mailed. The letters were sent to people in the news media and to members of Congress. Five people died from inhaling the anthrax in these letters. Officials did

not find a link between the anthrax letters and the September 11 attacks.

3. **How did the September 11 attacks affect the way Americans looked at life?**

_____

_____

The United States Responds

(pages1091–1092)

How has the United States fought back against terrorism?

After September 11, the United States asked for an international effort to fight terrorism. U.S. officials suspected that Osama bin Laden directed the September 11 attacks. Bin Laden was the leader of a terrorist group called al-Qaeda.

The U.S. government created the **Department of Homeland Security** in 2002. Its job was to organize the fight against terrorism in the United States.

U.S. officials began to search for al-Qaeda terrorists in the United States. In addition, U.S. officials arrested and questioned many Arabs and other Muslims. Critics said that arresting people because of nationality or religion was unfair. They said that some of the arrested people probably did not commit a crime.

The **USA Patriot Act** became law. This law allowed the government several powers to help chase and capture terrorists.

The Federal Aviation Administration (FAA) ordered airlines to put bars on cockpit doors. These bars would help stop hijackers from getting control of planes. National Guard troops began to guard airports. Trained security officers called sky marshals were put on planes. The Aviation and Transportation Security Act was passed. It put the federal government in charge of airport security.

4. **How was aviation security increased?**

_____

_____

Cultures Blend in a Global Age

TERMS AND NAMES

popular culture Cultural elements—such as sports, music, movies, and clothing—that reflect a group's common background

materialism Placing high value on owning things

BEFORE YOU READ

In the last section, you read about terrorism.

In this section, you will learn about the global blending of cultures.

AS YOU READ

Use the chart below to take notes on the blending of cultures around the world.

MAIN IDEA	SUPPORT
Sharing of cultures has speeded up	Television and other mass media have sped up cultural sharing

Cultural Exchange Accelerates

(pages 1093–1094)

What has speeded up the sharing of cultures?

Changes in technology have made it possible for people to share their cultures with one another. Television is one of the main forces in this trend. It allows people to see things that happen around the world. Movies and radio also have had an impact in bringing the world's people together.

As a result of these *mass media*, the world's popular culture now includes elements from many different cultures. **Popular culture** includes music, sports, clothing styles, food, and hobbies. American television shows have become popular around the

world. Broadcasts of some sporting events can reach millions of people in all corners of the globe. Music has also become international.

1. Name three aspects of culture that have become international.

_____

_____

_____

World Culture Blends Many Influences (pages 1095–1096)

What countries have most influenced cultural blending?

Cultural blending occurs when parts of different cultures are combined. In recent times, the United

States and Europe have been a major force in this blending. One reason is that Western nations dominate the mass media.

The political power of the West has also spread Western culture to other regions. For example, English is now a major world language. About 500 million people speak English as their first or second language. More people speak Mandarin Chinese. But English speakers are more widely spread throughout the world. Western clothes can be seen throughout the world.

Western ideas have also influenced world thought. The Western idea of **materialism**—placing high value on owning things—has also spread. Some ideas have also traveled from East to West. The worlds of art and literature have become more international in recent years.

2. What Western aspects of culture have spread throughout the world?

_____

_____

_____

Future Challenges and Hopes (pages 1096–1097)

How has the world responded to cultural blending?

Some people think the spread of international culture is a problem. They worry that their own culture will be swallowed up by other cultures. Some countries have adopted policies that reserve television broadcast time for national programming. In other countries, television programmers take Western programs and rework them according to their own culture. In some areas, people have returned to old traditions in order to keep them alive.

The people of the world are becoming more and more dependent on each another. All through human history, people have faced challenges to their survival. In the 21st century, those challenges will be faced by people who are in increasing contact with one another. They have a great stake in living together in harmony.

3. What problems or challenges can cultural blending bring?

_____

_____

_____

Glossary   CHAPTER 36   Global Interdependence

acid rain Rain with a high concentration of acids that destroy plant life and life in water

biological weapons Weapons that use disease-spreading microorganisms

chemical weapons Weapons made from chemicals, such as poison gases

conserving Saving

cultural blending Process of combining different cultures

DNA Basic material in chromosomes that transmits the genetic pattern

docked Joined together in space

European Union Powerful European trading bloc created to promote free trade

hijacked Took control of a moving vehicle by force

lasers Devices that give off light in intense, narrow beams

mass media Communications that

reach large numbers of people, including television and radio

Multinational corporations Companies that operate in many nations

nuclear weapons Weapons that use atomic energy

peacekeeping force Soldiers sent by the United Nations to help keep peace

unprecedented Never done before

AFTER YOU READ

Terms and Names

A. Write the term in each blank that best completes the meaning of the paragraph.

emerging nations

developed nations

free trade

global economy

sustainable growth

A new **1** _____ links the economies of many nations. Multinational corporations play an important role in this kind of economy. Often the offices of these companies will be found in countries that have already industrialized, known as **2** _____. The factories, on the other hand, may be found in **3** _____, because wages may be lower there. One thing that many people believe helps world economies to grow is **4** _____. This means that no barriers block goods from one country from entering another country. Some people are worried about the impact of this world economic growth on the environment. They support **5** _____, economic development that meets current needs but conserves resources for the future.

B. Write the letter of the name or term next to the description that explains it best.

a. genetic engineering

b. proliferation

c. terrorism

d. materialism

e. cloning

____ **1.** Placing high value on owning things

____ **2.** Process of creating identical copies of DNA for research and other purposes

____ **3.** Spread

____ **4.** Use of violence to force changes in societies or governments

____ **5.** Use of genes to develop new products and cures

AFTER YOU READ (continued)   *CHAPTER 36* Global Interdependence

Main Idea

1. Explain three major effects of technology on everyday living.

_____

_____

_____

2. How has technology changed world economies?

_____

_____

_____

3. How has technology helped speed up cultural blending?

_____

_____

_____

4. What is a UN peacekeeping force, and when and how is it used?

_____

_____

_____

5. Discuss three responses people make to cultural blending.

_____

_____

_____

Thinking Critically

Answer the following questions on a separate sheet of paper.

1. How does economic growth strain resources, and what results can this have?

2. Discuss three threats to global security, and explain the possible effects of each one.